The Fool's Excellent Adventure

A Hero's Journey
through the Enneagram & Tarot

by
Susan Rhodes

The Fool's Excellent Adventure

A Hero's Journey
through the Enneagram & Tarot

by
Susan Rhodes

All text, graphic design, and illustrations are by the
the author unless otherwise noted. Kimberly Crabtree provided
invaluable artistic consultation on cover revisions
and the tarot images introduced in Chapter 11.

ISBN: 978-0-9824792-5-4

©2017

Geranium Press

DIVINE MYSTERY.

THE MOON.

THE HERMIT.

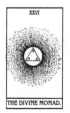

THE DIVINE MONAD.

THE STAR.

STRENGTH.

9

Divine Possibility

8

Ascension

MERKABA.

THE TOWER.

THE CHARIOT.

7

Liberation

Trust in the Goodness of Life

6

THE DIVINE FAMILY.

THE DEVIL.

THE LOVERS.

Wisdom

5

THE HIEROPHANT

KEEPER OF THE FLAME.

TEMPERANCE.

THE FOOL.

0

1

Alchemy

Intuition

2

Creativity

3

Individuation

4

Preface

An imprisoned person with no other book than the Tarot, if he knew how to use it, could in a few years acquire universal knowledge, and would be able to speak on all subjects with unequaled learning and inexhaustible eloquence.
– Éliphas Lévi

The enneagram is a universal symbol. All knowledge can be included in the enneagram and with the help of the enneagram it can be interpreted. Everything can be included and read in the enneagram.
– G. I. Gurdjieff

ABOVE WE HAVE TWO QUOTES, each on a different system but strikingly similar. In either quote, we could easily exchange the word "tarot" for "enneagram" or vice-versa and come up with the same meaning. And yet, little if anything has ever been written about the parallels between these two remarkable systems of the Western Esoteric Tradition. So that is my goal in this book: to explore similarities between the tarot and the enneagram, bringing the two together in a way that allows each system to more fully illuminate the other.

The central metaphor for this exploration is the *hero's journey*. It's an apt metaphor for tarot work because it reveals the not-so-hidden story line underlying the seemingly separate cards of the tarot. And it's also appropriate for enneagram work because the enneagram is by nature a story-telling system.

So my purpose here is to tell the story of the hero through the lens of both the enneagram and tarot, interweaving the two in a way that illustrates their many parallels.

I also rely upon principles of Pythagorean number symbolism, which is based upon two key propositions: (a) that numbers possesses qualitative information that is of universal significance and (b) that the single-digit numbers 1–9 are of special significance, because they are the "root" numbers from which all others are derived. Since the enneagram is a numerically-oriented system based on the numbers 1–9, it is naturally aligned with Pythagorean principles. The tarot, however is not based upon the number nine—at least not in an obvious way.

But a few years ago, author Hajo Banzhaf published *Tarot and the Journey of the Hero*, which describes the hero's journey as a nine-stage process. His model makes it easier for anyone to imagine the parallels between the tarot and the enneagram. However, even before I was aware of Banzhaf's work, I had already noticed many such parallels. What I did not know was whether they were systematic, not coincidental. Working on this book has only increased my conviction that they *are* systematic—and there is a profoundly meaningful connection between these two great systems.

Susan Rhodes, November 2017

Grateful thanks

to the many friends who have helped me over the years, both with reading, proofing, and editing books and with so many other things in life. You are loved and appreciated for your ongoing support. Special thanks to Norman Thompson, Pamela Silimperi, Joy Geertsen, Debbie Edge, and Kimberly Crabtree for your editorial help and thoughtful ideas on the manuscript of this book as it evolved.

Contents

I

The Tradition of the Hero's Journey

1:
An Overview

*You know what the issue is with this world? Everyone wants
a magical solution to their problems and no one believes in magic.*
– Mad Hatter in the TV series Once Upon a Time

IN 2016, A GROUP OF 12 PEOPLE WERE DEPOSITED *sans* clothing, food, or water into the wilderness of the African plain to see whether they could last for 40 days in a hostile environment. Could they make it to the end?

Most did not; only four succeeded. One of them was Stacey Osorio, a biology student from Stites, Idaho. Stacey had participated in a previous 21-day challenge with a single partner in Croatia, but was pulled from the competition after only eight days when a burn wound she'd acquired two days earlier became seriously infected.

When she signed up for the 40 day challenge, she was determined to succeed. And she did, despite a weight loss of 40 pounds (1 pound per day)! For Stacey, the experience wasn't just about redemption. It was about participating in a wilderness quest.

On the last day—despite her weariness, pain, and hunger—Stacey was in a jubilant mood. She joyfully proclaimed: "I was given the opportunity for a hero's journey. I took it, and I won!"

❖ ❖ ❖

"I won!"

Those two words capture a special moment, the kind we all yearn for in life. It's that moment when we know that everything we've had to take on—every obstacle, every defeat, every failure, and every torturous moment of self-doubt and recrimination—was worth all that effort. Against all odds, we managed to persevere. And now we know ourselves in a new way: as someone simultaneously heartened by our achievements and humbled by our limitations.

Of course, most of us aren't about to set forth naked into the wilderness, much as we might admire the fortitude of those who do. Nevertheless, the popularity of books like the Harry Potter series, modern hero films (e.g., *The Hunger Games*, *Divergent*, and *Star Wars*), and TV's *Once Upon a Time* testify to the admiration we feel for heroes and our secret longing to become a hero, too.

Consider the character of Henry, the 10-year-old protagonist in *Once Upon a Time*. Adopted as a baby, he starts out looking for someone to save his home of Storybrooke. He needs help because the town is populated by fairy tale characters who, due to a curse, don't remember who they really are.

Henry travels to Boston to find Emma, who is secretly his birth mother. Emma starts out as a reluctant hero, but gradually becomes the "savior" that everyone is hoping for, including Henry. But meanwhile, Henry is growing up. At some point down the road, he realizes he doesn't just want to sit on the sidelines; he wants to become part of the action. Finally, he gets sufficiently exasperated to proclaim: "I'm done reading about heroes. I want to be one!"

That's the moment when Henry's journey really begins.

But for most of us, the heroic quest seems like a dream. It's something we read about or see on TV, not something that happens to us. There are several reasons for this.

One is that we find it hard to imagine ourselves as heroes. This is often because we tend to see heroes as quite different than us—bolder, braver, and (usually) better-looking! This kind of Hollywood image is hard to live up to. In real life, nobody ever does—even heroes. Real heroes are not perfect people. They make mistakes, experience failures, and usually possess the same character flaws as the rest of us, flaws like laziness, impatience, jealousy, or timidity. What makes them heroes is not their strengths but their willingness to try—and to just keep on trying, no matter what comes. Anyone can decide to try—which means that we all qualify as potential heroes.

A second barrier to "hero-hood" is modern culture, whose cynicism informs us that heroism is a lost ideal, never to be found again. None of us start out cynical, but as we grow up, we grow out of our belief in myths, legends, and fairy tales, because we are informed that they're not real. Not wanting to be seen as a crazy person, we decide to forget about all that hero stuff—all about dreaming, magic, and questing after impossible goals. The new goal is to be successful in the consensus reality of flatland materialism.

Although this quest for success may bring material rewards, it's not very fulfilling. It leaves a hole that we're never quite able to fill. In the words of Matt Ragland in his blog on the Huffington Post, "Most days, our life's story does not feel heroic, but mundane. Even…with a happy family and meaningful work, the slow creep of the status quo invades our life….The question is: What are you going to do about it?"[1]

Cynicism is a big problem for Emma at the beginning of her Storybrooke quest. As a hip but hardened bail bondsman living in a Boston high-rise, she finds the whole "saving Storybrooke" story preposterous. No way does she believe that magic is real, much less that she was born to be a savior of anything, even herself. It is only the sweet innocence of Henry, her long-lost son, that begins to melt the armor around her heart.

A third barrier for would-be heroes is a lack of self-understanding. When we truly understand ourselves, we know what matters most and are motivated to act. But at the beginning of the hero's journey, almost no one knows him- or herself very well. However, any kind of motivation that gets the hero out the door will do. The main thing is that it's compelling enough to draw the hero onto his path and keep him there until he can't easily retreat. For when he can't go forwards and can't go back, he is forced to go within—and that's when he finally begins to understand what the journey really means.

When Henry first arrives at Emma's door, she sees herself as virtually worthless—as a modern-day survivor who is secretly ashamed of abandoning her son. So when she agrees to go with Henry to Storybrooke, it's out of guilt, not love. But once there, she becomes curious about the town and its strange inhabitants. Curiosity gives way to intrigue, and intrigue gives way to tenderness, as she becomes closer to Henry and motivated to ensure his welfare. At some point, she finds she cannot leave him. That's when she is compelled to face Ragland's pointed question: *What are you going to do about it?*"

This is the most important question we will ever ask ourselves: the question of how to throw off our social conditioning in order to discover who we really are and what we're meant to do in life. That's the hero's quest in a nutshell. It's not about retreating into fantasy to duck out on the realities of life but about reacquainting ourselves with the true nature of the world and our role within it so that we, like Henry, feel ready to jump into the story and make it our own.

The Modern Hero's Journey

Jungian author Sue Mehrtens contrasts the classical hero's journey—with its emphasis on physical courage, daring acts, and public rewards—with the modern hero's journey, which more often involves moral courage, inner work, and unsung acts. She observes that "the new hero is brave, but not in the sense of the firemen or soldiers under fire. Far more subtle, but no less arduous, is the bravery of the soul's journey into the 'mystery' that is man."[2]

The tarot provides a natural entryway into this mysterious hero's journey, which is why so many authors of tarot books allude to the hero's journey in their writings. In the world of the tarot, everyone is a potential hero. And the world is a place in which to have adventures.

As Karen Hamaker-Zondag, author of *Tarot as a Way of Life* (1997) notes, "the hero lives in each of us…we are the hero of our own lives" (p. 55). In the tarot, the hero is symbolized by Key 0, The Fool, who starts out as an "innocent abroad," full of anticipation but lacking life experience. As The Fool progresses through the 21 cards (Keys)[3] of the major arcana, he has the potential to become The Hero, depending upon how he responds to the challenges he encounters along the way. So it's not surprising to hear that "when this card appears in your reading, be ready for adventure."[4]

Anthony Louis speaks of the Fool's movement through the major arcana as an "archetypal story of human development," noting that each of the major arcana cards is associated with an archetypal experience in life. But he also notes that these archetypes only come fully to life when the Fool begins to consciously engage with them, citing Jung's comment that the archetypes are a "dry river bed that becomes active only when water begins to flow" (p. 45). The water is the pool of inner awareness, and it begins to flow as the Fool begins to awaken his inner hero.

In *The Tarot: A Key to the Wisdom of the Ages* (1947/1990), esoteric tarot author Paul Foster Case observes that

> the Tarot…is a symbolic wheel of human life. We might, indeed, arrange these twenty-two pictures in a circle, with the keys equally spaced, like figures on a clock face. Then, when we had gone round the circle from 0 to 21, we should, in completing the circuit, arrive at 0 again. This is an important clue to some of the deeper meanings of the Tarot. Ponder it well, and from within you will come to more light than we could shed in page after page of explanation (p. 26).

In the last sentence, Case is strongly hinting at the power of imagery (and the imagination) to connect us with the deepest part of our being. It explains why tarot is so much more than just a deck of cards.

Among Jungian tarot authors, the hero's journey is often associated with the process of individuation. Such authors often devote an entire chapter to the hero's journey, because it's a metaphor for that process. But German tarot teacher Hajo Banzhaf devotes an entire book to it: *Tarot and the Journey of the Hero* (2000). Initially, he describes the hero's journey as a path of healing marked by meaningful signposts "on the path to a treasure that is hard to find, …[the treasure of] wholeness or individuation" (p. 12). Later, he provides a more lyrical description:

> The journey of the hero is the oldest story in the world.…It is woven into myths, fairy tales, and legends that tell us how a person sets out to accomplish the great work. It is the story behind all these stories, which to this very day are always told in the same way under countless names in all languages and cultures over and over again.…As the oldest story in the world, it is also an exemplary story, a parable for the human being's path in life. This is what makes it so interesting, and this is why it must be told time and again: so that we never forget why we are on the Earth and what we have to do here (p. 17).

Here Banzhaf alludes to deeper dimensions of the hero's journey, dimensions that allude to the soul's purpose in life and the importance of discovering that purpose. His evocative style invites us not simply to read the words, but to experience their meaning as we are reading. To that end, the book contains many color illustrations of both tarot cards (Pamela Colman Smith's much-copied images of the major arcana), and works of art depicting the archetypal dimensions of each card. Even the paper is high-quality, making the book a pleasure to read.

It's not hard to see why this book is so popular with readers. However, for me, it contained an additional bonus: a way of explaining the 22 aspects of the hero's journey in a way that turns out to be compatible with another system that can describe our inner journey: the *enneagram* (**Fig. 1-1**).

Like the tarot, the enneagram can be used to describe the stages of the hero's journey (as the process enneagram). It can also be used to identify nine personality types (as the personality enneagram). As we will see, there is a direct relationship between the two approaches, such that Type 1 on the enneagram possesses traits that correspond to Stage 1 on the process enneagram. The same is true for every point on the enneagram.

If we take the example of Point 1, it is associated on the *personality enneagram* with focus, determination, and taking the initiative; it is associated on the *process enneagram* with the first stage in a new process or project. If we take the example of Point 2, it is associated on the *personality enneagram* with affection, caring, and nurturance; it is associated on the *process enneagram* with emotionally investing in a new venture (giving new ideas the care and support that they need to develop). If we take the example of Point 3, it is associated on the *personality enneagram* with enthusiasm, hard work, and goal achievement; it is associated on the *process enneagram* with productivity, synthesis, and perpetual motion.

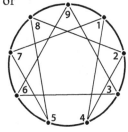

Fig. 1-1.
The Enneagram.

These parallels are consistent from Points 1–9, such that each point on the enneagram is associated with attributes that can be expressed on either the personality or process enneagrams (see Table 8-1 on p. 100 for details). I began to realize that these parallels can be explained numerologically by the principle that two things identified by the same number are usually similar in nature, assuming that the number has symbolic meaning.

In the case of both the enneagram and tarot, the numbers we see have definite symbolic meaning (see Chapter 9). As a result, we might expect to see meaningful correspondences between those points on the enneagram and the Keys in the tarot that have exactly the same number. And indeed, from the first time I looked at the two systems together, I saw parallels between Point 1 on the enneagram and Key 1 in the tarot, Point 2 and Key 2 in the tarot, etc.

But what happens when we reach the tarot Keys higher than nine?

That will take a little more explaining. One of the easiest ways to begin is by looking at the tarot using Banzhaf's approach for exploring the hero's journey. Banzhaf describes the journey by referring to three stages: the Arc of the Day, Arc of the Night, and the Return or Goal. The *Arc of the Day* describes nine "root" archetypes that are in need of development; the *Arc of the Night* describes nine archetypal challenges, each of which is associated with

Table 1-1. The Two Arcs.

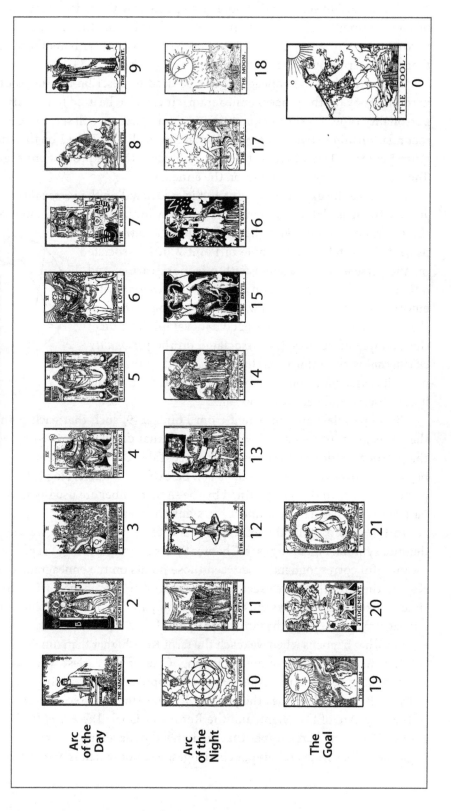

one of the nine archetypes. The *Return* (the goal) depict nine states of higher consciousness that are the result of integrating the "Day" qualities with the "Night" qualities. This approach is based on the Jungian idea of resolving or integrating the opposites within our nature.

Table 1-1 arranges these stages using the 22 cards of the major tarot. The rows depicts these three stages; the columns depict nine variants on the hero's journey, based on which archetype is being emphasized.

THE ROWS. In this table, Row 1 shows the tarot Keys in the Arc of the Day; Row 2, those in the Arc of the Night; and Row 3, the three "goal" Keys that depict their integration (the goal of the journey). The Fool is separate, for it is he who makes the journey through the 21 stages.

THE COLUMNS. There are nine columns of tarot Keys. All the Keys in the same column are meaningfully related, because the first depicts a particular archetype to be developed and the second a shadow quality of that same archetype. The two must be reconciled both for healing and the development of higher qualities. For example, if we look at the top card in the fourth column, we see The Emperor (4), a card which symbolizes an individual at the height of his powers. But if we look at the Key just below it, Death (13), a king lies dead on the ground, because no power can resist the call of Death. Together, these cards reveal that although it's natural to develop a sense of personal identity, we must eventually transcend it ("die" to it), in order to rediscover a sense of self that is more all-encompassing. On this table, this goal state is not shown for Columns 4–9, because there is no card in the tarot beyond The World (21). Later, we will explore what it would be like to completely fill in the third row (see the frontispiece for an overview and Chapters 10–14 for details). For now, it suffices to say that whenever we see an archetype and its shadow, there is always an implied resolution, whether seen or not.

Now to return to the idea of linking the enneagram and the tarot: if we want to look for correspondences between the nine enneagram types and the 22 tarot Keys, we have to come up with some way to logically associate the numbers over nine with the single-digit numbers. If we look at Table 1-1, we see that Key 1 (The Magician) is in the same column as The Wheel of Fortune (Key 10), and The Sun (Key 19). Does that mean that Enneagram Point 1 should be related to Tarot Keys 1, 10, and 19? Yes, it does, because they are all related *through their cross-sums*, where the cross-sum of a number greater than 9 equals the sum of each digit within the number, e.g.:

KEY 10 = 1 + 0 = 1   KEY 19 = 1 + 9 = 10 AND 1 + 0 = 1

So using cross-sum arithmetic, we can see that Keys 1, 10, and 19 all share the same single-digit value: 1. The same is true of the Keys in each column: they all reduce to one of the nine single-digit numbers. As a result, many tarot authors have discussed the similarities among tarot cards with the same "root" number (see Chapter 9).

What no one has yet discussed, however, is the possibility of linking the tarot with the enneagram through their shared root number. Since the enneagram is a system with nine points, it would make sense to check it out.

I was not aware of the cross-sums approach when I initially started working with these systems 20 years ago. Nevertheless, I began to notice parallels between tarot cards and enneagram points sharing the same number. I noticed, for example, how the Two of Cups in the tarot and Twos on the enneagram both focus on feelings of affection and close personal relationships; how the tarot's Hierophant strongly resembles the intellectual and teacherly Five on the enneagram; how the enigmatic Seven of Swords depicts one of the defining aspects of the tricky but clever Enneagram Seven; and how the Nine of Pentacles—with its lady at home in the garden—seems a lot like the nature-loving Type 9 on the enneagram. These are just a few examples; there are many more, as we will see.

At first, I only noticed the most obvious parallels; it took me longer to work out more subtle relationships. But when I discovered cross-sums, the pieces really began to fit together. The more correspondences I noticed, the more useful I found this understanding for my enneagram and tarot work. (See Appendix C for ways to use the enneagram in tarot work.)

My Own Journey in a Nutshell

My interest in the hero's journey goes back to a time in my life when I felt anything but heroic. I wasn't raised religious; in fact, I wasn't raised anything. So I grew up with a sense of living in a world without much depth or purpose. When adolescence hit, I suddenly saw the world "as it really is": full of hypocrisy and lies. Or so I thought, as a disillusioned teen. The truth was, anger and cynicism were my only defenses against a broken heart. How could I live in a world devoid of magic and mystery?

It turned out I couldn't. Within a month of leaving for college, I found myself in a Buddhist group. There I learned the most valuable lesson of my life: that there was something beyond the dense world of material life. My experiences as a newbie Buddhist gave me the motivation to discover more about this "something."

I learned a lot from Buddhism, but I didn't stay in that group forever. It turns out that I'm the kind of person that doesn't stick to one path. Instead, I pursue the same lessons from diverse perspectives. So I've followed many paths, with many interludes and changes of direction. In the late 1990s, I began a Sufi meditation practice which involved Jungian dream work. That woke up a desire to better understand archetypal imagery, which is how I became drawn to the tarot. But at the same time I was getting involved with tarot, I was also getting acquainted with the enneagram. I got far enough after several years of working with both systems to notice distinct parallels between them. But I could not go farther in my comparisons at that point, because they are both complex systems. I had to focus on one at a time.

I ended up focusing on the enneagram. Although I was at first a reluctant enneagram student, I eventually delved deeply into the system—deeply enough to write numerous articles and three books. I hadn't planned on writing any. But it turned out that I had a unique "take" on the enneagram that was not reflected in any book I read. So I wrote the kind of books that I'd originally hoped to read.

Let me explain. When I first encountered the enneagram in the early 1990s, I really didn't like it. It took me a long time to overcome that initial dislike, which was due to the negative way that most authors described the nine enneagram personality types. I was used to working with systems like the Jungian-inspired Myers-Briggs Type Indicator (MBTI), which describes personality using four preference pairs (introvert/extrovert; thinking/feeling; intuition/sensing; and judging/perceiving) to generate 16 personality types. The optimism seen in Jung's psychology is clearly reflected in books on the MBTI.

The MBTI helped me understand why I found it hard to settle into a conventional job. I discovered that I'm an INFJ[5] in that system, which means that I often have difficulty fitting into conventional careers: INFJ's have an abundance of creative energy but often find it hard to discover the right channel for it. And we like to work alone, not in a group.

Learning this gave me a great sense of relief; I'd been feeling like the proverbial square peg trying to fit into a round hole. It didn't solve all my career problems but it did help me stop questioning myself. I loved learning about personality with the MBTI, because it not only restored my faith in myself but helped me understand other people.

I wanted to learn more. That's how I got curious about the enneagram. One day, I was browsing in the personality section of a bookstore. I leafed through a couple of enneagram books. But I quickly noticed that the descriptions of personality types were less positive than the ones in the MBTI books. Instead of emphasizing personality differences, they emphasized personality deficiencies.

Why did they do that? Why so negative?

It took me years to find out.

The Personality Enneagram

What I discovered is that the negative personality descriptions in enneagram books can be traced back to the views of three extremely influential enneagram pioneers—Oscar Ichazo, Claudio Naranjo, and A. H. Almaas—who regard personality as a barrier to spiritual development. As a result, their teachings focus on its limitations rather than its assets. Ichazo was the first person to teach the personality enneagram, starting around 1969. However, Ichazo never called it the personality enneagram; he called it the *enneagram of fixations*. This is because he describes the nine points of the enneagram as ego fixations that gradually displace our essence [our pure and undefiled original state]. He believes that when ego-personality develops, "man falls from essence into personality....Once man is within ego consciousness he is driven by fear and desire. He can find no real happiness until desire is extinguished and he returns to his essence."[6] So Ichazo's enneagram work is designed to "destroy ego-dominated thought."[7]

Ichazo taught the enneagram of ego fixations for the first time in 1969 in Santiago, Chile, but is best known for the enneagram teachings disseminated to a group of Americans who traveled to Arica, Chile for a nine-month retreat. The group included dolphin researcher John Lilly and psychoanalyst Claudio Naranjo. Although the group was pledged to secrecy, Naranjo began teaching the enneagram to his students (also pledging them to secrecy), arousing Ichazo's wrath. However, the secret once again slipped out, coming to the attention of various interested parties, among them Helen Palmer, a gifted psychic, who began teaching enneagram classes all over the San Francisco Bay Area. Within a few years, the enneagram was being openly taught by individuals in the Bay Area and beyond, with an emphasis on identifying nine different mental fixations and emotional passions (imbalances).[8]

As a psychoanalyst with a neo-Freudian perspective, Naranjo has always been particularly interested in the passions and the role they play in creating mental illness and social dysfunction. To that end, he wrote *Character and Neurosis* (1994), a detailed neo-Freudian analysis of the character disorders associated with each enneagram type. But his view of ego seems to be as political as it is psychological. At the very beginning of another book, he says of his enneagram work that, "beyond [the] work of self-observation and [self-] confrontation...the work proceeds to a holy war against the ego."[9] To characterize the work of the enneagram as "a holy war" tells us that there is little chance of converting Naranjo to the view that personality is an asset.

A. H. Almaas was one of Naranjo's first students. He went on to found his own organization, the Ridhwan School, which has many students in the enneagram community. In his book on the enneagram, *Facets of Unity* (1999), he reiterates Ichazo's idea that we each begin life as infants in a state of unified awareness ("essence") but soon come under the influence of "delusions of separation that take nine separate forms" [i.e., nine fixation types]. These delusions, he says, develop as a result of "the inadequacy of the early holding environment." There is no possibility, according to Almaas, that our early environment might actually be good enough to produce a healthy personality. (Ironically, Donald Winnicott—who is the originator of the holding environment concept—held a very different view. Winnicott was an optimist who sought to reassure 1950s-era moms that they don't have to be perfect to provide "good enough mothering.")

These three individuals—Ichazo, Naranjo, and Almaas—view enneagram work as a means of helping us minimize the influence of our enneagram type. The goal is to replace our mental fixation with a "Holy Idea" and our passion with a virtue. From my perspective, such a goal is based on a conceptualization of personality that is rigid, narrow, and dualistic. To the extent that we buy into it, we are trapped in an unproductive "good vs bad" battle of inner forces. This is why I find it unproductive.

Compare this approach with Jung's approach to inner work, which focuses on the goal of achieving *individuation*: the complete integration of all aspects of the psyche. From this perspective, personality is an asset to be developed. He specifically calls for the development of "that fullness of life which is called personality," going on to note that "the great liberating deeds of world history have sprung from leading personalities."[10]

Jung is the great champion of personality because he sees it as the product of a well-differentiated psyche—the kind that is capable of assuming individual responsibility and exercising community leadership. For personality to become integrated, it is necessary to reunite all the psyche's fragmented parts, especially its despised shadow aspects. He sees these shadow aspects as the keys that hold the secret to wholeness, because the shadow is home to the primal material (*prima materia*) that "is never that which it appears to be, because it always contains the opposite."[11] By transforming our shadow qualities, we become capable of mental discernment, emotional compassion, and spiritual refinement.[12]

The Process Enneagram

Jung's ideas are the primary inspiration for my alternative approach to enneagram work. In order to develop this approach, I tried to learn as much about the enneagram as I could. What I discovered is that the personality enneagram was not the first one taught. It was derived from earlier enneagram teachings by G. I. Gurdjieff. It was Gurdjieff who first described the geometric figure of the enneagram, around the time of World War I. But Gurdjieff didn't use the enneagram to describe personality types; he used it to describe transformational processes. This is why it is often referred to as the *process enneagram*.

Gurdjieff implied that the enneagram, like the qabala, is a foundational system in Western occultism. But he also said it would never be found in historical records: "It was given such significance by those who knew, that they considered it necessary to keep the knowledge of it secret."[13] For reasons known only to himself, Gurdjieff decided that this was the right moment in history to reveal the enneagram to his students. When his teachings were later published by P. D. Ouspensky in *In Search of the Miraculous* (1949/2001), they became available to the general public.

This is why we now have two different enneagrams. In the past, these enneagram models have remained mostly separate, because the Gurdjieff teachings are sufficiently esoteric that the inheritors of those teachings tend to regard the personality enneagram as a degraded version of the process enneagram. Those who use the personality enneagram find it useful enough that most don't feel the need to link it to Gurdjieff's work. But I've found it valuable to work with both together. Using a "dual enneagram" approach is especially helpful for describing the hero's journey, because it gives us a way to look at it as a transformational process that can be characterized from nine points of view, according to one's enneagram type.

A Potential-Oriented Enneagram Approach

The conclusion I drew from my first several years of enneagram research is that the enneagram is a system that can be used for multiple purposes and taught from multiple perspectives. As someone interested in human potential, I decided to develop a potential-oriented approach to the enneagram. It is this approach that I develop in my books and articles.

In my first book, *The Positive Enneagram* (2009), I emphasized the positive qualities of the nine type and explore parallels between the personality enneagram and Gurdjieff's process enneagram. In the second, *Archetypes of the Enneagram* (2010), I interpreted the enneagram from a soul-oriented perspective based on the work of Carl Jung and James Hillman. In my third, *The Integral Enneagram* (2013), I looked at the enneagram through the prism of Ken Wilber's integral system, which depicts personality development as a necessary and progressive stage in inner work.

At the 2013 International Enneagram Association Convention—whose theme was about Wilber's work—I gave a well-received talk on this book. But it did not make the kind of impact necessary to shift the views of opinion leaders in the field. At the 2014 convention, I presented research on positive psychology that demonstrates the benefits of focusing on human potential rather than human limitation. Again, the talk was well-attended and the audience receptive; I was privately complimented on my work by several colleagues. But it was clear to me that the original paradigm that launched the field was still firmly in place—and probably would remain in place so long as those who originated the anti-ego paradigm remained active in the field. It was at that point that my thoughts began to turn once again to the tarot, in part because it is grounded in the potential-oriented philosophy of Hermeticism (see Chapter 3).

Re-enter the Tarot

When I started delving into the tarot again in 2013, my focus was on trying to see whether a case could be made for the idea that there are genuine correspondences between the cards in the tarot and the points of the enneagram. That's when I re-discovered Banzhaf's *Tarot and the Journey of the Hero*.

When I read the book in 2000, I did not have the background in either the tarot or the enneagram to fully grasp its significance. But when I re-read it 13 years later, its implications leapt out in a way that was impossible to ignore. In 2014, I wrote a 50-page article, "The Hero's Journey through the Enneagram," for the *Enneagram Monthly*, planning to follow up with articles looking at each of the nine types as heroes-in-the-making. That didn't quite happen, because I went through a period when I was simply unable to write. (After writing over 50 articles for *Enneagram Monthly* since 2006 and three books in five years, I was probably suffering from burnout.)

So instead, I read—adding yet more tarot books and articles to my burgeoning collection. I also joined several tarot study groups, which gave me a more practical education than could be gained from reading books or using the tarot for solo meditation. Two and a half years later, my vacationing "writing muse" suddenly returned. I re-read my original article, planning to use it as a template for the book. But I found it wanting, both because it was written entirely for an enneagram audience and because I had learned new things as the result of my forced sabbatical from writing.

As a result, I had to re-write the article from scratch, which took about four times longer than writing the original! Now that I knew more, I encountered more problems that required addressing, especially concerning the roots of the tarot and the numerical values that were associated with each tarot card. The result was Appendix E, which could easily have evolved into a book all by itself (more on this below).

I retain an interest in demonstrating the benefits of working with the enneagram from a more optimistic perspective. This shows up in the present book as an advocacy for adopting an approach for enneagram work similar to the Hermetic approach that informs most tarot work. Hermeticists see human nature as essentially divine, not sinful or neurotic. From a Hermetic perspective, the nine enneagram types might be described as nine kinds of divine potential and the hero's journey as a means of developing that potential.

At this point, there is very little written either on the hero's journey on the enneagram or on the relationship between the tarot and the enneagram. The only material on the latter comes from one online article by Richard Dagan that briefly explores the relationships between the enneagram, the Myers-Briggs Type Indicator (MBTI), and the tarot. Using the approach pioneered by

Angeles Arrien and Mary Greer, Dagan uses cross-sum addition to calculate his Destiny card (based on the sum of the digits of his birthday), in an effort to find out whether it might be the same as his enneagram type (which in his case, it was not).[14] It is not the same for me, either (my enneagram type is Four and my tarot Destiny card is Nine, the Hermit). But there *is* a relationship, in that I'm not just a Four, but a Four that leans towards Point 5 (such that Five would be called my dominant "wing" type).[15] On the enneagram circle, Point 9 on the enneagram is across from Point 4—and can thus balance the energy associated with Point 4. (Interestingly, Dagan appears to have the exact same configuration as mine; he identifies himself as a Four/Five and his Destiny card as The Hermit!)

It's possible that there are some interesting relationships to explore between the enneagram types and our Destiny card. But that will not be our primary focus here. For me, it's enough just to lay the groundwork for a numerical linking of the enneagram with the tarot.[16]

Why This Book?

My main goal in this book is to explore the parallels between the tarot and enneagram using the hero's journey as a metaphor for the process of individuation. But more specifically, it is to present readers with a background in either system with a way to see it from a different angle, thereby expanding their understanding. Readers with enneagram experience will no doubt find some of the information on the enneagram fairly basic; readers with a knowledge of the tarot will likely have the same experience with the tarot descriptions. Readers are cordially invited to skim the sections that cover familiar ground. (You are also invited to skim any material that seem overly esoteric or besides the point!)

Scope

In the interests of keeping the main focus on the interaction between the tarot and enneagram, I decided to include system-specific information on only those aspects of both systems that are particularly relevant to linking the two. In the case of the tarot, this means focusing mainly on the symbolism of the major arcana (not the minor arcana or court cards);[17] in the case of the enneagram, this means focusing on the numeric symbolism of the nine enneagram points (which is seldom discussed in enneagram books).

However, I include somewhat more information on the enneagram for three main reasons. First, the enneagram is a more inherently abstract system. Without a description of its nine points and their interrelationships, it's impossible to understand it. Second, the enneagrammatic approach that I use involves both the personality and process enneagrams, and few if any authors have attempted to describe the relationship between them, as I do here. Third, the tarot is an inherently more transparent system, because its images speak to most people, even tarot beginners. There is still ample material on the tarot, especially its 22 Keys; see Chapter 5 and 12–14 for the hero's journey in the tarot and Appendix A for a description of all 78 tarot cards.

Organization & Other Details

ORGANIZATION. The book is organized into four main sections plus five appendixes.

▶ PART I introduces the hero's journey, the tarot, and the enneagram. Chapter 1— the one you are reading right now—provides an overview of the book; Chapter 2 introduces the Western Esoteric Tradition that gave birth to the tarot; Chapter 3 introduces the magico-philosophical system of Hermeticism, because it is the basis for much tarot work; Chapter 4 explores the hero's journey as conceived by Joseph Campbell and mapped (by me) onto the enneagram; and Chapter 5 relates the hero's journey as it unfolds in the 22 Keys of the tarot.

▶ PART II offers a fairly detailed introduction to the enneagram as a system. Chapter 6 introduces the basic enneagram concepts, especially those relevant to the personality enneagram; Chapter 7 describes the nine personality types of the enneagram; and Chapter 8 describes the process enneagram and shows how the personality and process enneagrams are two applications of one system.

▶ PART III discusses number symbolism and how it can be used to generate a new nine-path, 27-Key tarot model. Chapter 9 focuses on number symbolism and why it matters; Chapter 10 introduces the idea of developing a 27-card major arcana and examines two decks that have 27 cards; and Chapter 11 introduces an enneagram-informed tarot model with its nine paths of three Keys each, plus The Fool.[18]

▶ PART IV presents detailed descriptions of the nine paths: Chapter 12 describes Paths 1–3, Chapter 13, Paths 4–6, and Chapter 14, Paths 7–9. Chapter 15 describes applications for the new model in enneagram and tarot work; and Chapter 16 discusses the broader implications of the model for modern culture and the Western Esoteric Tradition.

▶ APPENDIXES: Appendix A provides a brief description of all 78 tarot cards; Appendix B discusses ways to discover your enneagram type; Appendix C describes ways to use the enneagram in tarot work; Appendix D looks at one way to map the minor tarot onto the enneagram; and Appendix E describes the relationship between the tarot, enneagram, and qabala.

Appendix E is more complex than most of the chapters in this book, because it not only introduces the qabala and describes its potential relationship to the enneagram and tarot, but offers a detailed discussion about the fateful decision by the Order of the Golden Dawn to discard the traditional numeric values associated with the tarot in order to fit the tarot onto the paths of the qabalistic Tree of Life, a decision I've come to view as problematic for the reasons enumerated in this appendix.

Style Conventions. Below are key stylistic decisions that may require some explanation.

▸ As mentioned earlier, I refer to the 22 cards of the major arcana as *Keys*, rather than cards or trumps; so The Fool is described as Key 0, the Magician as Key 1, etc. I like the term "Key" because it reminds me that the function of the major arcana is to unlock the inner doors that enable us to find our way home.

▸ I don't capitalize the names of most systems or approaches—e.g., the enneagram, tarot, major arcana, minor arcana, hero's journey, qabala, sephira, sephiroth—although many people do. This is not out of a lack of respect for these systems but because these terms are used so many times throughout this book. When reading the same term over and over, it's becomes tiring to see Everything In Capital Letters. Exceptions include terms that are so generic that a non-capital might create confusion (e.g., "Tree of Life" for the qabalistic Tree of Life). However, in direct quotes, I use the style conventions of the person quoted.

▸ Cited sources are referenced by book title, author's name, year of publication and the publisher. There are chapter endnotes for cited materials and a reference section at the book's end for all books, articles, and major online articles. If a source is available online as a PDF, I try to indicate where to find it.

This book is about the hero's journey, but writing it was also a journey. For me, the journey started as scribbles on a piece of a Starbucks napkin. As the project evolved, I learned not only about the hero's journey on the enneagram and tarot, but about my own inner journey as a writer and a person.

One day, I was thinking about the nature of books. It came to me that there are really only two kinds of books: living and dead. Dead books are the ones that seem "flat"—without an animating spark (written-by-committee textbooks come to mind). While books like this may inform us, they seldom beckon us onward. Living books are the ones whose words seem to leap off the page, tugging at us to read further. This book came alive for me as I wrote. I hope it will for you, too.

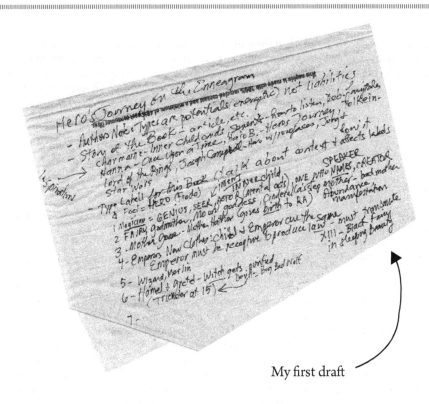

My first draft

Notes

[1] See http://www.huffingtonpost.com/matt-ragland/the-heros-journey-using-a_b_4893165.html.

[2] "Jung's Hero: the New Form of Heroism," The Jungian Center for the Spiritual Sciences; see http://jungiancenter.org/jungs-hero-the-new-form-of-heroism/.

[3] Like many tarot writers, I refer to the 22 cards of the major arcana as *Keys* to highlight their symbolic significance.

[4] Lerner, Isha & Mark. *Inner Child Cards* (Bear: 1992/2002), p. 42.

[5] In the Jungian-inspired MBTI, an INFJ = a Introverted Intuitive Feeling Judger.

[6] There is a logical problem with the impossibility of the idea of "returning to essence" that has been addressed both by Ken Wilber and tarotist Gareth Knight. Wilber critiques A. H. Almaas on this point (see *The Eye of Spirit,* Shambhala: 2001, footnote 11, p. 365); you can also read my condensed version of Wilber's argument on pp. 90–92 in *The Integral Enneagram* (Geranium Press: 2013). Gareth Knight comments that "no created being can attain to its essence. Were any created being to... [do so], ... it would by that very fact become uncreate" (*Qabalistic Symbolism*, Weiser: 1965/2001, p. 68).

[7] "Breaking the Tyranny of the Ego," an interview by Sam Keen, in *Interviews with Oscar Ichazo* (Arica: 1982), pp. 9–10, 13. It should be noted that Oscar Ichazo has never revealed exactly

where the idea came to him to look at the nine enneagram points as revealing distinctive differences among human beings. Every time he has been asked about it, he says something different. So it's doubtful if we'll ever really know the whole truth. The one thing that those of us who work with the system know for certain—and upon which we can all agree—is that it is a profound system that is extremely rewarding to work with, whatever perspective we adopt for that work.

[8] For a summary of Ichazo's enneagram teachings, see "The Arica Teaching," by John Lilly and Joseph Hart, in *Transpersonal Psychologies* (Harper & Row: 1975), pp. 329–352.

[9] *Ennea-type Structures* (Gateways: 1990), p. 1.

[10] "The Development of Personality," in *The Development of Personality* (Princeton Univ. Press, R. F. C. Hull, trans.: 1981), p. 167.

[11] See http://carljungdepthpsychology.blogspot.com/2015/03/carl-jung-on-prima-materia.html.

[12] Carl Jung is not the only who advocates the reconciling of the opposites; it is also a cornerstone of qabalistic thinking. Thus, in *Qabalistic Symbolism* (Weiser: 1965/2001), Gareth Knight says that the path of human beings "is one of equilibrium between the opposites" (p. 47). Interestingly, Knight also discusses vice and virtue in the context of the energy centers (sephiroth) on the Tree of Life, observing that "these are not…part of the Sephirah itself but are the reactions of the human psyche to it…really a Sephirah has no vice" (p. 48). So while we are free to speak of virtues or vices in relationship to the enneagram types, sephiroth on the Tree of Life, or in any other context, we are not speaking of a characteristic intrinsic to the thing itself.

[13] This quote of G. I. Gurdjieff's, like many of those on his enneagram teachings, comes from P. D. Ouspensky's account of Gurdjieff's work as related in *In Search of the Miraculous* (Harcourt: 1949/2001), p. 287.

[14] See http://richarddagan.com/zulu.php.

[15] See Chapter 6 for a discussion of the enneagram wing types.

[16] The material on the enneagram connecting points in Chapter 6 explains how we can use the connecting points to understand both our relationships with other people and the relationships among different elements within our own psyche.

[17] Appendix D describes how specific combinations of suits and numbers in the minor arcana demonstrate a potential link between the enneagram and tarot.

[18] In regard to The Fool, the approach I'm proposing generates 28 major arcana Keys if we include The Fool as part of the major arcana (see frontispiece). But The Fool is a funny character; there are times when it makes sense to see The Fool as one of the cards in the majors and other times when it makes sense to see The Fool as either separate (the figure who walks through all the stages) or as embodied in all the cards. The same can be said of The Fool's counterpart in the enneagram: Point 9, which can also be considered Point 0! For more discussions on The Fool, see Chapters 9, 14, 16, and Appendix E, Part II.

2:
The Emergence of the Tarot in the West

The tarot is a symbol code that depicts universal and natural laws and principles that are shared by all the world's great religio-spiritual traditions.
– Amber Jayanti

THE WESTERN ESOTERIC TRADITION consists of the mystical teachings of Europe, the Near East, northern Africa (notably, ancient Egypt), and potentially the Americas, to the extent these are known. It is more fragmented than its Eastern counterpart, mainly due to its widespread suppression by both religious and secular authorities during the last several millennia. As a result, it can be challenging to trace the development of its various traditions. In this chapter, we'll focus on the origins and development of the tarot.

Origins of the Tarot

The tarot is highly mysterious. In referring to the tarot's "seeming appearance out of nowhere," in the late 14th to early 15th century in Europe, Thomas D. Worrel has commented that "even the Gypsies are easier to trace than the Tarot."[1] But in his book, *The Tarot: History, Symbolism, and Divination* (2005), tarot historian Robert Place discusses what can be factually documented about the tarot; thus, everything in this chapter is derived from his ideas unless otherwise noted.

According to Place, starting in the 18th century, Western occultists claimed that the tarot originated as a spiritual text in ancient Egypt and that it was spread through Europe by the Gypsies. Others said that the trump cards—or *major arcana*, as they were later labeled by occultists—contain a type of secret code in which each of their 22 images is related to a letter of the Hebrew alphabet. In the Hebrew kabbalah, each Hebrew letter is associated with a planet, a sign of the zodiac, or an element. Therefore, correlating the major arcana with the alphabet added these associations to its repertoire (pp. 5–6).

Place goes on to add that there is little hard evidence to support the idea that the tarot is of Egyptian origin, an idea which he believes distracts us from its value as an imagistic system. Tarot can, however, be traced back to the early Italian Renaissance, when certain prominent Catholic families such as the Visconti family commissioned the creation of hand-painted tarot decks. The most famous early deck appeared around 1450, to celebrate Francesco Sforza and his wife Bianca

Maria Visconti, daughter of the duke Filippo Maria. Now known as the Visconti-Sforza deck, it has been widely copied and remains influential to this day.

Within about half a century, the tarot became more widely disseminated, especially around the area of Marseilles, France. The Marseilles tarot as we know it today, however, was not published until 1748 by Grimaud. This style of tarot became very popular, so popular that it serves as a model for many modern tarot decks, including the Rider-Waite-Smith (RWS) deck used in the present book.

Place documents the existence of Chinese cards that preceded the European decks, as well as Mamluk decks, which existed during the Mamluk dynasty that ruled Egypt and Syria from 1250 to 1517. The two Mamluk decks still in existence both date to the 1400s, although one or two cards can be traced back maybe another 100 years.

However, he pegs the year 1781 as the dividing line between the early and modern history of the tarot, for it was this year that the French esoteric writer Antoine Court de Gébelin (1725–1784) published the volume of *Le Monde Primitif* that made intriguing historical claims for the tarot, asserting that it is of Egyptian origin, a product of ancient Hermetic wisdom. Gébelin believed that these teachings were depicted as images in playing cards in order to disguise their esoteric origins.

According to Cynthia Giles, Gébelin first encountered the tarot six years earlier, in 1775, at a social gathering where the hostess showed him one of the major arcana Keys. She said that "as an avid student of mythology, archaeology, and linguistics, [he] became immediately enthralled,"noting his reaction to the first card to which he was introduced: "I glanced at it and as soon as I did, I recognized the allegory [to Egyptian teachings]."[2]

Gébelin's recognition must have been more intuitive than fact-based, because what was actually known about ancient Egypt was quite limited prior to the discovery of the Rosetta Stone in 1799. But the late 1700s was a period when there was nonetheless intense interest in ancient Egyptian culture.

In *Le Monde Primitif*, Gébelin also published a tarot article by his friend, Louis-Raphaël-Lucrèce de Fayolle, Le Comte de Mellet (1727–1804). Noting that there are 22 major arcana Keys and 22 letters in the Hebrew alphabet, Mellet proposed assigning one Hebrew letter to each Key. This proposal was designed to make it possible to link the tarot with the qabala, which was considered by many to be the most foundational system in the Western Esoteric Tradition. This idea of linking tarot and qabala proved to be so intriguing that it fired the imagination of French occultists for the next century. It also became a key feature in the Golden Dawn's qabalistic system.

One of Mellet's contemporaries, Jean-Baptiste Alliette (1738–1791), re-named himself Etteilla by re-arranging the letters in his name. He was interested in using the tarot for divination and commissioned the creation of a deck to be used for that purpose. Although Etteilla has often been denigrated by later occultists for making rather grandiose, hard-to-support claims, his *Grand Etteilla* deck, published in 1789, is often considered to be the first modern tarot deck. It was extremely popular for divination, and was the first deck to clearly relate the four minor suits to the four elements (fire, water, air, earth) and to provide illustrations for the minor arcana cards. Place notes that occultists after Etteila somewhat de-emphasized the connection between tarot and Hermeticism in favor of focusing on the connection between tarot and qabala (see pp. 52–53 for a discussion).

Tarot in the 19th & 20th Centuries

The next prominent figure in the history of the tarot was Alphonse-Louis Constant, who took the name of Éliphas Lévi (1810–1875) when he became involved in occult studies on magic, qabala, and tarot, about which he wrote numerous books in French. Lévi was a grand synthesizer, and according to Place, was interested in describing the links among many different occult systems: alchemy, ceremonial magic, Pythagorean number theory, astrology, qabala, Hermeticism, Egyptian symbolism, and tarot.

Like Etteilla, Lévi assigned the 22 Keys of the major arcana to the 22 letters of the Hebrew alphabet. For this purpose, he used the numbering system of the Marseille tarot, which pairs The Magician with One, The High Priestess with Two, and so forth; the only difference between his numbering scheme and that of most modern tarot decks is that he assigned the Fool the position between Judgment and the World. While the correspondences suggested by Lévi were mostly retained on the Continent, they were not retained in the English-speaking world (Great Britain and America) because of changes introduced by the Golden Dawn in the late 1800s (see Appendix E).

However, Lévi's influence remains strong in the tradition of magical Hermeticism. He was a highly imaginative artist with a particular talent for depicting the Hermetic idea of balancing the opposites. His depictions of the Chariot and the Devil obviously influenced the depictions in the RWS deck and all the decks based on the RWS. He also explored the possibility of assigning the 10 numbered cards in the minor arcana to the 10 cosmic emanations (*sephiroth*) on the qabalistic Tree of Life.

Although Lévi never developed his own tarot deck, Oswald Wirth (1860–1943)—a Swiss occultist and student of the French occultist Stanislas de Guaita—published a new deck in 1889 that incorporated many of Lévi's ideas in his illustrations; much later (in 1927), he published a related book, *The Tarot of the Magicians*. But in the same year that Wirth published his new deck (1889), tarotist Gérard Encausse (1865–1916)—better known as Papus—published *The Tarot of the Bohemians*, a tarot book inspired by Lévi's ideas.

Lévi also inspired a resurgence of interest in the occult societies such as the Freemasons and Rosicrucians and the idea that there are hidden, secret teachings that can help us unlock the mysteries of life. Those who started these societies valued secrecy and went about devising initiatory grades for their members; the most arcane secrets were reserved for those at the highest grades.

Although a number of occult groups started up in the late 1800s, the most well-known in the English-speaking world is the Hermetic Order of the Golden Dawn (GD), founded in 1888 by three English occultists: William Westcott, S. L. M. Mathers, and William Robert Woodman. Although the Order remained intact for only 15 years, while it lasted, its membership included some of the most illustrious occult figures of the day, figures such as William Butler Yeats, A. E. Waite, and Aleister Crowley (although many would regard Crowley as more notorious than illustrious).[3] The GD also served as the inspiration for others who later followed in a similar vein: Dion Fortune, Paul Foster Case, and Israel Regardie among them. Pamela Colman ("Pixie") Smith was introduced to the Golden Dawn by Yeats. In 1903, she became a member of Waite's GD splinter group, the Rectified Rite of the Golden Dawn.

The Golden Dawn strongly emphasized the use of the tarot as a tool for qabalistic work.[4,5] As far as tarot is concerned, one of its foremost legacies was the development of an esoteric deck that developed the symbolism used in their ceremonies and initiations. But the GD deck was never published; each member had to re-create and color the deck on his or her own, using a deck believed to have been designed sometime around 1888 to 1890 by either S. L. M. Mathers or his artistic wife Moina.[6] Modern versions of the Golden Dawn deck, such as those by Chic Cicero and Robert Wang, are based on information collected by Israel Regardie from *Stella Matutina,* one of the Golden Dawn's offshoots, after it more or less disbanded in the 1930s.

After Arthur E. Waite had established his Rectified Rite of the Golden Dawn group in 1903, he wanted to develop a new deck that incorporated some, but not all, of the symbolism of the Golden Dawn deck. In 1909, he hired Pamela Colman Smith to do the illustrations. Smith had experience not only as an artist but as a theater set designer. She was also an imaginative painter with an appreciation of nature.

As a result, Smith was able to create a deck with a very inviting appearance—so inviting that it eventually became the most popular tarot deck in history. Traditionally called the Rider-Waite deck (because it was designed by Waite and published by Rider), it is now more often called the RWS (Rider-Waite-Smith) deck, in order to give more credit to Smith, whose contribution may be greater than Waite implies. (Waite is well-known for emphasizing his own insights and de-emphasizing those of his colleagues!) Not much is known about the process by which the deck was created nor the degree to which Waite supervised its creation, because neither Waite nor Smith say much about this.

But its use of pictorial imagery for all 78 cards has made it a highly practical tool for divination. This is probably another reason that the RWS deck became so popular.

Waite was, however, only one of a number of Golden Dawn inheritors able to preserve and promote the original teachings of the Golden Dawn in some form. Other well-known figures include

▶ **ALEISTER CROWLEY** (1875–1947): After the Golden Dawn disbanded, Crowley became an influential and provocative figure in the occult community and an influential member of the Ordo Templi Orientis. He later went on to commission the development of a visionary "Thoth" tarot deck, a project to which he expected to devote six months. But due to its great complexity, the deck's development actually took place over five years (1938–1943). It was not actually published until 1969, 22 years after Crowley's death. However, its artistry is remarkable; it is said that Crowley had artist Lady Frieda Harris paint some of the cards as many as eight times. In 1977, Harris' paintings were re-photographed for a second edition and further revisions followed in 1986 and 1996.

▶ **PAUL FOSTER CASE** (1884–1954): Case founded the venerable Builders of the Adytum (B.O.T.A.) in 1922, which remains a resource for serious tarot work, offering both Case's books and a course of study for those interested in systematically working with the major Keys. Case also developed his own meticulously designed deck, which was illustrated by artist Jessie Burns Parke (although only the major arcana and court cards include pictorial scenes). It is widely considered to be one of the best esoteric tarot decks available for working with the symbolism of the major arcana.

▶ **DION FORTUNE** (1890–1946): Fortune initially joined one of the Golden Dawn splinter groups, Alpha and Omega. But in 1927, she founded her own group, the Community of the Inner Light—a group that lives on to this day as the Society of the Inner Light. She wrote what remains the most popular book ever published on the qabala: *The Mystical Qabala* (Weiser: 2000). One of her students, Gareth Knight, became a prolific author on the tarot and qabala.

▶ **ISRAEL REGARDIE** (1907–1985): Regardie was invited to become Aleister Crowley's secretary in 1928. Although he distanced himself from Crowley four years later, he remained respectful of his writings. Regardie is known particularly for his book *The Golden Dawn: The Original Account of the Teachings, Rites & Ceremonies of the Hermetic Order*, first published in 1937, which is notable for its never-before-published information about the inner workings of the Golden Dawn. He later collaborated with Robert Wang to create a tarot deck based on the original symbolism of the Golden Dawn which was published in 1977.

The Tarot Today

As mentioned above, the Western Esoteric Tradition was politically suppressed by both religious and secular authorities for many centuries. Thus, it's not surprising that before 1960, few people outside of esoteric groups knew much about practices such as tarot divination. But as Lee Irwin notes in *Gnostic Tarot* (1998), the consciousness revolution of the 1960s paved the way for a sharp upsurge of public interest in the occult and consequently the tarot (p. 16). Irwin goes on to provide a detailed commentary on landmarks in recent tarot history, including the publication of Eden Gray's *Complete Guide to the Tarot* in 1971 and Stuart Kaplan's impressive, four-volume *Encyclopedia of Tarot* in 1978. The 1980s and 90s saw a veritable explosion in the publication of tarot books and decks. By the turn of the 21st century, there were over 1,000 tarot decks in circulation, with more in the pipeline. Many came packaged with full-fledged books (not just the obligatory LWBs—little white books— that are included with every deck).

Today, interest in the tarot remains strong. Nevertheless, some people still view tarot work—and especially tarot divination—as something weird or creepy, probably because of the historical religious taboo against seeking hidden knowledge. Case in point: although my tarot teacher is a courteous professional who wouldn't attract attention in a crowd, when she tried to open a bank account for her tarot school, the clerk at her credit union refused to set it up in the name of the school. Why? Because "Tarot is a cult." That was three years ago.

But as one tarot author mildly observed, "The cards themselves are rather neutral. They are nothing more than 78 paper cards with images on them." If we go back far enough (to 14th century Europe), ordinary playing cards were repeatedly banned by European authorities because they were said to promote idleness, wickedness, and impious behavior. Nowadays, we see card playing as an innocuous pastime.

Tarot can be casually used for fortune-telling, but it can also be used for sustained inner work.[7] For tarot is an imaginal system in a world that tends to discount the value of imagination. It thus fills a gap that cannot be filled by more abstract systems. Its powerful images speak directly to the subconscious, providing instant access to the inner psyche. So it's a powerful tool with many applications: in meditation, in intuitive work, for the development of creativity, in depth psychology, and for Hermetic study. We'll take a look at each of these in turn.

Author Janina Renee says she believes that the tarot was originally designed specifically as an aid to *meditation*. She explores ways it can be used to help us contemplate paths to spiritual self-improvement, broaden our understanding of the human condition, and highlight the workings of archetypal forces in our lives. The simplest approach, she says, is to draw a card a day, and then meditate on the image.[8]

The tarot can also help develop our *intuitive faculties* by giving them a more tangible form. At tarot.com, the home page informs us that intuition is "that pure perception of truth we all have hidden deep inside...the inner voice of your higher self, telling you what is the right thing to do and hoping you won't ignore it."[9] Although we do sometimes ignore our inner voice, often we simply don't hear it. Life moves so fast and noise is almost everywhere. So it's helpful to have a tool that amplifies the message, the way that a speaker amplifies the music from a receiver. The tarot can translate the dream-like messages of the subconscious into a solid image that we can consciously work with. When a card like the Tower or the Devil appears, it's hard to ignore the message!

Tarot fosters *creativity* by providing images with the power to call forth new associations and inspirations. In the tarot classes that I attend, many participants are artists. They find inspiration in the images, and prefer to do inner work in a way that is more imagination-based than doctrine-based. They like the freedom of expression associated with the tarot tradition, a tradition that uses the imagination to expand human consciousness.

Tarot supports *deep psychological work* because its images tap into the deep psyche, allowing us both to detect unhealed wounds and discover unknown gifts. It is especially fruitful for anyone interested in the work of Carl Jung or James Hillman, both of whom worked extensively with imaginal archetypes. Jungian-oriented tarotists like Robert Wang, Hajo Banzhaf, and Art Rosengarten offer a number of ideas for using tarot that can be used to foster greater awareness of the psyche, to heal inner psychological rifts, and to resolve interpersonal conflicts.[10] Tarot work especially lends itself to the Jungian technique of *active imagination* (where we enter into a dialogue with one or more of the characters on the cards, in order to directly communicate with the unconscious). Tarot work can also be done in combination with Jungian *dream work*. Since working with the tarot, I've had a number of meaningful tarot dreams, featuring cards like Justice or The Tower.

In the Tower dream, I found myself in a struggle with two strong men, who were dragging me somewhere while I fought them tooth and nail. Then I saw we were at the top of a Florentine tower, very high up. It had a gaping hole in the side which they pushed me towards. I was terrified; it was so vivid. These men were strong, so they were ultimately able to shove me out the hole. But instead of falling, I found myself floating in the air. There was no more fear, just a peaceful feeling. Later that night, I felt as though the top of my head was coming off; there was so much energy there (as though I'd been struck by lightning!). The dream came to me the night before my tarot group was going to study The Tower.

A fifth use for the tarot is specifically *Hermetic*—to explore the nature of Hermetic philosophy and magical practices using the symbols of the tarot. The focus in Hermetic work is on exploring the deeper mysteries of life in a way that is both practical and transformational. Hermetic tarot work is often done in combination with related systems such as the qabala, alchemy, and astrology, because the use of multiple approaches facilitates the development of a rich interior source of symbolic imagery (which is why the tarot has often been called a Treasure House of Images). Tarot work facilitates the building up of ever-expanding symbolic associations that can be used in divination, qabalistic pathworking, ceremonial magick, art, writing, and Jungian-oriented inner work.

Although this approach can be initially challenging (lots of memorization required), these associations can eventually make the tarot cards come alive in ways that are hard to imagine. If we frame this idea in terms of the hero's journey, it's the development of such associations that allows the hero to move from ordinary life into the Special World where transformation is possible.

In this book, the hero's journey is presented mainly through the dual prisms of depth psychology and Hermetic philosophy. Depth psychology provides methods to help would-be heroes distinguish the conditioned from the unconditioned self; Hermetic philosophy provides an integrated set of life principles that support such a quest. These principles are explored more fully in Chapter 3.

Notes

[1] "The Quest of the Magus: A Summary of the Western Magical Tradition," in *The Inner West: An Introduction to the Inner Wisdom*, Jay Kinney, ed. (Tarcher: 2004), p. 114.

[2] *The Tarot: History, Mystery, and Lore* (Paragon House: 1992), p. 23.

[3] The Golden Dawn also included illustrious, but lesser known, female members such as Moina Mathers, Florence Farr, Annie Horniman, and Maud Gonne. They were finally given their due in Mary Greer's fascinating history, *Women of the Golden Dawn* (Dark Street Press: 1995).

[4] Here I am referring to the Hermetic qabala, which can be described in many ways. See Part I of Appendix E for a concise introduction.

[5] A readable introduction to the Golden Dawn and its principal players can be found in R. A. Gilbert's *Twilight of the Magicians: The Rise and Fall of a Magical Order* (Aquarian Press: 1983). For a more in-depth treatment of both the Golden Dawn and modern tarot, see *A History of the Occult Tarot, 1870–1970*, by Ronald Decker and Michael Dummett (Duckworth: 2008).

[6] See Emily Auger's *Tarot and Other Meditation Decks: History, Theory, Aesthetics, Typology* (McFarland: 2004), p. 6.

[7] For the record, divination is not the same thing as fortune telling. The goal in divination is to attune to the divine to align one's actions with divine will, not just to foretell the future.

[8] "Other Uses for Tarot: Meditation," by Janina Renée; see http://www.llewellyn.com/journal/article/1678.

[9] See http://www.tarot.com/tarot/readings-benefits.

[10] Robert Wang's book, *The Qabalistic Tarot* (Marcus Aurelius: 1978/2004), is a classic; Art Rosengarten's *Tarot and Psychology* (Paragon House: 2000) is an insightful Jungian-based exploration of the tarot.

3:
The Hermetic Spirit of the Tarot

A little science estranges a man from God; a lot of science brings him back.
– Sir Francis Bacon

ALTHOUGH HERMETIC TEACHINGS date back to at least 100 C. E, Hermeticism as a philosophy was eclipsed by Christianity after 400–500 C. E. But when a renewed interest in Classical Antiquity arose among the European *literati* during the 1400s, they were eager to understand this re-discovered philosophy. Although the Renaissance is often associated with Greek neo-platonism and the revival of the secular philosophy of humanism—naturally leading, it is said, to the modern scientific method—it was actually the magically-inspired philosophy of Hermeticism that sparked the great rebirth of art, philosophy, and science in 15th century Europe.

Hermeticism: The Inspiration of the Renaissance

Esoteric historian Peter Kingsley observes that "Western scholarship has managed to dismiss...[Hermetic teachings] as second-rate philosophy, devoid of real value."[1] It is dismissed, he says, because of its subtlety and emphasis on knowledge as *gnosis*, knowledge of the divine. But in recent years, scholars such as historian Frances Yates have begun to take a second look at Hermeticism and the pivotal role it played in Renaissance thought.[2]

Lynn Picknett and Clive Prince discuss the Hermetic revival in a more story-like form in their fascinating book, *The Forbidden Universe: The Occult Origins of Science and the Search for the Mind of God* (2011). A key player in this revival was Cosimo de Medici, who had a keen interest in the lost knowledge of the ancients and who dreamed of re-establishing a modern version of Plato's Academy in Florence. To that end, he sent agents searching for lost manuscripts and employed the great scholar Marsilio Ficino (1433–1499) to translate them. In 1463, just as Ficino was about to translate Plato's works from Greek to Latin, a monk returned from Macedonia with a Greek manuscript containing the first fourteen writings from the *Corpus Hermeticum*. Cosimo asked Ficino to translate this new manuscript first. When Ficino's translation of the *Hermetica* was published eight years later, it "sent seismic shock waves throughout the academic community in Florence and beyond, being widely and feverishly discussed" (p. 26).

Picknett and Prince cite several reasons for all the excitement over the *Corpus Hermeticum*. First, it offered a much more open and optimistic view of human nature (and nature itself), and thus radically departed from Christianity's "stifling view of creation and humanity's place in it" (p. 27). Second, it introduced the idea that there was a primordial religion, now lost, that served as the basis for all the religions that followed (an idea that later became known as the *perennial philosophy*.) Third, it hinted that this primordial religion was from ancient Egypt and that Moses himself learned "great secrets" from its teachings. Fourth, it attributed these teachings to an esteemed God/priest Hermes Trismegistus (the "Thrice-great"), who was considered to be a mysterious sage of mythic proportions.

Originally, Church officials (and even some popes) took a positive interest in Hermetic ideas because they were carefully presented by Hermeticists as laying the groundwork for the rise of the One True Church. But over time, Catholic support eroded for a number of reasons. One was Martin Luther's publication of his *Ninety-Five Theses* in 1517 and the Reformation it created, which undermined the authority of Catholicism. Another problem concerned three astronomical assertions made in Hermetic writings: that the earth (a) moves in space, (b) revolves on its axis, and (c) rotates around the sun. The fact that these assertions happened to be true (and that high Church officials knew them to be true) was besides the point; these astronomical observations did not accord with sacred Scripture, and the Church needed to buy time to somehow reconcile the two. Meanwhile, Church officials sought to quash independent speculation on the part of Renaissance thinkers who thought too freely. A third problem concerned the inherent power and beauty of Hermetic ideas, which moved men not just to dream, but to act.

Two of those men were Giordano Bruno (1548–1600) and Tommaso Campanella (1568–1639). They were visionary thinkers who sought to develop and share Hermetic ideas and to use those ideas to change the social order. Bruno was especially well known for his development of methods that used mental imagery to enhance memory. His work also had a magical dimension, "in which different symbols, shapes, colours, and materials are deemed to have specific properties and energies based on magical associations. The trick was to use those principles when forming the mental images" (*The Forbidden Universe*, p. 44).

The following quote, attributed by William Boulting to Bruno, captures the essential nature of the Hermetic spirit that animated him:

> I need not instruct you of my belief: Time gives all and takes all away; everything changes but nothing perishes; One only is immutable, eternal and ever endures, one and the same with itself. With this philosophy my spirit grows, my mind expands. Whereof, however obscure the night may be, I await daybreak…Rejoice therefore, and keep whole, if you can, and return love for love.[3]

Campanella was another man of action who so believed in the Hermetic vision that he attempted to organize an insurrection in 1598–99 with the aim of setting up a Hermetically-oriented state in Calabria (then ruled by Spain). According to Picknett and Prince, "Campanella shared Bruno's vision of the great magical transformation that was glimmering over the horizon and which was written in the stars. He also regarded the heliocentric theory as the trigger of the New Age of Hermetic enlightenment, and…believed it was destined to happen in 1600" (p. 77).

But this vision was not to be. Bruno was imprisoned in 1592, spending the next eight years languishing in an Inquisition cell; Campanella's Calabrian revolt failed and he was also clapped into prison to be examined by the Inquisition in November 1599. Campanella at least survived the experience (by feigning madness, even under torture). Bruno did not; he was burned at the stake three months later, on February 17, 1600. The timing of his death suggests that the Church was sending a very strong message to anyone who dared to challenge its authority.

Another telling blow to Hermeticism came in 1614, when Isaac Casaubon published a linguistic analysis of the *Hermetica* showing that these writings could not have been produced in ancient Egypt, because they used a form of Greek that could be dated to 100 C. E. Casaubon's analysis enormously damaged the credibility of the *Hermetica*, not only because he (correctly) dated the writings but because he accused the writers of getting all of their material from the New Testament. Much later, it was shown that they were not plagiarized—that Egyptian teachings did indeed have a major influence on the content of the *Hermetica*.[4] But in the short term, the effect was devastating. Although individuals such as Isaac Newton and groups such as the Rosicrucians and Freemasons continued to preserve Hermetic ideas, the brilliant Hermetic Renaissance was over.

However, on the Hermetic Fellowship website, the writer of its Home page takes a more circumspect view of the rise and fall of Hermeticism during the Renaissance, pointing out that the very reason why it was so influential is specifically because no one knew its true roots. For as soon as Christianity became the state religion of the Roman Empire, non-Christian teachings were ruthlessly suppressed and its texts destroyed. The Hermetic works so celebrated during the early Renaissance were simply those that had managed to survive the purge. He reminds us that "these were, after all, pagan texts. How was it that these pagan scriptures could be even passably acceptable in the very Christian world of *Renascimento* Italy?" Only because they were mistaken for much older teachings! (It makes one wonder whether this "mistake" was actually deliberate.)

The widespread popularity enjoyed by Hermeticism during the Renaissance may have been temporary, but its revival served to bring Hermetic ideas out into the open, even if only temporarily. This enabled enough people to be exposed to these ideas that it was no longer possible to stamp out their memory. A century and a half later, as the Enlightenment of the 18th century began to take hold, formerly banned ideas began to resurface. So it's no surprise that French occultists such as Gébelin were eager to explore these ideas and disseminate them in new publications like *Le Monde Primitif*.

What is Hermeticism?

Irwin provides the simplest answer to the question, "What is Hermeticism?," when he states that it is *the art of spiritual transformation*. From an alchemical perspective, it has been identified as "the transformation of the 'lead' of ordinary being into the 'gold' of true consciousness"[5] Yet another source tells us that Hermeticism explains "the Unity of the Cosmos and the sympathy and interconnection of all things."[6]

Hermeticism can also be explained by reference to its key propositions. *The Kybalion*, a concise work written around a century ago by three anonymous authors (the "three initiates"), lists seven key Hermetic propositions:

1. **Mentalism**: "All is mind." The physical world is a mental creation of "the All."

2. **Correspondence**: "As above, so below." There are multiple planes of existence, and what we see on the higher planes, we also see on the lower.

3. **Vibration**: "Everything is in motion." This idea applies not only to physical matter, but to thoughts and feelings.

4. **Polarity**: "Everything exists as a pair of opposites." These opposites can potentially be reconciled to create a new synthesis.

5. **Rhythm**: "Everything flows in and out." Nothing stays the same, everything changes state.

6. **Cause and effect**: "Everything happens according to Law." There is no such thing as chance; nothing "just happens."

7. **Gender**: "Everything is both masculine and feminine." All things in life have gender; everything masculine has some feminine qualities and vice-versa.

These seven propositions constitute a formal statement of the properties of Hermetic philosophy and are a good starting place for anyone interested in understanding Hermeticism. This list is complete in and of itself and extremely well-known among Hermeticists. In addition to principles already previously covered, it emphasizes the mental quality of all existence and the related ideas that everything exists (a) in motion; (b) in polarity; and (c) in rhythmic motion.

There are several other key characteristics of Hermeticism that show up in various descriptions and which also bear mentioning here:

▶ An **open-minded, optimistic view** of life and human nature that encourages **spiritual curiosity** and an **eclectic** approach to inner work (one that draws on diverse sources of wisdom).

▶ An understanding that **balance is essential** to inner work; this includes a respect for the balance within the natural world.

▶ A sense of **poetic whimsy**, a quality often associated with archetypes such as the Fool, Trickster, or Joker.[7]

These ideas speak especially to the value of a "hero's journey" view of life, because they remind us to lighten up and retain a sense of proportion when it comes to life's problems, so that can keep moving through them, rather than get bogged down.

Robert Place also lists a series of key propositions. Because he is writing about Hermeticism in relationship to the tarot, for each proposition, he states its implications for tarot work (see *italicized statements*):[8]

1. **The world is a living being that has a soul, the *Anima Mundi*, that holds everything else together.** "All of the world, including the rocks and streams, is alive and possesses a soul." *The World card is designed to illustrate the nature of the Anima Mundi.*

2. **Imagination is the key to psychic unity**, for it provides "the door for entering the reality of the soul or the unconscious mind." *Tarot images open the door to imagination.*

3. **Everything in existence is interconnected at every level of reality (the law of correspondences)**: Everything we see in our outer life is a reflection of our inner state. *Using tarot for divination allows us to experience this interconnection (synchronicity) for ourselves.*

4. **Everything can be changed (transmuted) into a higher state.** "Lead can be turned into gold and a common man into a sage." *The 22 Keys of the tarot describe how this transmutation can be effected.*

5. **The greatest truths are universal, and are expressed as universal archetypes.** "All cultures and religions share common…patterns and the same yearning for the mystical experience [divine union]." *The tarot embodies the "archetypal quest for enlightenment," which Joseph Campbell calls the hero's journey.*

6. **Spiritual truth is realized through transmission or initiation**, and is "accomplished by a reenactment of the hero's journey." *The 22 Keys can act as our guides (initiators) in the hero's journey.*

Here Place wants to show that the tarot embodies the spirit of Hermeticism. His last two propositions are particularly interesting because they point to the hero's journey as a specifically Hermetic model of transformation, an idea we will return to in the next section. But I first wish to mention a way to directly experience the energy of Hermeticism, which is through reading and/or reciting *The Emerald Tablet*, the complete text of which is given below:

> True, without falsehood, certain and most true, that which is above is as that which is below, and that which is below is as that which is above, for the performance of the miracles of the One Thing. And as all things are from One, by the mediation of One, so all things have their birth from this One Thing by adaptation. The Sun is its father, the Moon its mother, and the Wind carries it in its belly, its nurse is the Earth. This is the father of all perfection, or consummation of the whole world. Its power is integrating, if it be turned into earth. Thou shalt separate the earth from the fire, the subtle from the gross, suavely, and with great ingenuity. It ascends from earth to heaven and descends again to earth, and receives the power of the superiors and of the inferiors.
>
> So thou hast the glory of the whole world; therefore let all obscurity flee before thee. This is the strong force of all forces, overcoming every subtle and penetrating every solid thing. So the world was created. Hence were all wonderful adaptations, of which this is the manner. Therefore am I called Hermes Trismegistus, having the three parts of the philosophy of the whole world. What I have to tell is completed, concerning the Operation of the Sun.

This text is attributed directly to Hermes Trismegistus. There is something deeply evocative about this passage, despite its cryptic message. It is alive with meaning: we sense its vibrancy, even if its details elude us. Reciting it aloud (as is done in B.O.T.A. gatherings) can attune one's consciousness to a deeper dimension of reality, such that "the medium becomes the message." This experiential component is critical to genuine *gnosis*. And that is why the hero's journey is emblematic of a Hermetic process: because it is about lived experience, not just theory.

The Hermetic Tradition and the Hero's Journey

The claim that direct experience leads to spiritual wisdom may sound like an obvious truth to modern ears, but in previous centuries, to suggest such an idea would be hazardous to one's health. For if direct spiritual experience is superior to doctrine, study, or intercession by special personages (like popes), why do we need religions and religious doctrines at all?

This was the dangerous question implicit in Bruno and Campenella's work. (What is amazing is not that the Church punished them for having the temerity to raise such questions, even indirectly, but that it took so long for the Vatican to realize the true implications of Hermetic philosophy.)

Tarot can be viewed as a Hermetic approach because it translates Hermetic principles into imagery, imagery that can tell a story. The story of the hero's journey in the tarot tells us what life is about (transformation) and also shows us the kinds of archetypal challenges that can help us transform (the 22 Keys of the major arcana).

Robert Place makes the claim that, not only does tarot offer the perfect vehicle for experiencing the hero's journey, but that the tarot cards themselves can act as our spiritual guides:

> In modern practice, one may be initiated by one's inner guide, and if one truly believes in the perennial philosophy, ancient pedigrees are not necessary. It is the view of this book that the tarot trumps contain the archetypal myth of the hero and that they can serve as one's guide in initiation (p. 52).

Does it seem strange to suggest that the images on 22 paper cards could serve as one's spiritual guide? It's not the kind of idea you hear every day. But it's a view fully grounded in the Hermetic tradition, because it places our attention on the power of the imagination to free us from the limits imposed by cultural conditioning.

In *The Hermetic Tradition* (1931/1995), Hermetic scholar Julius Evola speaks to the idea of the hero's journey as the kind of myth that liberates us from self-limiting beliefs, particularly the beliefs imposed by religious doctrine. He starts by describing the journey as a myth that "speaks to us of an event involving fundamental risk and fraught with elemental uncertainty" (p. 6). Typically, in such a myth, he says, transcendental figures are portrayed as possessing a power that can be transmitted to anyone who is capable of attaining it. But it is far from certain whether such an effort will be rewarded with success or failure. So it's clearly a high-risk venture.

The most important question, according to Evola is, "How do we interpret the nature of such a venture and the one who undertakes it?" Evola cites two possible ways of envisioning the protagonist: as a *magical* hero or a *religious* saint. He characterizes these two views as "opposing," so that we will understand just how different they are.

Evola continues: If we view the hero (or heroine) as a *magical hero*, we see him as "a being whose fortune and ability have not been equal to his courage." In this case, the hero remains a sympathetic figure whose failure may only be temporary; we can imagine a scenario where he will set forth once more at a more propitious time, perhaps after acquiring the kind of skills that will allow him to ultimately succeed.

If, on the other hand, we view the hero as a [would-be] *saint*, his actions take on a moral dimension that radically changes the way we interpret the story. In this scenario, "[his] bad luck is transformed into *blame*, [and] the heroic undertaking is [transformed into] a *sacrilege* and damned not for having failed *but for itself* [italics mine]."[9]

In other words, when would-be saints fail in their quests, this failure (it is said) must be because that person is wrong—not misguided, inexperienced, or unlucky, but fundamentally wrong. This wrongness may be seen as so fundamental that it is intrinsic to the person himself (making him evil, like the devil); alternatively, the wrongness may be due to his actions and the attitudes underlying them (which at least allows for the possibility of redemption). But in either case, there is no possibility of a "re-do," for the nature of the story has radically shifted. The heroic quest has turned into a morality tale of sin and redemption.

Employing the Biblical story of Adam and Eve to further illustrate this point, Evola likens the story of The Garden of Eden to a heroic myth interpreted from a religious (rather than a heroic) standpoint. From a heroic point of view, the actions of Adam and Eve might be interpreted as a bold attempt to grow beyond the limits of their current understanding. But from a religious point of view, these acts are inherently wrong, because they are acts of disobedience to the Deity (which is all-powerful and all good).

Even many religious people now have a certain amount of trouble with this idea of obedience-as-the-ultimate-virtue, because they have seen the results of too much obedience in the absence of discernment. This is why Evola has reservations about doctrines that are based on a fixed idea about the nature of vice and virtue. Citing Berthelot, the writer of an 19th century book on alchemy, Evola tells us that "the knowledge of nature and the power derived from it can be turned equally to good or evil." He implicitly says that this is what distinguishes the Hermetic ethos with "the religious vision that subordinates everything to elements of devout dependency, fear of God, and morality" (p. 9).

❖ ❖ ❖

Evola would clearly prefer to see the protagonists in mythic stories as heroes rather than saints. For as heroes, they remain unburdened by the doubts that arise when one adopts a worldview rooted in the need to please some higher authority figure, on pain of death, expulsion from Paradise, or some other dreadful fate.

This raises the question: If we free the protagonist to be a hero, what is to stop him from making mistakes or developing the kind of over-confidence that leads to serious errors in judgment?

The answer is: absolutely nothing. Every experience we have in life represents an opportunity for learning. We try different responses and see what happens; over time, we tend to learn what works and what doesn't. When errors of judgment arise—as they surely will—we bear the consequences of those errors, hopefully using our lapses to avoid the same mistake in the future.

But learning to listen to our "little voice" can help us avoid many of the really serious lapses in judgment. I'm always struck by just how often it's possible to avoid such lapses if we acknowledge the power of our intuition to guide us in difficult and dangerous situations. See Gavin de Becker's *The Gift of Fear*,

(1999), for both cautionary tales and inspirational stories about the power of intuition to change our lives. It's one of the 10 best books I've ever read.

How Hermeticism Animates the Tarot

Robert Place has already given us some ideas for using the tarot to understand Hermetic principles. From my perspective, the tarot is naturally Hermetic in nature for the following reasons: (a) it depicts 22 archetypal experiences that we encounter in real life; (b) the images on the cards reveal the precise nature of these experiences and how to learn from them; and (c) tarot work involves contemplating these images, which fixes them in our memory, so we can apply their lessons in real-life situations.

We can use that understanding to develop practical strategies for problem solving. For example, let's say I have a problem completing a project at work. To get working again, I need to understand why I'm stuck (what role I'm playing in the current situation). I can lay out some or all of the cards of the major arcana and ask myself which of the following roles best describes me:

► **The Fool** (an optimistic but sometimes unfocused daydreamer who may not be paying enough attention to what's going on around him)

► **The Magician** (a highly focused but impatient figure who may be quick to judge and overly attached to idealized outcomes)

► **The High Priestess** (an empathic listener who can sense subtle changes around her but cannot easily justify her intuitions to others)

► **The Empress** (a prodigious creator who may be more focused on productivity than working out the fine details)

► **The Emperor** (a passionate individualist who may find it hard to work cooperatively with others)

► **The Hierophant** (a shy, detached thinker so absorbed in his mental world that he can find relationships hard to establish)

► **The Lover(s)** (someone whose fear of displeasing others may make it hard to speak up or break the rules)

► **The Charioteer** (someone burning with creative enthusiasm who can have trouble staying focused on just one project at a time)

► **Strength** (a strong-willed mover and shaker whose focus on power dynamics or bodily appetites may prove a distraction)

► **The Hermit** (an introspective worker who needs a quiet, harmonious environment to stay on track)

It is the *specificity* of the tarot Keys that enables us to pinpoint the nature of a situation and our role within it—two factors that combine to create what human factors psychologists call *situational awareness*. Cultivating situational awareness is the first step in solving any problem.

In this example, I only described typical roles associated with the first 10 major arcana Keys. If you're in the mood, you might try to describe the roles associated with the other 12 (or even do the same thing with all 78 cards). The point is that working with the tarot in this way helps create greater situational awareness, which in turn creates more options for resolution.

(The same thing can be said of the enneagram, but we'll get to that presently. However, readers familiar with the enneagram may already notice parallels between the descriptions above and the patterns associated with the nine enneagram types.)

❖   ❖   ❖

It's interesting to me that although Hermetic philosophy was a major influence on Renaissance thinking, the tarot did not enter into the picture in discussions of Hermetic philosophy at that time—a fact that tarot writer Cynthia Giles finds very curious:

> Consider this: During the Renaissance, the study of esoteric systems was a thriving enterprise. Alchemy, astrology, and natural magic were the preoccupations of many great men, such as Giordano Bruno, John Dee, and Isaac Newton; quantities of books were written on metaphysical subjects of all kinds—but *not a word* about the Tarot. And that is a very curious fact, because the Tarot deck seems so naturally suited to esoteric interpretation.[10]

She goes on to say that it's not until Gébelin and Mellet encountered the tarot in the last quarter of the 18th century that it became associated with "Egyptian ideas" which—based on the presumed correspondence between the Egyptian God Thoth and Greek God Hermes—are Hermetic in nature.

As discussed in Chapter 2, this idea was further developed by tarot writers such as Etteilla, Éliphas Lévi, Papus, and finally, the founders of The Hermetic Order of the Golden Dawn. But the incorporation of Hermetic ideas into tarot decks did not end with the Golden Dawn tradition or its successors. Most tarot teachers and authors embrace the idea that tarot is thoroughly grounded in Hermetic philosophy. Richard Roberts tells us that "Tarot is traditionally Hermetic."[11] P. D. Ouspensky says "it is the most complete code of Hermetic wisdom that we possess."[12] Mouni Sadhu said that, "in traditional Western occultism, the Tarot is recognized as the keystone of the whole philosophical system called Hermeticism."[13] In a modern book about Manly P. Hall's New Art Tarot, author Yolanda Robinson uses the principles of Hermetic philosophy to explain the meaning of the cards, and how they are related to the Western Esoteric Tradition, alchemy, astrology, magic, Pythagoreanism, Gnosticism, and Theosophy.[14] C. C. Zain's Brotherhood of Light Egyptian Tarot cards are clearly designed using the principles of Hermetic science.[15] The name of Godfrey Dowson's tarot deck—The Hermetic Tarot—speaks for itself. And last, there is Hajo Banzhaf, our inspirational guide in the hero's journey through the tarot and enneagram, who takes a thoroughly Hermetic approach in his description of that journey, noting that

> the alchemists, the Freemasons, almost all Western secret societies, and many esoteric societies call him their founding father or trace themselves back to [the teachings of Hermes Trismegistus] in some way (p. 84).

At this point, there are at least fifty decks listed under as occult on aeclectic.net, most of which incorporate key tenets of Hermetic wisdom into the images on the cards. Modern day tarot culture has reached the point where Hermetic principles are so interwoven with the card meanings—even in decks not considered "esoteric"—that we can truly say that tarot is animated by the spirit of Hermeticism.

In the next chapter, we begin the hero's journey. The first stop on the journey takes us into the world of its greatest champion, Joseph Campbell. From there, we enter the realm of the enneagram, with its nine transformational stages (Chapter 4), before proceeding to re-experience the journey through the 22 images of the tarot's major arcana (Chapter 5).

Notes

[1] "Knowing Beyond Knowing." *Parabola:* Spring 1997, pp. 21–25; available as a PDF from www.peterkingsly.org/cw3/Admin/images/knowing.pdf.

[2] Yates, Frances A. "The Hermetic Tradition in Renaissance Science," in *Renaissance Magic, Witchcraft, Magic and Demonology*, Vol. II, Brian P. Levack, ed. (Univ. of Chicago: 1992), p. 258. See also Yates' excellent book, *Giordano Bruno and the Hermetic Tradition* (Univ. of Chicago: 1964/1979).

[3] *Giordano Bruno: His Life, Thought, and Martyrdom* (Hardpress: 2012), p. 75.

[4] See the discussion in Chapter 7 of *The Forbidden Universe.*

[5] Smoley, Richard. "Hermes and Alchemy," in *The Inner West*, Jay Kinney, ed. (Tarcher: 2004), p. 30.

[6] See http://www.renaissanceastrology.com/hermestrismegistus.html.

[7] The source for the first two characteristics of Hermeticism are from the Hermetic Fellowship at http://www.hermeticfellowship.org/HFHermeticism.html; the third is my addition, based on the idea that as a Greek god, Hermes is known to be a trickster who would outwit the other gods, either for the good of humankind or his personal amusement.

[8] *The Tarot: History, Symbolism & Divination* (Tarcher: 2005), pp. 50–52.

[9] The material in square brackets is from my efforts to clarify Julius Evola's much terser treatment of the comparison between a religious vs heroic quest.

[10] *The Tarot: History, Mystery, and Lore* (Paragon House: 1992), p. 20.

[11] *Tarot Revelations* (Vernal Equinox: 1982), p. 46.

[12] See http://www.hermetics.org/pdf/ouspenski.pdf.

[13] *The Tarot: A Contemporary Course of the Quintessence of Hermetic Occultism* (Hermetica Press: 2007), p. 11. The book is available as a PDF at http://tarothermeneutics.com/classes/waite-trinick/books/Mouni%20Sadu-The-Tarot-A-Contemporary-Course-of-the-Quintessence-of-Hermetic-Occultism.pdf.

[14] Robinson, Yolanda. *The Revised New Art Tarot: Mysticism and Qabalah in the Knapp-Hall Tarot* (Kindle ed.: 2015), p. 6 or in the paperback edition (Circe's Whisper: 2015), p. *xx*.

[15] See the website of The Church of Light, based on C. C. Zain's teachings, at https://www.light.org.

4:
The Hero's Journey on the Enneagram

Modern man has himself disenchanted the world;
only his inner life harbors residues of enchantment.
–Philip Rieff

Archetypically, stories about the hero's journey start with a young male with more spunk than sense (the hero), a fair maiden (symbolizing the hero's lost feminine self or *anima*), the maiden's family (typically Royal, meaning she's worth fighting for), and a host of seemingly hostile characters (archetypal forces) that prevent the hero from marrying the maiden and inheriting the Kingdom.

In modern times, our vision of the hero's journey has been expanded. It not only tells the tale of heroes seeking to heal their hearts but heroines seeking to empower their minds.[1] For we are finally beginning to realize that it is only by honoring both the masculine and feminine aspects within us that we can develop the balance necessary to embody the heroic archetype in real life.

The hero's journey has never been easy, but modern life makes it seem especially elusive. It's not just that most of us are living in a high-tech world divorced from nature, it's also that we've collectively lost sight of the heroic *ethos* that gives the hero's journey its meaning and dignity. Belden C. Lane, a professor of religious studies, comments that "the whole history of Western culture can be seen as a history of demythologization. The dominant Western story we have been telling ourselves for 3,500 years has been a painful tale of children who, in their progress toward maturity, have steadily cast off their illusions."[2]

But in 1988, something interesting happened. PBS launched a six-part series called *The Power of Myth*, along with a companion book by the same name. It featured a series of Bill Moyers' in-depth interviews with Joseph Campbell, a well-known mythologist who related spellbinding stories about culture, mythology, and the hero's journey. The two men looked like close friends deeply absorbed in an intimate conversation, completely unaware of the world around them. But this was a conversation witnessed by millions of TV viewers.

The Power of Myth was popular—so popular that it sparked something of a mythic revival in American culture. On the Facebook page of the Joseph Campbell Foundation, the most-heard remark from people who have seen the series or read one of Campbell's books is "Joseph Campbell changed my life."

Campbell brought a sense of wonder to the study of classic myths—wonder that permeates the interactions between Campbell and Moyers. Their shared encounter with mythology invites the viewer to participate, as well.

There is a certain poignancy to these discussions, as both parties jointly come to the conclusion that modern American culture is sorely impoverished when it comes to myths, rituals, and genuine rites of passage.

Although *The Power of Myth* made Joseph Campbell a household name, it was in an earlier book, *The Hero With a Thousand Faces* (1940/2006) in which Campbell first explored the fascinating journey of the hero. In *Hero*, he explains the significance of myths and rites of passage:

> It has always been the prime function of mythology and rite to supply the symbols that carry the human spirit forward, in counteraction to those constant human fantasies that tend to tie it back (p. 10).

By distinguishing myth from fantasy, Campbell is attempting to draw a line between the kind of stories that bring us closer to the truth of our nature and those that embroil us in an inner labyrinth from which there is no easy escape. Even in 1940, he was aware of the perils of modern culture and its addiction to stimuli which condition, adulterate, and artificialize so much of our lives. Campbell's aim was to demonstrate the power of myths to "break through [our conditioning] to the undistorted, direct experience and assimilation of what C. G. Jung has called 'the archetypal images' "(p. 16). The iconoclastic power of these archetypes is why myths matter: *because their power is real*.

The power of the hero's journey lies in its ability to transform not only the protagonist but the lives of all those he touches. As Campbell notes,

> a hero ventures forth from the world of [the] common day into a region of supernatural wonder: fabulous forces are there encountered and a decisive victory is won: the hero comes back from this mysterious adventure *with the power to bestow boons on his fellow man* (p. 28, emphasis mine).

So while the hero's journey may sound like the tales we remember from childhood, what it symbolically represents is the most profound of truths: that the transformation of a single individual has the power to transform the whole world.

This explains why the hero's journey is not just a children's story. It's the story of humankind and its ongoing quest for understanding. While this path is not an easy one—Campbell calls it the "dark interior way from tragedy to comedy"—it's a path that potentially leads to the kind of "psychological triumphs" whose effects are more far-reaching than we could ever imagine (p. 27). The events it describes seem fantastic because they speak a different language, the language of psychic symbolism [the language of the tarot—SR].

As I was writing this section, I took a coffee break at my local Starbucks, where I was reading the story of a couple hiking the Continental Divide Trail from New Mexico to Canada. At the very beginning of the trip, Stopwatch (the author's trail name) fell ill with a bad cold. It was made worse by heatstroke and nausea caused by daily temperatures of up to 120°. Each day was a grueling struggle to make the miles to the next camp. Even her training as a long-distance runner wasn't enough to keep her going at that point. She was at the end of her rope; what could she do?

What she did was to consciously decide to become a hero—and yes, that's the word she used. By consciously embracing her Inner Hero, she was able to embody it at a time when only a heroic effort would see her through. And it did see her through, all the way to the end of a 3,000-mile trek (from *A Long Way from Nowhere*, 2014, by Julie Urbanski).

Heroism is contagious. People who become heroic inspire others to do the same. Maybe not everybody and maybe not every day. But it happens enough to keep the spirit of heroism alive. According to Campbell,

> the effect of the successful adventure of the hero is the unlocking and release again of the flow of life into the body of the world…[thus creating the kind of culture that is] nurtured in mythology…and made alive with symbolic suggestion (pp. 37–40).

The Way of the Hero in Archetypal Stages

In *Hero*, Campbell reflects at length on the various aspects of the hero's journey. However, he does not neatly summarize the stages in that book or elsewhere. But many other writers, inspired by Campbell's observations, have extracted versions of the hero's journey and broken it down into stages. The 10-stage model we'll talk about here is adapted from several existing versions of the hero's journey, combined with my understanding of the enneagram.[3] The ten stages are as follows:

0. **Ordinary Life** (the hero is introduced as a participant in ordinary life)

1. **The Call** (the hero grows restless; change is in the air)

2. **Refusing the Call** (force of habit & loved ones try to keep the hero home)

3. **Mentor Appears** (the hero receives encouragement to answer the Call)

4. **Crossing the Threshold** (getting ready & crossing into the Special World)

5. **Adjustment to the Special World** (getting acclimated, acquiring skills & allies)

6. **Escalating Challenges** (tension grows as the hero prepares for the Ordeal)

7. **Elation** (the hero has faced his fears & triumphed in his quest)

8. **Recognition & Rewards** (the hero is honored for his deeds)

9. **The Journey Home** (the hero returns home & integrates what he has learned)

You'll notice that the numbering of these stages begins with a zero, not a one. There's a reason for that. It has to do with the nine points on the enneagram, where transformational processes begins at Point 0, not at Point 1. There is not much live action there (that's why it's Point 0) but there is a subtle stirring that foreshadows what is to come.

To translate these steps into story form, we begin with a hero who lives an ordinary life but who is beginning to feel rather stuck and in need of a change (0). His restlessness and yearning attract an opportunity to get involved in something new; in the classical form of the hero's journey, this usually involves travel to a strange and distant land (1). At first, the hero is excited by the prospect of change; but his initial elation soon gives way to doubts, as he considers the problems he might encounter. His travel plans are disparaged by friends and family, who can't imagine him as a brave adventurer (2). Just as our would-be hero is about to throw in the towel, something happens to change his mind: perhaps a wise mentor appears to encourage him or perhaps circumstances make the status quo impossible to sustain (the tornado approaches or his family home burns down). One way or another, he decides to say yes to the journey (3). But making the decision and setting forth are not the same thing; before he goes, he must prepare himself for the journey, whether that means getting in better shape, gathering supplies, or emotionally preparing himself for the rigors ahead. Only then is he ready to Cross the Threshold into the Great Unknown (4).

The Special World is very different from ordinary life; it operates by different rules, rules unknown to the hero, but which he must quickly master, if he is to survive. The strangeness of the Special World tests his adaptability to the max and mercilessly exposes his weaknesses. But he does manage to survive, gradually acquiring the skills, allies, and resources he needs to prosper in this new environment (5). Once word of his accomplishments gets around, people starting thinking he may be able to solve some big problem that nobody else has been able to solve (not that he's looking for that kind of a challenge). At that point, he is asked to (or tricked into) taking on an impossible task involving forces that are sure to inspire terror in the heart of even the most intrepid hero. Whatever the task, it will always target the hero's greatest fears (heights, darkness, fire, water, snakes, caves, being buried alive...you get the picture). Nevertheless, he somehow manages to screw up his courage, face his fears, and succeed at vanquishing whatever bedevils him, often with synchronistic assistance from mysterious forces (6). The moment of triumph catapults him into a new state of being; it's as though a tiny space has just exploded into limitless multiverses. The hero is flooded with relief, followed by feelings of amazement, joy, and gratitude (7). His success is subsequently given formal recognition by the Powers That Be and soon becomes part of the mythology of the Special World (8). But the hero is still far from home, and he can't remain in the Special World forever (Special Worlds all seem to be like that—good for a visit but not an extended stay.) The last stage of the journey, the return home, is often a whole journey in itself (like Homer's *Odyssey*). But we seldom hear about it in detail. However, heroes who successfully negotiate the trials and tribulations of the journey home are the ones who have what it takes to truly "live happily ever after" (**9**).

The Hero's Journey on the Enneagram

Fig. 4-1 maps the 10 stages of the hero's journey onto the enneagram. Now you can see why I use a 10-stage model: because Point 0 on the enneagram represents the pre-journey status quo. It is included here because it sets the stage for what comes after. It also symbolically represents the results of all previous efforts made by the hero up to the point where the story begins. And this explains why Fig. 4-1 depicts the journey as a *spiral*: because transformation is a never-ending process in which each individual circuit is part of an endless developmental process. But the first and last steps of each circuit—which occur at Point 0/9—are special, because they "bookend" the journey. They represent a point of resonance, which is why they always overlap. This overlap is necessary in order to "close the circle," to make it complete (the same way that the two *do*'s in a musical octave bookend the octave. We sing both of them, because if we stop at the seventh note, the octave sounds incomplete).[4]

Notice also the bottom of the circle (the nadir). This is another special place that marks the irrevocable crossover of the hero into the Special World; see also pp. 47, 98–99, and 256–57 for more on the significance of the nadir.

In the previous section, we explored the hero's journey by breaking it into ten sequenced stages that show how the *plot* unfolds in a prototypical version of the journey. Next we'll look at those same ten stages from the viewpoint of *theme*, using the enneagram to explore both the purpose for each stage and the qualities it represents when translated into a personality type (see the the *italicized text* at the end of each stage description). If you're already acquainted with the enneagram, this juxtaposition should give you the means to begin linking each stage with each enneagram type. If you're new to the system, they offer a preview of the material in Chapters 6–8.

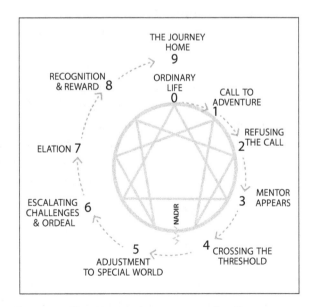

FIG. 4-1. The Hero's Journey on the Enneagram.

The Nine Stages on the Enneagram

0–ORDINARY WORLD: Point 0 on the enneagram is the place of the "everyman," nature, and the daily rhythms of life. So it provides the baseline against which all subsequent experiences are measured. At this point, the hero is not yet a hero; he's an ordinary person with aspirations to greatness. But his aspirations are still fantasies because he has not yet done much to actualize them. He fits in well with the world around him, but does not stand out in any way. His challenge is to realize that he's just treading water at this point and to allow his curiosity to outstrip his desire for an uneventful life. *(Enneagram Nines are generally agreeable types who value harmony and enjoy the small pleasures of daily life but who often procrastinate when it comes to making big decisions that could potentially disrupt their routines.)*

1–THE CALL TO ADVENTURE: Point 1 is a place of new beginnings. So the hero is presented with a new opportunity in life: the opportunity to discover his true *dharma* (his life's purpose). Awakening to *dharma* is an intense process that produces an intense response: a one-pointed desire to discover the truth about himself. The impulse is to act, but he has no idea what to do. But this impulse is so strong that it produces a sense of conviction—conviction that can actually interfere with the message. The challenge is to maintain momentum (the determination to answer the Call) while also maintaining the attunement necessary to actually hear what the Caller is saying! *(Enneagram Ones are focused, passionate idealists with a keen desire to act on their beliefs, but they can find it tough to open to new ideas or to allow processes to unfold naturally, rather than being forced).*

2–REFUSING THE CALL: Point 2 is particularly associated with friends, family, and intimate relationships. But the hero's journey is about breaking away from other people (at least for a time), in order to discover one's own path in life. At this point, heroes tend to find themselves confronted with friends and family who try to keep them home, offering convincing arguments that slowly begin to erode the hero's resolve. His challenge is to cultivate the discernment necessary to tell the difference between arguments that have real merit and those that are meant to play upon his emotions. *(Enneagram Twos cherish their relationships but can sometimes let their desire for intimacy or reliance on other peoples' opinions override their better judgment.)*

3–MENTOR APPEARS: Point 3 is associated with outside help that enters a situation to move the process along. Such help is necessary at this point because nascent heroes don't typically have the strength or resolve necessary to break the spell of cultural conditioning. They need someone or something that can support their decision to move ahead, whether it's a fairy Godmother, ancient wizard, and just a guy they meet on the street (but who may not be quite what he seems). Good mentors instill enough confidence in the hero to renew his resolve. The challenge for inexperienced heroes is to listen carefully to what the mentor has to say, because the advice offered at this point often turns out to be crucially important later in the journey, when the mentor is no longer available to consult. (*Enneagram Threes are decisive actors with a creative flair whose optimism and drive get them over many obstacles in life; their experience as overcomers makes them good advisors for heroes-in-training.*)

4–CROSSING THE THRESHOLD: Point 4 is a "threshold" point on the enneagram due to its position just shy of the nadir of the circle (see Fig. 4-1), which is associated with irrevocable change. So although the hero has made a mental decision to say yes to the journey, he must still come to terms with it *emotionally*, and that's no small task. It's hard to portray in films (and even books), so it can be easy to miss what's going on here. However, heroes who don't get themselves emotionally prepared for the intense pressures of the journey—and especially the Ordeal—tend to crumble at a critical point in the action (like Luke Skywalker when Darth Vader announces "I am your father"). (*Enneagram Fours are associated with emotional commitment, authenticity, and a tolerance for the emotional trauma of others.*)

5–ADJUSTMENT TO THE SPECIAL WORLD: Point 5 on the enneagram is associated with a complete change in polarity and viewpoint due to the crossing of the nadir from Point 4 to 5. So it symbolizes a world that is completely alien to the hero. Anyone arriving in such a world will feel totally clueless, like a baby who must relearn everything from scratch. But the Special World also gives the hero a once-in-a-lifetime opportunity to remake himself into a new person, unencumbered by the social conditioning of his previous life. In the process, he acquires knowledge, skills, and allies who know him as the person he is becoming, not the person he has been. He also becomes aware of new dangers and acquires enemies who feel threatened by his developing powers. His challenge is to stay on track and continue to hone his skills, rather than getting complacent or succumbing to hubris. (*Enneagram Fives are iconoclastic knowledge-seekers whose genius for puzzle-solving and calmness under pressure makes them invaluable contributors in difficult situations.*)

6–ESCALATING CHALLENGES & ORDEAL: The Ordeal is the dramatic high point of the hero's journey. But what happens plotwise—while exciting—is of less import than what it means for the hero, the inhabitants of the Special World, and (eventually) the people back at home. For the challenge of the Ordeal—and what it takes to face it—represents not only the overcoming of fear by a single person but the kind of overcoming that can change an entire people (like those who tore down the Berlin Wall in 1989): what one person does, others can do, too. Thus, Point 6 represents not only the high point in the plot but the sacred core that gives the journey its meaning. It is exactly two-thirds the way around the enneagram circle, and the two-thirds marker is well-known in psychology as the point in any process where people tend to encounter the greatest psychological resistance: if they can get past that point, things start to get easier. The two-thirds marker is also where the greatest synchronicities are possible, if only we have the strength of heart to risk everything for the sake of some greater good.[5] (*Enneagram Sixes are a psychically sensitive type who can apprehend the subtle psychic currents around them; this sensitivity unfortunately makes them apprehensive, such that they tend to see danger everywhere they look. But this makes them the type most motivated to overcome fear with faith.*)

7–ELATION: Point 7 represents the moment when the hero who has conquered his fears and come through the Ordeal suddenly realizes the Ordeal is over: he has succeeded in his quest. The sudden release of tension causes an immediate expansion of consciousness, as the soul breaks through its ordinary level of consciousness to experience a whole new level of being—like a Zen *satori* experience. This state may not last, but while it does, it allows the hero to directly experience what he can aspire to. Whatever tangible rewards he may be given later, nothing quite compares to the sweetness of this fleeting moment. (*Enneagram Sevens are the most joyous and fun-loving on the circle but their highs are indeed fleeting; to experience a more sustained sense of inspiration, Sevens—like youthful heroes—must learn how to slow down, center themselves, and find some worthwhile ideal with the power to inspire them on an ongoing basis.*)

8–RECOGNITION & REWARD: Point 8 is the top of the mountain, the place of honor and acclaim, where all the inhabitants of the Special World (except maybe the villains) assemble to honor the hero for his valor and to bestow upon him tangible rewards. Smart heroes will realize that this moment is not just about them and their achievements but about the idea that anyone who aspires to greatness can achieve it and that, in so doing, can inspire others to do the same. (*Enneagram Eights are known for their strength and fortitude, as well as their respect for personal honor and hands-on leadership; they are also known for their temper and tendency to try to "own" the people around them, so they can especially benefit from cultivating respect for others and gratitude for the higher powers that provide them with the ability to act.*)

9–THE JOURNEY HOME: Point 9 at the end represents the descent from the mountaintop to the valley below (the return from the Special World to ordinary life). As in real-life mountaineering, this part of the journey can be especially perilous, in part because it seems so easy (we're going with gravity, right?). But gravity (the force of habit) can sweep us right off the mountain if we're not careful. Also, as we descend, the grand view from the top becomes gradually obscured, leaving us less clear about how to proceed. It's painful to return to a world where we "see through a glass, darkly." (It may be even more painful if we retain our vision, but must live among those who are blind.) Nevertheless, we must return home, because what the journey is ultimately about is the soul coming home to itself. Accepting this truth, wherever it takes us, brings the serenity that comes when we are able to fulfill our *dharma* in life. (*Enneagram Type 9 at the journey's end is associated with selfless service, appreciating the "ordinary," being fully present in the moment, and a mystical connection with all life.*)

The Three Phases of the Journey

As we have seen, the hero's journey has nine "active" stages (1–9). These can be broken into three main phases—The Call, The Response and The Outcome—each of which involves a different kind of challenge:

▶ In *Phase I* (The Call), the challenge is *moral*, because it causes the hero to ask himself "What do I really value in life?" How much does he value comfort (Point 9), his existing beliefs (Point 1), or the opinions of others (Point 2)? If he values them too much, he will never embark on the journey.

▶ In *Phase II* (The Response), the challenge is *psychological*, because it requires the hero to develop himself as fully as he is capable: emotionally (Point 4), mentally (Point 5), and physically (Point 6). The physical outcome depicted as Point 6 rests upon the emotional and mental work done before. (Even the synchronistic help at Six depends upon the hero's willingness to invest himself fully in the outcome.)

▶ In *Phase III* (The Outcome), the challenge is *spiritual*, because of the freedom it gives the hero to decide how far he will allow the journey to take him. That's why it's the most variable and hard to pin down: for while we can describe the plot easily enough, the significance of each stage—Elation (7), Recognition (8), and The Journey Home (9)—depends entirely upon the hero, who must decide what to do with the power he now possesses.

One reason I wanted to mention these three phases is that virtually all transformational processes revolve around them, processes that go by many names. If we look back to the discussion on Hermeticism, we'll see that one of the main Hermetic principles is the principle of *polarity*: the idea that *everything exists as a pair of opposites that can potentially be reconciled to create a new synthesis.* In the coming chapters, this idea reappears again and again. In enneagram work, it is referred to as Gurdjieff's Law of Three (affirmation-denial-reconciliation). It is graphically depicted on the enneagram by the figure of the triangle, which is discussed at greater length in Chapter 8. **Fig. 4-2** shows the three phases on the enneagram; **Table 4-1** summarizes the three phases and nine stages.

FIG. 4-2. The Three Phases.

Table 4-1. The Hero's Journey in a Nutshell.			
THE CALL (MORAL)	0	Ordinary Life	The hero is introduced in his role as a participant in the ordinary world.
	1	The Call	The hero grows restless; change is in the air.
	2	Refusing the Call	Force of habit and opposition from friends and family make the hero try to forget the Call.
	3	Mentor Appears	Someone or something appears to encourage the hero (willing or not) to begin the Journey.
THE RESPONSE (PSYCHOLOGICAL)	4	Crossing the Threshold	The hero prepares for the crossing, deals with potential "threshold guardians," and at exactly the right moment, crosses into the unknown (the "Special World").
	5	Adjustment to the New World	The hero gets his bearings, meets potential allies, and discovers the properties of the Special World.
	6	Escalating Challenges & Ordeal	The hero and his allies overcome challenges that gradually increase in intensity, but the supreme challenge—the Ordeal—must be faced by the hero alone.
THE OUTCOME (SPIRITUAL)	7	Elation	At the moment of victory, the hero experiences a moment of supreme elation and a sense of liberation.
	8	Recognition & Reward	The hero is recognized and rewarded for his achievements; his deeds become part of the folklore of the Special World.
	9	The Journey Home	The way back often introduces new twists and turns that provide additional opportunities for transformation.
	9+	Integration ("chop wood, carry water")	The hero must find a way to integrate his experiences into ordinary life.

Notes

[1] See Maureen Murdock's *The Heroine's Journey* (Shambhala: 1990) for a take on the hero's journey from a feminine perspective.

[2] "The Power of Myth: Lessons from Joseph Campbell," (*The Christian Century*: July 5–12, 1989, pp. 652–654); available at http://www.religion-online.org/article/the-power-of-myth-lessons-from-joseph-campbell/.

[3] These adaptations of the hero's journey are derived from three sources: http://www.thewritersjourney.com/hero%27s_journey.htm, http://mythologyteacher.com/documents/TheheroJourney.pdf, and Christopher Vogler's excellent *The Writer's Journey* (Michael Wiese: 2007).

[4] A. G. E. Blake, author of *The Intelligent Enneagram* (Shambhala: 1996), tells us that "the importance of the affinity of points 0 and 9 cannot be overemphasized….This is the key mystery of the enneagram, and all others are subservient to it (p. 185)."

[5] Blake says that Point 6 is where we realize that we cannot complete self-realization without divine assistance; this realization is what attracts exactly the kind of help that we need (Ibid, pp. 61–63); see also my discussion in *The Integral Enneagram*, pp. 270–271.

5:
The Hero's Journey in the Tarot

Nothing is impossible; the word itself say "I'm possible."
– Audrey Hepburn

NOW THAT WE'VE LOOKED AT the hero's journey on the enneagram, we can look at it using the 22 images of the major arcana, images I have referred to as *Keys*. Maurice Nicoll, a writer on Gurdjieff's teachings, spoke of the power of imagery to transform human consciousness, noting that "pictures are formed out of the powerful force of imagination and govern us all...[They]can replace the actual by the imagined."[1] This is why the images of the tarot are not just ordinary pictures but symbols with the power to change our lives.

As tarot pioneer Eden Gray (1970) notes, these symbolic keys have the power to unlock "mystic powers and esoteric wisdom."[2] She later goes on to observe that

> symbolic keys, like material ones, are expected to fit locks and open doors. Systems like the qabala or Tarot, however, do not accomplish this in a simple or direct manner. Here we find keys that fit more than one lock and locks that can receive more than one key....Here there is no "final authority"— everything that is part of the living stream moves and changes (p. 13).

This passage alludes to the dynamic nature of life and the diverse perspectives from which we can envision it. The hero's journey sequentially links the images of the tarot in a way that allows us to explore the process of transformation in a fun and adventurous fashion. So that's the main focus of this chapter. But first, let's take a brief look at the tarot as a system.

A Tarot Overview

Tarot decks are divided into three parts consisting of the *major arcana*, *minor arcana*, and *court cards*:

▸ THE MAJOR ARCANA: 22 "MAJOR" CARDS, depicting archetypes of 22 transformational opportunities/challenges from the perspective of the Western Esoteric Tradition. All the numbers higher than nine are reducible to a single-digit root number (see p. 9 or 113 for details on how to derive the roots).

▸ THE MINOR ARCANA: 40 "MINOR" CARDS, consisting of four suits (Wands, Cups, Swords, and Pentacles); each suit's cards are numbered 1–10, as with normal playing cards. Wands are associated with *fire*, Cups with *water*, Swords with *air*, and Coins/Pentacles with *earth*.

▶ **Court Cards: 16 cards** (Pages, Knights, Queens, and Kings), associated with personal qualities, personality types, or people we know; the court cards are usually not assigned numeric values, but when they are, the numbering usually continues the 1–10 sequence of the minors, such that Pages=11, Knights=12, Queens=13, and Kings=14.

Appendix A provides an overview of the 78 cards in a traditional tarot deck, as well as my proposed additions to the major arcana (as depicted in the frontispiece and in Chapters 11–14). The discussion below explains the approach I use in this book for discussing these three types of tarot cards.

The major arcana represents the major archetypal forces that govern imaginal reality and are my major focus in this book. The majority of the images are closely related to the images in older tarot decks such as the Marseille or Sola Busca decks, although some Keys are modified by Waite either to incorporate ideas from Golden Dawn symbology (like astrological symbolism) or from mystical Christianity (like the Edenic imagery in The Lovers).

Chapter 1 contains a brief introduction to the major arcana, focusing mainly on how it can be used to tell the story of the hero's journey, a story expanded later in the present chapter. Starting in Chapter 11, the major arcana is described in the context of a proposed 27-Key model of the tarot. The idea is to use Banzhaf's Jungian model as a jumping off point for developing a three-octave model with nine Keys per level (see the frontispiece or Table 11-1). Chapters 12–14 flesh out this model by describing nine variants of the hero's journey; Chapter 15 describes applications of the model in our tarot and enneagram work; and Chapter 16 describes its wider implications. These variants were developed based on the attributes of the numbers 1–9 as seen in the context of symbolic numerology and embodied in the teachings of the enneagram.

The minor arcana describes how the archetypal forces represented by the major arcana are stepped down in intensity and expressed in the activities of ordinary life. Although they are sometimes denigrated because of being perceived as less important than the majors, I see the two as equal partners that serve different purposes. While the majors focus on the archetypal forces that shape our lives, the minors direct our attention to situational details that the majors may miss. And as we all know, the devil is in the details.

Despite my respect for the minors, they are not our main focus in the present book. Although there are several reasons for this, the most compelling is that the symbolism associated with the minors has become somewhat muddied ever since the original Order of the Golden Dawn sought to link them with the qabala. Whereas the minors have traditionally derived their meanings primarily from their *numeric value* and secondarily from their *suits*, the Golden Dawn (GD) decided to add two more variables to the mix: *astrological meanings* and the meanings associated with the ten *sephiroth* (emanations) on the qabalistic Tree of Life. That makes four potential symbol systems to sort out.

Adding astrological meanings might not be a problem, had the GD used a system grounded in mainstream Western astrology. But they instead devised a new and (to me) unintuitive system that is sufficiently strange to elicit apologies from two very well-known writers on the Qabalistic tarot, Robert Wang and Lon Milo Duquette.[3] Linking the minors to the sephiroth is another questionable practice, because it flies in the face of the idea that the minors focus on...well, matters that are *minor*, while the sephiroth—as Cosmic Emanations—do not. So there's a definite mismatch in meaning here.

Meanwhile, there seems to have been little interest by the GD (or creators of GD-inspired decks like the RWS) to highlight possible correspondences between major arcana Keys and the minor cards sharing the same root number. Whatever numerological links may exist between the two, they don't show up in the images we see in the RWS minors (at least not in any obvious or systematic way). For example, the images in the four Fives in the minor arcana don't call to mind the figure of The Hierophant; nor do the images of the four Sevens have much to tell us about The Chariot (etc.). While it's certainly possible to develop one's own correspondences, such correspondences are known only to the person who notices them and files them away in his or her memory. Anyone trying to learn them by looking at the cards will not find help there.

These are some of the reasons that I rely mostly on the major arcana Keys—not the minors—when trying to meaningfully link the tarot with the enneagram. But I do not ignore the minors entirely. Appendix D depicts a way to link the minors with the enneagram based exclusively upon looking at the numbers printed on the cards and the elements associated with each suit.

THE COURT CARDS. These are excluded from our discussion because they have no clearly assigned numerical value. Although they are sometimes assigned the values of 11, 12, 13, and 14, this is an approach that does not enjoy consensual support among tarot readers. Elizabeth Palladino calls it problematic to number the court cards this way, because "this does not really work in either standard Pythagorean numerology or in the Kabbalistic numerology that is the underlying structure of many tarot decks, such as Rider-Waite or Thoth."[4] Angeles Arrien believes that the court cards are best used to describe levels of mastery with their suit indicating the qabalistic world in which that mastery occurs.[5] Mary Greer points out that the court cards are especially liable to be assigned divergent meanings by the creators of tarot decks [a problem that also afflicts the minors; see the discussion above]. Although Greer is talking about the RWS vs. Thoth decks, the same problem crops up with other decks, as well.[6]

❖　❖　❖

This concludes our brief introduction to the tarot as a system. For more detailed descriptions of the RWS deck, check out Hajo Banzhaf's *The Tarot and the Journey of the Hero*, Rachel Pollack's *Seventy Eight Degrees of Wisdom*, or Eden Gray's *A Complete Guide to the Tarot*.

The Three Arcs

At this point, we are just about ready to commence our hero's journey in the tarot, using Hajo Banzhaf as our inspirational guide. I rely on Banzhaf here because he not only offers an eloquent description of the journey but proposes a new way of viewing the journey that can be mapped very nicely onto the enneagram. As described in Chapter 1, he breaks the journey into three stages: the Arc of the Day, Arc of the Night, and The Return. The Fool (0) is the traveler who makes the journey.

The *Arc of the Day* (Keys 1–9) introduces us to the archetypal forces at play during the entire journey; the *Arc of the Night* (Keys 10–18) shows us the archetypal challenges that arise when we get serious about inner work. The last stage, *The Return*, depicts the results of reconciling the two Arcs: the return of the light (The Sun, Key 19), the meaning of the journey (Judgement, Key 20), and what we become as a result (The World, Key 21).

In later discussions, I retain Banzhaf's descriptors for the first two arcs but elevate *The Return* (Banzhaf's "goal of the journey") to the status of a full arc, which I call the *Arc of the Goal*, even though it has only three cards. I offer three justifications for this change. First, these three cards describe momentous events that are deserving of greater emphasis. Second, three cards are enough to establish the foundation for a complete arc because they represent the thesis-antithesis-synthesis pattern that is the basis for all forms of transformation (see the discussions in Chapters 10 and 11). Third, they are well-suited to describe three overarching phases of a proposed 27-Key model with nine-Key Arc of the Goal (see the frontispiece for an overview).

The next section presents the hero's journey of The Fool through the 22 Keys of the major arcana. Unless otherwise mentioned, all quotes are Banzhaf's. Each quote is from the chapter in *Tarot and the Journey of the Hero* that deals with the card under discussion.

The Hero's Journey through the Keys

In the beginning was **THE FOOL** (0): the youthful, androgynous adventurer with big ideas but little worldly experience. He is "close to Heaven" (note the high mountains on the card), but in the processing of stepping into life (in fact, he looks like he may be stepping off a precipice!). But it's hard to believe that he'll come to

any harm, because—as we know—"God protects children and fools." Although Banzhaf calls him the hero of the Story, he also points out how strange it is that, "of all people, The Fool should be the hero that succeeds in the great journey," in that he violates all our stereotypes about what a hero should be. But at the beginning of the story, The Fool doesn't seem to have much to offer; he is like the youngest son of the King, who is much loved but little respected. However, his very simplicity and lack of pretense make him open to something new.

As **THE MAGICIAN** (1), the hero has become more focused. He retains the mystical idealism of the Fool but is much more focused and goal-oriented. He has

learned that nothing can be accomplished without inner conviction (the insistently pointing finger) and practical means of moving towards one's goals (the tools on his table). Like the Fool, he retains a sense of connectedness to something greater than himself; but he sees himself as a conduit for this "something greater," standing "in the pose of the master who does not act on the basis of his own strength, but receives his energy from above and makes it effective on earth." The gifts of the Magician allow the hero to remember why he is on his journey, so that he doesn't get sidetracked along the way.

THE HIGH PRIESTESS (2) represents the Magician's deeply mysterious feminine side (*anima*). While The Magician looks for inspiration from "the Above," The High Priestess meditates within "the Below."

She is the source of our deepest feelings and intuitions, which well up from the subconscious. She understands the cyclical nature of life (note the moon under her left foot). She also receives insights from dreams, visions, and subtle intuitions. The High Priestess understands much more than she can express, and so her wisdom is often underestimated. Nevertheless, she safeguards the secrets of life (the Tora scroll) under her blue (devotional) robe. Her gifts allow the hero to attune to his inner wisdom, especially in times of danger.

THE EMPRESS (3) sits on a lush seat in a beautiful garden surrounded by flowers, water, and trees. A field of wheat lies at her feet and her loose gown hints at pregnancy. She is the epitome of fruitfulness. Banzhaf likens her to Mother Nature; thus like the High Priestess, she is well aware of the cycles of nature. But she only comes into being once The

Magician has begun to integrate his feminine side to the point when a "pregnancy" can occur (i.e., where the energies of The Magician and The High Priestess can combine to create Christ Consciousness—a more integrated way of being in the world). The Empress protects and nurtures this new kind of consciousness within her womb until it is the time for it to be "birthed" into the outer world. The gifts of The Empress allow the goal-oriented hero to appreciate the natural cycles of life and the need for timing and care in creative work.

If The Empress represents nature, **THE EMPEROR** (4) represents the cultivation of nature. For in Banzhaf's words, "while Mother Nature is the quintessence of cyclical changes, The Emperor constantly attempts to balance and regulate these fluctuations," by imposing some sort of structure on them—a process described as the creation of *civilization*. The Emperor is also an in-

novator who seeks to put nature to work, i.e., to develop innovations rather than doing the same things the same way, over and over again. His is a disciplined but solitary approach that emanates from a place above and beyond from the lushness of the valley (note the desert setting and arid mountains in the background). His solitude, while sometimes difficult, allows him to appropriately reflect on his decisions before putting them into effect. He represents the mature *animus* figure whose gifts are a sense of independence, personal dignity, adult responsibility, and natural authority.

THE HIEROPHANT (5) is associated with the education of the hero (*hieros* = "holy" and *phantes* = "teach"). So the Hierophant is the teacher who imparts the holy wisdom ("quintessence" or direction) to the hero. In short, he blesses the

hero (notice the hand gesture) and thereby helps him discover the inner meaning of his journey. The Hierophant represents a higher level of the self—the level in which knowledge becomes *gnosis*; the two smaller kneeling figures represent the masculine and feminine aspects of the learning self. They are not yet integrated and therefore tend to project the image of their Higher (integrated) Self onto an external figure (such as a spiritual hierarch); that is why they kneel before him. The gifts of the Hierophant allow the hero to begin to understand his true nature and the purpose of his life.

THE LOVERS.

The RWS deck depicts **THE LOVERS (6)** as an (innocently) naked couple overshadowed by a large Angel: the man (consciousness) looks to the woman (subconsciousness) who looks to the Angel (superconsciousness). Thus, the image depicts both the necessity of including the subconscious in any spiritual quest and also of balancing all three aspects of our being. However, in older tarot decks, this card depicts a male figure with two female figures overshadowed by an arrow-shooting Cupid. Often, one of the female figures is older, suggesting a choice between mother and lover—and the Key itself is labeled "The Choice." So it is at this point that the ego (ordinary self) must make a choice between the status quo ("mom") or the love of his life. Banzhaf notes that "the associated determination and resolution is not only the theme of this card, but also the pre-requisite for any hero's journey." He also highlights the notion that this is a choice made using free will (not a conditioned response). The gifts of the Lovers allow the hero to declare "his heartfelt loyalty to one path, one person, one task."

THE CHARIOT.

Having made his choice, the hero is ready to depart on his journey. **THE CHARIOT (7)** depicts his departure in his impressive-looking vehicle. Like the previous Key, this Key is about making choices, but the choice here is more specific, because our hero is beginning to gain *clarity* about exactly what he is seeking. Clarity, Banzhaf notes, is inherently one-sided; thus, The Chariot is not so much about integrating the opposites as about holding them in check through the power of the will (note that his hands hold no reins to guide the Sphinx): "Now he looks completely like a knight, the symbol of the higher, more mature human being. However, the charioteer continues to wear his Fool's clothing beneath the armor. In order to do justice to the external impression, he will have to grow on the inside." So the task here is to "master contradictions, risking something new." The gifts of The Chariot enable the hero to move boldly into the world, where he can learn about life via his diverse experiences.

STRENGTH.

STRENGTH (8)[7] is about love (the woman) overcoming our animal instincts (the lion). Archetypally, the lion is often called the Red Lion of Desire; it is also associated with force (it is called "La Force" in the Marseilles deck) because love is the only force stronger than the force of raw instinct. Banzhaf associates this Key with hubris—which indeed is a possibility, if love does not sufficiently temper instinctual desire. But he also associates it with "the helpful animal," which makes sense, in that our animal vitality—once curbed—can become a great source of support. Traditionally, the hero's journey involved killing a lion, dragon, or other great beast (i.e., killing desire, which is the path of asceticism). But in modern times, we understand the advantages of cultivating, rather than killing, our instinctual energy. The gifts of Strength give the hero the strength, fortitude, and heart needed to persevere on the journey.

THE HERMIT (9) is the last of the single-digit numbers—and as such, represents the end of the Arc of the Day. Thus, the figure of a hermit stands in

the fading light holding a lamp to guide travelers through the coming night. He stands above the mountains—and is obviously quite alone. So this card speaks to the need for the Hero to cultivate solitude—to go into the wilderness of his own being—in order to find himself and (in Banzhaf words), his "true name...[for] the perception of true identity is the fruit that can only be found in silence and retreat." His inner light is shown in the symbol of the lantern, the light by which he illuminates the way for others on the path. He is old, because developing our light is the work of a lifetime. The gifts of the Hermit give the hero the ability to go within to discover his true nature, in preparation to fulfill his higher calling in life.

THE WHEEL OF FORTUNE (10) depicts a circular form inscribed with many curious symbols. It symbolizes the hero's life path or destiny. The challenge is to situate oneself in the center (where it is still and one can see the entire circle) rather than on the edges (where the circle is in constant motion, making it hard to gain perspective). Banzhaf sees The Wheel of Fortune as the force of *dharma* (our life's purpose). He goes on to say that it "corresponds with the setting sun on the Western horizon, an image of turning the light to the dark and previously neglected polarity." In other words, it represents the point where it becomes

necessary for the hero not only to develop his strengths, but to face his weaknesses, especially the ones he has so far ignored (to engage in shadow work). Often, though not always, this involves feminine surrender (although for unassertive heroes, it could involve the opposite). In either case, the Wheel invites the hero to broaden his view of life and his beliefs about his own potential. It also confers the confidence he will need to move into the Arc of the Night. The gifts of the Wheel confer an expanded world view, new opportunities for growth, and an understanding of how to remain centered despite changing conditions.

JUSTICE (11) is about becoming more mentally aware, conscientious, and fair in one's dealings with others. The figure of Justice sits upright with a sword in one hand and a scale in the other, between two gray (balanced) pillars: the very epitome of the archetype she represents. If the Wheel of Fortune is about *dharma*, Justice is about *karma*: about developing the ability to appropriately respond to life's challenges via the cultivation of both mental discernment (the sword) and balanced judgment (the scales). The absence of a blindfold shows that true justice is about becoming consciously aware of our responsibilities in life. So at this point, the hero must surrender immature rationalizations and other tactics previously used to "duck out" on responsibility. He must willingly open his eyes so he can see what is really going on in his life. But he must do so without developing the kind of "judging" attitude that would interfere with his ability to use his new tools in balanced manner. The gifts of Justice are objectivity, fairness, and the ability to make fine distinctions.

THE HANGED MAN (12) shows a curious figure: a man hanging upside-down by one foot. But he has a halo around his head and a peaceful expression on his face. So he does not appear to be upset (so to speak) by his "reversal" of position. On the hero's journey, there comes a point where the hero must come apart from the crowd in order to find himself—to dance to his own tune, not someone else's. (If we turn the card upside down, we will see that he indeed

looks like he is dancing!) However, Banzhaf also calls this card "the great crisis," implying that this upside-down dancing (i.e., going against the tide of public opinion) is not easy. (The soul may be elated, but the ordinary self—not so much.) Like The Hermit, The Hanged Man is separated from the masses around him. But where the Hermit retreated to learn his true name, The Hanged Man hangs upside-down in order to "let fall" everything that rings false. So the focus here is more on purging than meditation. The gifts of The Hanged Man are the ability to let go of control, find patience, and willingly sacrifice that which no longer serves.

DEATH (13) is one of the most interesting—and scary—images in the RWS tarot deck: a menacing skeleton covered in black armor, advancing upon both the great and the small. When people turn up this card in a tarot reading, they immediately wonder if physical death is imminent. But this is almost never the case. Nevertheless, when the hero discovers that the journey will involve a descent into the Underworld—whether to retrieve a lost treasure, rescue a

maiden, or slay a dragon—he realizes that this is not just any journey: it's one that involves actual danger and the very real possibility of death. But it's really more about the *process* of dying (which takes place over the entire Arc of the Night). Banzhaf notes that "truly letting go means letting go with our entire attention" (which is how we move from The Hanged Man to Death: by becoming present to our current situation rather than trying to deny or escape it). If the hero encounters Death but fails to allow it to transform him, he tends to fall back into the position of The Hanged Man—and remains there until he becomes genuinely open to change. The gifts of Death are the willingness to tolerate the intolerable, to accept the unacceptable, and to let go of all that is impermanent in life.

When something dies, it must be replaced by something else—something more refined. Thus, "after death has dissolved the boundaries that the ego previously had to build, from now on it will be important to unify what had been separate before." TEMPERANCE (14) depicts the refining process: the act of balancing the opposites, which is done by the proper *mixing* of our inner energies by the Higher Self (the "Holy Guardian Angel"). This action takes place in the Underworld; we know that's where we are because of the conspicuous presence of irises, which are said to grow in Hades. This mixing can only happen at this deepest level of the psyche, where the ordinary self isn't able to interfere with its

operations. Banzhaf says that the hero often finds himself there as the result of life experiences that so overwhelm the ego self that it experiences a sense of complete hopelessness and doom. Nevertheless, there is a light in the darkness. This is where the hero first becomes aware of a power beyond himself, a power that can sustain him through his trials. He is amazed to find guidance that he hadn't known existed. And so—as if by magic—he finds that he is saved, after all. The gifts of Temperance are a deeply experiential sort of knowing and the ability to allow one's energies to become balanced at a profound level of the psyche.

However, the hero's trials are far from over. For the next character he meets is the ultimate denizen of the Deep: THE DEVIL (15). He's a scary-looking creature, featuring horns, bat-wings, a bare, flabby chest and cloven hooves. And he's not alone. Beneath him are two human-like creatures (a naked not-so-innocent-looking male and female) bound by loose chains. Like the Devil, the man and the woman sport horns, indicating their sympathetic tie to him. Unlike lesser adversaries encountered by the hero, The Devil poses a special challenge because he symbolizes the kind of psychic force that binds us through alternating cycles of *attraction* and *repulsion*. This is the Ultimate Adversary, our own personal Dweller on the Threshold. Defeating The Devil cannot be done via opposition, only by acceptance. With acceptance, the hero stops projecting his "devil" energy onto other people and instead sees them as he sees himself: a vulnerable human being whose faults also make him human. The gifts of The Devil are humility, compassion, and tenderness.

Dealing with The Devil is an ongoing process; it doesn't really happen in one fell swoop. But accepting the task gets the hero on the right path. However, he's not out of the woods just yet. He's still in the Underworld, so there are dangers lurking about—like the entrenched but outworn beliefs, habits, and emotional reactions that can function like a prison without a door. Unlike The Devil, which actively tempts the hero to do things he knows he shouldn't, **THE TOWER (16)** limits his freedom by keeping him locked up in entrenched response patterns that appear rock-solid (and thus, impossible to destroy). This is why liberation must occur from the intervention of an active, external force that is more powerful than the passive force of habit. In hero sagas, the intervening power is often a natural force, such as an earthquake, exploding volcano, deluge of water, or—as here—a lightning bolt from On High. It knocks the crown (mental arrogance) off the top of the tower (our inflexible belief system). Banzhaf remarks that in some old tarot decks, The Tower is knocked off by just a feather—indicating that heros who seek to cooperate with the process may

find their values crumbling in a more organic (and less traumatic) fashion. The gifts of The Tower are liberation from outworn thinking, the throwing off of old restrictions, and the possibility of divine inspiration (the sudden "ah-ha" of a completely new idea).

After liberation from the Tower, the hero is elated but exhausted. He has been through a lot. But still he remains in the dark. So it would be easy at this point to fall into despair. But if he allows himself to look upwards, he will see something wonderful: a sky is full of stars (inspiration). One of them is especially bright (the Great Star of his own Higher Self). By the light of **THE STAR (17)**, he detects a small spring from which issue the Waters of Life: the secret spring with the power to make us immortal. The naked maiden on the Key (innocence regained) is pouring the

Waters of Life into both the pool (to replenish it) and onto the earth (to make it fertile). This flow of blessings restores his energy and helps prepare him for the last leg of his journey. The gifts of the Star are hope, vision, and a renewed sense of innocence (inner sense).

Now that the hero has found the source of life, he is ready to return home. **THE MOON (18)** has risen, and he can use its light to find his way. But moonlight is not sunlight—and the moon in the Moon Key is partially blocking the sun (which should make him doubly cautious). Although the hero has regained his innocence, he is still vulnerable to any unresolved issues lurking in the psyche (the turbulent pool). If he mistakes the half-light of the moon for the full light of the sun, something may crawl out of the pool when he least expects it. He must rely primarily on his inner light (The Star) to find his way. He must be alert to the forces—the crab, the wolf, and the two ominous Watchtowers—that may challenge his resolve but also to be aware of potential gifts (the marked path) and allies (like the friendly dog signifying devotion). The gifts of the Moon are inner discernment (to stay on the path), remembrance (of what matters most), and longing (the poignant desire to return home).

THE SUN (19) represents the return to the Light: "The hero has won the victory. He has followed the path of the sun, crossed Heaven and Hell, passed all the

tests, and truly returned again." On the RWS Key, the hero is pictured as a young, naked child astride a white horse, triumphantly carrying a red banner under the bright light of the rising sun. Sunflowers grow along the top of a stone wall, adding even more warmth to the image. It's a simple image that symbolically reflects the inner simplicity of the regenerated hero. "He began his journey as a dumb fool, but soon become adult, very clear, and extremely competent. Here now, at the end of the path, he is once again humble, modest and…truly mature." The gifts of the Sun are vitality, nobility, and goodwill.

JUDGEMENT (20) is about "the wonder of transformation" that can occur now that "all the preconditions have been fulfilled.…The treasure that the hero has fought for in the realm of the shadow—the elixir, the water of life, the blue flower, or whatever was so hard to find—can now bring healing." So contrary to what we may think, this Key has nothing to do with the Christian doctrine of having one's sins assessed by God on the Day of Judgement. In that sense, it is strangely named—which is why some tarotists have called it Resurrection, Deliverance, Healing, or Aeon. Judgement is a card that depicts being liberated once and for all from the heavy weight of "sin and the sense of sin" that we carry throughout life as the result of our perceived imperfections and failures. It represents the point where we finally get to experience the upliftment that takes us beyond the reach of any trace of guilt, shame, or self-judgment—and transports us to a place of ineffable wonder. The gifts of Judgement are healing, rebirth, and realization.

The last Key, **THE WORLD (21)**, is "paradise regained." It depicts the result of the transformative process that began with The Fool (0), accelerated at The Hanged Man (12), and led from there into the darkness of the subconscious (Keys 13–18). At The World, the upside-down Hanged Man becomes the joyful World Dancer—the one who dances in the clouds within an oval wreath of celebration. The oval wreath represents the rebirth of the self through the uniting of the opposites. So the World shows us the results of combining the brightness of the Sun with the healing power of Judgement: we can now move through life with a sense of lightness and wonder. The paradise created is not, however, a state of perfection. For in Jung's words (cited in Banzhaf), "[even] the united personality will never quite lose the painful sense of discord. Complete redemption from the sufferings of this world is and must remain an illusion." Here Jung refers to the idea that, as long as we remain in embodiment, the limitations of that state cannot be completely transcended. The gifts of The World are spontaneity, a zest for life, and joy.

Two Archetypal Paths

Banzhaf has something interesting to say about the first four Keys: The Magician, The High Priestess, The Empress, and the Emperor. Like all of the major arcana Keys, they describe four stages of the hero's journey. But according to Banzhaf, they also describe two archetypal paths of development: the *masculine* and the *feminine*:

► **THE MASCULINE PATH OF THE MAGICIAN (PATH OF THE WILL)**
Allows us to separate from the womb (The Empress), and to develop the self.

► **THE FEMININE PATH OF THE HIGH PRIESTESS (PATH OF THE MYSTIC)**
Allows us to transcend the masculine to become whole (the Emperor).

Banzhaf further observes that The Magician's path can be thought of as the one we take during the first half of life (the Arc of the Day) while The High Priestess' path as the one we take during the second half of life (the Arc of the Night). This idea goes along with the Jungian notion that the path of individuation requires us to establish a firm sense of self during youth and early adulthood and then to surrender that sense of self-identity later in life, in order to experience whatever transcends it.

However, please note that this model was developed by Jung—a male. This may be why he associates the first half of life with the masculine. From a female perspective, the first half of life could be more feminine than masculine, because it's the period when many women rely on their feminine qualities to attract a partner and to nurture children, especially if they marry and/or have children at a young age. Even young women who focus first on a career often rely more on feminine qualities like friendliness and cooperation to initially make their way in life as opposed to masculine qualities like assertiveness and leadership. (This is not to say that all women start out unassertive, it's to say that the Jungian "masculine-first-feminine-second" pattern may not hold true for all individuals, whether they are male or female.)

But Banzhaf's idea of two sub-paths is interesting. We start out on one path, the universal Path of the Hero, with its symbol of The Fool, an androgynous figure. But depending on our nature, we proceed along one of two sub-paths—the masculine or the feminine. On the *masculine path of the Magician*, we develop the qualities that allow us to assert ourselves in the world of outer activity (the Arc of the Day). It culminates in Key 19, The Sun, which symbolizes outer dominion. *On the feminine path of the High Priestess*, we cultivate feminine qualities that help us become more sensitive to the subtle and invisible aspects of life (the Arc of the Night). It culminates in Key 20, Judgement, which symbolizes inner healing and a state of equanimity.

Ultimately, both paths converge at The World, where another androgynous figure dances in the sky (the Cosmos), but a sky firmly anchored to the material world by the four symbols depicting the fixed signs of the zodiac. The dancer moves within a *vesica piscis*, a sacred geometrical symbol that shows us the integration of the masculine and feminine (**Fig. 5-1**).

Banzhaf's approach reveals two alternative variations on the hero's journey based on sexual polarity. As we will see, the enneagram offers another way to generate variations on the hero's journey—nine of them—based on differences in individual temperament. But to understand these nine variations, it's necessary to have some background in the enneagram. Section II provides that background, discussing the enneagram as a system in Chapter 6, the personality enneagram in Chapter 7, and the process enneagram in Chapter 8.

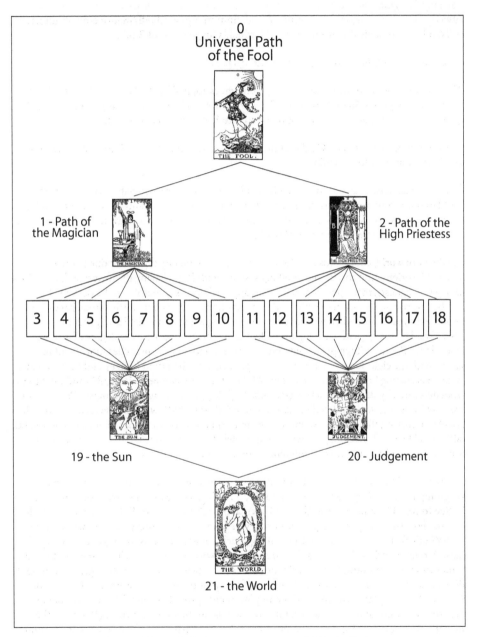

FIG. 5-1. Paths of the Magician and High Priestess.

Notes

[1] See *Psychological Commentaries on the Teaching of Gurdjieff and Ouspensky, Vol. 2*, (Weiser: 1995), p. 458, available online at https://selfdefinition.org/gurdjieff/maurice-nicoll-directory/Nicoll-Psychological-Commentaries-Gurdjieff-Ouspensky-Vol-2.pdf.

[2] *A Complete Guide to the Tarot* (Bantam: 1970), p. 5.

[3] For a discussion of the astrological correspondences applied by the Golden Dawn to the minor arcana, see pp. 44-50 in Wang's *The Qabalistic Tarot* or Chapter 9 in DuQuette's *The Chicken Qabalah*, 2001). See also the discussion in Endnote 1 of Appendix D, p. 264.

[4] "Introduction to the Court Cards," at https://www.academia.edu/7433595/Introduction_to_Court_Cards?auto=download.

[5] Using the qabalistic approach of the Golden Dawn, *Wands* are associated with fire and the world of pure spirit and inspiration; *Cups* are associated with water and the world of creativity and feeling; *Swords* are associated with air and the world of mental intention; and *Pentacles* are associated with earth and the physical world.

[6] In the tarot world, court cards are often described as personality types. But due to their monarchial orientation and implicit ranking system (with Pages having the lowest rank and Kings having the highest), many people feel that this approach leaves something to be desired. This may be one reason why even experienced tarotists often find the court cards somewhat difficult to work with, especially when we move beyond looking at the two variables of gender (male vs female) and maturity (with each higher-ranked card representing a greater degree of maturity or wisdom). For describing personality types, I have found other approaches more helpful. I started with the eight Jungian temperament types discussed by David Keirsey and Marilyn Bates in their fascinating book, *Please Understand Me* (Prometheus-Nemesis: 1978/84) and the MBTI types described by Isabel Myers Briggs in *Gifts Differing* (Consulting Psychologists' Press: 1980); later, I enjoyed Keirsey's updated *Please Understand Me II* (1998), which converts the classically oriented Greek mythological descriptors used in the first version to modern language equivalents (although I like both versions). However, I ultimately found the enneagram to offer the most penetrating insights into the core differences among personality types.

[7] Here we will temporarily depart from Banzhaf, as he uses the Continental approach of assigning Justice to Key 8 and Strength to Key 11, while Waite assigns Strength to Key 8 and Justice to Key 11, following the Golden Dawn approach (see Tables E-2a/E-2b in Appendix E to see how the change in assignment occurs). I follow Waite, simply because we are using his RWS deck. However, the Continental approach could also be used to good advantage, because Strength and Justice have a shared theme: the wise use of power. The power of Strength comes from unconditional love, while the power of Justice comes from strategic discernment. We can assign Strength and Justice to either of two points on the enneagram—Points 2 or 8—in order to explore how these different placements provide somewhat different perspectives on the nature of power and what it can teach us on the hero's journey. (Point 2 is the appropriate placement for a card assigned the value of 11 based on the cross-sum reduction of 11 to 2.) For more on the 8-11 controversy, see Endnotes 24 and 25 in Chapter 9.

II

The Hero's Journey and the Enneagram

6:
Introducing the Enneagram

The enneagram tells a dramatic story. In fact,
it is archetypal of all stories that capture our interest.
– A. G. E. Blake

THE ENNEAGRAM IS AN AMAZING SYSTEM. Gurdjieff said that "the understanding of this symbol and the ability to make use of it gives man very great power... The enneagram...is the *philosopher's stone* of the alchemists [italics his]."[1]

Wow. It's hard to know what to make of a claim like that.

But when I first encountered the enneagram, I didn't know anything about its philosophical depth or alchemical heritage. I was just curious to see whether it was a useful tool for understanding myself and my relationships with other people.

Although my first exposure was from books, I soon found myself attending enneagram retreats and conferences, so I could experience the enneagram for myself. I was particularly attracted to *type panels*, meetings where a group of people of the same type would talk about their experience as that type. I not only listened to the panels but talked with people at breaks and meals, trying to get a deeper sense of the differences between the types.

What really surprised me was how deep the enneagram turned out to be— how it didn't just focus on outer behavior but on something deeper and more definitive. I became intrigued with the system and began to study it in earnest. After awhile, I started introducing it to friends. Sometimes they were receptive but sometimes they seemed annoyed.

Much later, I asked one of the more annoyed friends if she found any value in the system. She surprised me by her heartfelt response. She said that it had really helped her understand both herself and her family relationships. Another friend described how enneagram work had made it easier to understand the dynamics of his workplace, which increased his confidence and ability to work with abrasive people. As for me, it's improved my ability to get along with many different kinds of people.

In this chapter, we'll take a look at its main elements, mostly from a personality perspective. If you're new to the system, that's usually the best way to start getting acquainted with it.

Origins of the Enneagram

As far as anyone knows, esoteric teacher G. I. Gurdjieff (1879–1949) was the first person to openly teach the enneagram as part of the information he imparted in 1916 to his students in Moscow and St. Petersburg. He told them that they would not find the enneagram in any historical teaching. And this has proven to be the case: despite the efforts of many earnest scholars and seekers, no one has yet to unearth a clear historical reference to the enneagram figure as we know it today. However, rumors abound. There have been attempts to link the enneagram to a number of historical figures and movements:

▶ Pythagorean teachings, which focus on sacred geometry and its role in creating the cosmos

▶ Sufi teachings through the Naqshbandi lineage

▶ Plotinus and his Enneads

▶ the sephirothic triangles on the qabalistic Tree of Life

▶ Christian asceticism and monk Evagrius Ponticus' teachings on the Christian virtues

▶ Mystic Raymond Llull's nine-pointed figure

▶ Athanasius Kircher's nine-pointed book frontispiece

Additionally, in his book *The Commanding Self* (1994), Naqshbandi teacher Idries Shah (1924–1996) said that the enneagram has long existed "in disguised form" (as a double octagon with a dot in the center symbolizing the ninth point). Interestingly, Shah's publishing company is called Octagon Press.

All of the foregoing ideas about the origins of the enneagram have merit, but none of them can be proven. What's interesting to me is how similar this discussion on the origins of the enneagram is to discussions on the origins of the tarot, the qabala, Hermeticism, Rosicrucianism, Freemasonry, and Sufi mysticism. All of these entities "appeared" at some point in history, but efforts to definitively pin them down never quite seem to work. It is as if their true origin has been magically erased from history.

Why are such systems so hard to pin down? When Sufi mystic Irina Tweedie was asked about the origins of Sufi mysticism, she used to tell people "Sufism is the ancient wisdom. It always *was*."

But such wisdom can take different forms, depending upon the needs of the time. If so, the enneagram must be very timely, for it was introduced only one century ago. And the personality enneagram was introduced by Oscar Ichazo only 50 years ago. Thus, as esoteric systems go, the enneagram is still in its infancy. Its true nature and ultimate potential for helping people transform their lives is only beginning to be understood. It will be exciting to see what unfolds during the coming decades.

The next few pages offer a brief description of the personality enneagram and its main elements: the nine types, the core energy that motivates the type, the three energy centers, the subtypes, the wing types, the connecting points, and the "look-alike" types. There is also a brief discussion of shadow types—the ones we either strongly dislike or like too much! Because these descriptions are based on an optimistic view of human nature, they may differ from ones encountered in other enneagram books (this is even more true for the descriptions in Chapter 7).

The Personality Enneagram: Basic Concepts

What makes the enneagram unique is its geometry. As a geometrically-based system, the enneagram has dimensions unknown to most personality assessment tools. We have only begun to scratch the surface of what is possible.

An easy way to think about the personality enneagram is to envision nine people standing on the nine points, looking towards the center. If there's an elephant in the middle, each of us will see it from a different angle. Each of us will describe different features, depending on our outlook (**Fig. 6-1**). This is why the nine types are also called *points of view*: because each type responds to the same situation in a different way.

The idea of having a point of view clues us into the idea that the entire enneagram can be looked at as a map of the psyche of a single human being. Thus, although we each have one dominant point of view (our type), we also have all the other eight points of view within us. So in order to develop a balanced psyche, it's important to understand all nine points of view.

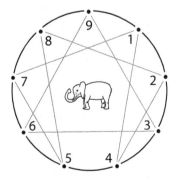

Fig. 6-1. Nine Points of View.

THE NINE TYPES. Here's a thumbnail sketch of each type:

Type 1: High-minded idealists with a focus on principle and passion for justice.

Type 2: Tender-hearted nurturers who freely express their emotions.

Type 3: High-energy achievers whose aspirations and work ethic know no bounds.

TYPE 4: Unconventional individualists willing to sacrifice the ordinary for the possibility of experiencing the extraordinary.

TYPE 5: Thoughtful observers with the ability to come up with ingenious solutions to unusual problems.

Type 6: Service-oriented skeptics alert to danger; loyal protectors of family, friends, and community values.

Type 7: High-spirited optimists with multiple talents and a quirky sense of humor.

Type 8: Powerful leaders whose directness and lust for life often require a bit of tempering.

Type 9: Peace-loving mediators who avoid taking sides and love to blend in with a group.

CORE ENERGY. Most systems designed to look at individual differences describe personality by reference to innate predispositions, observable behaviors, or expressed attitudes. They are often aimed at helping people make better career choices (e.g., the Kuder Navigator or Strong-Campbell Interest Inventory), determining the state of their mental health (the MMPI = Minnesota Multiphasic Personality Inventory), or providing a general temperament profile (the MBTI = Myers-Briggs Type Indicator). All these systems work from the "outside in": they look at what's on the outside (attitudes and behaviors) rather than at whatever it is that *underlies* those behaviors.

The enneagram does just the opposite; it works from the inside-out. Each point symbolizes a master archetype, and each archetype represents a different way of relating to life. While these archetypes can be generally associated with characteristic attitudes and behaviors, that is not what defines them. Rather, it is a unique energy or motivation that is at the core of each type, an energy that gives rise to all observable behaviors.

I call the unique energy of the types their *core energy, core motivation*, or *energy signature*. My operating assumption is that each person is born with a core motivation associated with one of the nine types, a motivation that is with that person for life. Thus, our type never changes. Nevertheless, it can evolve, a process which Jung calls *individuation*. The enneagram supports that process by allowing us to become aware of the precise nature of the inner forces underlying our outer behaviors. With that awareness comes the opportunity for transformation.

THE THREE ENNEAGRAM ENERGY CENTERS. A simple way to initially approach the enneagram is through its three energy centers: the Body Center (Points 8-9-1), Heart Center (Points 2-3-4), and Head Center (Points 5-6-7):

► The **Body Center** is associated with fire, anger, gut instinct, tension, fairness, balance, the five senses, ethical action, the gut and hands, and the natural world. Body types tend to be practical but prone to irritation. So they especially benefit from physical exercise, which helps them dissipate tension and channel their energy in a constructive way.

► The **Heart Center** is associated with water, depth, empathy, flow, caring, sorrow, love, the heart, and the feminine world. Heart types tend to be sociable but prone to self-consciousness. So they especially benefit from cultivating emotionally satisfying relationships and finding ways to enhance their sense of self-worth.

► The **Head Center** is associated with air, wind, logic, awe and fear, planning, systematization, ideas, the head, and the mental world. Head types tend to be analytical but detached. They especially benefit from translating their ideas into something tangible (a project, book, or invention); this allows them to ground their energy and also create something of lasting value.

To balance the centers within us, it is necessary to cultivate not only the energy of our dominant center, but the energies of the non-dominant centers. Usually, one of those centers will be relatively easy to cultivate while the other will be more difficult. We could call the latter our "shadow" center.

Fig. 6-2 depicts the three energy centers. If you're new to the enneagram and aren't sure of your type, you might start by focusing on the centers, trying to see which one seems most like you. The easiest way to do this is often to think about your instinctual reaction to stress. When the going gets tough, what is your "go to" response? Do you tend to feel angry (Body Center), anxious (Head Center), or emotionally deflated (Heart Center)?

One thing I've noticed about the centers is that *the position of the types within each center influences how they express the energy of that center.* If we think of progressing around the circle in a clockwise direction, the first point we encounter in each center (Points 2-5-8) tends to *extrovert* the energy of that center (such that Twos tend to seem overtly emotional, Fives seem overtly idea-oriented, and Eights seem overtly sensate). The second point we encounter (3-6-9) tends to *introvert* the energy (such that Threes' emotions tend to be less visible, Sixes' mental activity tends to more subtle, and Nines often seem more disembodied than embodied).

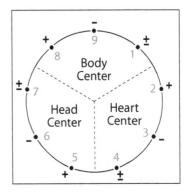

Fig. 6-2. Enneagram Energy Centers.

The third point (4-7-1) tends to *synthesize* these two modes of expression, which means that these types feel motivated to outwardly express their inner experience (such that Fours seek to translate emotions into artistic works, Sevens to translate mental processes into tangible inventions, and Ones to tangibly embody ethical ideals in their outer actions). Fig. 6-2 uses *plus* (+), *minus* (–) and (±) *plus/minus* signs to graphically depict these different roles.

THE ENNEAGRAM SUBTYPES. The enneagram subtypes are related to the *three arenas of life* in which we all participate: the arena of individual action (self-preservation subtype = SP), the arena of intimacy (sexual or one-to-one subtype = SX), and the arena of community (social subtype = SOC). Although we encounter these three arenas throughout our lives, most of us are more comfortable in one of them than the other two (although it's possible to have two strong arenas, with the last one a distant third). When we combine the three arenas with the nine types, we can generate 27 subtypes (**Table 6-1**).

One way to identify your type is to start with your most preferred subtype arena. Here are key characteristics associated with each arena:

▶ **SP subtype**: independence, individualism, self-reliance, a need for privacy, practicality, the love of comfort, personal responsibility, steadiness, calmness, unflappability, earthiness, directness, an appreciation of tradition

▶ **SX subtype**: intensity, sexuality, charisma, the need for intimacy, a love of secrets, creativity, mystery, magic, intrigue, darkness, depth, drama, spontaneity, impulsivity, dauntlessness, provocation, an attraction to the taboo, temper

▶ **SOC subtype**: sociability, cooperation, teamwork, organization, sensitivity to social standards, diplomacy, manners, indirection, maintaining reserve, carefulness, stylishness, social causes, planning, civilizing, community values

For a more in-depth treatment of all 27 subtypes, please see my book, *Archetypes of the Enneagram: Exploring the Life Themes of the 27 Subtypes* (2013).[2]

THE ENNEAGRAM WING TYPES. The wings of a given type are the two types on either side of it. In the example in **Fig. 6-3**, the type is Seven, and its wings are Six and Eight. Most people "lean" more towards one wing than the other; this is called their *dominant wing*. Since we have nine types, there are 18 possible wing types.

Taking the example of Type 7, Sevens tend to be high-energy thinkers who are interested in anything new and different. They have a zest for life and can adapt to a wide variety of situations. But Sevens with a Six wing (7w6) are more skittish and funny while Sevens with an Eight wing (7w8) are more hard-driving and focused. Some people feel they have equal access to both wings, and are thus said to be "bi-winged." One way to think about the types is as

TABLE 6-1. The 27 Subtypes.		
TYPE	**SELF-PRESERVATION** (INDIVIDUALITY)	**SEXUAL** (1-TO-1 INTIMACY)	**SOCIAL** (LARGER CULTURE)
1	detail-oriented craftsman	intense idealist & fiery orator	precise arbiter of standards
2	devoted caregiver	romantic lover	humanitarian & social organizer
3	Horatio Alger bootstrapper	magnetic mentor & performer	cooperative coordinator
4	hands-on independent crafter	disciplined & refined artist	social & artistic critic
5	"my home is my castle" thinker	investigator of arcane ideas	thoughtful teacher & philosopher
6	family champion & preserver	warrior for the underdog	dutiful community supporter
7	appreciator of the good life	charming but elusive lover	utopian visionary ahead of her time
8	powerful but gentle doer	dominant, charismatic leader	populist participatory leader
9	sensible lover of simple living	mystical but impassive lover	seeker of world harmony

a combination of their wings, such that the Seven in our example could be considered a combination of Types 6 and 8.

We'll see another use for the wing types in Chapter 8, in "Wings Around the Enneagram," where I use descriptions of the 18 wing types to connect the personality and process enneagrams; I also position them on the enneagram circle in Fig. 8-4.

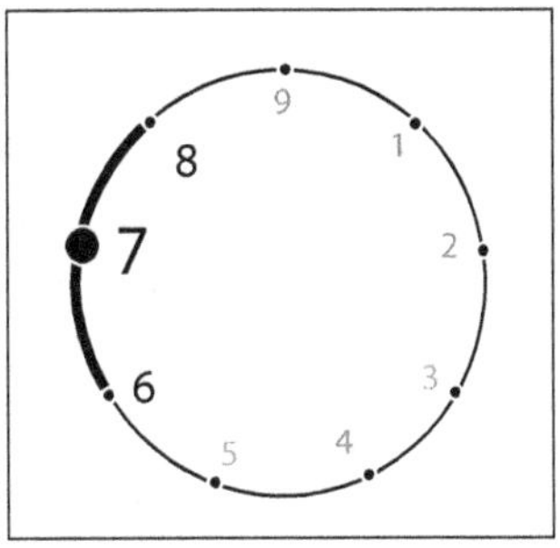

Fig. 6-3. Enneagram Wing Types.

THE ENNEAGRAM CONNECTING POINTS. The enneagram connecting points are the two points on the enneagram circle to which each type is connected by the inner lines of the circle (**Fig. 6-4**). Just as each type has exactly two wing types, it also has exactly two connecting points.

Like the wing types, the connecting points represent the types whose energy we can especially connect with. But usually, that connection is not quite as accessible, because the connecting points are further removed. We usually access the energy of our connecting points in situations where the energy of our type isn't quite the right energy for a particular situation. For example, Fives tend to be socially inhibited while Eights tend to be socially dominant. However, one of Type 5's connecting points is Type 8 (note the line between them on Fig. 6-4). So if a Five finds himself in a challenging social situation, he may temporary "go to Eight" in order to take more control. Alternatively, he could "go to Seven," becoming more energized, entertaining, and "go with the flow." I have two Five friends who both teach school. One relies more on going to Eight (becoming a leader) and the other on going to Seven (becoming an entertainer). Both strategies seem to work pretty well.

There is just one caveat. The energy of the connecting points is not as familiar to us as the energy of our own type. Therefore, we can have more difficulty using it (much as a beginning driver has to concentrate because he has no muscle memory of where the controls are). So when we move to one of our connecting points, we can easily become clumsier versions of that type. For example, the Five moving to Eight may become domineering rather than dominant; the Five moving to Seven may become more silly than funny. So although the energy of our connecting points is available, it is not necessarily balanced! It may "pop out" suddenly (especially in stressful situations), seemingly changing our personality for a time. But it's not a permanent change; as soon as things are back to normal, we revert to acting more like our type.

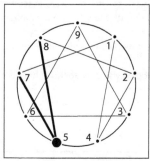

Fig. 6-4. Enneagram Connectng Points.

LOOK-ALIKE TYPES. Many types look similar on the surface. For example, our wing types and types with whom we share a connecting point may seem similar to our own. But even types that are not directly next to us or connected through the inner lines may look similar for various reasons.

For example, Types 2, 7, and 9 all tend to be initially friendly and curious. But once we scratch the surface, we find a different motivation driving the behavior: Twos are friendly because they seek to understand themselves through their relationships; Sevens are friendly because of their innate interest in all things new; and Nines are friendly because they seek harmonious relationships. Types 1, 3, and 5 are all known for their competence when it comes to work. But at Point 1, competence is about perfecting their abilities; at Point 3, it's about achieving their goals; and at Point 5, it's about achieving and demonstrating competence (understanding) regardless of the situation. Types 4, 6, and 8 tend to confront conflict directly (and often bluntly). But Fours are motivated by an inner mandate to be authentic, Sixes by the desire to "nip it in the bud" (before it escalates), and Eights by the gut instinct that they have the power to control the situation.[3]

So this brings us back to the importance of core motivation. With many systems, you diagnose personality on the basis of behavior; with the enneagram, you *trace behavior back to the motivation that sets it into motion.* From the perspective of traditional enneagram teachers, however, this core motivation is said to be inherently unbalanced (hence the Freudian slant to such teachings; see Chapter 1). From my perspective, the type is simply an energy potential: the way it's expressed depends upon us. We have the ability to balance both the dominant energy that creates our type and the other eight energies associated with the remaining types. For no type is really isolated from any other, because as mentioned earlier, we contain all of the types within us. That said, it's also true that we probably work most with (a) our type energy, (b) the energy of the two wing types, and (c) the energy of the connecting points.

PERSONALITY, TEMPERAMENT & CHARACTER. I usually discuss the enneagram types as personality types because it is conventional within the field to do so. But they are technically *temperament types*, because they are innate. Although not everyone would agree with me, I have always maintained that we are born with our type; it is not something we acquire later on. There are many reasons for taking this position, but the foremost among them is that our enneagram type never changes (and that is a proposition about which there is universal agreement).[4]

David Keirsey, creator of an MBTI-based theory of temperament types, explains the differences between personality, temperament, and character as follows:

> There are two sides to personality, one of which is temperament and the other character. Temperament is a configuration of inclinations, while character is a configuration of habits. Character is disposition, temperament pre-disposition."[5]

I agree with Keirsey's definition, with one potential modification. I prefer to reserve the word *character* to describe the strength and resolve that we acquire as the result of consistently acting in a way that is in alignment with our inner nature. Thus, I see personality development as involving three factors: (a) temperament (nature); (b) our experiences throughout life (nurture); and (c) how we respond to those experiences (free will). It is our response to experiences—and particularly challenging experiences—that determines the development of our character.[6]

SHADOW TYPES. This is not a topic covered in any enneagram book. However, I have noticed that most people have one or more "shadow" types: types that are particularly hard for them to get along with or whose motives seem completely incomprehensible. What determines our shadow type(s) seems to vary from person to person. (If there is a pattern, I'm not sure what it is.)

For me, the shadow types were those of my parents (Three and Six). All the time I was growing up, I just never understood where they were coming from; they seemed very competent but not very responsive to my constant "why" questions as a child. The enneagram helped me better understand their motives, which made me more tolerant of their choices in life.

I mention this here because it may be worth contemplating as you read through the type descriptions in Chapter 7. If there are any that elicit a very strong reaction, it may be worth asking yourself why. A strong positive reaction may point to a "bright shadow" (the sense that certain types represent some kind of perfect but unobtainable ideal); a strong negative reaction may point to a "dark shadow" (the sense that certain types are "less than" or "not okay"). In either case, one thing is certain: a strong reaction reveals aspects of the psyche that are unhealed and therefore in need of ongoing compassion, acceptance, and realignment.

Notes

[1] Ouspensky, P. D. *In Search of the Miraculous: the Teachings of G. I. Gurdjieff* (Harvest: 1949/2001), p. 294.

[2] My treatment of the subtypes is decidedly potential-oriented, which is why it differs from the less-than-positive treatment they receive in much of the enneagram literature. For a discussion, see Chapter 9 of *Archetypes of the Enneagram* (Geranium Press: 2013).

[3] Much more could be said about this particular configuration of "look-alikes" (1-3-5, 2-7-9, 4-6-8), which was originally discussed by Don Riso, who called them *harmonic triads*. The harmonic triads and energy centers are two of the many triadic patterns that we can find in the enneagram.

[4] See the discussion on the innateness of the nine enneagram types either in my article, "The Enneagram of Individuality," available on my website (http://www.enneagramdimensions. net/) or in Chapter 7 of *The Integral Enneagram* (2013), pp. 121-122.

[5] See http://www.keirsey.com/temperament_vs_character.aspx.

[6] In *Character and Neurosis* (Gateway: 1994), Claudio Naranjo uses the word "character" in a very strange way. He speaks of enneagram types in terms of "character" differences, where "character" is defined as our "fundamental mode of [psychological] defense" p. *xxxvii*). In my opinion, this usage presupposes that (a) character = neurosis; (b) neurosis is inevitable; and (c) that the appropriate framework for conceptualizing character development is rooted in the ideas of Freud, his neo-Freudian successors, and the Gestalt psychology movement associated with Fritz Perls, Claudio Naranjo, and Esalen Institute. See *Jeffrey Kripal's Esalen: America and the Religion of No Religion* (University of Chicago: 2008) for a discussion, especially pp. 141–144; see also my discussion in *Archetypes of the Enneagram*, pp. 65–66.

7:
Enneagram Type Descriptions

The enneagram is a living thing.
– Maurice Nicoll

THIS CHAPTER DESCRIBES each of the nine enneagram types, including its subtypes, wing points, connecting points, and look-alike types. Each graphic depicts the "family constellation" for each type: its location, wing types, and connecting points.

Type 1 – The Perfecter

Ones are born idealists who find the imperfections of the world hard to bear. As a result, they often feel caught between their ideals and the less-than-perfect world in which we all live; this can create frequent feelings of tension and frustration. But their one-pointed work ethic and attention to detail makes them sought-after workers in any field that requires an eye for detail (e.g., mechanical engineering, legal drafting, detail carpentry, technical editing, publishing, surgery, or political satire). They can find it a challenge to develop and maintain satisfying intimate relationships because of their somewhat prickly nature and their tendency to show love by trying to "improve" those they care for. Thus, Ones tend to do best with partners who have a thick skin and forgiving nature. But they will also stand up for what's right and refuse to back down in a fight, so they often leave their mark on history as reformers, revolutionaries, and even martyrs. Mature Ones often have a witty sense of humor, a carefully-cultivated sense of patience, and great observational powers that can make them excellent teachers and strict but fair parents. They particularly benefit from making time for fun, regular physical exercise, and channeling their intense energy into creative projects and hobbies.

SUBTYPES: *SP Ones* are extremely diligent, and they typically demand that same diligence from those who work for them. So they can be tough bosses to please. They are naturally ascetic and thus often identified with the Pilgrim/Puritan/Shaker archetype (especially with a Nine wing). They do not bend easily but are solid "salt of the earth" types whose values do not waver, no matter what the provocation. *SX Ones* are fiery, intense, and passionate about their convictions; think fire-and-brimstone preacher or born activist (especially with a Two wing). They can sometimes be extreme in their beliefs and assertive about promoting them, but their heartfelt sincerity often wins them converts. *SOC Ones* are harder to read than other subtypes because they are typically more reserved. They understand the value of social formalities as a means of ensuring civilized behavior and will actively promote favored forms of social etiquette, codes of conduct, and the legal codes; think Emily Post or other mannerly advice-givers. Despite their reserve, SOC Ones are a still a fiery body type, so there is more heat there than first meets the eye. This subtype is often drawn to the legal and political systems, where they prosper as lawyers, judges (Judge Judy), or legislators.

WING TYPES: 1w9 and 1w2. *Ones with a Nine wing* tend to be introverted, reserved, and fairly even in temperament; they can be hard to identify as Ones at first because they seem outwardly more like Nines, although they are more assertive and decisive than a typical Nine. *Ones with a Two wing* are more outgoing, sociable, and outspoken in their beliefs. They can be somewhat possessive of others, especially those closest to them. This wing type is often attracted to popular social and political causes that promote their values (especially with a social or sexual subtype).

CONNECTING POINTS: Points 4 and 7. When *Ones go to Four*, they can access their innermost feelings, which can truly enhance both their self-acceptance and empathy for others, once they have gotten over their shock at seeing themselves as they really are. When *Ones go to Seven*, it can bring a sense of lightness that allows them to forget about their serious concerns and just enjoy the moment. Ones who figure out how do this can develop a quirky sense of humor that's hard to beat (think John Cleese or Harrison Ford).

LOOK-ALIKE TYPES: 3, 5, 6, 8. Ones look like Threes when they "work 'til they drop"; they look like Fives when they are dry and dispassionate (when applying rules); they look like Sixes when they become tense (although the same "tension" in a Six is actually anxiety); and they look like Eights when they get angry and explode (although they tend to be more apologetic afterwards).

Type 2 – The Emotional Intuitive[1]

Twos are generally warm, emotional individuals who tend to wear their heart on their sleeve. They like helping others, and many enjoy family life and a wide social circle (think Princess Diana), although they can also be self-conscious at times. Many Twos love animals and see their pets as important members of their family. They seek to maintain close ties with intimate others and tend to be sentimental when it comes to birthdays and holidays. Twos are often drawn to humanitarian careers or causes where the personal touch is required (nursing, social work, counseling, teaching, or veterinary care).

Overwork is possible, because they are capable of exhausting themselves in the service of those they love, whether at home or work. But they can also become a bit nosy, possessive, or gossipy, because of their tendency to get over-involved in other people's lives. This tendency is strongest in Twos who secretly feel that they may not be deserving of love and thus seek out people who can reassure them otherwise. But the more they seek out love from others, the less they look for it within themselves. This can set up a "giving to get" dynamic that slowly poisons their relationships, especially with those closest to them. So the greatest challenge for Twos is learning how to love unconditionally—starting with themselves. To do so, it is necessary to spend time alone; this is how they discover how to tap into their deep inner resources. Twos who learn how to befriend themselves naturally attract the love of others, as well. Then they can give and receive love freely, with no strings attached (Mother Teresa).

SUBTYPES: *SP Twos* are natural nurturers who enjoy providing tangible help to others, in the form of food, shelter, or financial support. They often occupy a matriarchal role or some other pivotal position in the household that allows them to take responsibility for the family as a whole. Women have traditionally been expected to play this role, and many still do in families from traditional cultures (although non-Two females may find this role rather unappealing). *SX Twos* are the great romantics of the enneagram. They are in love with love; they especially enjoy the process of falling in love. They make affectionate partners who are especially attentive to the needs of intimate friends and partners. They tend to be very good at reading the emotions of others and intuitively know how to respond to their needs. *SOC Twos* enjoy being part of the larger community and make superlative organizers of events of all shapes and sizes. They generally have a hard time staying at home, preferring to be out and about with friends. So they tend to over-commit themselves, which can result in burnout or physical illness. They benefit from learning the difference between enjoying their relationships vs using them to avoid "alone" time.

WING TYPES: 2w1 and 2w3. *Twos with a One wing* are more serious and concerned about social responsibility than Twos with the opposite wing. They are particularly apt to take an interest in health care or social causes and also tend to have greater powers of concentration. *Twos with a Three wing* tend to be extroverted and sociable; they enjoy social gatherings and can be more personally ambitious and prone to overwork. They are often drawn to careers as party organizers, event coordinators, entertainers, and people-oriented managerial jobs.

CONNECTING POINTS: Points 4 and 8. When *Twos go to Four*, their "feeling" side is greatly amplified, which is a plus, provided they have the maturity to transform surface-level emotions into deeper energies with the power to heal. When ***Twos go to Eight***, they become extra dominant, especially when it comes to household management or family affairs. This jump can make them pretty bossy, unless they can cultivate the detachment necessary to direct their energy in a strategic fashion.

LOOK-ALIKE TYPES: **9, 7, 4, 1.** Twos look like Nines when they help others in order to create more harmonious relationships; they look like Sevens when they are optimistic and friendly; they look like Fours when they feel things deeply; and they look like Ones when they crusade for the fair treatment of others.

Type 3 – The Self-tester

Threes are high-energy, "Type A" achievers who are great multi-taskers with excellent time management skills. I call them Self-testers because, although they are naturally competitive, their biggest competition is always themselves; they constantly seek to exceed their personal best. They quickly adapt to changing conditions but can sometimes be over-accommodating, in an effort to win the approval of those they look up to. This "people-pleasing" tendency comes from the need to feel good about themselves, which young Threes learn to do by performing well at home and at school. Later, they become the kind of employees who will bend over backwards to meet deadlines and maximize productivity. As a result, they tend to adjust well to the demands of the modern world, where productivity is everything. However, Threes who focus too much on the bottom line miss out on the joy that comes from learning to do something for its own sake (and how to appreciate themselves for who they are, not what they do). So it's important for Threes to learn how to cultivate self-respect, to nurture their inner lives (with meditation, yoga, walking, or other "slow" activities) and to make time for important relationships (rather than considering them secondary to work projects).

SUBTYPES: *SP Threes* are firmly grounded in the physical world; they are careful with their resources and seek out solid investments with long-term potential. For SP Threes, success in life must be built on a solid financial foundation. *SX Threes* are charismatic individuals who are often found in the performing arts; whatever their line of work, they always know how to "own the stage" (think Heidi Klum or Adam Levine). Once they're established, they often enjoy acting as mentors to those they take under their wing. *SOC Threes* are particularly adept as leaders, politicians, and group coordinators. They are often inspired speakers who can make us feel like we're all on the same team (Bill Clinton), but they need to be careful not to promise what they may not be able to deliver.

WING TYPES: 3w2 and 3w4. Type 3 is in the middle of the Heart (water) Triad, and yet they can seem like the least watery of types, because their water has gone underground, so to speak, where it nurtures all that activity that we see on the surface. Both wings bring greater access to emotion. But the emotionality shows up in *Threes with a Two wing* as warmth, conviviality, and the ability to enjoy social activities; it shows up in *Threes with a Four wing* as a desire for greater depth, authenticity, and meaning in life.

CONNECTING POINTS: 6 and 9. When *Threes go to Six*, they become more careful and cautious in their general approach and less apt to make overreaching promises. But they can also become overly cautious (and even fearful) if they lack the ethical or spiritual foundation with the power to keep them grounded in the "now." When *Threes go to Nine*, it's often in a state of collapse, for that's what it takes for them to spend large chunks of time just "being" instead of "doing." Threes benefit from learning how to go to Nine consciously (rather than, say, by sleeping 14 hours after an exhausting week), so they can kick back, relax, and enjoy simple pleasures like being in nature, getting a massage, or listening to music.

LOOK-ALIKE TYPES: 1, 2, 6, 7. Threes look like Ones when they work hard to get the job done; they look like Twos when they are friendly and cooperative; they look like Sixes when they become worried about meeting others' expectations; and they look like Sevens when they are high-energy and optimistic.

Type 4 – The Deep Sea Diver

Fours are emotionally intense individualists who tend to be more oriented to the workings of their inner world than to the demands of outer life (especially with a Five wing). Ironically, their emotions run so deep that they can actually have a hard time directly accessing them, which is why they are called Deep Sea Divers: because the emotions are buried deep in the sea of the unconscious. This is why Fours so often feel as though there is "something missing" in their lives: the "something missing" is the sense of wholeness that comes from fully integrating the psyche. Fours find fulfillment when they can translate their innermost creative energy into tangible form, thus bridging their inner and outer worlds. So it's not surprising to find professional artists, writers, and actors (especially method actors) who are this type. When Fours create, they create with their entire being. They also have the capacity to endure emotionally intense interactions based on the expression of authentic feelings, whether it's pain, fear, or anger. Thus, it's common to find Fours working in crisis centers, as depth psychologists, or in other roles that require a tolerance for emotional intensity. But don't seek out a Four if you're inclined to make a mountain out of a molehill; they have no time for "fake" drama—or for that matter, for small talk in general.

SUBTYPES: *SP Fours* are hands-on crafters who like to literally feel the medium they're working with, so they excel as weavers, potters, mosaic artists, and others who like a visceral approach to art. They prefer to work alone or with a small group of intimates. *SX Fours* are very emotionally intense and dramatic; this subtype is often drawn to performing, and they bring great emotional authenticity to those performances (think Adele, Nicolas Gage or Kate Winslet). They also excel as dancers (especially ballet) but can find it difficult to sustain a sense of equanimity. This can make for stormy but steamy partnerships. *SOC Fours* are the most reserved and least overtly emotional. They are painfully aware of in-group/out-group dynamics, and can keenly feel the loneliness of being on the "outs." While most Fours have a hard time with loneliness, it's the SOC Fours who feel it most keenly, so they generally try harder than the other two subtypes to find communities where they can fit in and experience a sense of belonging.

WING TYPES: 4w3 and 4w5. *Fours with a Three wing* are more business-like, competitive, and able to fit into the social fabric; they tend to be less intense and more involved in outer activities. *Fours with a Five wing* are more introverted, introspective, moody, and non-conformist (think Goth); they are often deeply intellectual but more communicative than Fives with a Four wing.

CONNECTING POINTS: 1 and 2. When *Fours go to One*, they cultivate the ability to be disciplined, focused, and emotionally restrained; this can be helpful in developing one's artistic gifts to a professional level. When *Fours go to Two*, they can learn how to value relationships and how to emotionally give of themselves to others. They can also learn how to relax and enjoy their relationships, which helps them feel more at ease in a larger group.

LOOK-ALIKE TYPES: 1, 2, 5, 8. Fours look like Ones when they are disciplined in their creative work; they look like Twos when they become relaxed and affectionate; they look like Fives when they become fascinated with new ideas; and they look like Eights when are bluntly direct.

Type 5 – The Puzzle-solver

Fives are energetically unique in a way that often makes them the easiest of the nine types to recognize; they are the type most likely to stand out from the crowd, because of a sense of "other-ness" that is hard to describe—a combination of child-like innocence and deep curiosity about life. Fives tend to be shy, private, and socially awkward, so they're not easy

to draw out in conversation. But if you're patient, you'll find out just how deep they go—and how much extraordinary information they have collected on unusual topics. Their opinions seldom accord with cultural conventions, because they prefer to do their own research and arrive at their own conclusions. They have a knack for coming up with innovative solutions that seem obvious once expressed. This makes them intellectual and artistic pioneers (think Nikola Tesla or Georgia O'Keeffe). But it also makes them people that often don't easily fit into the world around them, because they have no respect for the status quo (or the powers that maintain it: once Tesla said he could provide free energy to all, his research funds were summarily withdrawn). Fives need their space, and appreciate those who respect that need. They also appreciate those who are interested in their ideas, and enjoy teaching motivated students. Although their social circle tends to be small, they are extremely loyal to those they trust.

Subtypes: *SP Fives* are the shyest and most self-contained of the subtypes; they're the ones often referred to as "castle Fives," for they often regard their home as their castle—and they don't let just anybody over the drawbridge! It takes a lot of patience to get to know them well, but they are actually very warm and caring once they let you in. They're particularly gentle with children, because they instinctively understand how to make them feel safe and loved. *SX Fives* are the most secretive Fives; but they also like to share their secrets with special friends. They enjoy mysteries (Sherlock Holmes), and often take an interest in strange and unusual subjects. (I'm guessing that many secret societies in history have been formed by SX Fives.) Alternatively, they can express their inner world as artists, poets, shamans, or researchers on obscure topics. *SOC Fives* are the least Five-like subtype, for they enjoy social interactions and seek ways to connect with people that allow them to share what they know; so they are often found as college "Mr. Chips" type professors, in think tanks, or in other roles that allow them to share knowledge in a group of like-minded others.

Wing Types: 5w4 and 5w6. There is a noticeable difference between these two wings, because the *Five with a Four wing* leans towards the "abyss" at the enneagram's bottom while the *Five with a Six wing* leans toward the larger community that is associated with Point 6. So the 5w4 is much more emotionally intense (as well as subject to abrupt mood swings) while the 5w6 is more emotionally detached, but also more interested in community affairs, politics, and economic trends (especially males).

Connecting Points: 7 and 8. When *Fives go to Seven*, they become funnier, more playful, and less inhibited than usual; this tends to happen when they are with children or on the stage. I once saw a stage magician who adopted a Seven persona while performing; another Five friend said she used the same approach when teaching high school. When *Fives go to Eight*, their energy suddenly expands and they become a force to be reckoned with. I speak from experience when I say it's not fun to see a Five lose their temper; it's enough to make people run the other way! But most of the time, this energy remains inside, a source of quiet authority that helps Fives compensate for their social shyness.

LOOK-ALIKE TYPES: **6, 7, 8, 9**. Fives look like Sixes when they are quiet and retiring; they look like Sevens when they play the role of performers; they look like Eights when they lose their temper; and they look like Nines when they are impassive and non-responsive.

Type 6 – The Steward

Sixes are a service-oriented type with strong ties to friends, family, and community. As rational thinkers with a skeptical bent, they are often attracted to scientific and engineering specialities that require the detailed breakdown of data into analyzable categories. Although Sixes are cautiously open to new ideas, they are quick to note the possible "down" side of any untried proposition. As a result, they tend to be associated with conservative political values. In truth, their political views tend to depend on the extent to which they view a particular platform or candidate as facilitating a safer, more secure world (unless they are counterphobic, in which case they may take the exact opposite tack of supporting revolutionary causes; see the discussion below).

The sensitivity of Sixes to danger makes this the type most in need of developing the faith that overcomes fear. It's not that Sixes are less courageous than other types (if anything, the opposite is true); it's just that facing their fears is a central issue for them. This accounts for the sizable number of Sixes who seek out hazardous work (e.g., as police officers, firefighters, and EMTs); jobs like these give them opportunities to confront their fears and develop strategies for dealing with them. Often, these strategies are initially based upon instituting a set of rules designed to ensure that "things run smoothly" (bedtime routines for children or policies and procedures at work). But they tend to discover over time that no amount of rule-making is a substitute for the kind of inner work that helps them identify the One Big Fear behind all the little anxieties. Once they are willing to consciously face that fear, they discover the inner resources that allow them to do so.

Some Sixes exhibit what are termed "counterphobic" tendencies, based on the strategy that "the best defense is a good offense." That's why counterphobic

Sixes are so often found in the ranks of military volunteers, as participants in high-risk expeditions, or engaging in edgy sports that others avoid. These activities require so much concentration that there is no room for fear (at least until they're over!).

SUBTYPES: *SP Sixes* are generally quiet, shy, and protective of home and hearth. But they are also warmly welcoming of guests, for they enjoy providing a safe haven for friends and family. They can sometimes become quite sentimental about past events that remind them of cherished family moments or other times when life was good. Not surprisingly, they are more risk-averse than risk-seeking. *SX Sixes* are often the opposite: risk-seeking rather than risk-averse. It's here that we most often see the counterphobic tendencies, because SX Sixes are the ones that try to overcome fear by acting exactly the opposite of fearful. Their challenge is to avoid getting addicted to the temporary high that comes from such experiences (so that they don't keep thrill seeking to burn off anxiety). *SOC Sixes* are less overtly nervous than the other two subtypes, possibly because they take comfort from community-building activities which keep them busy and make them feel they are creating an environment that is safe, stable, and supportive. We see many SOC Sixes in the military, police forces, and civic organizations dedicated to keeping the homeland safe.

WING TYPES: 6w5 and 6w7. *Sixes with a Five wing* tend to be studious, careful workers who often have a scholarly bent; they are very detail-oriented and thorough in any undertaking. But their retiring demeanor and natural modesty may prevent them from receiving the kind of recognition that their efforts merit. *Sixes with a Seven wing* are more extroverted, witty, and nervous; they usually have a pretty good sense of humor although it can be self-deprecating at times (think Woody Allen). Both wing types tend to have the kind of unassuming manner that other people appreciate.

CONNECTING POINTS: 3 and 9. When *Sixes go to Three*, they become more focused, grounded, and forward-moving. This helps them put their nervous energy to good use in creative projects, home renovations, or community work. When *Sixes go to Nine*, they feel calmer, clearer, and more in control; they find out how to be more in sync with the natural rhythms of life.

LOOK-ALIKE TYPES: 5, 8, 1, 2. Sixes look like Fives when they are studious and intellectually cautious; they look like Eights when they become counterphobic warriors; they look like Ones when they become anxious (because they seem tense); and they look like Twos when they reach out in friendship or participate in community activities.

Type 7 – The Improviser

Sevens are high-spirited innovators who like to get the most out of life. They are a fascinating blend of mental quickness, creative imagination, and insatiable curiosity. They are especially good at improvisation, bringing together diverse elements in a way that creates something new and useful. Sevens also tend to have an appealing quality that makes them attractive to others, a magnetism arising out of their youthful attitude and zest for life. As a result, most Sevens lead very full lives (complete with multiple backup plans, so that they are never without options). They often have many talents, including a talent for taking on jobs for which they are not necessarily qualified—and succeeding in spite of their inexperience! Their challenge is to settle down to long-term projects that require an ongoing sense of commitment, because of their almost insatiable need for novelty. Despite all their options and talents, Sevens can find lasting fulfillment elusive, unless they can find a way to move beyond the surface of life, to a place of greater depth, focus, and conviction. Once they find one thing to truly care about in life, they can use their diverse interests and talents to accomplish something that will stand the test of time.

SUBTYPES: *SP Sevens* are somewhat atypical for self-preservation subtypes in that their idea of self-preservation has less to do with literal survival and more to do with survival in a more refined sense (complete with gourmet food, exquisite libations, and delightful surroundings). It's amazing the "home" that an SP Seven can patch together, using only a handful of resources and a lot of ingenuity. *SX Sevens* could be called the party-animals of the enneagram: they love pleasurably intense experiences that satisfy their desire for every kind of sensory stimulation (and must therefore take care to avoid "edgy" activities that could be dangerous or addictive). But when they are at their best, they are extraordinarily productive thinkers with a passion for creative work. *SOC Sevens* are visionary thinkers whose minds reach far into the future, in an effort to anticipate challenges and solve them before they arise. They enjoy imagining alternative futures and multiple problem-solving strategies.

WING TYPES: 7w6 and 7w8. *Sevens with a Six wing* are pretty high-strung, fast-thinking, and funny (think Robin Williams); they have a hard time sitting still and often become "class clowns" to let off all that nervous energy. They are born entertainers but also do well in any job that requires mental alertness, quick reflexes, and extreme adaptability. *Sevens with an Eight wing* are more realistic, business-oriented, and adventure-seeking; they excel as adventure travel guides, airplane pilots, innovative architects, urban planners, or entrepreneurs.

CONNECTING POINTS: 1 and 5. When *Sevens go to One*, they became less scattered and more focused; but they also can become a bit rigid in their ideas. So the trick is to integrate Seven's flexibility with One's single-mindedness (and not to go overboard in either direction). When *Sevens go to Five*, they become quiet but withdrawn; as with the shift to One, it's a bit jarring for the extroverted Seven to find herself "confined" by the energies of a less expansive type. Again, the key is learning how to integrate the two: to mesh the mental quickness of Seven with the mental thoroughness of Five.

Look-alike Types: **9**, **2**, **3**, **4**. Sevens look like Nines when they are agreeable and travel for the sake of travel; they look like Twos when they are curious about other people; they look like Threes when they are high energy and enthusiastic; and they look like Fours when they avidly pursue creative projects.

Type 8 – The Master

Calling Type 8 the "Master" doesn't mean that Eights are perfect—just that they have the kind of expansive energy that requires considerable mastery to properly contain, develop, and balance. Mature Eights are probably the most magnetic of all the types; their natural leadership abilities tend to attract followers. Assertive, protective, and quietly intense, they have 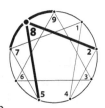 great stamina and the ability to follow through on whatever projects they attempt. But they also tend to have thick skins that are hard to penetrate, so it's a challenge to get to know them really well. However, under their thick skins, they are perhaps the most sensitive of the nine types. That sensitivity can often be seen in the tenderness they display towards vulnerable innocents, like children, the elderly, or pets. But they can be less open to strangers and are easily aroused to anger, especially in response to perceived betrayals; the desire for vengeance can become a major life theme if they allow it to. As an intense and high-energy "fire" type, they can have problems holding their temper or resisting the urge to overindulge in sensual pleasures. That's why they benefit from developing the ability to balance extreme arousal with extreme self-control.

SUBTYPES: *SP Eights* are the epitome of what used to be called the strong, silent type (think John Wayne). They are quietly powerful and often physically imposing. But whatever their physique, they have a gentleness, kindness, and quiet forbearance that allows them to be the "rock" in any kind of high-pressure situation. *SX Eights* are arguably the most charismatic type on the enneagram. Intense, magnetic, and highly sensual, they easily attract a following, whether in love or battle. They also have a tremendous appetite for physical pleasures and the stamina to persist at tasks that would defeat mere mortals. However, they are potentially the most romantic and chivalrous Eights, always seeking a cause truly worth championing. *SOC Eights* are probably the most approachable and diplomatic Eights, because they are interested in how to create a cohesive group and ways to draw out the best in group participants. They are also more open to feedback than other Eight subtypes and often enjoy mentoring juniors with leadership potential.

WING TYPES: 8w7 and 8w9. *Eights with a Seven wing* are swashbuckling adventurers with a brash tongue and quick temper; they can easily overstep whatever limits they encounter and must therefore learn self-control at an early age. *Eights with a Nine wing* are less flashy and more self-contained (think Marlon Brando as the Godfather). Like Fives, they like to watch things from a distance and make decisions only after gathering a complete picture of the entire situation. But once they make up their minds, they are not likely to change them. As leaders, they commonly disguise themselves as a non-entity (allowing a subordinate to impersonate them), in order to observe the reactions of others without being observed.

CONNECTING POINTS: 2 and 5. When *Eights go to Two*, they display conspicuous generosity and a magnanimous heart (think the Ghost of Christmas Present in *A Christmas Carol*). They become warmly affectionate and willing to cooperate wth others. When *Eights go to Five*, they become very private and introspective, whether to recover from emotional wounds or to focus their attention on something that requires their undivided attention.

LOOK-ALIKE TYPES: 1, 3, 4, 5. Eights look like Ones when they become suddenly fiery; they look like Threes when they exert leadership in a group; they look like Fours when they see through people's deceptions; and they look like Fives when they protect their hearts by retreating into silence.

Type 9 – The Storyteller

Kind, dreamy and imaginative, Nines make very good storytellers, especially if the story is a fairy tale, fantasy, myth, or adventure. For they love the world of magic and possibility, and delight in sharing it with others. They value harmony above all else and will go to great lengths to promote it—which is why they often seek out employment as mediators, musicians, fantasy writers (like J. R. R. Tolkien), singers, yoga teachers, massage therapists, or other alternative health care providers. They also enjoy anything to do with nature, such as gardening, hiking, kayaking, or nature conservancy. What they do not enjoy is making decisions—or doing anything else that makes them feel separate from other people or the natural world. Nines prefer to live in a world of oneness, not separation, and they easily become perturbed by the kind of activities that chop up that oneness into discrete units. (Clocks, alas, are not their friends.) So the Nine is very like the Fool in the tarot, wandering happily in his own world, hoping to avoid unpleasant encounters. While this often works for youthful Nines, eventually most of them encounter situations that compel them to give up their rose-colored glasses. The challenge at that point is to come to terms with the fact that true harmony is not obtained by ignoring what we dislike in life, but in finding a way to maintain inner harmony despite the disappointments and disillusionments we encounter.

SUBTYPES: *SP Nines* are the most comfort-seeking SP type; they especially enjoy the pleasures of home and would happily spend time puttering around the house, doing small chores or attending to their gardens. They can, however, find it hard to get out of the house, because they are so easily distracted by tasks that make leaving a complicated process. *SX Nines* are introspective mystics who are especially dreamy and otherworldly in temperament. They are natural channels for invisible energies, and often have talents as healers or "messengers of the Gods"; they particularly benefit from time alone for introspection. *SOC Nines* enjoy participating in social activities, especially the kind that allow them to blend into a larger group for some harmonious or spiritual purpose (Chrismas caroling, folk dancing, musical jams, group hikes, or candlelight vigils). They seek out a wide circle of diverse friends, because they like to meet different people with different interests in life.

WING TYPES: 9w1 and 9w8. *Nines with a One wing* tend to be more forward-moving and curious about life. But they are also more annoyed by the prospect of decision-making than the other wing, because they feel pulled between the desire to get going and the desire to stay where they are. *Nines with an Eight wing* are more solid, implacable Nines who cannot be moved unless they so choose. They make decisions, but in their own time and in their own way. They are more solidly grounded than the other wing but slow to change or adjust to sudden changes in the immediate environment.

CONNECTING POINTS: 3 and 6. When *Nines go to Three*, they become more decisive, motivated, and action-oriented: once they make the move, they can stay moving indefinitely, allowing them to get a lot done. When *Nines go to Six*, they get more antsy, second-guessing themselves with "What if's" and "But maybe's." It's hard to stay grounded, because of the "airiness" of Six. But this move can also motivate them to work on unresolved worries that they've been trying to ignore.

Look-alike Types: 1, 2, 3, 5, 6. Nines look like Ones when they become tense or obstinate; they look like Twos when they are helpful to others; they look like Threes when they get into gear and work to complete a project; they look like Fives when they don't outwardly react to negative stimuli; and they look like Sixes when they become anxious from too much ruminating.

Please note that Nines have an extra look-alike type; I could have included a couple more, as well. For Nines look like many other types in their quieter moments. And they often identify with them, too. This is consistent with one of the unspoken assumptions in the enneagram community: that Nines are the "root" type for all the other types, the original matrix for human consciousness. That may be why the type seems so open to experience (just like The Fool, Key 0, on the tarot). This does not mean that Nines are less evolved than other types, just that they are less specialized. They seem to have a more "all-around" set of tools with which to work. On the tarot, they are associated with The Hermit: the wise meditator and wayshower to others lost in the wilderness.

❖ ❖ ❖

As you can see from this brief introduction to the enneagram personality types, the enneagram is a powerful vehicle for exploring the nature of personality. When I first checked it out, I never dreamed I'd be writing books about it; I was just curious about a new way to explore human potential. Nobody was more surprised than me to find myself so deeply immersed in the system.

In the next chapter, we'll look more closely at the other variety of enneagram—the process enneagram—where the nine points represent nine stages in a transformational process. It continues the discussion begun in Chapter 5, where we saw how the hero's journey could be envisioned as one spiral around the enneagram circle.

Notes

[1] In previous publications, I have called Type 2 the People Person because of this type's emotional intelligence and focus on interpersonal relationships. But I have also been aware that their attraction to social interaction is in many ways a substitute for the ability to develop a fully functional relationship with the inner self. It's not that Twos lack the ability to develop that kind of inward relationship; it's that such a relationships are not particularly valued in modern American culture. As a result, Twos are seldom encouraged to develop their intuition or rewarded for their emotional sensitivity. As a result, they often suffer from low self-esteem and a sense of insecurity which they attempt to remedy with "helping behaviors." The tarot, however, esteems the archetype of the High Priestess, associating it with Cosmic memory, emotional wisdom, and unconditional love. Re-naming Type 2 the Emotional Intuitive better captures the essential nature of the type and also makes it easier to see the link between Point 2 on the enneagram and Key 2 in the tarot.

8:
The Process Enneagram

The digits 1 through 9 symbolize the stages through which an idea must pass through before it becomes a reality. All manifestation is the result of these nine stages.
—Faith Javane and Dusty Bunker

WE HAVE ALREADY ENCOUNTERED the process enneagram in Chapter 4, where we talked about the nine points as stages in the hero's journey. Seeing the process enneagram from that perspective provides a highly intuitive way to understand what makes it unique and how it can be used to tell a story or explain a process. But it does not delve into the history of the enneagram or the theory that informs it, which—to put it mildly—turns out to be deeply esoteric.

So this is one of those chapters in which I make an effort to respect the nuances of the system but at the same time to make it as understandable as possible. I don't want to oversimplify, however, because it's important to get across the idea that the enneagram is a truly profound system.

It's not hard to grasp its profundity when G. I. Gurdjieff —the first teacher of the enneagram—is talking, because nothing about his teachings or writings is oversimplified. He was never someone who would say something straight-out; he was much more likely to hint and tease, providing half the information needed to understand the topic at hand. He was also extremely fond of arcane allusions and neologisms in his writing (e.g., "stopinder," "Harnel-aoot," and "legominism"). So reading Gurdjieff can be like trying to learn Esperanto (only harder).

He wrote very little about the enneagram; what little we know about it comes to us primarily from one source: P. D. Ouspensky's *In Search of the Miraculous* (*ISM*), which consists of Ouspensky's accounts of lessons that Gurdjieff gave to his students. Although it mentions many topics in passing, the main focus is on the importance of the musical scale as a symbol of transformation and how it can be mapped onto a geometrical figure of great esoteric import: the enneagram (see Chapter 9 and Appendix E for more on the role of the scale).

Although most of Gurdjieff's explanations of the enneagram are hard to fol-low, he makes sure to get across the fact that it is much more than its simple geometry might indicate. This is why he refers to it as "the philosopher's stone of the alchemists," "a diagram of perpetual motion," and "the fundamental hiero-glyph of a universal language." He also tells us that a knowledge of the enneagram confers "great power," but that it requires a teacher ("a man who knows") to fully unravel its true meaning. Gurdjieff himself notes in *ISM* that the enneagram teaching is incomplete.[1] Unfortunately, most of us are not in direct touch with a "man who knows," which is why most people find the process ennea-gram so hard to decipher. This is probably what leads Richard Smoley and Jay Kinney to comment that "it is not clear how...[the] ideas [associated with the process enneagram] can be taken further into practical application."[2] Despite efforts of Fourth Way teachers[3] like J. G. Bennett to relate the enneagram to transformational events that occur in ordinary life, such as cooking a meal, the model has never really been presented in a way that allows the average person outside a Gurdjieff group to integrate it into his or her spiritual practice.

(The most interesting application I've encountered is learning the arcane but beautiful dances that involve the enneagram in the sense that they require participants to do different motions with their hands, feet and heads simul-taneously, a practice said to balance the three energy centers in the body. I have attempted this and can testify as to its difficulty. But I saw that it can be mastered and I suspect it does exactly what Gurdjieff claims for it. YouTube contains multiple examples of enneagram dances that are worth checking out; alternatively, rent the movie *Meetings with Remarkable Men* (1979) to see the dances in the context of Gurdjieff's lifelong quest to find the truth about life.)

We have seen in Chapter 4 how the process enneagram can make the hero's journey more memorable. The present chapter delves more deeply into the pro-cess enneagram as Gurdjieff taught it, especially its structure and the three ele-ments that comprise it: the triangle, the hexad, and the circle. It also focuses on aspects of the system that are especially relevant for exploring the hero's journey.

The Structure of the Enneagram

Chapter 6 introduced the three geometric figures that make up the ennea-gram: the triangle, the hexad, and the circle. Each has many symbolic mean-ings, some of which we'll explore below. But one simple way to think of them is as follows:

▶ The *triangle* represents the thesis-antithesis-synthesis framework which gives rise to all of creation (akin to the statement: "This is how all creation works").

▶ The *hexad* represents the flow of psychological projections and reflections that occur during a transformational process (akin to the *theme* of a story or the inner thought processes of the protagonist).

▶ The *circle* represents the actual movements of the individual participating in a transformational process (akin to the *plot* of a story or the physical moves made by the protagonist as he proceeds around the circle).

Fig. 8-1 gives us a reference point for the discussion of these figures.

THE TRIANGLE. The *triangle* embodies what Gurdjieff called the *Law of Three*, the idea that all transformational processes involve three forces: a positive or affirming force, a negative or "denying" force, and a neutral or "reconciling" force. Because the process enneagram depicts the process of transformation, and transformation is the key to all evolution, the triangle is a central feature in the geometry of the enneagram. It also represents the higher intelligence that underlies all of creation and its power to tangibly transform the world.

If we place the triangle on the circle, its three vertices hit Points 3, 6, and 9 on the enneagram circle. These points represent places where new information enters a transformational process. This "new information" is anything that re-energizes the process and takes it to a higher level—raw materials, shocking news, a compelling insight, or outer encouragement or help. In the oft-cited example of making a meal, it's the raw food that is delivered to the kitchen at Point 3 and the attention paid to ensure that the food prepared by the chef is exactly what the diners order at Point 6. (We'll talk more about what happens at these points in the discussion of shock points below.)

Gurdjieff did not invent Law of Three. It is a well-known principle that has been described in

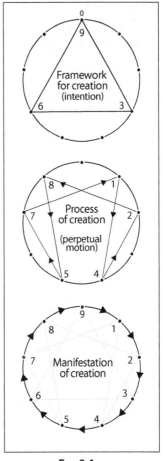

FIG. 8-1.
The Triangle, Hexad & Circle.

many ways, depending on the field: as Thesis-Antithesis-Synthesis (philosophy), Masculine-Feminine-Androgynous (gender), Attractive-Repulsive-Neutralizing (electromagnetism), Protons-Electrons-Neutrons (physics), Black-White-Gray (as symbolic colors in both the qabala and tarot), and Archetype-Shadow-Reconciliation (Jung). It describes the nature of all transformational processes. We will revisit this principle many times in future chapters, particularly when discussing the three octaves of transformation in Chapters 10 and 11.

THE HEXAD. The *hexad* embodies Gurdjieff's *Law of Seven*, based on the idea that 1/7 = .142857, a recurrent sequence that endlessly repeats. As we can see Fig. 8-1, the hexad is a literal representation of the idea that life is always in motion, always perpetuating itself (moving along the 1-4-2-8-5-7 path (see also Chapter 9). But for this perpetuation to occur requires diverse energies, which is why "there are seven quite different qualities or states that have to be gone through in order to complete an action," according to A. G. E. Blake.[4] He cites the days of the week, colors of the rainbow, and notes of an octave as examples of this principle.

In his short but informative book, *Enneagram Studies* (1990), J. G. Bennett tells us that the arrows we see on the hexad represent "the way in which the processes correct and reinforce one another to obtain self-renewal"(p. 21). So he is talking about how a system sustains its balance through both anticipatory mechanisms and feedback loops. In human beings, it refers both to the way that we think ahead to make new plans and the way we reflect back on past outcomes, so that those future plans can benefit from previous lessons learned.

On p. 29, Bennett cites the example of a cook preparing a meal, in which the hexad represents "what goes on in the mental vision of the cook…in the cook's mind that travels around the 1-4-2-8-5-7."[5] The flow of energy on the hexad thus contrasts with the flow of energy around the circle (see below) in that the former is *mental* and the latter is *physical*.

THE CIRCLE. If the Law of Three states the nature of transformational processes and the Law of Seven depicts the process in action, the circle defines the cosmos in which these two Laws interact. In Blake's words,

> the circle represents a unity, a whole. It is a definite region in space, time, and form.…Hence,…[it] is like an enclosure. The circle also represents a *present moment*, proper to the given whole: around the circle [on the outer perimeter], there is a successive movement, a "flow of time," while the circle as a whole is always "now." Finally, as an autonomous whole, it has its own pattern, or "signature".…It is a *unity in multiplicity* (p. 25).

Thus, the circle symbolizes a cosmos that can be viewed as both a *space* in which events happen and the physical events as they unfold in *time*, commencing at Point 0 and ending at Point 9. This unfolding of events is something we've already seen in Chapter 4, where the hero's journey was mapped onto the enneagram. You may recall from this previous discussion that the circle is actually a *spiral* (see Fig. 4-1), which is why it can symbolize both an enclosed area and the expansion of that area as the cosmos evolves.[6]

❖ ❖ ❖

All three figures of the enneagram are essential to the completion of a transformational process because all such processes are the combined result of intention (the triangle), mental construction (the hexad), and manifest action (the circle). Intention gives rise to mental construction which eventually produces tangible results in the physical world.

Enneagram Shock Points & the Hero's Journey

In Chapter 4, where we looked at the hero's journey and how it can be mapped onto the enneagram, I divided the journey into three parts: The Call, The Response, and The Outcome. Those divisions occur at Points 3, 6, and 9 (shown in Fig. 4-2). These are the same places on the enneagram associated Gurdjieff's *shock points*. Below we'll look at what this means.

Fig. 8-2 depicts the shock points on the enneagram. As mentioned above, the shock points are where new information enters the process, information that bumps it up to another level. At Point 0/9, the hero begins to experience subtle changes that make it necessary to contemplate a change of direction in life. There is no shock yet, because nothing much has happened. But by Point 3, *the first shock point*, he must make a decision: to accept the Call or not. He usually has some help from a mentor to make this decision, so there's a pretty good chance he'll say yes. It's for this reason that this shock is referred to in the enneagram literature as "mechanical": because it happens almost automatically.

Once he says yes, there is a clear shift from an internal, mental process to external physical activity involving travels to strange lands, meeting allies, and developing necessary survival skills. All this activity reaches a dramatic crescendo at Point 6, *the second shock point*, where the hero's success depends solely upon his ability to overcome fear with faith. To do so, he must make a conscious decision to move forward, however great his fear. The act of making this courageous decision gives him both the inner fortitude he needs to face the Ordeal and attracts help from higher forces, the kind of help that makes the impossible possible.

After successfully coming through the Ordeal, the hero receives his rewards but must still face the journey home, which is not without its dangers. And if he makes it home, he must face the more subtle challenges of gracefully integrating his experiences into ordinary life. So the *third shock point* at Point 9 symbolizes his ability to truly learn from his experiences, not just to file them away as an exciting memory.[7]

In formal enneagram theory, the shock points are said to represent *discontinuities*, where "the process starts again, but from another point [of view]" (p. 59). So the shock points represent situations in life when things have reached a point where there must be a shift if something more is to happen.

In the enneagram literature, discussions about the third shock point are quite arcane. Fourth Way teacher Maurice Nicoll

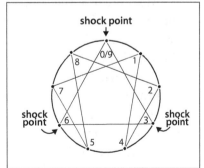

FIG. **8-2**. The Enneagram Shock Points.

comments that neither the second nor third shock are about something we do, but about something in which we agree to participate.[8] About the third shock, he says it is "looked after very carefully by the cosmic influences that wish to keep life on earth constantly multiplying."[9] Blake, citing Gurdjieff, says it has to do with the transmutation of negative emotions. He also alludes to the idea that it is at this point that "we go beyond the opposites" (p. 356). Fourth Way commentator Ian MacFarlane says that the third shock may have to do with the "intentional enduring of unavoidable suffering."[10]

All three of these comments allude to the idea that the third shock is about moving beyond one level of life into a higher level through integrating the opposites. MacFarlane's idea reminds me of the Buddhist observation that life on earth is suffering. It would thus make sense that a complete acceptance of suffering would free us of the desire to avoid suffering—and thus take us beyond the opposites.[11] The third shock could also be the hidden impetus for the next transformational cycle that will commence when the time is right.

The Turn at the Bottom: the Point of No Return

Anthony Blake is intrigued by the role of the process enneagram in explaining the structure of dramatic stories. Since the hero's journey is the ultimate dramatic story, it's useful to hear what he has to say.

One thing he particularly stresses when discussing the enneagram in that context is the importance of what he calls the "turn" and "latch." The *turn* represents a decisive turning point in the action and the *latch* represents the completion of the story (the point at which it truly "clicks shut"). On the enneagram, the latch is "set" at Point 0 and is completed at Point 9, 360° later. The turn is located 180° from the latch at the *nadir* between Points 4 and 5 (**Fig. 8-3**). In enneagram books which liken the transformational process to the preparation of food, the nadir is the point where the food gets "cooked" (i.e., irrevocably transformed).

More broadly, the nadir can be associated with the entire area on the bottom of the circle. It is sometimes considered the entire zone between Points 3 and 6 (*The Intelligent Enneagram*, p. 186). Even in the personality enneagram, the bottom of the circle is associated with chaos or voidness.[12]

If we relate this "turn and latch" notion to the hero's journey, it may help us understand one of the important hidden dynamics that the plot does not necessarily reveal: the internal shift that must take place within the protagonist in order to transform a *would-be hero* into an *action hero* (someone who is prepared to act on his convictions).

By Point 4, the hero has made the mental decision to set forth on the journey. But before he can actually do so, he must make the inner transition from mentally

deciding to truly committing. And this requires
working through the psychological resistances that
Point 4 represents.

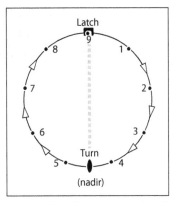

That kind of inner work is typically reflected in
outer life by a kind of ambivalence, where one day
we say, "Yes, I can do it," and the next we feel un-
certain and unable to commit. This kind of "going
back and forth" pattern often shows up in heroic
tales as a venturing forth into the Special World
by day, followed by a return home each night (like
the children in the *Chronicles of Narnia*, who cross
back and forth into Narnia through the closet).

FIG. 8-3. The Turn and the Latch.

This "trying out" of a new (and potentially heroic) role allows new protagonists to gain skill and confidence before they make a full commitment to cross
over once and for all.

The moment of the final crossing is seldom determined by a conscious decision. In stories, it usually takes place when a two-way door finally slams shut
or when the hero has "accidentally" wandered too far into the Special World
to find his way back. It may be when he discovers that he cares so much about
the troubles of the people in the Special World that his desire to help them is
greater than his fear or attachment to life back home (e.g., Emma, the "savior"
in *Once Upon a Time*). However it happens, once the hero has crossed over, he
cannot return home until he completes the quest or fails in the attempt. So the
crossing from Four to Five is a critical event in any hero's journey.

In the tarot, this crossover is represented by the transition from The
Emperor (4) to The Hierophant (5), where The Emperor represents the mastery
of the egoic self and The Hierophant represents the gaining of higher wisdom
from sources beyond that self. In order to make that transition, The Emperor
must grapple with his ego resistance (the idea that "ego is king"), so that he can
"die" to himself at a higher octave of his being (Death, Key 13). Once he accepts
the idea that "the king must die" (i.e., that the ego must serve some higher
purpose than self-perpetuation), the crossover can take place. The Hierophant
looks rather grand like the Emperor, but his role is very different, because he
serves as a representative of Spirit, not the personal self. The robes, three-fold
crown, etc., symbolize the sublime quality of spiritual truth; the person who
wears them is the mouthpiece of truth, not its source. This is why popes and
other high officials in the Church who were sincere about their work often wore
hair shirts under their outer finery: to remind them of that distinction.

Thus, the nadir of the enneagram *may be where the greatest transformation
occurs on the enneagram*, even though it's not one of the nine enneagram points.
It's for that reason that future chapters often include a jagged line at the nadir:
to remind us of its pivotal role in the hero's journey.

Nathan Bernier's "Rosetta Stone"

Blake's *Intelligent Enneagram* was my first introduction to the process enneagram. But it was not from Blake that I gained the understanding that allowed me to see the parallels between the personality and process enneagrams. It was from another author, Nathan Bernier, who wrote *The Enneagram: Symbol of All and Everything* (Gilgamesh: 2003).[13]

While I found much of Bernier's book fascinating but obscure, I discovered one nine-page section that was crystal-clear. It detailed what happens "when our endeavors fail" (pp. 325–333). It contains blow-by-blow descriptions of the challenges associated with each point on the enneagram circle. Bernier's descriptions of these challenges were similar to the descriptions of the challenges faced by the nine personality types—similar enough to allow me to bridge the gap between the two enneagrams. As the result of reading this very small section of a very big book, I was able to make the mental leap necessary to link the nine personality types with the nine process stages; see **Table 8-1**.

This table shows us the similarities between the personality type associated with each number and the transformational challenge associated with the same number. For example, if we take the number *zero*, on the process enneagram, Point 0 is where we begin to feel a vague restlessness that gradually coalesces into dreams and imaginings. On the personality enneagram, it's where we find Type 9, the one most associated with dreams, imaginings, and flights of

TABLE **8-1.** Parallels between the Process and Personality Enneagrams.

Pᴛ	Process	Personality Attributes
0 9*	Dreaming about a new project	Dreamy, imaginative, open-minded, animated
1	Starting a new project & developing goals	One-pointed, fiery, goal-oriented, specific
2	Nurturing the "baby" & seeking support	Nurturing, caring, supportive, organizing
3	Developing a real-life working prototype	Enterprising, ambitious, adaptable, concrete
4	Emotionally committing to move ahead	Determined, intense, deep, brave, dauntless
5	Solving problems with innovative thinking	Objective, analytical, ingenious, detached
6	Overcoming the biggest obstacle(s)	Feisty, persevering, "try try again" attitude
7	Refining the details to create a refined work	Artistic, refined, creative, flexible, playful
8	Presenting the final product for appraisal	Grounded, concrete, hard-driving, pragmatic
0/9	Integrating the experience into the self	Receptive, integrating, harmonizing, impassive

*Recall that on the process enneagram, although the point at the top of the enneagram is usually labeled 9, it plays two roles (beginning and end) because of the overlap of cycles (see Table 4-1). So Point 0 and 1 are the same on the personality enneagram, although in the context of this chart, it's possible to think of Type 0 as the personality of a Nine in youth and Type 9 as the personality of a Nine with some degree of life experience.

fancy. The correspondences between the two are unmistakable. If we take the number *one*, it's associated on the process enneagram with a new cycle and the need to be clear about one's vision and goals; it's associated on the personality enneagram with a type that is one-pointed in focus and determined to align its goals with those of a higher will. If we take the number *two*, it's associated on the process enneagram with nurturing a new, not-fully-developed venture; it's associated on the personality enneagram with a type that is known for its devotion to nurturing, healing, and offering encouragement.

The parallels exist for all nine enneagram points. They should appear even clearer once we look at the archetypes of the tarot in Part III. But there is another way to explore the relationship between personality and process that we'll look at below, by examining the relationships between the 18 enneagram wing types (**Fig. 8-4**).

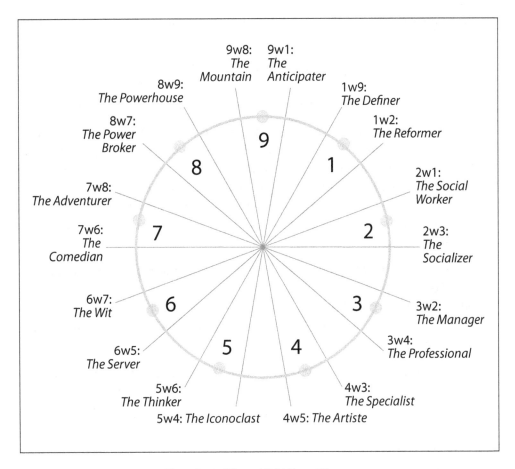

FIG. **8-4.** The 18 Wing Types.

Wings Across the Enneagram

The 18 wing types divide each enneagram point into two "zones." They thus enable us to make finer distinctions between them and to bridge the gap between adjacent points. Studying the wings gave me the idea to illustrate the underlying unity of the two forms of the enneagram by using them to tell a little story in which we, the readers, imagine ourselves as the hero in the story. We start at the top (9w1) and proceed through the entire enneagram, having different experiences at each of the 18 points we encounter. While I'm not sure that my little story would ever be nominated for a literary award, it does provide a practical way to understand the wing types and to link the personality and process enneagrams.

If we start at the very top of the enneagram, we find ourselves in a space of anticipatory expectation. At this point, we're just about to start a new project or cycle, but haven't quite done anything yet. We're simply being in the moment, content but alert. Slowly, something begins to stir. It's subtle, and it creates a slight but definite ripple of interest. We become **The Anticipator** *(9w1).*

Energy begins to gather and move. It starts to swirl around without much form. This is a time of excitement, but also tension; we sense the need to develop a definite and precise matrix for imposing some sort of order. We are becoming **The Definer** *(1w9).*

Imposing order on chaos is not an easy task; it requires discipline and concentration. It can also be nerve-wracking, because whatever we do at the start of a project will affect that project all the way through to completion. So it's a serious business. In order to minimize mistakes, we strive to find a way to judge whether we're really on track by establishing clear standards by which to separate truth from error. Once these standards are in place, we want to ensure they'll be taken seriously. We become **The Reformer** *(1w2).*

Our efforts to this point have been based on an idealized abstraction. In order to take the next step, we need to involve others in order to humanize our ideals and also enlist support for them. As we do this, we begin to see how those ideals translate into plans with the power to help real people, especially those in need. We become **The Social Worker** *(2w1).*

Part of the joy of helping others is knowing that we're not alone. We not only enjoy the companionship of others, we also see how other people can act as mirrors for our developing self-image. Each relationship mirrors back different aspects of ourselves, and this gives us an incentive to make more friends and contacts. We're now **The Socializer** *(2w3).*

We soon realize how having a social network helps us accomplish our goals in life. But we now have so many friends and contacts that we're having a hard time keeping them straight; we have to organize our relationships. As our social proficiency and organizational skills grow, we increasingly find ourselves in positions of organizational responsibility. We're becoming **The Manager** (3w2).

Managing people is something we're good at, but we find that relationships can sometimes become messy and even interfere with getting things done. As we become increasingly intrigued by our work, we also become more aware of ourselves as individuals. We seek to develop the skills that enable us to shine as **The Professional** (3w4).

Over time, we find that being a successful Professional, while rewarding, is not satisfying our deeper needs. Once we've achieved our goals, what next? We realize that we need more than ideals (Point 1), more than contacts (Point 2), or even more than outward success (Point 3). We need a sense of significance or meaning (Point 4). So we begin to engage in our work for its own sake, getting more and more knowledgeable as a **Specialist** (4w3).

Despite our special skills, we feel increasing dissatisfied with living on the surface of life. We want to delve deeper, to get to the bottom of who we actually are. We continue to hone our skills but to use them in the service of self-discovery, becoming ever more focused on ways to express our deepest selves. We are now the exquisitely skilled but highly sensitive **Artiste** (4w5).

Finally, as we encounter the chaotic zone at the bottom of the enneagram, things reach a breaking point, and there's a dramatic collapse of the self as we have known it. The sense of "self-as-role" disappears, replaced by a new and curiously impersonal self that is less constrained by the need for social approval. We find ourselves without the need to adhere to social norms or even to maintain social appearances. We are now **The Iconoclast** (image-breaker) (5w4).

However, we soon discover that it's exhausting to go around breaking other peoples' images all the time. Also, they don't seem to like it very much. So for the sake of convenience, we allow our natural curiosity to lead us in a new direction, into a space of pure thought and reflection. We find it extremely satisfying to become **The Thinker** (5w6).

The more we think about things, the more we realize how complex life really is. This understanding begins to make us a bit nervous. It also slows us down, giving us a tendency to hesitate before we act. Finally, it makes us feel our own aloneness and realize that we need companionship to avoid feeling alone and afraid. We seek ways to reestablish our social ties. How can we do this? Perhaps by volunteering to serve the needs of our family and community. We become **The Server** (6w5).

Through serving, we get used to being around people without feeling uncomfortably intimate. It's easier to relax if we can play a well-defined social role in the family or at work. Later, we begin to explore ways to step outside those roles. We're a little nervous about this but find that humor helps us relax in social situations. It makes other people laugh, too. We've become **The Wit** (6w7).

The more social approval we get, the more confident we become. We start actually enjoying life, so much so that we tend to brush aside anything that might ruin the party. We don't, after all, want to go back to that place where we felt awkward or apprehensive. We amp up our entertaining skills even more, becoming the life of the party—**The Comedian** (7w6).

Of course, even humor has its limits. If we're going to continue to grow, we'll have to find new venues for expansion. It's an exciting time. New worlds are opening up for us; we're dazzled by all the things that life has to offer. Buoyed by confidence and the sense that life is an adventure, we become increasingly innovative and entrepreneurial. We're now **The Adventurer** (7w8).

We travel to the four corners of the world, garnering every possible experience we can. We find that we adapt easily to whatever environment we encounter. We collect interesting experiences the way that some people collect stamps. But eventually, so many adventures takes its toll—we can't go on like this forever! We settle down enough to master "the art of the deal." We become **The Power Broker** (8w7).

But we haven't quite reached the pinnacle of achievement. We realize that while we've mastered the ability to accomplish a lot of different things, it's much more interesting to focus on just One Big Thing. We turn our entire will in one direction to accomplish some great work that will stand the test of time. As we place the final brick in the edifice we have built, we know we have finally arrived: we are **The Powerhouse** (8w9).

We are now enormously powerful and influential. We've managed to climb out of the laboratory of ideas (Point 5), to apply those ideas to serve others (Point 6), to expand our horizons (Point 7), and to bring all our experiences together to manifest something of substance (Point 8). We've accomplished all of our goals and have nothing left to do.

Ironically, in bringing forth our great accomplishment, we no longer have the freedom we had at earlier stages of our journey. We are now so massively powerful that we literally can't move without affecting everything around us. We're obliged to simply stand still, to be the symbol that inspires others to follow their dreams. We've become **The Mountain** (9w8).

But even the highest mountain doesn't remain a mountain forever. Mountains wear down and dissolve into dust, until eventually there's nothing left. This is the end of the journey. It comes as a relief, because no matter how great the accomplishment, once it's done, it's done. There's nothing left to do, no place left to go. We can't ascend *any further—at least not for the moment. All we can do is return whence we came: The Primordial Sea (Point 9).*

In this timeless place we remain for a period, assimilating our experiences and recovering our sense of oneness with life. There are no borders or edges here; we bask in the primordial atmosphere of light and love. We experience a sense of Allness that seems to satisfy all our needs.

Then one day, there's a stir. Something begins to arise—something new, something that beckons us onward. We become vaguely irritated. We begin to anticipate some sort of change (9w1), and the whole cycle begins once more.

In the section above, I have transformed the personality enneagram into a process enneagram by describing the characteristics of the 18 wing types and linking them together to create a plausible story. It is the last of several efforts I have made in this chapter and earlier to weave together these two enneagrams in a way that suggests they are really a single enneagram seen from different perspectives.

Why does this one enneagram model matter so much? Because in the next section, we look at parallels between the enneagram and the tarot, using the hero's journey as our central metaphor.

The major arcana of the tarot can be described as either 22 independent archetypes or as 22 stages on a hero's journey; people who work with the tarot move seamlessly between these two perspectives, viewing them both as valid, depending upon their purposes. In a tarot reading, the Keys (and the rest of the tarot deck) are usually viewed as separate entities, although meaningful relationships often appear in the reading. In a book describing the tarot, depicting the 22 Keys as stages in the hero's journey often helps people to better understand and remember the archetypes.

I've tried to show in this section that the enneagram can also be described as either nine independent archetypes (of personality) or as nine stages in a hero's journey. Understanding the parallels between the two perspectives on the enneagram (personality and process) is useful for three reasons. First, I believe it is the most accurate way to describe the enneagram: as one system, not two. Second, it marries the simplicity of the personality enneagram with the more optimistic focus of the process enneagram. Third, it makes it easier to understand how the enneagram and the tarot can meaningfully inform one another.

The discussion on number symbolism in Chapter 9 builds upon this foundation to explore how the ability to relate to numbers as symbols has the power to open Huxley's "doors of perception" into new dimensions of experience. We'll see what the tarot and enneagram may have to tell us about these new worlds, both alone and together.

Notes

[1] *In Search of the Miraculous* (Harvest: 1949/2001), p. 294.

[2] *Hidden Wisdom: A Guide to the Western Inner Traditions* (Quest: 2006), p. 225.

[3] Gurdjieff teachers and groups follow what they call the Fourth Way, because while many schools focus on just one of the three energy centers that govern our lives—body, mind, or emotions—Gurdjieff focused on integrating the three in daily life.

[4] *The Intelligent Enneagram* (Shambhala: 1996), p. 39.

[5] According to A. G. E. Blake, if we envision the enneagram as a dramatic story, the journey around the outer circle is characterized as the protagonist's movement through "the world of blind experience" (p. 181) while the inner lines reveal both the protagonist's anticipation of future events (or reflections on past ones) and the special knowledge of mentors who are "in the know" (and thus able to help the protagonist make better decisions at key points in the story).

[6] J. G. Bennett also notes the spiral nature of the enneagram circle in *Enneagram Studies* (Weiser: 1983), p. 29.

[7] Archetypal journeys are always ideals. Real journeys are much messier, inevitably involving delays, misunderstandings, detours, and incomplete transformations.

[8] *Psychological Commentaries on the Teaching of Gurdjieff and Ouspensky*, Vol. 2 (Weiser: 1996), p. 390; available as a pdf at: http://www.gianfrancobertagni.it/materiali/gurdjieff/nicoll_commentari2.pdf.

[9] Ibid, p. 437.

[10] See http://www.endlesssearch.co.uk/philo_is_talk_ae2005.htm.

[11] A. G. E. Blake, Maurice Nicoll, and Ian MacFarlane have all discussed a third shock as occurring at both Points 6 and 9. The confusion arises because Gurdjieff speaks of the enneagram as depicting an octave on a scale, with the shock points inserted where the half-step intervals occur between *mi-fa* and *si-do*. However, when he positions the shock points on the enneagram, he places them between *mi-fa* and *sol-la* (at Points 3 and 6), remarking on this strange placement with this mysterious comment: "The apparent placing of the interval in *its wrong place* itself shows to those who are able to read the symbol what kind of 'shock' is required for the passage from *si* to *do*" (*In Search of the Miraculous*, p. 291). This is a deeply mysterious topic; see Gurdjieff's discussion on pp. 288–294 in *ISM*; see also Chapter 9 and Appendix E.

[12] On the personality enneagram, the nadir has the same chaotic associations as on the process enneagram, even though it is seldom mentioned in personality enneagram books. But there is something disturbingly void-like in the vertical center of the circle. Judith Searle, a noted personality enneagram theorist, wrote an article that explores the mysterious properties of the nadir (which she calls "The Gap at the Bottom of the Enneagram," available at http://personalitycafe. com/enneagram-personality-theory-forum/180553-gap-bottom-enneagram.html. See also my article, "The Circle, the Triangle, and the Hexad," (available at: http://www.enneagramdimensions.net/articles%5Ccircle_triangle_hexad_pt1.pdf) or pp. 153–155 of *The Integral Enneagram* (2013) for a discussion.

[13] "Nathan Bernier" is apparently a pen name; his book is available as a PDF at http://www. lemma-coaching.hu/docs/ajanlott_irodalom/Nathan%20Bernier%20-%20The%20Enneagram,%20Symbol%20of%20All%20and%20Everything.pdf.

III

The Hero's Journey by the Numbers

9:
Number Symbolism
in the Enneagram & Tarot

The world is built upon the power of numbers.
– Pythagoras

One for unity and the movement of power
Two for duality and coming together
Three for creation, whatever is born
Four for structure, the directions of Earth
Five for bodies, and roses, and Venus
Six for the love that moves generations
Seven for spheres and music and color
Eight for infinity and eternal return
Nine for gestation, the moons of our birth
Ten for our fingers and the toes of our feet.

RACHEL POLLACK COMPOSED THE ABOVE VERSE especially for her marvelously comprehensive book, *Tarot Wisdom* (2015). It's an invocation in recognition of the key role played by numbers in the tarot. She says that although she loves the images painted by Pamela Colman Smith, she's glad that newer tarot decks often depart from Smith's imagery, because it shows us the many different ways that people can understand numbers. And yet, her verse reflects the idea that numbers possess identifiable qualities, qualities that are archetypal in nature.

This chapter focuses on numbers in their role as *universal symbols*, especially the single-digit numbers 1–9. The idea that these numbers are inherently meaningful is the basis for the idea that we can link the enneagram with the tarot based upon the numbers that they share. So before looking at how they can be linked, let's take a look at the nature of numbers and what they mean in the enneagram and tarot.

The Mystery of Numbers

Number mysticism is very old. We don't know how old, but probably older than written tablets can record. For the Pythagoreans, numbers were not a mere subject to study, but a way of life. Thus, numerologist Michael Schneider quotes the Pythagorean philosopher Philolaus as observing that "Truth...is inherent in the nature of number."[1] And in *Homage to Pythagoras,*[2] Christopher Bamford notes that

> the Pythagorean philosopher thus strove to align his being [and] unite his thinking...with the thinking and being sources of the Kosmos, i.e., the Gods, Numbers or Archetypes (p. 15).

The idea that Numbers, Gods, and Archetypes are equivalent (and all deserving a capital "A") reflects the Pythagorean reverence for the archetype of number. This same idea informs the thinking of modern esoteric writers:

▶ Carl Jung considered numbers to be archetypes, and as such, "pre-existent to consciousness." In other words, we did not invent numbers but, rather, *discovered* them.[3]

▶ Esoteric tarotist C. C. Zain, the founder of the Brotherhood of Light, tells us that "the universe sprang into differentiated existence in conformity with the law of numbers."[4]

▶ Faith Javane and Dusty Bunker tell us that numerology is "the art and science of understanding the spiritual significance and orderly progression of all manifestation,"[5] going on to observe that "every word or name vibrates to a number and every number has its inner meaning. The letter and number code...brings us into a direct and close relationship with the underlying intelligence of the universe."[6]

▶ Robert Lawlor says that numbers are not just abstract ideas but are intimately associated with "the laws and relationships observable in light and sound."[7,8]

People with synesthesia—the ability to "mix the senses," such that they can, e.g., hear colors, feel sounds and taste shapes—often express a "felt" awareness of what numbers mean. In a *Scientific American* interview, number savant Daniel Tammett (who can calculate *pi* to 22,514 places) says that

> I have always thought of abstract information—numbers for example—in visual, dynamic form. Numbers assume complex, multidimensional shapes in my head....They have form, color, texture, and so on. They come alive to me, which is why as a young child I thought of them as my friends."[9]

He's not alone. As much as 4% of the population has some form of synesthesia, and number synesthesia is by far the most common—which lends credence to the claim that the concept of Number is a "master archetype."

Numbers as Archetypal Qualities

If 4% of us are synesthetic, the other 96% are not. Therefore, it's hard for most of us to really understand numbers as symbols. I can understand the concept, but that's very different from understanding it experientially. Most of the time, I only think of numbers when I need to calculate a tip or measure a room. And this way of thinking is very typical: as Karen Hamaker-Zondag observes, "We employ numbers every day without stopping to think that they could have a *meaning*" (p. 72). The idea that numbers are both quantitative and qualitative doesn't come to mind. John Opsopaus, creator of *The Pythagorean Tarot*, explains why:

> In the historical, conscious development of number, the West has favored the quantitative and abstract structural aspects, which has led to the development of modern science, whereas the East has favored the qualitative and affective (feeling-toned) aspects....When the qualitative aspects are included in our conception of numbers, they become more than simple quantities 1, 2, 3, 4; they acquire an archetypal character as Unity, Opposition, Conjunction, Completion.[10]

His observations remind us that meaning is an essentially feminine idea—and we all know how undervalued feminine archetypes are in Western culture. I suppose a good motto for this position would be "When in doubt, quantify!"

What is thought-provoking is just how deeply entrenched this "quest for quantification" really is—so deeply entrenched that even those who would in theory embrace the feminine (like modern-day spiritual seekers) have difficulty translating theory into practice.

A story from Drunvalo Melchizidek illustrates this idea very well. Druvalo is a well-known teacher of sacred geometry. His Flower of Life (FOL) workshops were particularly popular in the 1980s and 90s. Participants learned how to activate their *merkaba*, a powerful energy field which is the light body of a human being—and which remains dormant unless consciously awakened.[11] There were two parts to the teaching. The first focused on how to open the heart, which participants are told is essential to the second part: performing a detailed, step-by-step meditation. But when Drunvalo taught the work this way, only women came. After four years, his guides instructed him to reverse the order. When he did, men began to attend the workshops. However, reversing the order gave some participants the idea that they could just do the (masculine) meditation without opening the heart. But participants who did only the masculine practice became mentally unbalanced, sometimes gravely so. In 2011, Drunvalo made a video to explain what had happened, in order to prevent future problems.[12]

This example illustrates the idea that, not only do we discount the power of feminine receptivity to create the proper attunement for masculine action—we also discount the power of the masculine to produce transformational results. For no one would knowingly perform a meditation that would make them crazy. If they do, it's because they don't really understand the very real "power of Number"—or how to work with it safely. This is why genuine mystery schools don't casually reveal their secrets to outsiders: because they teach techniques that can be powerful and dangerous to apply unless you know exactly what you are doing. This may also explain the reason behind the idea that members of the Pythagorean school were rumored to have done away with Hippasus, the man who discovered irrational numbers (or perhaps revealed their existence to outsiders), or that, according to Drunvalo, "if you even uttered the world 'dodecahedron' outside the School, they would kill you on the spot."[13]

Stories like these might sound crazy to modern ears. But are they? It's quite possible the ancients knew something about the true nature of numbers that we have now forgotten—and could potentially benefit from remembering. Especially since we seem to be coming into a time when all kinds of lost knowledge is resurfacing, whether we're ready for it or not.

If we believe what Pythagoras and his followers through the ages tell us, then *numbers literally create the world we live in.* If so, that's a very good reason to see them as more than just practical tools for measuring things. To the Pythagoreans, they were not just *quantitative* measures but *qualitative* symbols, symbols that reveal the story of creation.

The Archetypal Numbers 1–9

Now that we've looked at number symbolism in general, let's take a look at the nine single-digit numbers that serve as the basis for all others. As we know, numbers are infinite; there is no limit to how many exist. But to Gurdjieff and other explorers into the mystery of number symbology, there are really only nine numbers (or 10, if you add in the zero). All the other numbers are derivatives of these nine. Here is what Western numerological scholars have had to say about these unique numbers:

▶ Numerologists Faith Javane and Dusty Bunker tell us that "the digits 1 through 9 symbolize the stages through which an idea must pass before it becomes a reality," and that "all manifestation is the result of these nine stages."[14]

▶ Sandor Konraad begins his book on numerology and the tarot with this statement: "Our study of numerology properly begins with the first nine numbers. These are known as root numbers. The numbers 1 and 9 actually comprise all the numbers in the world."[15]

▶ Carl Jung said that the numbers 1–9 possess "numinosity and mystery"; he thought of them as sacred, because they connect us with something larger than ourselves—some greater reality that is divine, cosmic, mysterious. Their significance will thus always elude the grasp of our logical minds.[16]

▶ Eden Gray, the author of one of the first modern books on the tarot, notes that "there are 9 digits and hence 9 root influences....The Tarot Keys that are numbered above 9 embody both the meanings of their sequential number and the aggregate [cross-sum] of their digits."[17] This is an interesting comment, because it brings in the idea that, while larger numbers may in some sense be reducible to a root number under 10, they also retain their original character—an idea that we see reflected in the way that Angeles Arrien and Mary Greer later developed the concept of tarot constellations (see Chapter 10).

▶ C. C. Zain notes that "any number above 9 is merely one of the root numbers, to which 9 has been added a given number of times. This adding multiples of nine to some number is called Theosophical Evolution, not because it derives from any particular group of people[18] but because Theosophy means Divine Wisdom, and because…the number 9 is the key to Divine Wisdom insofar as numbers and cycles are concerned."[19]

▶ G. I. Gurdjieff speaks of the importance of the first nine numbers, telling us that one transformational cycle—which can be characterized as an octave—consists of seven notes plus two shock points, making a total of nine steps in all.[20]

If 1–9 represent archetypal numbers (and an archetypal sequence), it certainly makes sense to think that the number archetypes which cluster around each of these nine numbers (those whose cross-sums yield the same single-digit number) should have a very strong "family resemblance."[21] It's also the basis for supposing that we would find similarities between the tarot cards and enneagram points sharing the same digital root.

Reducing Numbers to Cross-sums

As we saw in Chapter 1, the digital roots 1–9 are calculated by adding up their cross-sums until we obtain a number between 1 and 9. To review how this works, let's look at a couple of examples:

Number = 2,438
Step 1: $2438 = 2 + 4 + 3 + 8 = 17$
Step 2: $17 = 1 + 7 = 8$

∴ the digital root of 2,438 is **8**

Number = 94,135
Step 1: $9 + 4 + 1 + 3 + 5 = 22$
Step 2: $22 = 2 + 2 = 4$

∴ the digital root of 94,135 is **4**

In an online article, "Nine, the Ultimate Mystery," Joe Dubs explains more about this process:

> The process of reducing a number down to one digit is called many names. It is common practice not only in numerology but also in mainstream science. The great geometric genius (alliteration aside) of the 20th Century, Buckminster Fuller, called this subset of math "integrated digits" or "indig 9." It is also recognized in computer science. They call it a "digital root" or "digital sum" or "quantum bit." This process has also been called Kabbalistic reduction or Pythagorean addition. Some other names for this practice include: decimal parity, quantum numerology, theosophical addition, indig, integrated digit, indig 9, modulo nine arithmetic, number essence, reduced ordinal values, horizontal addition, and numeric reduction.[22]

The same approach was also used by school children in the 19th century who employed the mathematical shortcut of "casting out nines" to do various arithmetic operations.

As we discussed in the previous section, the idea of reducing numbers to single digits by their cross-sums is rooted in the idea that *the first nine numbers are esoterically unique,* that they each represent a unique archetypal energy that is symbolically meaningful. That's why it is often said that there are really only nine numbers.

To understand more deeply what this means, we can turn to Hermetic philosophy. The idea that a relationship exists between numbers with the same cross sum is broadly based upon the Hermetic principle, "As above, so below," also known as the Law of Correspondences: the idea that life exists in many different dimensions which, while essentially separate, nevertheless interact or overlap in various meaningful ways.[23] This is the same idea alluded to by Gurdjieff when he speaks of the musical octaves, noting that the *do* of each octave overlaps with the *do* of the corresponding lower and higher octaves, an idea we'll look at shortly.

Number Symbolism in the Tarot

In the tarot, number symbolism is widely regarded as an important topic of discussion. This is why just about every well-known tarot author has weighed in on the subject when discussing the meaning of the numbered cards in the major and minor arcanas. It is taken seriously enough that there are even a number of disagreements among authors about what the numbers signify or what numbering system is best. For example, one of the most famous ongoing debates about the symbolic significance of the tarot Keys concerns the "swap" made by A. E. Waite of Key 8 (Strength) with Key 11 (Justice).[24, 25] Another topic concerns the best numerological approach to use for interpreting the cards and whether or not to try to map them onto the qabalistic Tree of Life (see Appendix E). Below are some comments on number symbolism in the tarot from well-known tarot authors:

▶ Manly P. Hall tells us that "the Pythagorean numerologist will…find an important relationship to exist between the numbers on the [tarot] cards and the designs accompanying the numbers."[26]

▶ Paul Foster Case speaks of the importance of the numbers 0 through 10 in tarot work, going so far as to develop a B.O.T.A. meditation, The Pattern on the Trestleboard, based on these numbers.[27]

▶ Eden Gray tells us that "there is a universal language that speaks to us through numbers," and then describes the numerological meanings associated with all 22 of the major arcana Keys.[28]

▶ Karen Hamaker-Zondag describes numbers as "symbols in the world of the psyche, and therefore much richer in content than words can express."[29]

▶ Tracy Porter talks about number sequence as symbolically significant: "Each card was placed in its sequence for a particular reason. Each card has a story to tell, and its placement within the suit shows where we are in the cycle of our evolution. Therefore, the numerical significance of each card is paramount when giving a meaningful [tarot] reading."[30]

▶ Hajo Banzhaf believes that the numbers of the major trumps are symbolic in nature, but is not sure whether the minors are also symbolic. He notes (citing A. E. Waite) that "no occult...writer has attempted to assign anything but a divinatory meaning to the minor arcana," p. 5. However, Robert Place speaks of the role of Pythagorean mathematics in linking the 10 suits of the minor arcana with the 10 sephiroth on the qabalistic Tree of Life (p. 92).

▶ Art Rosengarten explores a number of ways in which numbers cluster together to demonstrate different principles of number symbolism; he also alludes to the "root connection" between numbers such as 21 and 3, observing that "such numerological connections are never lost in the tarot."[31]

▶ Ronald Decker describes the tarot as a system in which number symbolism is widely used, but points out the considerable divergence in the way that different authors describe the symbolic quality of numbers as applied to the tarot. He wonders aloud how tarot designers are supposed to decide which approach to use when assigning numeric symbolism to tarot cards.[32]

▶ Richard Roberts, Art Rosengarten, Angeles Arrien, Mary Greer, and Shirley Gotthold all see the numbers 1–9 as having special properties, such that tarot cards sharing the same numeric value when reduced to numbers 1–9 constitute a kind of "numerological family"—what Arrien and Greer call a *tarot constellation* (see Chapter 10). This is also my view, and it serves as the basis for my exploration of parallels between the enneagram points of view and tarot Keys.

▶ Rachel Pollack takes the discussion of number symbolism to another level when she notes that the numbers of the major arcana may mean different things, depending upon whether we treat the cards as (a) a set of independent entities [separate archetypes] or (b) a series of sequential events [like the hero's journey]. If we treat each card as independent, the numbers are "part of their symbolic language [such that] the number 1 belongs to the Magician not because he comes first but because that number signifies ideas—unity, willpower—appropriate to the concept of the Magician." If we treat the numbers as a progression, we can see "where each card fits in the overall pattern" because "each new trump builds upon the previous one and leads the way to the next."[33]

Rachel Pollack's comments particularly caught my eye because of the two ways she says we can view the numbers of the tarot Keys—as either independent cards or as part of a sequence. This exactly parallels the two ways the numbers on the enneagram can be viewed: either as the names of independent entities (the personality enneagram) or as a sequence (the process enneagram).

Number Symbolism in the Enneagram

Unlike the tarot, the enneagram contains no pictorial symbols (unless you see the geometry itself as pictorial, like some sort of formal, abstract painting). All we have are the numbers 0–9 and the three figures of the circle, triangle, and hexad. Thus, all the meaningful information in the enneagram is expressed solely by its numbers and geometry.

However, to precisely pin down the numeric symbology of the enneagram is something of a challenge, because Gurdjieff did not spell it out in plain English. Thus, although the following discussion explores Gurdjieff's ideas about the number symbolism of the enneagram, it is far from a straightforward account. It does, however, demonstrate that Gurdjieff clearly saw the enneagram as a system entirely based on number symbolism—symbolism so profound that it has the power to utterly transform human consciousness.

Fig. 9-1 is a replica of the enneagram shown on p. 288 in *In Search of the Miraculous (ISM)*. The triangle is dashed to distinguish it from the hexad. The numbers are arranged in the same order that we see them on any enneagram in use today. **Fig. 9-2** is an exact copy of the enneagram on the following page; what is curious about it is that it includes the notes of the diatonic scale, the one we know from *The Sound of Music*. We'll return to the second figure momentarily.

As mentioned above, Gurdjieff was well-aware of the idea that all numbers reduce to the root numbers 1–9, a process he knew as theosophical addition. He placed these nine root numbers on a circle, in the configuration we see in Fig. 9-1, together with the two geometric figures of the triangle (said to embody the Law of Three) and the hexad (said to embody the Law of Seven).

We have already discussed these figures in Chapter 8, but to briefly review that discussion, the enneagram *triangle* is symbolic of the foundational nature of the Law of Three, because it has three vertices, which symbolically represent the Affirming-Denying-Reconciling forces that are necessary for any kind of evolutionary change. Gurdjieff said that "change can only happen when three independent forces come together." When the third [reconciling] force enters, "the two forces are no longer locked together....There is an extra degree of freedom and a higher level of awareness"(p. 81). These three forces are thus imbued with "higher elements" (will and intelligent purpose) that inform lower-order processes and give them meaning.[34] He thus affirms that the law that governs the Cosmos is both *intelligent* and *intentional*.

If we take the fraction 1/3 and convert it to decimal form, this generates the recurrent sequence .333...; multiplying .333... by 2, we get .666...; multiplying it by 3, we get .999....Symbolically, the repeating of the same numeral at each vertex emphasizes the unchanging and eternal structure of transformational processes.

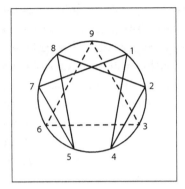

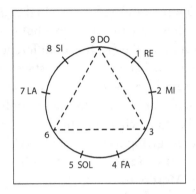

FIG. 9-1. Gurdjieff's Enneagram.   **FIG. 9-2.** The Scale on the Enneagram.

The figure of the *hexad*, which symbolizes perpetual motion, is said to embody the Law of Seven. This sounds puzzling until you realize that it comes from an infinitely repeating sequence that is generated by dividing 1 by sevenths:

$$1/7 = .1\ 4\ 2\ 8\ 5\ 7\ ...$$
$$2/7 = .2\ 8\ 5\ 7\ 1\ 4\ ...$$
$$3/7 = .4\ 2\ 8\ 5\ 7\ 1\ ...$$
$$4/7 = .5\ 7\ 1\ 4\ 2\ 8\ ...$$
$$5/7 = .7\ 1\ 4\ 2\ 8\ 5\ ...$$
$$6/7 = .8\ 5\ 7\ 1\ 4\ 2\ ...$$

If we multiply .142857 x 7, we don't get "1", but instead .999....This explains why the hexad includes the sequence 1-2-4-5-7-8 plus Point 9: because nine is the stable beginning and ending point (the apex of the triangle) that contains or structures all that moves in life (the hexad). That is why it must be placed at the top of the enneagram circle, where the two figures meet, "because it is the ninth step that closes and again begins a cycle" (p. 288).[35] Gurdjieff goes on to say that the number 9 also "closes the duality of its base, making possible the manifold forms of its manifestation." So the number nine plays a unique role, because it participates in both the triangle and the hexad. As such, it serves as the linchpin for everything that happens on the enneagram circle.

The numbers are placed in a clockwise progression on the nine points of the circle, as shown in Fig. 9-1. Gurdjieff does not tell us why he positions them in this way, but it is doubtful that any other arrangement would be appropriate. For as enneagram scholar Nathan Bernier tells us,"Gurdjieff did not give us the option to put the numbers in the enneagram in any other way."[36] Gurdjieff himself refers to the fact that the enneagram is divided into nine parts "in a certain order" (*ISM*, p. 285).

Now turning to Fig. 9-2, it clearly equates the enneagram with the seven-tone diatonic scale, a scale that describes one musical octave, which begins with a lower *do* and ends with a higher *do* one octave later, making eight notes total. Both *do*'s are the same note but in separate octaves; the place where they meet represents the meeting of different dimensions of experience. This scale represents the Law of Seven, the stages of evolution within a single octave of experience, where one cycle can refer to, e.g., the building of a house, the serving of a meal, or the transformation of human consciousness. This is why Gurdjieff talks so much about the properties of octaves before introducing the enneagram (giving rise to Ouspensky's comments that "the law of octaves naturally gave rise to a great many talks in our group and to much perplexity," p. 135).

Most of us can relate to their perplexity, for the topic is arcane and Gurdjieff's discussion does little to make it less so! But by introducing his students to the musical octave, Gurdjieff seeks to explain the nature of transformation, starting with the idea that everything in life is a matter of *vibration* (p. 122), where the implicit goal is to move from a lower to higher vibratory state. Each note in the octave represents an identifiable move up the evolutionary ladder.

According to Gurdjieff, the ability to identify the steps in an octave allows us to contemplate the idea that life is governed by the principle of "unity in diversity"; he cites the qabala, tarot, and astrology as examples of systems that show us how to organize diverse elements into a single, unified system.[37] He goes on to say that it is difficult to capture the idea of unity in diversity without distorting it in some way (e.g., by using words to describe it). He tells us that he has sought an objective (undistorted) way of expressing this concept, and found it in the figure of the enneagram, which is based purely on number symbolism (p. 283).

In summary, Gurdjieff is saying that the enneagram figure provides us with a geometric symbol that depicts the way that intelligent life evolves, so that what we normally see as random patterns ("diversity") can be understood as the product of two Laws—the Law of Three and the Law of Seven—where the Law of Seven depicts the dynamic motion of life processes and the Law of Three depicts the stabilizing force of intelligent will that acts upon these processes. The enneagram circle represents the cosmos in which these two laws interact, which is why it represents the relationship between unity and diversity.

One thing that Gurdjieff does not bring up are the specific properties associated with the individual numbers on the enneagram circle, although associating each one with a specific musical tone gives us a good starting point for investigating those properties.

When it comes to the personality enneagram, there has historically been little interest in looking at the symbolism of the numbers 1–9. This makes sense, considering the fact that the types have usually been presented as either categories of psychological imbalance or character defects. However, this does not mean that enneagram teachers and users actually experience the numbers as meaningless. On the contrary—because each type is almost always referred to by its number, not its name. As a result, when an experienced enneagrammer hears "Type *x*," a rich array of symbolically meaningful associations immediately comes to mind. So number symbolism is powerfully present, but is not talked about as such. There are no discussions in enneagram books or during enneagram panels that focus specifically on what the numbers actually *mean*. One advantage of pairing the enneagram and tarot is that it is likely to make enneagrammers more consciously aware of the symbolic dimension of the system.

The Enneagram, Tarot, and the Quantum Zero

The discussion above clearly demonstrates that both the tarot and the enneagram are number-oriented systems in which the numbers serve a symbolic purpose. But they emphasize different aspects of numerology. In the tarot, the focus is on the nature of individual numbers and the symbolic associations between numbers, colors, and imagery. So it offers a more lyrical and intuitive approach to exploring number symbolism and how it is related to both personal and collective archetypes.

In the enneagram, the focus is more on numbers as coordinates in a geometric matrix and the relationships between these coordinates. It thus provides us with a method for exploring number symbolism in the context of a dynamic, interactive system. Once we know the system, we have an amazingly practical tool for exploring interpersonal relationships and intrapsychic dynamics.

Essentially, I would characterize the tarot field as adopting a more intuitive, feminine approach to numerology and the enneagram field as adopting a more masculine, formalized approach. Thus, bringing these two systems— the feminine tarot and the masculine enneagram—into relationship with one another has the potential to help us develop a more integrated approach to symbolic numerology. Combining the two has significantly enhanced my understanding of number symbolism.[38]

However, in the writing of this book, I realized that there is something which brings together these two systems in an even more numerologically significant way: *the fact that they both possess a zero.*

Zero is not like other numbers. Most of us non-mathematicians don't think much about that, because we use zero the way we use all the numbers: to accomplish some practical end. Most of what we know is stuff we memorized for school or use in arithmetic operations. Nobody really talks about what zero really means.

But maybe there's a reason that it's not talked about—or thought about, either. In his book *Zero: The Biography of a Dangerous Idea*, (Penguin: 2000), Charles Seife relates the deep suspicion with which our European ancestors regarded the zero and its twin concept, infinity. This intense dislike of zero goes back at least 2,500 years, to ancient Greece (and later, Rome), where they so disliked the zero that they refused to use it, even as a placeholder (ignoring the

Babylonian system, which did use zero as a placeholder, thus making it much more efficient for complex calculations). The Greeks strongly preferred Pythagorean geometry and its elegant use of ratios, in which the number zero can play no part. Later, the concept of zero was discarded by Aristotle on the grounds that both zero and infinity were mere mental concepts that were not needed to explain anything in the real world. His theory that the heavenly bodies move around the earth in crystalline orbs bounded by the starry heavens was hugely embraced by the Catholic Church, because it could be used to prove the existence of God (based on the idea that someone or something of great magnitude was needed to set the celestial orbs into motion).

When a bright merchant's son, Leonardo Pisano Fibonacci, brought back the zero to the West in 1202, it was eagerly embraced by Italian merchants involved in trade, because it made complex calculations so much easier. Although Florence tried to ban the system a century later (ostensibly because Arabic numbers could easily be changed, e.g., a 3 could be made into an 8), Italian traders continued to employ them; gradually, Europe began to move from an Aristotelian, Greco-Roman numbering system to a more modern system based on Arabic numerals and a zero imported from further East (either India or Southeast Asia). But it was a slow back-and-forth process. Support for zero surged ahead when Renaissance artists such as Filippo Brunelleschi (1377–1446) conceived of using the vanishing point—a zero-dimensional object—to create realistic-looking, perspectival drawings, thereby transforming the art world (pp. 78–87).

At the same time, Copernican notions of astronomy made increasing inroads into Aristotle's theory of the spheres, causing forward-thinking individuals such as Giordano Bruno to write that the earth was not the center of the universe and that there were an infinite number of worlds like our own. This was the last straw; toward the end of the 16th century, the Church went on the offense, against both these new ideas and those who promoted them, such as Bruno and Galileo. From that point on, "zero was a heretic...the void and the infinite [that] must be rejected" (pp. 91–92).

Of course, the Church could not suppress zero forever; it came back with the emergence of the Enlightenment and thinkers like Descartes, Pascal, Kepler, and Newton. But the *fear of zero*—and of its ability to introduce paradox and uncertainty into the world—remains with us still. In modern times, we suppress it by "forgetting" about its symbolic dimensions, relegating it to the role of placeholder or focusing only on its practical use in calculus or (more recently) quantum mechanics.

But zero is not a concept that is easily suppressed or forgotten, at least not forever. Like a bad penny, it has turned up once again in quantum physics to bedevil us with the same kind of paradoxes that our rationalist ancestors sought to avoid—paradoxes like the idea that "Fullness is emptiness," "Nothing is real," "Boundedness is freedom," or "Chaos is unity."

For better or worse, quantum physics is here to stay and so is the zero. We'll return to the topic of quantum physics in Chapter 16; what is immediately relevant to our discussion of number symbolism is the fact that both the enneagram and the tarot possess something precious and rare: a true zero. In the enneagram, it's the top point on the circle (0/9); in the tarot, it's the first card in the major arcana: The Fool (0). And these are not placeholder zeros, but *symbolic* zeros, which means they tend to have multiple (and potentially opposing) meanings. This is what makes zero a paradoxical number.

In the process enneagram, zero is the first *do* in the scale, the note that determines the key for that scale and therefore its frame of reference; in the personality enneagram, it is Type 9 in childhood and early adulthood and is as close as you get to a "blank slate" when it comes to personality. It would make complete sense to call young Nines "Type 0" and more mature Nines "Type 9," thus conveying the symbolic idea that a person begins life with zero experience (as Type 0) but acquires a variety of life experiences (as Type 1, Type 2, etc.), finally "arriving" back at Point 9, having learned about life from nine different vantage points in the interim.

Also, the enneagram itself is a circle, which can be considered a zero. Its two variations are paradoxical, because although the actual figure never changes, one version is about *space* while the other is about *time*. On the personality enneagram, the points are points in space (remember the elephant in Fig. 6-1)? On the process enneagram, they are points in time. So the enneagram is a visual depiction of *space-time*—a concept straight out of the new physics!

In the tarot, the zero has many paradoxical meanings: it can represent both emptiness and fullness; both boundedness and expansiveness; both interiority and externality; both the beginning and end of a journey (and all stages in between). Its association with The Fool gives this Key its whimsical and paradoxical character, its ability to symbolize all the Keys or none of them.

Because both systems possess a symbolic zero, they can serve an important purpose: to help people make the psychological transition from the finite world of Beingness, Order, Aristotelean Logic, and Newtonian Physics to the infinite (and paradoxical) world of Non-being, Chaos Theory, Crazy Wisdom, and Quantum Mechanics. Our cultural predecessors were unsettled by the paradoxes raised when we contemplate both worlds at the same time. They even went so far as to create a monolithic world model dedicated to the avoidance of zero—and to the paradoxes it creates. But now the zero has caught up with us. To deal with it is going to require a 180° shift in the way we relate to nature, each other, and our own interior lives.

Fig. 9-3 translates these paradoxes into several visual metaphors involving (a) still images that won't stay still (see the jumping dots?); (b) impossible figures that can't be mentally processed; (c) images whose figure/ground relationship can't be resolved; and (d) stereograms whose 3-D image can only be seen if we use both sides of our brain to process it. Figures like these may inexplicably distress us, but they hint at deeper truths that are intriguing, if only we can get past our fears.

Symbolically meaningful systems like the enneagram and tarot provide excellent introductions to the significance and power of numbers. And they do so in a way that is self-empowering. Many of us are afraid of power because we don't want to misuse it. But there is a kind of power that cannot be misused: the power of the number zero. This is because the power of zero is the infinite power of wholeness. Systems that embrace the zero can be used to re-discover that wholeness.

The process by which we move towards wholeness involves three parts, three octaves of experience. In Chapter 10, we'll focus on that trifold process and how it has been previously used in the tarot in combination with the numbers 1–9.

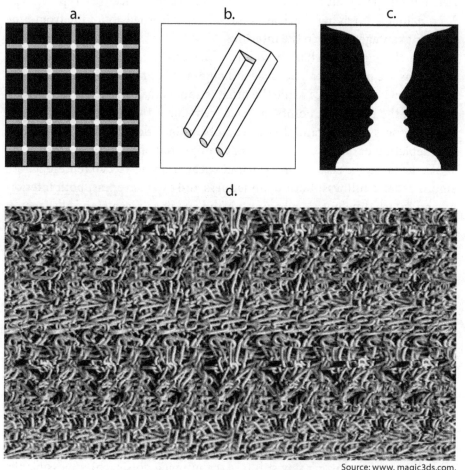

Source: www. magic3ds.com.

FIG. 9-3. Paradoxical Images.

Notes

[1] *A Beginner's Guide to Constructing the Universe: The Mathematical Archetypes of Nature, Art, and Science* (HarperPerennial: 1995), p. *xxii*.

[2] Introduction to *Homage to Pythagoras* (Lindisfarne: 1980), p. 15.

[3] Many Jung quotes on number archetypes were collected by Sue Mehrtens; see "Jung on Numbers," http://jungiancenter.org/jung-on-numbers/.

[4] *The Sacred Tarot* (CofL Press: 2005), p. 28.

[5] *Numerology and Divine Triangle* (U. S. Games: 1971/1980), p. 8.

[6] *Ibid*, p. 8.

[7] "Pythagorean Number as Form, Color, and Light," *Homage to Pythagoras*, p. 188.

[8] Here Robert Lawlor is referring exactly to the same principle behind Gurdjieff's Law of Seven, which governs light (as the rainbow) and sound (as the octave of a musical scale).

[9] "Inside the Savant Mind: Tips for Thinking from an Extraordinary Thinker" [an interview with Daniel Tammett by Jonah Lehrer]; available at https://www.scientificamerican.com/article/savants-cognition-thinking/.

[10] See http://wisdomofhypatia.com/OM/BA/PT/Intro.html.

[11] *Merkaba* means "chariot" in Hebrew. According to Drunvalo, in Egyptian, "mer" means a counter-rotating field of light; "ka" means spirit, and "ba" means the physical body. "Merkaba" is also one of the third-octave Keys in my new model (see Chapters 11 and 14 for details); see Part I of Appendix E, for a discussion of the sacred geometrical properties of the *merkaba*.

[12] The talk is "Information on Ascension and the Merkaba," available at YouTube at https://www.youtube.com/watch?v=7ix149wD_IU&feature=you.tube.

[13] *The Ancient Secret of the Flower of Life, Vol. I* (Clear Light Trust: 1998), p. 167.

[14] *Numerology and the Divine Triangle* (U. S. Games: 1971/1980), p. 9.

[15] *Numerology: Key to the Tarot* (Para Research: 1983), p. 9.

[16] Sue Mehrtens, "Jung on Numbers," see http://jungiancenter.org/jung-on-numbers/.

[17] *The Complete Guide to the Tarot* (Crown: 1970/1972), p. 184.

[18] C. C. Zain is presumably referring to the Theosophical Society.

[19] *The Sacred Tarot* (CofL Press: 2005), p. 99.

[20] *In Search of the Miraculous* (Harvest: 1949/2001), p. 283. See also Chapter 8 in the present book for a discussion on the enneagram shock points.

[21] Here is another cross-sum example: although all the numbers 12, 93, 30, 66, 426, and 87534 seem unrelated, they all reduce to the digital root of 3.

[22] Courtesy of Joe Dubs at http://blog.world-mysteries.com/science/nine-the-ultimate-mystery/. Dubs includes a very nice graphic of an enneagram in this article.

[23] See, e.g., p. 8 in Nicholas Goodrick-Clarke's *The Western Esoteric Traditions* (Oxford: 2008) for a discussion on the nature of correspondences.

[24] The nature of the controversy regarding the positioning of Keys 8 and 11 is summed up by Madhavi Ghare as follows: "Traditionally, the Justice card was numbered 8th in the Major Arcana, while the Strength card was numbered the 11th. However, when A. E. Waite published the Rider-Waite-Smith Tarot card deck, he changed all that. He put Strength as the 8th trump and Justice as the 11th trump in the Major Arcana sequence. Naturally, he was quite criticized for this. Following that, when Aleister Crowley published the Thoth Tarot deck, he put the Strength and Justice cards back in their former positions." (See http://www.taroticallyspeaking.com/knowledge/strength-and-justice-cards-in-tarot/.)

[25] Waite's swapping of Strength and Justice was not done on his own initiative but on the basis of teachings he received as a member of the Golden Dawn. But at the time that Waite's deck was published (1910), the GD teachings were still secret, so he could not cite their source, which is probably why his descriptions in his accompanying book, *A Pictorial Guide to the Tarot,* sometimes seem so cryptic (see Part II of Appendix E for a discussion of secrecy and the Golden Dawn; see Endnote 7 in Chapter 5 for a brief discussion of the 8-11 controversy).

[26] *The Secret Teachings of All Ages* (Philosophical Research Society: 1977), p. *cxxix*.

[27] For additional information on the Pattern on the Trestleboard, check out the entry at http://untothegate.com/the_pattern/.

[28] *A Complete Guide to the Tarot* (Bantam: 1970), p. 183.

[29] *Tarot as a Way of Life* (Weiser: 1997), p. 74.

[30] *The Tarot Companion: An Essential Reference Guide* (Llewellyn: 2000), p. *x*.

[31] *Tarot and Psychology: Spectrums of Possibility* (Paragon House: 2000), p. 106.

[32] See "Numinous Numbers," in Ronald Decker's book, *The Esoteric Tarot* (Quest: 2013).

[33] *Seventy-Eight Degrees of Wisdom* (Red Wheel: 1980/2007), pp. 20–21.

[34] A. G. E. Blake explains more about the triangle, and threefoldness in general, noting that "the threefold division [of the enneagram] means that the process is not just happening *but is coming about purposefully*," (emphasis mine, p. 32). On pp. 26–27, Blake reminds us of Gurdjieff's comment that although each organism can be viewed as an enneagram, only those with higher consciousness possess the inner triangle.

[35] It is interesting to note that tarot author Richard Roberts says that [it is] "the triangle [which]...channels the spiritual forces of the universe into the mundane" *Tarot Revelations* (Vernal Equinox: 1982), p. 73.

[36] *The Enneagram: The Symbol of All and Everything* (Gilgamesh: 2003), p. 149.

[37] *In Search of the Miraculous* (Harvest: 1949/2001), p. 283.

[38] When I call the tarot feminine and the enneagram masculine, I mean that, as a pictorial system, the tarot is naturally artistic and impressionistic (feminine); it is also widely used in divination, which is associated with feminine intuition. As a geometrically-based system based on Gurdjieff's esoteric teachings, the enneagram started out as more abstract (and hence masculine), but when used to understand personality and relationships, it is more emotionally-based and hence feminine.

10:
Developing a 27-Key Tarot

The sun rotates on its axis every 27 days; the moon orbits the earth every 27 days; the Hebrew alphabet has 27 letters (22 plus 5 finals); 27 is a perfect cube; there are 27 astrological nakshatras (sun signs) in Vedic astrology.

"THERE ARE ONLY nine numbers." This idea, introduced in the last chapter, serves as the basis for our discussion in this chapter. It's an idea embraced by a number of tarot authors, including Richard Roberts, Art Rosengarten, Shirley Gotthold, Angeles Arrien, and Mary Greer. The last chapter also focused on Gurdjieff's Law of Three: the idea that all transformational processes involve three sub-processes that go by many different names (**Table 10-1**).

This chapter brings together the idea that "Nine-ness is primary" and "Transformation is a three-part process" to lay the groundwork for creating an enneagram-informed, 27-Key major arcana. The focus here is on looking at what has already been done along these lines by previous tarot innovators.

Table 10-1. The Three Octaves.

▶ **OCTAVE 1 (ARC OF THE DAY)**
= THESIS / AFFIRMING / FIRE / LIGHT/ ACTIVITY / MENTAL INTENTION / CONSCIOUS KNOWING / MALE PRINCIPLE
(The nine archetypes that embody the energy of the nine paths)

▶ **OCTAVE 2 (ARC OF THE NIGHT)**
= ANTITHESIS / DENYING / WATER / DARKNESS/ STILLNESS / EMOTIONAL RECEPTIVITY / TACIT KNOWING / FEMALE PRINCIPLE
(The "shadow" side of each archetype that must be recognized, accepted & integrated)

▶ **OCTAVE 3 (ARC OF THE GOAL)**
= SYNTHESIS / RECONCILING / AIR / INNER-OUTER BALANCE / MENTAL-EMOTIONAL BALANCE / EMBODIED KNOWING / ANDROGYNOUS PRINCIPLE
(The highest potential that can be realized as the result of integrating the archetype with its shadow)

Nine Tarot Constellations

A number of tarot authors have become intrigued with the idea of using cross-sum reductions to look at the relationships between tarot cards that reduce to the same single-digit number. In *Tarot Revelations* (1982), Richard Roberts clearly articulates his goal is to demonstrate that "the Keys of the Tarot Major Arcana depict numerical archetypes" that are the "powers behind material manifestation" (p. 41). He goes on to allude to the "magical properties of the number nine," which he—like the sources already cited—sees as foundational to the idea of "number":

> If the Tarot code is to yield to the magic number nine, then the relation to nine should persist throughout. Furthermore, another dimension of meaning opens before us as we explore the idea of the archetype of each number raised to another level by the addition of nine....Let us proceed from the One, and move through the entire Major Arcana to show how the addition of nine preserves the original archetypal meaning of the number to which it is added, and yet transforms that number as well (p. 60).

Elsewhere, Roberts notes that this approach provides "the deepest esoteric meaning of the twenty-two Keys," (p. 59)—an approach that generates what Angeles Arrien and Mary Greer call *tarot constellations*. A tarot constellation is a grouping of tarot cards that share the same root number. Thus, the constellation based on the number One includes The Magician (1), The Wheel of Fortune (10), The Sun (19), all four Aces and all four Tens. Greer's formulation of the constellations is shown in **Table 10-2.**[1]

Angeles Arrien is the originator of the concept of tarot constellations, which she discusses in *The Tarot Handbook* (1987/1997). According to Mary Greer, Arrien got the idea from Joseph Campbell when the two were co-leaders of an Esalen workshop. To make use of them, Arrien taught her students to use cross-sum addition to determine the numbers most influential in their lives. Linking these numbers to tarot cards allows them to be associated with meaningful images.

Mary Greer was one of Arrien's students. At the same time Arrien was writing *The Tarot Handbook*, Greer was writing *Tarot Constellations*, both of which were initially published in 1987. (Later, Greer updated and republished it as *Who Are You in the Tarot*, 2011; all pages cited below are from this version).

Greer says that the tarot constellations "are made up of cards that resonate to the same theme" (p. 10). She fleshes out the constellation idea in more depth, noting that "the tarot cards associated with your birth date and name form your individual mandala: *your pattern of personal destiny*" (emphasis mine, p. 3). So if someone is born on 2-05-95, her personality number = 21 (The World), because $2 + 5 + 9 + 5 = 21$; her soul number = 3 (The Empress), because 21 reduces to 3. The two may be the same or different, depending upon

KEYS	CONSTELLATION	PRINCIPLE
	TABLE **10-2.** Mary Greer's Nine Tarot Constellations.	
1-10-19	Constellation of the Magician	The Principle of Will & Focused Consciousness
2-11-20	Constellation of the High Priestess	The Principle of Balanced Judgment through Intuitive Awareness
3-12-21	Constellation of the Empress	The Principle of Love & Creative Imagination
4-13-22	Constellation of the Emperor	The Principle of Life Force & Realization of Power
5-14	Constellation of the Hierophant	The Principle of Teaching & Learning
6-15	Constellation of the Lovers	The Principle of Relatedness & Choice
7-16	Constellation of the Chariot	The Principle of Mastery through Change
8-17	Constellation of Strength	The Principle of Courage & Self-esteem
9-18	Constellation of the Hermit	The Principle of Introspection & Personal Integrity

one's date of birth.[2] In this example, the person also has a "Hidden Factor" number of 12 (associated with The Hanged Man, 12) because 12 is "hidden" in 21. According to Greer, the hidden factor card challenges us to go beyond our usual limitations. That would make it akin to the *shadow* in Jungian terms.

In Chapter 1, I mentioned an online writer who has wondered whether there might be a connection between soul/personality cards and enneagram types. Perhaps—but if there is a relationship, it's not a straightforward 1-to-1 relationship, because my soul/personality number is nine and I'm pretty sure I'm Enneagram Type 4, not a Nine. However, there are many ways in which the qualities associated with the The Hermit are especially meaningful to me: I work alone, have a meditation practice, and often prefer solitude to company. During the last two decades especially, I've spent most of my time alone.

In Table 10-2, the first four constellations have three major arcana Keys while the last five have only two. This is because there are 22 Keys in the major arcana. To have three cards per constellation would require us to have 27 Keys—five more than is customary. Such an approach would make all the constellations the same size, which I'm guessing she would see as an advantage. It's certainly useful for someone who's exploring possible links between the enneagram and tarot.[3]

Setting the Stage for a 27-Key Tarot

A 27-Key tarot—whether physically manifest or simply existing as a guiding principle—allows us to imagine nine developmental paths with three full octaves. We can label these octaves various ways, according to our purpose. The idea of octaves has already been introduced in the discussion of the process enneagram in Chapter 7; **Table 10-3** shows the three octaves using Banzhaf's Arc of the Day and Arc of the Night plus my Arc of the Goal addition.

This three-octave breakdown of the hero's journey is another formulation of Gurdjieff's Law of Three. According to A. G. E. Blake, it states that

> change can only happen when three independent forces come together. If there are only two forces, they either affirm or deny each other, and the situation is static. When a third force enters, the other two forces are no longer locked into each other in the same way as before.[4]

This third force is associated with the third octave of the journey. On one level, it represents the intention we hold as we move through the first two octaves, the intention that motivates and inspires us throughout the hero's journey. This intention matters, because without it, there would be no journey. However, as we change, that intention changes, too. We usually start the Arc of the Day with the desire to achieve a specific goal. But we eventually come to realize (usually during the Arc of the Night) that the journey is not about achieving anything; it's about finding the path to inner balance. Because inner balance is what attracts divine grace (Blake's "third force") that allows profound transformation to occur.

Table 10-3 shows the Arc of the Day, Arc of the Night, and the Arc of the Goal. The only thing we're missing are Keys 22–27. But we won't fill in the blanks until Chapter 11. First we'll take a look at the only two tarot decks that I know of that have 27-Key decks: The Transformational Tarot (Shirley Gotthold) and The Tarot of the Nine Paths (Art Rosengarten).

Shirley Gotthold's 27-Key Transformational Tarot

Shirley Gotthold did not just develop a 27-Key tarot; she developed a 100-card tarot with 27 majors, 72 minors, plus The Fool. She notes that these three elements constitute a triad of energies. Each of her minor suits has cards 1–10, the four Court cards (counted as having the values 11–14), plus four additional cards: the Teacher/Student, Reformer, Oracle, and Sage (15–18). This is how we get 72 cards (4 suits x 18 minor cards).

Notice the central role of the number 9 here: the number of majors (27) and minors (72) are inverses, and both reduce to 9. If we add them together, we also get a cross sum of 9 (27 + 72 = 99 = 18 = 9); this is true even if we include The Fool, because it has a value of zero.

TABLE 10-3 . A 27-Key Major Arcana with Six Missing Keys.				
KEYS	ENNEAGRAM PATH	ARC OF THE DAY	ARC OF THE NIGHT	ARC OF THE GOAL
1-10-19	Path of the Magician	1 Magician	10 Wheel	19 Sun
2-11-20	Path of the High Priestess	2 Priestess	11 Justice	20 Judgement
3-12-21	Path of the Empress	3 Empress	12 Hanged Man	21 World
4-13-22	Path of the Emperor	4 Emperor	13 Death	22 ? ? ?
5-14-23	Path of the Hierophant	5 Hierophant	14 Temperance	23 ? ? ?
6-15-24	Path of the Lovers	6 Lovers	15 Devil	24 ? ? ?
7-16-25	Path of the Chariot	7 Chariot	16 Tower	25 ? ? ?
8-17-26	Path of Strength	8 Strength	17 Star	26 ? ? ?
9-18-27	Path of the Hermit	9 Hermit	18 Moon	27 ? ? ?

Gotthold observes that her expanded deck reflects the expanded opportunities created by moving from the Piscean to the Aquarian Age (she was writing in 1995, when the idea of a "New Age" still symbolized the amazing new possibilities we imagined would unfold in the 21st century). She says that in her new deck, "every card…fits within the orderly pattern reflected by the numbers one through nine." She goes on to say that "to be aware of the fundamental meanings behind all the numbers develops our awareness of the rhythmic quality of the cosmic and creative processes" (p. 12).

All the cards in the deck (minus The Fool) can be laid out in a pattern of nine rows of 11 cards each row; all 11 cards in each row are related in meaning because they all reduce to one of the nine root numbers. While the logic she used to develop her deck is intriguing, our focus here will be mainly on her 27 major arcana Keys.

In answer to the question, "Why are the Major Arcana cards in the Transformational Tarot challenging?," Gotthold says that

it is because each of them represents archetypes that operate beyond the limitations of ordinary human experience, while also representing opportunities for us to move toward fuller expressions of that same human experience (p. 97).

According to Gotthold, the 27 Keys represent "major opportunities for change or for shifts of major importance"; The Fool is the catalyst that "activates the entire mechanism of self" (p. 13) and is not part of the major arcana. Elsewhere, she tells us that The Fool carries the Breath of Life from Spirit, the energy of *prana* that "enlivens the whole human condition" (p. 16).

Table 10-4 shows Gotthold's 27 Keys; the card descriptors are mine, but they are directly based on her discussion. Early on in her book, Gotthold characterizes Column 1 as the *powers* that influence our form of self-expression; Column 2 as the *critical choices* that determine the degree to which we transform; and Column 3 as the *resolution* that reflects the degree to which we take responsibility for our choices. Another approach she takes is to call Column 1 the cycle of *Nature*, Column 2 the cycle of *Man* (where we learn how to take responsibility), and Column 3 the cycle of the *Superhuman* (where we experience the mystery of transcendence); see p. 15.

Gotthold's Exploration of the Numbers 1–9

To better understand each of the 27 descriptions in Table 10-4, let's take a brief look at the attributes Gotthold associates with each of them, organized by root number (the rows on Table 10-4). These descriptions are exact quotes or very close paraphrases.

1–10–19: THE MAGICIAN – THE WHEEL OF FORTUNE – THE SUN. "The journey begins with the Magician." We began with **The Magician (1)**, who showed us the importance of drive, singleness of purpose, and of active concentration....Then through **The Wheel of Fortune (10)** we came to know life's continual movement through cycles of alternating expansion and contraction....The card of **The Sun (19)** represents our opportunity to move into a final, natural expression, to decide either to implement our own flowering or to allow our potential to shrivel and decay (p. 34).

2–11–20: HIGH PRIESTESS – JUSTICE – JUDGEMENT. "The number two is about division, difference, polarity, diplomacy, association, and partnership." **The High Priestess (2)** carries the Akashic record of all life, while **Justice (11)** makes certain that the law of karma is fulfilled. **Judgement (20)** divides karmic memory into three parts: automatic memory (all the material from the past that is replayed with total recall); logical memory (related facts and facts whose effects we now feel); the third part is moral memory (events and material that reveal moral values (p. 52).

3–12–21: THE EMPRESS – THE HANGED MAN – THE WORLD. "Three moves us into the field of manifestation." The card of **The Empress (3)** gave

	POWERS OF SELF-EXPRESSION	CRITICAL CHOICES	RESOLUTION
	TABLE 10-4. Shirley Gotthold's Transformational Tarot.*		
1	1 The Magician (PURPOSEFULNESS)	10 The Wheel (CYCLICAL MOVEMENT)	19 The Sun (FRUITFULNESS OR STERILITY)
2	2 The High Priestess (CO-CREATIVITY)	11 Justice (RESPONSIBLE CHOICE)	20 Judgement (TRANSCENDING DUALITY)
3	3 The Empress (FERTILITY)	12 The Hanged Man (INNER GROWTH)	21 The World (CREATIVE LIFE)
4	4 The Emperor (FOUNDATION)	13 Death (STRIPPING AWAY)	**22 The Master** (INTEGRATED POWER)
5	5 The Hierophant (BRIDGE BETWEEN WORLDS)	14 Temperance (GUIDED CHANGE)	**23 Galactic Force** (MYRIAD WORLDS)
6	6 The Lover (HARMONIZING DUALITY)	15 The Devil (PSYCHIC SPLIT)	**24 The Androgyne** (SERVICING HUMANITY)
7	7 The Charioteer (DRIVING FORCE)	16 The Tower (DIVINE WILL)	**25 Mystical Life** (SACRED MYSTERY)
8	8 Strength (NATURAL FORCE)	17 The Star (GUIDING LIGHT)	**26 Transcendent Mind** (HIGHER CONSCIOUSNESS)
9	9 The Hermit (INNER LIGHT)	18 The Moon (BODILY WISDOM)	**27 Universalized Wisdom** (INTEGRATED WISDOM)

* The names of each tarot Key in Gotthold's deck are based on the descriptions in her 180-page book, The Transformational *Tarot (Foolscape: 1995).*

us our first and most literal awareness of our creative potential....**The Hanged Man (12)** upended our perspective in order to open us to a deeper aspect of creativity....Finally, we have **The World (21)** where creativity comes to a beautiful, whole, rhythmic completion (pp. 65-66).

4–13–22: THE EMPEROR – DEATH – THE MASTER. "The number four completes a pattern." We began our study of the fours with **The Emperor (4)**, who represented a worldly, authoritarian figure of responsible power....The card of **Death (13)** [is] a card of transition and transformation of power through redirection....Now we have come to the final four, that of **The Master (22)**, who represents access to integrated power over all that has form as well as all that is formless (p. 80).

5–14–23: THE HIEROPHANT – TEMPERANCE – GALACTIC FORCE. "Introducing the action-oriented fives." Our journey through the fives of the

Transformational Tarot deck began with **The Hierophant (5)**, who showed us how to bridge the space between our outer world of the senses and our inner world of knowing....[Then] came **Temperance (14)**, whose promise dealt with the change that occurs within us when we respond to guidance and inspiration....We come now to **Galactic Force (23)**, and it represents our awareness of the changing form and movement of our own (p. 96).

6–15–24: THE LOVERS – THE DEVIL – THE ANDROGYNE. "Six, a rhythmical incomplete number." It was through **The Lovers (6)** that we explored the masculine and feminine principles involving duality....[Then] came **The Devil (15)**, the Great Teacher who sets before us the lessons that required us to translate our inner intent into practice in our daily lives....Now **The Androgyne (24)** brings the final coming together of the various dualities into a complete whole (p. 113).

7–16–25: THE CHARIOTEER – THE TOWER – MYSTICAL LIFE. "The inner mystery of the number seven." From **The Charioteer (7)**...we learned that how we *think* about our lives and circumstances directly affects what we actually experience....**The Tower (16)**...taught us to prune away the deadwood from our concepts so we can see and appreciate only what is true to our expression of life...the card of **Mystical Life (25)** offers us an expansive world of love and life that goes far beyond any we have yet experienced" (p. 131).

8–17–26: STRENGTH – THE STAR – TRANSCENDENT MIND. "Number eight, symbol of flowing activity." **Strength (8)** taught us lessons about dealing with the primitive part of self naturally....**The Star (17)** showed us that meditation is key to the achievement of effective use of mind and brain....[But] only through the **Transcendent Mind (26)** do we reach the apex of the figure eight and the mind's amazing potential (p. 146).

9–18–27: THE HERMIT – THE MOON – UNIVERSALIZED WILL. "Nine is the number of wisdom and completion." We began our series of nines with the card of **The Hermit (9)**, whose assistance and benevolence are always available as we struggle upward on our individual paths....**The Moon (18)** taught us to value our physical bodies and to prepare them for the lessons of will that lay ahead.... **Universalized Will (27)** represents great power—power that is awesome in its totality (pp. 163–164).

❖ ❖ ❖

Gotthold's deck was published in 1995. When I found it some years later, I was delighted by its originality. But I was even more intrigued by its emphasis on the number nine, because of my work with the enneagram. While it's beyond the scope of our discussion to look at these paths in greater detail, many of the descriptions echo those in both Art Rosengarten's Tarot of the Nine Paths and my own enneagram-based approach to the tarot (and vice-versa). They are included because the original book is out of print and hard to get. The descriptions here provide at least a brief outline of the developer's thought processes.

Art Rosengarten's Jungian Approach

Art Rosengarten is a Jungian psychotherapist who uses the tarot to help people become more aware of the archetypal energies that impact their inner and outer lives. In his excellent book on the tarot from a Jungian perspective, *Tarot and Psychology* (2000), Rosengarten notes that "the Tarot is built around the laws of opposition, and every card will contain a suggested energetic polarity" (p. 80). Later, he notes the advantages of using the tarot to reveal the nature of diverse polarities, as opposed to trying "to paint a word picture." He cites the example of asking someone, "How do you feel on your fiftieth birthday?" and getting the reply "Happy/Sad." Such an answer may be accurate, but it requires additional explanation to make sense. The tarot, however, uses visual symbols to communicate polarities at a glance. He cites the following Keys as prime examples:

- ▶ The Emperor: Forming the Opposites
- ▶ The Lovers: Combining the Opposites
- ▶ Strength: Embodying the Opposites
- ▶ Justice: Balancing the Opposites
- ▶ Temperance: Blending the Opposites
- ▶ The Devil: Separating the Opposites
- ▶ Judgement: Proclaiming the Opposites
- ▶ The World: Integrating the Opposites

Rosengarten also introduces the idea that the tarot can be conceptualized as a wheel, as suggested by the phrase "rota" (Latin for "wheel") in Key 10, the Wheel of Fortune, and by the many symbols of circularity in the major arcana, as seen in The Chariot, the Wheel of Fortune, The Sun, The Moon, and The World (p. 72). In a discussion on the hero's journey in Chapter 8, Rosengarten makes it clear that his purpose in characterizing the tarot as a circle is to liberate tarotists from the idea that the hero's journey is a linear sequence that occurs in a set order: by conceptualizing that journey as a circle with no set order of stages, he is seeking to open us to the idea that every hero's journey is unique.

I agree with his uniqueness hypothesis. I also share his concern about getting so attached to a particular approach that we cling to it dogmatically. However, unlike him, I have no problem with the hero's journey as a linear sequence, because I see it as a useful scaffold for inner work, just as long as it is not taken too literally. Like all systems of mental organization, the hero's journey is meant to provide an orienting framework: it's a map of the territory, not the territory itself.[5]

But to return to Rosengarten's idea of seeing the tarot as a circle: for me, this immediately brings to mind the idea of mapping the hero's journey onto the enneagram. In addition to showing the cyclical, spiral nature of the journey, this also allows us to look at relationships between different stages of the journey.

Rosengarten's Tarot of the Nine Paths

In 2009, Art Rosengarten published a 27-Key tarot entitled The Tarot of the Nine Paths (TNP); Rosengarten's nine TNP paths describe nine variants of the hero's journey depicted at three octaves of development which follows the Jungian pattern of depicting an archetype (Octave 1), its shadow or opposite (Octave 2), and the integration of the opposites (Octave 3).

In the LWB ("little white book") for his deck, Rosengarten speaks of the "twenty-seven principles believed to be instrumental in all processes of psycho-spiritual development," and says that in the development of the tarot, the well-known Marseilles deck (which has 22 Majors) created the blueprint for all future decks.[6] He makes the case that the tarot stopped evolving after that point, and states that this new deck is based on a "special regard for the magical properties of [the] number nine."[7]

Because I have a similar regard for the number nine, I was interested to discover what more he had to say about the new deck. At the time it was first published, there was no additional information available. But shortly before *The Fool's Excellent Adventure* went to press, I was delighted to discover that Rosengarten has been working on a new book on the deck: *Tarot of the Future: Raising Spiritual Consciousness* (Paragon: 2018).

The pre-release publisher's review describes the approach as offering a new version of tarot that is "re-tuned" for the 21st century based on Jungian, Eastern, and Western metaphysical and scientific principles. The author was kind enough to send me an advance copy of Chapter 13, "The Re-tuning," which describes key aspects of the model (but which has no page numbers; this is why the citations below are not page-referenced).

Essentially, the idea is to set forth a template (The Matrix) which reveals the mechanism underlying the tarot's operation during a divination session. As alluded to above, this template is based on essentially the same three-stage, Law of Three model that governs all transformational processes (see Table 10-1). But he uses a fresh metaphor to describe this idea, likening divination to the experience of being in an airport, a place that is like an "in between" dimension of experience; he calls this dimension *Terminal 9* (**Table 10-5**).

Using this metaphor, he divides his Matrix into three stages: Departures, Transfers, and Arrivals. He paints the picture of tarot divination as a natural, unstructured process that allows "the freedom for things to arise of their own accord in their natural wholeness and simplicity." The tarot is a vehicle for exploring "the intermediate territory." This takes us from Ken Wilber's stage of vision-logic—which is the transition stage between ordinary awareness and something more transcendent—to higher stages of consciousness (the psychic, subtle, and causal stages), ultimately culminating in the experience of *shunyata* (non-duality).[8]

The addition of the five cards allows us to "re-tune" the tarot, where re-tuning is said to be "a small but critical adjustment," as is necessary when fine tuning a stringed instrument. By expanding the deck from 22 to 27 archetypes, Rosengarten seeks to create a deck that incorporates archetypes that represent "emergent archetypal agencies of our time"—that is, archetypes that transcend the symbolism of The World.

He asserts that this addition does not change anything essential about the historical tarot, but instead uses its Renaissance roots as a foundation upon which to build. His purpose is not to change the tarot but to extend its Hermetic

TABLE 10-5. Art Rosengarten's Tarot of the Future.			
PATH	DEPARTURES	TRANSFERS	ARRIVALS
ONE: MASTERY	1 The Magician (INTENTION)	10 The Wheel (SYNCHRONICITY)	19 The Sun (CONSCIOUSNESS)
TWO: INSIGHT	2 The High Priestess (INTUITION)	11 Justice (BALANCE)	20 Judgement (AWAKENING)
THREE: JOY	3 The Empress (PASSION)	12 The Hanged Man (SURRENDER)	21 The World (INTEGRATION)
FOUR: TRANSFORMATION	4 The Emperor (DOMINION)	13 Death (DISSOLUTION)	22 The Well (RENEWAL)
FIVE: PEACE	5 The Hierophant (SPIRIT)	14 Temperance (SYNERGY)	23 The Ring (WHOLENESS)
SIX: RELATIONSHIP	6 The Lover (UNION)	15 The Devil (SEPARATION)	24 The River (FLOW)
SEVEN: THE SEEKER	7 The Chariot (CHALLENGE)	16 The Tower (UPHEAVAL)	25 The Dragon (INITIATION)
EIGHT: THE UNIVERSE	8 Strength (LIFE FORCE)	17 The Star (ESSENCE)	26 The Web (INTERBEING)
NINE: THE SAGE	9 The Hermit (WISDOM)	18 The Moon (IMAGINATION)	27 The Fool (POSSIBILITY)

correspondences, with the assistance of well-known Hermeticist Lon Milo Du-Quette. He characterizes the final result as "nine, three stepped, rites of passage for the transformation of consciousness extending the original Tarot map."

There are a number of intriguing things about Rosengarten's approach. First, like Banzhaf's, it is based on a three-stage, Jungian model. (Of course, Banzhaf did not complete the third Arc, which is why I chose to do so.) Jungian approaches are inevitably integration-oriented, and as such, focus on healing rather than fixing.

Second, Rosengarten echoes Gotthold's idea that, as cultures evolve, so will the tarot. His comments indicate that he is trying to walk the fine line between honoring tarot traditions and introducing changes that seem appropriate to changing circumstances. He characterizes the number nine as a spiritual number and wondering whether now is the time for its emergence as a spiritual influence. My experience with the number nine suggests that it has been extremely (and strangely) de-emphasized in the past. I've spent years looking for the roots of the enneagram, and never found them—just as Gurdjieff predicted. Any sort of references to the number nine are rare, as compared with most other numbers. Why is this? Is it because the "Age of Nine" is just now arriving?

Rosengarten may be correct in believing that now is the time for its emergence, for the 3 x 3 quality of Nine suggests motion and Gurdjieff called the enneagram a "perpetual motion machine" when he introduced it 100 years ago. Nikola Tesla claimed to have discovered a source of free energy just about the same time Gurdjieff introduced the enneagram. The idea of perpetual motion is arising again with the revolution in physics and the discussion of unlimited zero-point energy. (If you've read Chapter 9, I don't have to tell you the close relationship between zero and nine.) The fact that the enneagram is just now coming into its own lends support for the idea that the symbolism of 0/9 is of special import in the 21st century.

And speaking of zero, Rosengarten (thirdly) emphasizes the importance of the number zero, announcing with one subhead "Key Zero Remains Supreme." Indeed. This is spookily synchronistic for me as a writer, since just last week—after mostly completing Chapters 9 and 16—I was suddenly inspired to completely rewrite both of them in order to incorporate new material on zero in Chapter 9 and the concept of nothingness in Chapter 16. Rosengarten notes the "supreme importance" of the zero as the tarot's "alpha and omega,"

> the place wherein the story begins, ends, and begins anew" [which provides] a never-ending spiral of Beginningless Time and Open Space, within which The Journey only deepens, in keeping with the wisdom doctrines of East and West."

Fourth, Rosengarten talks about the third tier ("Arrivals") as referring to a point of completion rather than some kind of final state. He associates completeness not with some kind of ultimate destination but with a state of wholeness in which we are no longer creating new karma. This offers a useful way of thinking about the nature of transformational processes.

Fifth and last, Rosengarten laments the absence of a completion phase for all the cards in conventional tarot decks; he even uses the word "sad" to describe the fact that Paths 4–9 have no way to reach completion with 22-Key decks, but are instead "left hanging dualistically...with no further passage." I don't know whether I find it sad, but I too see any duality as an incomplete passage that begs for resolution—which is what drove me to complete the sequence for Paths 4–9, just as Rosengarten did.

❖ ❖ ❖

In this chapter, I presented the three-octave model and explained how it shows up in Robert's "magic nine," Arrien and Greer's tarot constellations, Gotthold's Transformational Tarot, and Rosengarten's Tarot of the Nine Paths (which he calls "The Tarot of the Future"). Anyone interested in transformational processes who looks at each approach will find in them many similarities. I would estimate that there is, at a minimum, a 65% agreement as to the specific symbolism of certain numbers and numbered paths, and more like an 80–90% agreement about number symbolism in a more general sense. I believe that working with the enneagram and tarot together would make those percentages converge to an even greater degree.[9]

Chapter 11 introduces an enneagram-based approach to the tarot; Chapters 12–16 discuss it in more detail.

Notes

[1] Mary Greer assigns The Fool the value of 22 in the major arcana.

[2] For some people—me included—the personality and soul cards are the same. This is the case if the results of the first calculation are over 21 (since the tarot cards only go to 21).

[3] Both Mary Greer and Angeles Arrien include a discussion of the court cards, but since they have no number, they must be assigned numbers on some basis. Arrien considers the court cards to indicate *types and levels of mastery*. She assigns each of them a rank, based on their suit and position in the royal hierarchy. She then converts these ranks to numbers which can be interpreted by linking them to the number of letters in a person's full name at birth (see pp. 102–103 in *The Tarot Handbook*). Greer considers the court cards to indicate *personality characteristics*. She does not assign them numeric values but takes their total number (16 = 4 cards x 4 suits) and uses 16 as the basis for linking them to The Chariot (7); see the discussion in Chapter 16 of either edition of her book. Neither Arrien nor Greer include court cards in their actual constellations, which makes me suspect that although they were interested in translating the symbolism associated with the court cards into numerical form, they were not entirely certain about the best way to do so.

[4] *The Intelligent Enneagram* (Shambhala: 1983), p. 80.

[5] My solution for the problem of getting overly attached to any particular approach for describing the hero's journey in the tarot is not to avoid using any "set" Key sequences such as 0–21, but to instead use multiple sequences, not just one. For example, in the present book, I describe the classic 0–21 sequence in Chapter 5 but describe nine enneagram-based sequences in Chapters 11–15. Another approach would to be use David Allen Hulse's sequence of the 22 tarot Keys to map the hero's journey in the tarot onto the Cube of Space, which is basically what Hulse does. His approach is so compelling that I was able to memorize most of the positions of the cards in the major arcana cards on the Cube after just one reading of his book. See his *New Dimensions for the Cube of Space: The Path of Initiation Revealed by the Tarot upon the Qabalistic Cube* (Weiser: 2000).

[6] The Marseille deck is not a single deck but a series of Continental decks put out starting in the 15th century. However, the most well-known deck was put out by Grimaud in 1748 (Source: Robert M. Place's *The Tarot: History, Symbolism, and Divination*, Tarcher: 2005).

[7] Art Rosengarten's tarot deck uses montages of Sand Play images to portray the archetypal theme associated with each card. Sand Play is a Jungian technique used particularly in therapy with children, where they are asked to play with little figures and talk about what they mean.

[8] My previous book, *The Integral Enneagram* (Geranium Press: 2013), is an in-depth analysis of parallels between the enneagram and Ken Wilber's Integral System, so I'm familiar with this approach. I did not have access to the full text of Rosengarten's book before my book went to press, but Wilber's books offer a number of useful models for thinking about the nature of transformational processes.

[9] There will always be some divergence in the interpretation of number symbolism, simply because each number has multiple meanings, and different systems can emphasize one meaning rather than another. The main requirement in a system based on the numbers 1–9 (e.g., the enneagram) is that it needs some way to include all the major archetypes within it. One reason I find it so satisfying to work with the enneagram is that it seems to have an appropriate niche for any symbolic idea I've been able to imagine.

11:
Nine Tarot Paths on the Enneagram

The events in your life develop around myriad patterns or themes, in a way similar to the themes of ancient myths. Once you begin to perceive such patterns, you realize that your life is not meaningless but has great mythic and spiritual significance.
– Mary Greer

IN CHAPTER 5, WE WALKED THROUGH THE HERO'S JOURNEY in the tarot from beginning to end, encountering all the challenges such a journey entails. But if I were to ask each reader which of the experiences—as symbolized by the cards—made the biggest impression, no two answers would be the same, because we all see our experiences from different points of view.

The enneagram has the ability to powerfully depict diverse points of view. This is why it is has so much to offer to any nine-based model of the hero's journey. I tried to visually capture this idea in Chapter 6, by placing an elephant in the center of the enneagram circle and showing the nine types facing it, each from a different angle. Although the elephant never changes, each viewer sees it differently, because each has a different "energy signature" that gives rise to distinctive values tied to our life's purpose. These values determine what is most salient ("what matters most") in any given situation.[1]

In this chapter, we'll look at a 27-Key model based on insights derived from the enneagram. That's what distinguishes it from any previous model.

The only thing that is missing from this model is a physical tarot deck—a Tarot of the Enneagram. This is because my ability to write about this approach easily outstrips my ability to generate a 78-card deck. (It was enough of a challenge to generate six additional images!)

I would suggest that readers approach this model the way you would approach the tarot constellations model or approaches designed to associate the tarot with any other symbol systems, like the paths on the Tree of Life: as a tool for developing an enhanced set of associations with each card in the tarot. Anyone who has worked with tarot over time usually has a rich set of symbolic associations for each card that draw from many different traditions: astrology, shamanism, multiple mythological traditions, the I Ching, Jungian dreamwork, alchemy, runes, Egyptian symbolism—the list goes on and on.

But at present, virtually no one has suggested an approach for integrating the symbolism associated with the enneagram into tarot work. That's my purpose here. (However, Chapter 15 includes practical suggestions for using this approach with a conventional tarot deck.)

TABLE 11-1. An Enneagram-based Approach to a 27-Key Tarot.

ENNEAGRAM TYPE & PATH (CORE MOTIVATION)	ARC OF THE DAY (ARCHETYPAL POTENTIAL)	ARC OF THE NIGHT (SHADOW POTENTIAL)	ARC OF THE GOAL (INTEGRATION OF ARCHETYPE & SHADOW)
1 – Path of Alchemy (LETTING OUR LIGHT SHINE FORTH IN LIFE)	1 Magician (MASCULINE INTENTION)	10 Wheel of Fortune (FEMININE RECEPTIVITY)	19 Sun (DIVINE LIGHT ILLUMINATES THE WORLD)
2 – Path of Intuition (ALLOWING THE FLOW OF LOVE TO NOURISH & HEAL US)	2 High Priestess (FEMININE MEMORY)	11 Justice (MASCULINE DISCRIMINATION)	20 Judgement (DIVINE LOVE LIFTS UP THE WORLD)
3 – Path of Creativity (BRINGING IN NEW LIFE TO RENEW THE WORLD)	3 Empress (CREATIVE IMPULSE)	12 Hanged Man (SACRED STILLNESS)	21 World (CHRIST CONSCIOUSNESS RECREATES THE WORLD)
4 – Path of Individuation (SELF-IMAGE BECOMES TRUE SELF-AWARENESS)	4 Emperor (SELF-DOMINION)	13 Death (SELF-DISSOLUTION)	22 Wellspring (TRUE SELFHOOD BRINGS ORIGINALITY INTO THE WORLD)
5 – Path of Wisdom (DISCOVERING THE LOVE OF WISDOM)	5 Hierophant (NATIVE GENIUS)	14 Temperance (ALCHEMICAL PRESSURE)	23 Keeper of the Flame (THE FLAME OF GNOSIS ENSURES CONTINUITY OF MEMORY)
6 – Path of Trust in the Goodness of Life (ALLOWING LOVE TO CONQUER DREAD)	6 Lovers (ATTRACTION)	15 Devil (REPULSION)	24 Divine Family (INTEGRATING THE OPPOSITES CREATES UNION & COMMUNION)
7 – Path of Liberation (BREAKING THROUGH THE SPIRITUAL VEILS)	7 Chariot (HUMAN WILL)	16 Tower (DIVINE INTERVENTION)	25 Merkaba (Divine Vehicle) (THE LIGHT BODY BRINGS ACCESS TO HIGHER CONSCIOUSNESS)
8 – Path of Ascension (FULLY EMBODYING THE SELF AS A WHOLE)	8 Strength (POWER UNDER LOVE)	17 Star (PURITY OF INTENT)	26 Divine Monad (OUR CONSCIOUSNESS ENCOMPASSES ALL THAT IS)
9 – Path of Divine Possibility (OPENING TO LIFE & ITS EXPERIENCES)	9 Hermit (MEDITATION)	18 Moon (IMAGINATION)	27 Divine Mystery (THE INEFFABLE BEYOND THE VEIL BECKONS US HOME)

Table 11-1 on the opposite page shows the completed model. The six blank spaces from Chapter 10 have now been filled in with the names of six new Keys. In this chapter, we'll look at the six new Keys, the images that accompany them, and the nine paths they create to complete a transformational model that includes three complete octaves: the Arc of the Day, Arc of the Night, and Arc of the Goal.

Six New Keys

The six new Keys represent the outcomes of reconciling the opposites in six developmental paths. Their characteristics are briefly described below.

Wellspring (22): A wellspring is "an original and bountiful source of something." It's the fount of energy that wells up from deep within one's being, healing and renewing the soul. In many people, this fount is inaccessible due to psychic blockages that prevent access. To find its source means becoming fully, consciously receptive to the energy of the soul. And this requires the blocks to be cleared, so that the Original Self can fully incarnate. Wellspring represents the reconciliation of Self-dominion (The Emperor) and Self-surrender (Death).

Keeper of the Flame (23): When the desire for knowledge is tempered by love, it ripens into wisdom. The wisdom keepers teach the truth when the culture is enlightened and hide it away when the loss of wisdom seems imminent, embodying the esoteric motto, "To know, to will, to dare, and to remain silent." Keeper of the Flame represents the result of allowing Alchemical Pressure (Temperance) to elevate Native Genius (The Hierophant) to its most noble and refined expression.

The Divine Family (24): Integrating the opposites is the key to balanced living. When love is greater than hatred, faith is greater than fear, and the power to act is greater than the tendency to react, then anything is possible; individuals find peace, families embrace, and civilizations prosper. The Divine Family represents the reconciliation of Attraction (The Lovers) and Repulsion (The Devil).

Merkaba (25): Inner balance initiates the activation of higher structures of consciousness within the psyche (the *merkaba*), structures that enable us to access higher states. Merkaba represents the transformation of the spiritual explorer, The Chariot(eer)—whose vehicle is initially powered by personal will—into the kind of explorer whose vehicle can traverse multiple dimensions of consciousness (and whose inspirations can transform those dimensions in striking, unexpected ways).[2]

The Divine Monad (26): Self-actualization represents the ability to fully manifest one's potential as a sovereign and divine being. It displays the powers of a single individual and at the same time transcends them. Great power requires great humility; great knowledge requires great powers of observation; great love requires great courage. All three come together in The Divine Monad, which represents Power (Strength) infused with Purity of Intent (The Star).

Divine Mystery (27): "To be *and* not to be": this expresses the innate nature of life. Out of mystery comes manifestation, birthed by curiosity and imagination; out of manifestation comes experience, ever expanding the mystery. Mystery is the divine antidote to cynicism, boredom, and the failure to thrive. It is always present in life but can be lost to conscious awareness. The experience of Mystery deepens in response to Self-awareness (The Hermit) infused with Imagination (The Moon).

❖ ❖ ❖

Each of these six Keys represents a synthesis of the first two Keys in the their respective paths. They are designed to make it easier to envision each path. However, it's possible that some people reading these descriptions will have a somewhat different vision of the third-octave goals for their type than the ones presented here. This is because each type—and each path—is multifaceted; it can thus be characterized from multiple perspectives. The goal is to provide a starting point for inquiry and an impetus to self-discovery. The key question is this: "What do I care about so much that I'm willing to go on a hero's journey to find it?"[3]

Creating the Images

Fig. 11-1 shows the six Keys translated from ideas into images. I did not originally plan to develop images for these Keys, because I'm a writer, not an artist. It seemed an impossible task to devise images to represent the archetypes in a convincing way. At first, I couldn't even imagine coming up with them. Later, I wanted to, but didn't know how. For months, I sat with blank rectangles by the Key descriptions. Eventually, I came up with something. And in the process, it moved something inside me. I think the breakthrough came the night I stayed up until six in the morning trying to get the stupid Fool's hands to look like hands, not claws. I literally redrew them hundreds of times.

In the end, the drawings I unearthed, traced, or otherwise devised seemed satisfactory for conveying symbolic information in picture form, including the cover drawing of The Fool. I am realizing just now, as I write, that coming up with these drawings was my hero's journey with this book. It was the "impossible task" that I couldn't imagine completing. Many people would consider writing a book to be a hero's journey. And it is (especially this chapter,

WELLSPRING.

KEEPER OF THE FLAME.

THE DIVINE FAMILY.

MERKABA.

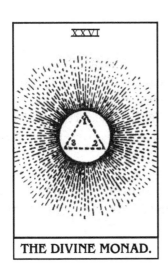

THE DIVINE MONAD.

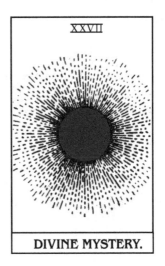

DIVINE MYSTERY.

Fig. 11-1. The Six New Keys.

which has been the hardest to write). But although it's hard work, and even grueling at times, it's not fearsome. It doesn't bring me face to face with my deepest insecurities.

Here is a brief rundown of how I came up with the following images. *Wellspring (22)* is modeled on The Emperor (4), except that now the throne has become a well enclosing a burbling spring that is beginning to replenish the desert and The Emperor has become a figure who stands gazing into (or meditating upon) the water, in which his Original Self is reflected. *Keeper of the Flame (23)* is a tracing of Albrecht Dürer's "Hand Study with Bible," which I chose because the hands show the regard in which the sacred book is held. *The Divine Family (24)* is modeled on The Lovers (6), completing the three-figure sequence for this path, although because the Angel is internalized, we now have a temple in the background; in the foreground is a family. The integration of male and female has created not only a child (Christ Consciousness; see Path 3), but a threefold unit upon which to build an enlightened culture. *Merkaba (25)* refers to a star tetrahedron, which is a sacred geometric form associated with traversing the dimensions; it also happens to be the enneagram when converted from 2-D to 3-D (see the discussion in Appendix E, Part I). The last two figures come from a single 19th-century print that captures the awe and beauty of divine consciousness. *The Divine Monad (26)* is designed to depict unity consciousness as embodied in a human being; *Divine Mystery (27)* is designed to depict the Great Mystery that gives rise to human consciousness and all else in the created world.

Nine Enneagram-based Tarot Paths

Now let's see how these new Keys fit into the nine-path model. The descriptions below are brief, because the goal is to provide an overview that facilitates easy comparisons.

TYPE 1 ON THE PATH OF ALCHEMY

"Masculine intent + feminine attunement to natural cycles allow the sun to illuminate the Earth."

Magician Ones (1) are naturally idealistic, impassioned individualists who seek through their actions to make the world a better place. But the quest for perfection can also make them overly critical, especially of themselves. Making the discovery of *dharma* (destiny) the goal, rather than perfection, can help them temper their self-critical tendencies and set attainable goals for themselves. **The Wheel of Fortune (10)** throws Magicians off balance, for it is the Wheel of Life, which requires no perfecting. The lessons of The Wheel are about developing the kind of flexibility, patience, and timing that allows them to live in harmony with the world around them (so that they find the spiral that leads to the center of the Wheel, where there is perfect peace). Integrating the masculine intent of the Magician with the feminine energy of The Wheel produces **The Sun (19)**, the solar energy (gold) so prized by aspiring alchemists.

TYPE 2 ON THE PATH OF INTUITION

"Feminine memory + masculine discrimination allow us to remember we are divine and to be healed of the sense of sin once and for all."

Although **High Priestess Twos (2)** are known for their desire for emotional connection and intimacy, they actually have a deeper, intuitive side that can be hard to fully cultivate in our extroverted and rationalist culture. So they may end up focusing so much on intimacy with others that they neglect to cultivate the most importance relationship: a relationship with their inner self. If they try to wield the sharp sword of **Justice (11)** without first finding their own inner center, they may end up using it in a manipulative way, to "goad" others into fulfilling their emotional needs. But if they can first discover how to drink from their own inner waters, Justice will provide the detached discernment necessary to balance intuition with rationality. Meeting both challenges is how they can find lasting healing at **Judgement (20)**.

TYPE 3 ON THE PATH OF CREATIVITY

"Outer productivity + inner stillness allows the birth of the world dancer (the one who knows when to move & when to be still)."

Empress Threes (3) are active, adaptable individuals known for their productivity and enjoyment of being "in the flow." They like to stay busy and tend to feel edgy when things slow down. **The Hanged Man (12)** represents that moment when the effort to manifest change via outer activity no longer works—when the only appropriate response is to go within and find the stillness that gives rise to all action. The Hanged Man is learning that all meaningful action arises out of the conscious awareness of Source (the *Tau* from which he hangs); his acceptance of this truth brings unexpected bliss (the halo). Integrating inner stillness with outer action transforms us into **The World Dancer (21)**, the one whose outer activity becomes the natural expression of inner bliss.

TYPE 4 ON THE PATH OF INDIVIDUATION

"Self-dominion + self-dissolution leads us back to our origins (the wellspring of our being) so we see the face of our original self."

Emperor Fours (4) are decisive individualists for whom independence is a priority. So they often hold themselves apart from others (on a high plateau, far from the waters below). Though they yearn for the lushness of the Empress' garden (the paradisiacal state), they find it hard to locate (much less drink from) the waters of life. As a result, immature Fours can seem like rulers without a kingdom who need to take self-dominion by growing up, facing life squarely, and accepting the need to serve the purposes of life before serving themselves (discovering that "the King must die"). **Death (13)** requires complete surrender of human willfulness, in preparation for rebirth into a higher form. Only then is it possible to experience a true sense of origin (awareness of the Original Self) that is the **Wellspring (22)** of our being.

TYPE 5 ON THE PATH OF WISDOM
"Native genius + alchemical pressure transform mental talent into spiritual wisdom, creating the preserver of the flame."

Hierophant Fives (5) typically have a thirst for knowledge and the ability to assimilate vast amounts of information at a time, which they enjoy systematizing, teaching, and sharing. However, they tend to separate themselves from the object of their attention, which can ultimately separate them from themselves, as well. **Temperance (14)** is all about "mixing it up"; it's where all the separate categories in our being get rearranged so that we can't wall off the aspects of the self we don't like but instead have to allow them to be remixed, rebalanced, and redistributed (not the easiest thing for a diffident Five, but necessary for healing). Fives that allow the Temperance angel to "mix them up" gradually discover a deeper, more meaning kind of understanding—and a love of wisdom as spiritual *gnosis*—that inspires a person to serve as a **Keeper of the Flame (23)**.

TYPE 6 ON THE PATH OF TRUST IN THE GOODNESS OF LIFE
"Reconciling the extremes in our nature (attraction + repulsion) brings communion."

Lover Sixes (6) have the nascent awareness of an inner world of awe-inspiring potential (the Garden). But with awe comes fear: the fear that they will not be able to harmoniously make peace between ego consciousness (the man), subconsciousness (the woman), and superconsciousness (the Angel). If Sixes react to the budding awareness of their inner awesomeness with fear instead of love, they will gradually turn this positive potential into a negative projection: **The Devil (15)**. (If The Devil looks scary, it's because he's the product of our amazing human imagination.) The challenge is to see through this projection and begin to work with the fear that drives it, so that the original vision of The Lovers in the Garden can be fully realized in **The Divine Family (24)**.

TYPE 7 ON THE PATH OF LIBERATION
"Aligning human will + divine will create a container for consciousness (merkaba) that can take us anywhere we want to go."

Charioteer Sevens (7) have the vehicle (the chariot of the will) that allows them to enthusiastically set forth in life, where they learn about their inner selves through their outer experiences. These experiences become organized into some kind of structured mental model, creating The Tower. If that model remains flexible, then the lightning that strikes **The Tower (16)** will represent some kind of breakthrough to another level (for those who don't mind having their "crown"/mind blown too much). If the model becomes too rigid, the lightning strike may seem more like an unwelcome shock that destroys outworn mental and energy structures. Whatever the Tower experience, the end goal is the same: to transform the ordinary vehicle of consciousness (driven by personal will) into a **Merkaba (25)**, a Cosmic Chariot with the power to liberate human consciousness from the material plane.

TYPE 8 ON THE PATH OF ASCENSION

"Instinctual wisdom + childlike innocence aligns the lowest & the highest within our nature, allowing us to embody the divine monad."

Strength Eights (8) are naturally dominant individuals that tend to possess unusual powers of will, strength, and physical stamina. The Strength card depicts the Eight-related idea that our natural instincts are a source of great power, but power that must be tempered by love and gentleness if it is to be used for constructive purposes. **The Star (17)** is the inner awareness (inner-sense or innocence) that comes to Eights whose devotion is sufficient to draw down the grace of Heaven (the stars), which can confer upon them great purity and a sense of renewal. **The Divine Monad (26)** symbolizes the combination of love and strength that enables human beings to fully embody the Divine Self.

TYPE 0/9 ON THE PATH OF DIVINE POSSIBILITY

"Self-reflection + imagination brings awareness in the moment & curiosity about the new possibilities that life has to offer."

Fool Nines (0) are youthful, imaginative, and naturally curious about life. As such, they are the closest thing we see to a "blank slate" when it comes to personality. As a result, they easily get caught up in the flow of outer events and other peoples' agendas. Becoming more aware of themselves as separate individuals with their own inner life is therefore a priority. Coming "home" to themselves as **The Hermit (9)**—gaining insight into themselves in a conscious, reflective way—helps them tap into their deeply imaginative side at **The Moon (18)** without getting lost in the process. Developing their imaginative and reflective faculties transforms the foolish Fool into the Divine Fool, capable of embodying the **Divine Mystery (27)**: the mystery of Being arising out of Non-being.

The nine paths above describe nine hero's stories. The protagonists in each story have "hero potential," but what constitutes heroism differs for each type. One of the biggest challenges is to determine which path will enable us to fully develop our "hero" potential in life. One of the ways that we sometimes duck out on our hero's journey is to take somebody else's path and call it good. Doing "good works" for others if you're a Two is a no-brainer (sorry, Twos, but it's true!); doing "good works" if you're a Seven (because you found yourself suddenly caring about orphans in Tibet—say, during a snowboarding tour) is quite another scenario. An Eight standing up to a bully is great, but it's a lot more impressive if the one standing up is a Six overcoming her fears or a Nine overcoming his inertia. This is why it's helpful to have some sort of idea of what the hero's journey looks like for each type: so we don't find ourselves pursuing a perfectly good path that is perfectly good for *somebody else*, not us!

To use the model above, it can be helpful to remind ourselves that although heroic stories tend to depict events in outer life, the real hero's journey takes place internally. It's for that reason that heroes of different types involved in the same events will experience them quite differently (remember the elephant?).

Nine Heros, Nine Journeys

One of the easiest ways to express this idea of people in the same situation having very different experiences is by looking at an example with which many of us are familiar: the Fellowship of the Ring, from J. R. R. Tolkien's *Lord of the Rings*. The Fellowship consists of nine characters who set forth from the Elvish town of Rivendell to accomplish the seemingly impossible task of saving Middle Earth from the evil entity Sauron, whose powers are tied to the One Ring of Power, which must be destroyed in the Cracks of Doom within Sauron's domain of Mordor. Frodo carries the ring; the others in the company are sworn to help and protect him. Each of the characters arguably represents one of the nine points on the enneagram (try typing them yourself or see Endnote 5, at the end of this chapter, for my best guess).

Although the Fellowship appears to share many experiences in common, its members are actually living in very different inner worlds. Among the four hobbits, Frodo is preoccupied with the burden of the Ring; Sam is preoccupied with Frodo's welfare; Pippin is a carefree traveler who is still enjoying the adventure without fully realizing its somber implications; and Merry is an unknown quantity whose heart has yet to be tested.[4] The two men, Boromir and Aragorn, are preoccupied with protecting the group, although soon enough Boromir will fall into madness because of his growing obsession with the Ring and Aragorn will be called upon to confront his greatest fears in the Halls of the Dead. Like the men, elf Legolas and dwarf Gimli serve as protectors, but are quick to squabble over ancient elf/dwarf disputes (Legolas' irritations arising out of a sense of subtle superiority and Gimli's coming from an intolerance for pretense and the inability to hold his tongue). Despite the prescient warnings of Aragorn, wizard Gandalf is forced by circumstance to lead the group into the evil mines of Moria and there confronts his nemesis, the Balrog (a creature originally of the same wizardly order as Gandalf, but now turned to darkness). Gandalf saves the Fellowship but dies in the process, transforming from Gandalf the Grey to return as Gandalf the White.

Each of the nine members of the Fellowship play a key role in the battle for Middle Earth, a hero's journey of mythic proportions. But each role is unique, as each hero grapples with a different kind of unseen struggle, leading to a dramatic ordeal precisely tailored to his inner nature.[5]

Fig. 11-2 depicts the Arc of the Goal (and its images) for each of the nine paths. It's designed to show how the vision we imagine at the beginning of the journey is fulfilled at its end. It also shows the nadir "crossover" that represents a major transition point in every octave; see Chapter 4 for a discussion.

Chapters 12–14 offer detailed discussions of each path. Chapter 15 provides an overarching view of the three-Arc model and its potential applications in enneagram and tarot work.

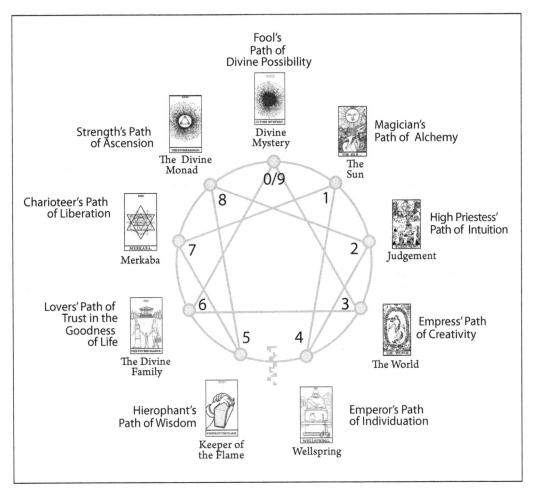

FIG. 11-2. The Arc of the Goal on the Enneagram.

Notes

[1] "What matters most" can either be what we consciously value most or what is most important to our lives, whether or not we are consciously aware of it. In a person who is truly awake, the two are the same. But for many of us, they are not. I tend to see "what matters most" as the experiences that encourage an individual's evolution—the kind that will help him or her to evolve rather than devolve.

[2] The idea of the *merkaba* was introduced in Chapter 9; it's based upon Ezekiel's vision of "wheels upon wheels" in the air, which has been likened to the human light body that enables us to transcend ordinary consciousness. It's discussed at greater length in Appendix E, in a section linking the enneagram and the qabalistic Tree of Life through sacred geometry. However, I should also mention that the enneagram is a two-dimensional representation of the three-dimensional *merkaba*; this idea is also discussed in the same section.

[3] What happens when we become impassioned about something enough to start out on a hero's journey to get it, only to discover later that it's the "wrong" goal? Well, this "mistake" matters very little at all. What matters is that we embark on the journey. The truth is that virtually no one has the right goals at the start. Sooner or later, the truth begins to dawn, and we redirect our efforts. Likely as not, we go astray again. This process happens over and over again, which allows us to become very proficient at admitting mistakes and changing course when necessary. So the very process of making mistakes is what teaches us how to correct them. Anyone who perseveres eventually ends up headed in a more promising direction. (The same thing applies to discovering our enneagram type: whatever type we "try out" initially, we will learn a lot about ourselves in the process, whether we pick the right one or not.)

[4] At this point in the story, Pippin and Merry symbolically represent undifferentiated parts of the psyche related, I believe, to Points 6 and 7 on the enneagram. Later, the two get separated because of Sevenish Pippin's careless interest in investigating things he doesn't understand (although he later demonstrates his growing maturity by pledging himself to the cause of Gondor). Meanwhile, Sixish Merry discovers within himself a fierce desire to serve as a warrior; he admirably acquits himself as the defender of slain King Théoden and his wounded daughter Éowyn in the Battle of the Pelennor.

[5] When J. R. R. Tolkien published *Lord of the Rings* in 1954, the personality enneagram had not yet been taught. But it's interesting that the Fellowship of the Ring that sets out from Rivendell is composed of nine individuals and that the terrifying Nazgul (clearly shadow figures) are also nine in number. The latter are not named, which makes sense, since shadow qualities usually have an undifferentiated but menacing quality about them. My best guess for the enneagram types of the characters: Frodo–9, Legolas–1, Sam–2, Aragorn–3, Boromir–4, Gandalf –5, Merry–6, Pippin–7, Gimli–8.

IV

The Hero's Journey
through the Enneagram & Tarot

We've already looked at the hero's journey as a universal path of transformation. Now we'll look at it as nine variants on that journey, each associated with an enneagram type and the tarot Keys sharing the same root number. My aim is to show how each Arc of the Day tarot Key expresses the core motivation of its associated enneagram type, while the Arc of the Night tarot Key expresses its challenges. When integrated, they generate the third octave of transformation: the Arc of the Goal.

12:
Enneagram Paths 1-2-3

Type 1: Path of Alchemy
The Magician (1) – The Wheel of Fortune (10) – The Sun (19)

THE MAGICIAN (1) symbolizes the fiery masculine path of action. So it's not surprising to see a figure on this Key that looks serious, goal-oriented, and naturally self-directed. It's pretty obvious that his quest is to bring some higher ideal into tangible manifestation. Fortunately, it looks like he's got what he needs for the job: a passion for action (the red outer garment), purity of intent (the white inner garment), and the alchemical tools necessary to accomplish the work (the magical implements on the table). In addition, his pose suggests an understanding of the Hermetic principle, "as above, so below": the idea that ordinary consciousness originates in superconsciousness. The Magician understands this truth and thus strives to serve as a conduit for the energy of heaven, so that it may manifest on earth. His reverence for Divine Law is shown by the positioning of his wand (like a lightning rod ready to receive divine inspiration) and two symbols of eternity: the figure-8 lemniscus over his head and the Ouroboros (snake eating its own tail) encircling his waist.

Like Magicians, enneagram Ones have the fiery will to make things happen and the innate understanding that their actions must be guided by some greater law or principle. They live in an intense inner world of ideal forms, which they are always comparing with the outer world of the real; the latter is usually judged to be inferior (in need of correction). Thus they are

THE MAGICIAN.

WHEEL ⑤ FORTUNE.

THE SUN .

very ethically-minded; but whether this makes them more ethical in practice depends upon their ability to translate their ideals into action. Because their very quest for perfection can potentially cause them to mistake personal ideals for a Divine Edict, the Will of the People, etc. So it's especially important for this type to cultivate a sense of proportion, in order that their upright stance does not become the rigid pose of a martinet. Perhaps if they take a look at the garden around them, with its beautiful bowers of roses and lilies, it will remind them that the world is already a magical emanation of Divine creation—a creation which they can enhance, but need not correct.

Continuing now with the journey of The Magician, his meticulous attention to mastering the tools of manifestation can allow him to become a skilled practitioner of the magical arts. But his direct and single-minded approach to life has its limits. To grow further, he needs an entirely different kind of experience—the kind that allows him to balance masculine initiative with feminine intuition. What could be more perfect than a ride on the whimsical but unpredictable Wheel of Fortune?

THE WHEEL OF FORTUNE (10) is very different in appearance from Key 1. The central image is circular (not linear); the arrangement of images looks disorderly (not tidy); the sky is cloudy (not clear); and there are strange creatures doing strange things (like reading books). There are also mysterious symbols on the Wheel (not just four workman-like tools). And don't even get me started on the Sphinx, the unfurled Ouroboros, or the weird-looking Hermes-Anubis figure lounging lazily on the side of the Wheel (surely a pose The Magician would not approve of).[1]

Unlike the world portrayed in Key 1, where it's clearly The Magician's efforts that make things happen, Key 10 depicts a reality where things appear to move on their own (or are moved by a hidden but powerful force). In short, Key 10 is the chaotic world of everyday life. And it's a pretty crazy world that can seem a lot like a roulette wheel in Vegas.

Our upright Magician is now on a Wheel that makes it impossible to maintain an upright stance, because it is constantly turning him upside-down! This is of course upsetting, but there is little can do to alter the rotation of the Wheel. He must instead learn to adapt to its movements, to "go with the flow" (maintaining a balance between principle and practicality). At first, this tends to drive a Magician crazy. But if he is willing let go a little, he may start to feel the motion of the Wheel (the rhythms of life) in his physical body and begin to appreciate what the natural world has to teach him about how to live, not just from the "top-down" but from the "bottom-up. And if he's *really* fortunate (and the Wheel is exactly the right place to discover good fortune!), the Magician will come to enjoy the motion of the Wheel for its own sake and to regard life's curve balls with humor instead of resistance.[2] (While it may seem strange to think of a sense of humor as an asset on the hero's journey, the ability to laugh in the face of adversity often has the power to transform a situation.)

Enneagram Ones would find it easy to understand The Magician's initial difficulty with the Wheel. For they are probably the most serious, rule-oriented type on the enneagram. Many times they even look the part: all sharp angles and straight lines, especially in the face. (Margaret Hamilton's Wicked Witch of the West is a perfect example.) As a result, they don't have an easy time transitioning from rule-oriented living to a more spontaneous, in-the-moment lifestyle. Youthful Ones can seem like "old heads on young shoulders": overly mature for their age, and very literal-minded. They are the children who actually follow the rules and expect others to do the same. (They're also the ones who can earn the ostracism of others by tattling, because they see rule-breaking as a serious offense.) However, once they grow to adulthood, Ones often begin to become more aware of the down side of a rule-bound life and to seek out new possibilities. Those who don't may eventually find themselves in a "bend or break" situation, where the only sane course is to cultivate greater openness and flexibility.[3]

The Magician who allows his masculine logic to be informed by the love and laughter of the feminine becomes more balanced—which of course is the whole purpose of life on the Wheel. The more balanced he gets, the more he naturally migrates from the Wheel's precarious edge towards its still center. As he approaches the centermost point, a wonderful surprise awaits him: the dawning light of his inner SUN (19), a light that rapidly increases in intensity.

Symbolically, The Sun represents the marriage of the masculine and feminine; that's why it has both straight and wavy lines. Once the two are integrated, The Magician is able to revel in the glory of his own inner light and to love himself exactly as is, no corrections needed. At the beginning of the journey, The Magician was looking for self-discipline, control, and a cause that would justify his powerful need to manifest a more perfect world. What he finds at its end is pure joy.

Enneagram Ones who learn how to combine the self-discipline of The Magician with the ability to roll with the punches (and a good sense of humor) find that life is warmer and sunnier than they could ever have imagined. The more they allow themselves to relax and accept life for what it is, the more life shows them its everyday treasures. The personal happiness that they experience is as welcome as it is unexpected.

Type 2 – Path of Intuition
The High Priestess (2) – Justice (11) – Judgement (20)

THE HIGH PRIESTESS (2) symbolizes the female principle; she is the feminine consort of The Magician. Sitting quietly between two black and white pillars (in a place of balance), The High Priestess is calmly serene. She wants or needs nothing because she already possesses the sacred waters of life (the blue garment). Behind her is a tapestry depicting the Tree of Life in which each sephira on the Tree is depicted by a pomegranate (a symbol associated with the myth of Persephone and thus the idea that the hero's journey always includes a Descent into the Deep).

Unlike The Magician, who is an assertive force for change in the outer world, The High Priestess' influence lies in her unmoving stillness, presence, and silent awareness of what is unfolding. In her resides the awesome but hidden power of the subconscious to hold the imprint (memory) of everything we have ever experienced. The subconscious also informs our intuitions, inspires our dreams, and wells up as psychic impressions that seem to arise out of nowhere.

In cultures in which the feminine is venerated, The High Priestess is the most sacred of archetypes, for she possesses the power to rejuvenate herself and others, using the healing energy of the waters of life. But because the West does not venerate the feminine, those who embody this archetype have never found it easy to do so. There is simply no social role that now corresponds to The High Priestess in Western culture. The closest counterpart is the "Mary" archetype of the Virgin Mother, but she is valued for her devotion and piety, not her powers.

What's amazing is that the image of the High Priestess even existed in the 15th century tarot, when the idea of a female spiritual leader was unthinkable (at least according to the Church; whoever conceived the tarot obviously had a different idea). Although a handful of women may have been recognized in the West for their achievements in life, what person—male or female—has ever been honored as a representative of the Sacred Feminine?

In the enneagram world, Two is the type most closely associated with the High Priestess. As tenderhearted feelers, Twos naturally want to connect with others. But they often try to do so without having first connected with their own inner wisdom. Due to cultural conditioning, many do not even realize that such a connection is possible. As a result, when they direct their energies outwards—"doing for" their families, friends, and others they love—they tend to do so out of the perceived need to have their self-worth validated (as opposed to the desire to give freely without conditions). This kind of conditional giving can create the kind of co-dependency that is a substitute for true intimacy.

The image on High Priestess Key reminds us that the feminine needs no external validation; it is complete unto itself. Twos who tap into their inner

High Priestess discover the true source of their power and become the pioneers who can help resurrect the Divine Feminine in Western culture.

At **JUSTICE (11)**, we see The High Priestess at a higher octave of development. She still sits between two pillars, unmoving and impassive, as before. However, in Key 11, her expression has changed. She looks straight at us, with an unwavering gaze. Her accessories have changed, as well: she now bears a sharp sword (a discriminating intellect) which is in her right hand because she is fully conscious of her decision-making abilities. In her left hand are a set of scales—the scales of justice, which allow her to balance her feminine intuition with masculine discernment. This is seen in the transformation of her silvery "moon" headdress into a golden crown (wisdom); the light behind the curtain is also golden. Her blue gown (the color of the sea) is now red (the color of inspired thinking); the purple curtain represents their higher synthesis (blue + red = purple). The solid gray pillars imply a complete synthesis of the black and white pillars we see at Key 2. Overall, these symbols suggest a feminine figure in the process of successfully cultivating masculine discernment.

Not that this is an easy task. For it is the first impulse of the feminine to nurture life, not to be harsh or critical. And yet, in her role of Justice, The High Priestess must strike a balance between compassion and critique, because the role of Justice is to restore cosmic balance to life. On the Tree of Life, Justice is associated with the fifth sephirah of Geburah, representing the force of Severity. This points to the Divine Feminine in its Kali-like role of Destroyer, where the Divine Feminine severs from creation anything that threatens the structures defining the world of form.

Most Twos on the enneagram would probably be more drawn to the magnetic mystique of The High Priestess than to the stern and sharp-looking figure of Justice. They don't want to develop the kind of intellectual acuity that tends to cut things apart because they far prefer to bring things (and people) together. That's why Justice is a shadow Key for Twos.

THE HIGH PRIESTESS

JUSTICE .

JUDGEMENT.

To the extent that they manage to develop both feminine archetypes, they will often kept them separate. Twos who develop their intellect tend to alternate between the two extremes of ultra-rationalism and ultra-emotionalism. It's a challenge for them to completely integrate these seemingly opposite functions. The greatest opportunity to develop their rational side often comes either when Two parents have children (who require a balance between love and limit-setting) or when they take on some kind of leadership role at work in which they are required to make hiring/firing decisions and to give corrective feedback to employees.

JUDGEMENT (20) represents the highest octave of the Path of Intuition. It depicts the ultimate integration of The High Priestess (2) and Justice (11). The title of "Judgement" can be confusing, because it sounds a lot—and seems a lot—like Justice, because the words *Justice* and *Judgement* seem very similar. But in the tarot, the imagery is very different. While Justice is a somber and spartan card, Judgement is very dramatic. Although it is obviously based on the Christian idea of "Judgement Day" (complete with Gabriel blowing his horn to raise the dead), its symbolism is entirely triumphant. The sky is blue; the mountains are brilliant; the angel is glorious; and the "dead" are rejoicing. So we know something awesome is happening here—something welcomed by all who seek eternal life.

Key 20 represents the reconciliation of the feminine potential to heal with love (Key 2) with the masculine authority to make this healing fully manifest, once all that stands in the way has been eliminated or balanced (Key 11). At Key 20, this vision can be fully realized. Gabriel announces the descent of divine grace, which has the power to heal us of our wounds (Gabriel's red cross is a universal symbol of healing.) It also restores our memory of the Divine (access to the Akashic record as symbolized by the TORA scroll half-hidden under The High Priestess' robe), thus raising us to the highest state (the magnificent peaks in the distance).

Twos are the type most associated with healing and the healing professions, especially as nurses and counselors. The healing that occurs at Key 20 comes to Twos at the point where they fully embrace the dictum, "Physician, heal thyself." Not all wounds can be healed through simple self-care, but without it, no permanent healing can occur. The Two that learns to care for herself creates the conditions that attract the kind of healing we call "miraculous" (the kind associated with Lourdes or other "Mary" sightings). While it *is* a miracle, it is also the natural result of integrating the opposites. Its mysterious quality comes from the mystery that is always associated with the Sacred Feminine. The Two who fully embodies that archetype is able to both heal and be healed (and all without the need to demand anything from anybody).

Type 3 – Path of Creativity

The Empress (3) – The Hanged Man (12) – The World (21)

The High Priestess symbolizes the feminine potential to bring forth life, but at Key 2, it exists as a hidden potential. It's not until The High Priestess gets together with The Magician that fertilization can occur. So **THE EMPRESS** (3) is The High Priestess in the process of becoming a mother (Mother Nature)—hence, the emphasis in Key 3 on the creative process.

The card depicts a radiant Empress attired in a flowing pregnancy gown full of juicy pomegranates (no longer half-hidden in the background but now displayed front and center). She loves life (Venus symbol on the heart) and enjoys relaxing in her beautiful garden—a garden she tends using the waters that flow from The High Priestess' robe. So it's clear that there's a close relationship between the two.

In modern, high-tech cultures, Mother Nature is an idealized archetype (although we often leave off the "Mother" now when speaking of the natural world). The natural world is distinguished from the civilized world, much to the detriment of the latter. In the minds of many people, nature is better off without human intervention, which is often seen as interfering with "natural processes." This same mindset leads us to split life into two categories—work and play—and to associate creativity with the latter, not the former. Or to think of creativity at work more as productivity (work done to produce something that can be sold in the marketplace, not work done for its own sake).

But from both a Hermetic and quantum perspective, we are not separate from nature; we literally create the world around us. Similarly, there is no meaningful way to separate activity into work and play; these are arbitrary, culture-driven categories. The truth is that creative imagination brings everything into manifestation and that embodied consciousness is its source.

THE EMPRESS.

THE HANGED MAN.

THE WORLD.

Enneagram Threes know all about work. As industrious Type A's, they fit right into modern culture. Enthusiastic, imaginative, and enterprising, they are always up for a challenge. But the jobs they are asked to do often require them to sacrifice creativity for results. They usually manage to do this, because (like Mother Nature), they are highly adaptable.

But although they work hard, this kind of work can wear them down over time, because there are limited opportunities to experience what Mihaly Csikszentmihalyi calls *flow*: an inner state of joyful absorption associated with creative inspiration. The experience of flow comes from making creativity a priority instead of an afterthought.[4]

Although Threes enjoy being in the flow, many work situations focus so much on results that there's very little flow, only the constant grind of new goals and deadlines. Even Threes, who have a lot of tolerance for high-pressure work, eventually burn out under these conditions. Sometimes the only way they manage to break the cycle of constant work is to subconsciously attract the kind of life events—illness, injury, or failing—that will break them out of unhealthy work situations. Getting away from work allows them to get a different perspective on life.

THE HANGED MAN (12) depicts that moment in life when activity stops and reflection begins. It represents the stillness that serves as the counterpoint to the state of flow. At The Hanged Man, the creative motion of The Empress comes to a standstill. At first, this abrupt halt is usually regarded as unfortunate, because the generative Empress—like the mother producing child after child—has no experience of non-doing. Every day is full of activities. When the activity slows down (as during beachy vacations), they often feel disoriented instead of relaxed.

A good example would be an empty-nester alone at home for the first time. When she first confronts a house without children, the place seems eerily quiet; her first impulse is to get busy with something—housework, errands, or even a home remodel. But if she resists that impulse (instead allowing herself to just "hang out" for a while), she eventually stops trying to merely fill up the time and instead looks for activities that are more naturally fulfilling.

For a Three, Hanged Man situations can seem like their worst nightmare—at least at first. Doing nothing seems akin to dying. So they must cultivate patience at the beginning, because it takes time to realize the benefits of stillness: the ability to experience a different kind of flow, the kind that sustains them in ways that outer activity never can.

The figure on the card has obviously reached that point; that's why he looks so blissed-out, despite his upside-down stance. His head is encircled by the halo of illumination because he is filled with peace. The numeral Four formed by his legs foreshadows the principle of Fourness, which is about manifestation in the physical world. It tells us that the highest form of manifestation requires a combination of outer activity and inner stillness. It also foreshadows the dancer at The World, where the upside-down Hanged Man becomes the right-side-up dancer. The difference is that the World Dancer doesn't need to be mechanically restrained to remain still; she can maintain her inner stillness while engaged in outer activity.

The dancing figure at **THE WORLD (21)** moves within an oval that represents a *vesica piscis*: the intersection of two circles that symbolizes the creative principle (and also the vaginal opening of the Goddess through which new life emerges). Key 21 resembles Key 10, the Wheel of Fortune; it includes both the Hebrew letter *Caph* that is associated in the Golden Dawn system with Key 10 (as the drape that surrounds the dancer) and the four fixed figures of the zodiac (symbolizing the fixed principles that stabilize the world of Creation). Just as the four figures emerge from clouds, the busy world of Creation emerges from the still world of Non-being. Integrating the principle of productivity at Key 3 with the principle of stillness at Key 12 produces the dancer at Key 21: the human being whose outer actions express her inner being. This Key also symbolizes a world in which we not longer see the world in terms of opposites, but instead as their union.

Threes are often seen as more superficial than other enneagram types, because they often appear to be motivated by secondary gains like money, success, or social prestige. However, their focus on work and the rewards it brings is often a cover for the subconscious fear that they really have no intrinsic identity or value; hence, the belief that "I am what I do." The cultivation of stillness gives Threes access to their inner world, perhaps for the first time. And this enables them to know with conviction that, not only do they have a unique identity as a soul, but that they are celebrated for exactly who they are. So they do not have to produce anything to prove their value. This is the joyful, life-changing discovery that we see embodied in the dancing figure at Key 21.

Notes

[1] There are many interesting features of Key 10 that The Magician might find worth exploring, if he could get over his initial suspicions. He might notice that, like his tools, many of the symbols on the Wheel are also in fours—we have the T-A-R-O letters, the four letters of the Tetragrammaton, and the four beasts said to symbolize the four creatures of Ezekiel: the man, the lion, the ox, and the eagle. (The latter's studious demeanor suggests they are trying to learn something; maybe The Magician also has something left to learn?) Older decks often show the four stages of life, which suggest a move from focusing on space in Key 1 to time in Key 10. The unfurled snake—often said to represent the monstrous Typhon—might also symbolize the Scorpionic potential for finding transformation on the Wheel. (And for The Magician, the unfurling of the Ouroboros could have something to do with his need to unbend, just as the Hermes-Anubis figure is doing!) The feminine Sphinx with the sword looks an awful lot like Justice (11) but she could also be the lady we see in Strength (8), now merged with her friend the lion. She can remind us that it's the feminine principle (Binah) that rules the world of manifestation and its wheel of time—something that The Magician may not yet know. For other possibilities on the symbolism of this very complex Key, see the discussion at http://www.nextiermedia.com/jennifer/tarotcards/article3.html.

[2] The need of the Magician to learn how to "go with the flow" reminds me of a trip I took across the North Atlantic on a small student ship in high school. At first, the motion of the boat made me queasy, but once I got used to it, I found it incredibly soothing. Back on land nine days later, I was surprised by how much I missed the rocking motion of the waves.

[3] You might be wondering at this point how a Key that helps us learn to enjoy life can be part of the Arc of the Night, when that Arc is all facing the dark and disowned parts of ourselves. It's because not all shadows are dark. Jung spoke of the "bright shadow" as all of the positive qualities in our nature that we have disowned, because we're afraid of them, don't think we deserve them, or disapprove of them. The Wheel is a bright shadow for anyone whose focus is mastery and perfection, because it represents those aspects in life that we can't control but that have the power to open us up to new possibilities.

[4] Csikszentmihaly, Mihalyi. *Flow: The Psychology of Optimal Experience* (HarperCollins: 1983).

13:
Enneagram Paths 4-5-6

Type 4 – Path of Individuation
The Emperor (4) – Death (13) – Wellspring (22)

THE MOVE FROM THREE TO FOUR represents a major shift, because it takes us beyond the trinity that sets the stage for physical manifestation. If the first three paths are about the process of manifestation, the fourth is about its tangible results on the physical plane, as represented by **THE EMPEROR** (4). That is why this card is so often associated with taking dominion in the physical world.

However, The Emperor as depicted in most decks is quite old—much older than his pregnant consort, The Empress. Why is this? It is because physical manifestation is the end of the road for the process of involution (the process whereby we descend from spirit into matter). Thus, as soon as we come into physical manifestation, we begin aging, which anticipates our eventual death in the physical sense. But it also anticipates our spiritual rebirth and all that is necessary to bring this about.

So this Key is extremely complex. It has three aspects: the connection between process and actual manifestation, taking dominion in physicality, and the preparation for a return to spirit. Ironically, the meaning most attributed to it—taking dominion in the physical world—is the least interesting from a transformational point of view, which may be why it's not actually depicted on the card. We don't see The Emperor at the height of his powers but at their waning. Yes, he's the still boss. But just what is he the boss of? A kingdom of flesh and blood that is only temporary. To truly take dominion will require more than the ability to seize and hold worldly power. It will require the ability to truly understand why we incarnate and what makes our lives matter.

The Empress gives us a clue about why life matters. As the consort of The Emperor, she is also the mother of his child. He initiates the life that she brings forth; he also protects her and her unborn child; and when the child is born, he protects his family and teaches the child the responsibilities of a ruler. His last role is to recognize when the child is ready to assume the responsibilities of adulthood and to step back, allowing his role to be assumed by the next generation. Thus, the mature Emperor is the one who understands that the role of ruler is to serve the nation, protect its integrity, and hand over the baton when the time is right.[1]

As applied to human consciousness, The Emperor symbolizes the executive function of the self: the egoic mind that is responsible for the coordination the "empire" (the human body) and its "subjects" (thoughts, emotions, and acts). It is The Emperor who must take care of the everyday self, keeping it not only physically safe but motivated to stay engaged with life, despite the relative dryness of life on the physical plane (the desert setting). That is why this Key is so full of red (impassioned action), yellow (solar power), and Aries symbolism (four rams on the throne and an embroidered ram on The Emperor's cloak).

But how can an Emperor sustain himself in such a dry, stark place? The answer is, he can't—at least not without help. The dryness of the scene tells us that Emperor's ability to stay motivated depends upon his ability to connect with The Empress, whose gardens are fed by the magical waters we see far below in the valley. Visiting her gardens can help him remember how beautiful life can become when we plant the earth with love (recall The Empress' Venusian heart).

Like The Emperor, the enneagram Four is strong-willed and independent-minded. Also like him, he tends to experience feelings of aridity and isolation. Fours have the kind of aristocratic sensibilities and artistic tastes that often sets them apart from the crowd. At the same time, they have an innate sense that something is missing in life, something vital and life-giving. Caught between a desire for to be completely independent and a longing for "something missing from life," they can find it very hard to feel at home in this world.

A key reason for their discomfort is that they embody that point in human evolution when the ego self has reached its developmental apex. A person at this point must grow beyond ego in order to prosper—which means allowing it to be superseded by something greater. This does not mean renouncing the ego; it only means renouncing **our exclusive identification with it**. But initially, it's the only self we know. So renunciation is difficult.

Difficult, but not impossible. Looked at from another angle, Key 4 provides a symbolic depiction of what this process involves. The isolation of the

THE EMPEROR.

DEATH.

WELLSPRING.

desert provides a suitable environment for change. For its isolation separates us from collective conditioning; its harsh light strips us from our mental illusions; and its temperature extremes break down habitual responses that no longer benefit us. Fours who allow themselves to open to this transformational process gradually slough off enough of their conditioning to allow the nourishing energy of the soul to well up within them.[2]

The move away from ego identification prepares us for the transition from involution to evolution (from a life grounded in the material world to a life grounded in spirit). But there is a transition between the two. It is the transition we call DEATH (13).[3]

Death is one of the most misunderstood Keys in the tarot. At first glance, it looks entirely uninviting: a skeleton carrying a black flag before whom all mortal beings cower. These are the images upon which people fixate when they first gaze upon this card.

But a closer inspection reveals several symbolic hints that the Death Key is not quite what it appears to be. For it includes a magnificent sun on the horizon, a majestic white horse (the same horse we see in The Sun?), and a giant white rose of pure-hearted intent. There is a barge on the river which symbolizes the carrying of a soul from one life to the next. Among the people is a very young girl who—alone in the crowd—welcomes Death with open arms (probably because she remembers what it really means). Death even sports the same red feather we see in The Fool and The Sun, which symbolizes the life force. Granted, it's a little wilted here (which tells us that rebirth isn't happening right away). But it's still an indicator that death is the champion of life, not its enemy.

Death certainly comes to the physical body, but on the hero's journey, this Key is about transformation, not physical demise. It symbolizes the surrender of the notion that our ego self is the hero in the hero's journey. But ego can never be the hero, because its abilities are simply too limited. Once we really understand its limitations, it gets easier to discover its primary purpose: to serve as the conduit for a Cosmic Force greater than itself. (Initially, I wrote "Comic Force"; it was tempting to retain the typo!)

Death is a symbol of the first stage we pass through when moving from ego development to ego transcendence. Reflecting deeply on the nature of life and death is one of the ways that Fours come to terms with the sobering truth that transformation is not a game. It is a process that, once set into motion, will continue to its logical end. The Four has a choice to make: either to realize the limits of a self-centered life (and to willingly open to whatever experiences are necessary for transformation) or to persist in a conditioned path (which will make life increasingly seem like a "house of mirrors" from which there is no escape). Choosing to open to something new brings the welcome discovery that Death is not the end of life but the gateway to a greater reality.

WELLSPRING (22) is the first of our Keys to go beyond the 21 Keys that we already know. On the Arc of the Goal, the first three Keys (19, 20, and 21) represent the outcome of three primordial paths: the Masculine Path of Alchemy (Keys 1-10-19), the Feminine Path of Intuition (Keys 2-11-20), and the Androgynous Path of Creativity (Keys 3-12-21). These paths are primordial because, in numerology, the number One represents oneness, Two represents duality, and Three represents the multiplicity. Every number after Three describes a different aspect of the multiplicity.

As mentioned above, the number Four represents the aspect of material manifestation. In the case of human beings, this relates not only to the physical world and the body, but the manifestation of consciousness *within* the body. It also relates to the characteristics of manifest vs unmanifest consciousness and how the two are related. For most people, our manifest consciousness is limited, both because of the limitations of the human body and social conditioning. Few of us remember what it is like to experience unlimited, unconditioned consciousness.

As the third octave of the Path of Individuation, Wellspring (22) depicts what it is like to cease identifying with conditioned consciousness. This is the path where we get the chance to reconnect with the soul self, which can exist as either an individual or as part of a larger whole.

The imagery in Key 22 symbolizes the reconnection with our soul identity. This comes about as the result of letting go of our identification with ego, which allows a more foundational understanding of self to emerge from deep within the psyche. Key 22 is set in the same desert as Key 4, but the figure once known as The Emperor now has no clearly-defined social identity; we cannot even tell whether it is male or female. He or she is clad in a pure white garment (symbolizing fully purified desire manifest in form). There is also no outward ornamentation because none is needed: this figure has regained its primordial wholeness. Its downward gaze into the water symbolizes a connection with something deep inside the psyche; this is the kind of connection capable of drawing up the hidden waters of the feminine subconscious to re-vivify the everyday consciousness of the ego self.

The throne from Key 4 (the conditioned belief in the supremacy of ego) has been transformed into a burbling spring (soul identity) enclosed in a square well (meaning that this connection is experienced in outer conscousness). The well is more lightly built than the throne, because it is not "set in stone" (based on rigid, inflexible beliefs). Unlike the Emperor's throne, which served only the The Emperor, the well serves all who venture into the desert, providing life-giving water to thirsty travelers. Moreover, the water is so abundant that it overflows from the tap on the side of the well. As a result, the desert is beginning to bloom.

Wellspring (22) depicts the truth that transforming the world begins with transforming the individual. Enneagram Fours are the type most aware of this truth and thus the great champions of personal authenticity and individuality. Their challenge is to learn to distinguish the willful and defiant individuality of the conditioned self from the true individuality of the Original Self, which is as natural as a spring that flows out of the depths of the earth.

Fours are known for their ability to sense when something is missing in life. That "something missing" is the Original Self—the "face before they were born." In reality, this Original Self never really leaves us. But it commonly becomes obscured by conditioning in early life. The Path of Individuation is about allowing that conditioning to be gradually stripped away, so that we can reconnect with the Original Self. Wellspring (22) shows the nature of that reconnection, which brings not only the ability to deeply experience our inner nature but to powerfully change the environment around us (not because of what we **do** but because of what we **are**).

Path of Wisdom – Type 5

The Hierophant (5) – Temperance (14) – Keeper of the Flame (23)

THE HIEROPHANT (5) features an authoritative figure presiding over two kneeling acolytes. This Key is sometimes described by tarot writers as a symbol of the forces of orthodox religion (i.e., the pope). However, the symbolism associated with the number five points to a more esoteric concept. The Pythagoreans say it is about *"hieros gamos,"* the marriage between heaven and earth; others attribute it to the mystery of the *quintessence*—the power that transcends the four elements of earth, air, fire, and water. So despite the pope-like image on the card, which suggests the authority of established religion, at a higher level, The Hierophant symbolizes the kind of teacher whose knowledge transcends religious doctrine. This is the embodied knowledge of a shaman, real guru, or esoteric teacher. The pillars on either side can be seen as portals of initiation, the kind we'd find at the formal entrance to an ancient mystery school. Along the same lines, The Hierophant's right hand is in a position widely known as the "gesture of esotericism," in which only three of the fingers are fully visible, while the other two are hidden (compare this to The Devil's completely open palm, where "what you see is what you get," i.e., the gross rewards of the material world).

The qualities of The Hierophant mesh well with the qualities of the Fives on the enneagram, for Fives are the type most associated with scholarly, academic knowledge. They are the ones who are often found as teachers of advanced concepts requiring highly abstract or metaphysical knowledge. While this knowledge may be impressive, it is often solely theoretical, divorced from either emotion or practical application. Enneagrammatically, the challenge for Fives is to integrate their intellect with the wisdom grounded in their emotions and body. If they cannot or will not do so, then their intellectual discoveries—which start out fresh and original—can turn into dogma, especially once they reach a position of authority. (So they really **can** turn into the pope, at least in their own mind.) This is why it's so important for Fives to learn how to translate book knowledge into something more vital and life-giving.

For The Hierophant, TEMPERANCE (14) is both a trial and an act of deliverance. Temperance depicts the alchemical blending of all the aspects of our being, so that we do not remain one-sided. The Temperance angel is Archangel Michael, the great protector of the faith. His eyes are closed, as if in deep meditation, for the process of alchemical blending is complex and requires great precision. And rather than appearing in the clouds above (as the angels in Keys 6 and 20), he is right down here on the same level as us human beings, straddling the earth and the water. So the theme of *mixing* shows up in many ways: mixing heaven and earth, angel- and human-kind, water and earth, and the contents of the right and left cups. The ultimate mixing involves the united of the opposites within our nature. The irises just next to the pool are yet another symbol of mixing, for they refer to the Goddess Iris, who links the earth with both the heavens and the "depths of...the underworld."[4]

The Temperance Key represents the process by which an enneagram Five experiences the decompartmentalization of his once-separated mental, emotional, and physical selves. The fact that the active figure here is an Archangel tells us that the action is not being performed by the Five himself, but by greater forces within his being—forces outside his conscious control. So from his perspective, something is being done to him; his role is to try to cooperate with the process.

The term "mixing" may sound fairly neutral, but the experienced of "being mixed" by an Archangel is not exactly an ordinary sort of event, for the blending at Temperance is alchemical. The four colors of alchemy are black, white, yellow, and red. We see the color black in Key 13, in which Death wears black armor and carries a black flag. This symbolizes the first stage of alchemical change, the *nigredo*, where all that is impermanent begins to decay and die. In Key 14, we see the other three colors. Archangel Michael's robe is white, symbolizing the stage of *albedo*, or "whitening," where the light begins to emerge out of the darkness; it is often associated with the (silver) light of the moon and with the separation of elements into their opposites. The Archangel's hair is yellow, as are the irises in the background. Yellow is associated with the *citrinitas*, "yellowing," where the silver light of The Moon begins to yellow in the light of the dawning sun (as well as the golden crown in the distance). The sunrise begins the process of reconciling the opposites (as symbolized by the "marriage" of the moon and sun), a process completed in the *rubedo*, "reddening," symbolized by the intensely red angel wings. It is this last process that heralds the return of the light.[5]

Alchemical processes are often likened to the practice of tempering metals, especially swords. This involves alternately heating the sword to a red-hot state and then plunging it quickly into cold water, a process that is done repeatedly, in order to make the sword strong but supple. The sword is an apt symbol here, since it is associated in the tarot with mental processes: about how our ideas and mental processes are subjected to real-world testing in order to see whether they survive the process intact.

Another symbol of alchemical transformation is the image of cooking food like beans or meat over a low flame for a long time, in order to soften the food and break it down into its constituent elements, a process that eventually produces the reblending that creates a superior meal. An example would be Rumi's description of the cooking of chickpeas, which entails both slow simmering of the beans and the adding of additional ingredients designed to make the final dish perfectly balanced.[6] In shamanism or temple rites, the same process involves tests and trials designed to assess a candidate's readiness to take on the arduous training of a shaman or initiate. If this challenge sounds daunting, the presence of Archangel Michael—the Great Protector—ensures that this doesn't happen until a person is properly prepared.

This process of alchemical blending depicted at Key 14 is particularly relevant to enneagram Fives because they are almost certainly the type that is most compartmentalized, and thus the type most in need of an alchemical "make-over" to help them blend together the disparate elements of their psyche. On one hand, Fives seek privacy, solitude, and the ability to act without outside interference; on the other, they long for connection,

THE HIEROPHANT

TEMPERANCE.

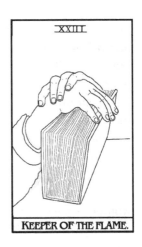

KEEPER OF THE FLAME.

although they can seldom express this need in words. Despite the fact that they may see themselves as capable of living almost entirely within their minds, they are not exempt from the need to meaningfully connect with the world around them. But they also need to connect with the world within. It's not easy to "blend" these very different worlds; hence the need for alchemical intervention. Fives who are sufficiently open will attract whatever experiences are needed to produce alchemical changes that will allow them to reconnect both internally and externally. (One Five friend of mine who had no particular desire to marry managed to attract a wife and family who completely transformed his world.)

The role of the **Keeper of the Flame** (23) is to so thoroughly understand a teaching that it becomes part of one's very being. It is the role of the teacher in all oral wisdom traditions, where the greatest teaching is conveyed not by one's words, but what they are and how they act. The Flame is of course the Flame of Wisdom, and wisdom cannot be acquired by study alone. The image on the Key is a simplified version of Albrecht Dürer's 1506 drawing, "Hand Study with Bible."

The transition from knowledge to wisdom involves a "course of study" that is not just mental but experiential. And the experiences, as indicated above, are typically intense. So only those individuals capable of withstanding the impact of such forces can fulfill the role of Keeper of the Flame. (I once met a Native American shaman who, like many before him, accepted shamanic training very reluctantly. He understood all too well its nature, and was not eager to undergo the tests and trials involved. He did eventually say yes, but only after being shown very clearly that this was a calling that could not be denied.)

As indicated above, enneagram Fives are typically introverted and thus find it difficult to freely mingle with others in whatever society into which they are born. They tend to stand apart, acting as dispassionate observers of all that goes on around them. So their challenge is to somehow become involved not only as observers but as participants in that world, despite their inability to easily fit into the social fabric. What is frequently not perceived about Fives is their potential to serve in a role that is powerful and fundamental: as silent channelers of elemental forces and neutralizers of negative energy. As natural channelers of elemental forces, they can use those forces to transform the lives of those around them, even when they are unaware of it. As neutralizers of negative energy, they have a natural ability to "soak up" negative energy in a way that renders it harmless to others—not by doing anything overt, but simply by being fully present in the situation.

In cultures that recognize the importance of such roles, their innate talents are often recognized early in life by the previous generation of wise men and women. They or their parents are then informed that it is their natural role in life to undergo the training that will help them maximize their potential. In cultures that do not recognize such roles, they may grow up feeling divorced from the community around them, believing they have no special role to play. Nevertheless, they are often drawn to situations in which their patient presence helps others to feel calmer, clearer, and more tolerant of life's difficulties.

Path of Trust in the Goodness of Life – Type 6
The Lovers (6) – The Devil (15) – The Divine Family (24)

THE LOVERS (6) depicts a beautifully naked and innocent-looking couple being blessed by Archangel Raphael, the angel of healing, under a glorious sun. The couple seems to be in the Garden of Eden, complete with a flaming Tree of Life and an apple tree with twining snake. A tall mountain rises in the background—a symbol of the Great Work of transformation. It is a magnificent image of life's perfection. It can also serve to symbolize the harmonious interaction of archetypal energies, one in which the opposites of masculine and feminine are completely reconciled within the human being. When individuals are in harmony, they can come together to create a harmonious union, which in turn gives rise to a harmonious family, community, and national culture.

Enneagram Sixes are instinctively drawn to activities and organizations that create stable bonds between people. They have a natural service ethic and a respect for others which helps them bring together diverse individuals under a single banner. They are the natural guardians of culture and who are sensitive to the potentially disastrous consequences of cultural disruption (anarchy, revolution, etc.). As a result, they are often attracted to activities that support the larger community, as police officers, fire fighters, EMTs and community volunteers. They are often willing to sacrifice individual rewards or recognition for the sake of their community values (however they define these values) and are loyal and steadfast in their commitments. However, they can be too loyal and conventional at times, because of an instinctive trust for the Known and distrust for the Unknown. From a Sixish point of view, if Adam and Eve had simply obeyed God's command not to eat from the Tree of the Knowledge of Good and Evil, we might still be in The Garden of Eden.

But would this really be a good thing? What would it be like to stay in The Garden of Eden forever, experiencing only love and ease?

If we look a second time at The Garden, we might begin to see it in a different light. These lovers may be undefiled but they seem awfully passive; the angel is the only dynamic figure here. And what about their nakedness, meant to symbolize innocence? If these were small children or even a single figure alone, this might make sense. But what we have here are two fully-grown adults on a card entitled The Lovers. What adult couple wanders about naked, barely aware of each other's body? Only those living as brother and sister, not husband and wife. At what point do these adults get to discover what love (and life) are really about?

It's at the point where they develop the courage to reject blind obedience as a childish virtue. Unquestioned obedience to outer authority figures, however benevolent, deprives people of the chance to discover their inner divinity—to discover that they have the potential to actually *become* the the glorious Angel depicted in Key 6. Once a person realizes that, The Garden has served its purpose (to give us an outer vision of what is possible in our inner lives). So what happens next? He gets thrown out of the garden, of course! Not because of sin but because *it's time*. When The Call comes, it catapults us out of The Garden and onto The Road to Adventure.

The Lovers' card shows us everything in life that is good. But it is only good to the extent that we actually make it our own. To to that, we have to leave The Garden so we can rediscover life's goodness within ourselves. The Lover's Path shows us what this involves: the vision, the shadow, and the tangible outcome of reconciling the opposites.

THE DEVIL (KEY 15) shows what happens if we try to prop up "good" by denying "evil": the "evil" grows and grows until it becomes too powerful to be contained within the unconscious. That's when it starts to leak out into our everyday lives. If we continue to deny evil, it eventually "possesses" us, and we become The Devil. That's why The Devil Key is the mirror image of The Lovers. Considered together, they clearly convey the message that human consciousness can be either angelic or devilish: whether we create Heaven or Hell depends on the choices we make. These choices can be fearful, because of the possibility of making a mistake that has dire consequences. But to allow fear to paralyze our thinking (because we

THE LOVERS.

THE DEVIL .

THE DIVINE FAMILY.

cannot bear to choose) means that we get Hell by default, because living in fear is like living in Hell. The antidote to fear is *trust*: trust in life, trust in ourselves, and trust in other people. If we look to The Lovers yet a third time, we will see that it shows us how to develop that trust. The man (consciousness) looks to the woman (subconsciousness), and the woman looks to the Archangel (superconsciousness). This tells us that the road to higher consciousness inevitably begins with a descent into subconsciousness, where we become aware of our wounds and develop the self-compassion necessary to heal them.

The problem of fear is familiar turf for most Sixes, because they are the type most obviously prone to worry and anxiety. Many are extremely sensitive to energy, and pick up on psychic impressions very easily. So they are all too aware of the subconscious. What they are typically less aware of is how to work intelligently with it, allowing their dreams, visions, or other experiences to illuminate their inner world. In the absence of understanding, they may see such experiences as either signs of mental illness or demonic possession. So it's little wonder that they are often reluctant to delve beneath surface of life, relying on mental props like rules and routines to keep life "safe."

Staying on the surface of life can reduce anxiety but doesn't make it go away. The only way to defeat fear is with courage, which is based on love (from the French, *coeur* = heart). Courage can be cultivated, along with patience and humor. Patience defeats panic (by slowing down time) and humor defeats negative projections (by showing them to be the gross exaggerations that they really are)! The founders of the Golden Dawn gave us a clue about the true nature of The Devil when they assigned him the quality of *mirth*. This tells us that they saw him more as funny than bad. Meditating on the quality of mirth may be helpful for seeing through The Devil's disguise.

THE DIVINE FAMILY (24) depicts the outcome of integration, both within an individual and a relationship. The Lovers is a beautiful card, but the paradise it depicts is based on the illusion that it's possible to remain like children for our entire lives. Its real purpose is to give us a vision of what we can create once we have reconciled our quest for Light with our fear of Darkness. The truth is that both are two sides of the same coin: we cannot have one without including the other. How we resolve the problem of "Light vs Dark" determines whether our journey through life takes us into the realm of *myth* or the realm of *fantasy*.

Dreams can provide clues about the difference between the two. The night prior to the 2016 U. S. presidential election, I had a dream where a pink house on a glass foundation slid down a mountain, damaging other houses at the bottom. I did not understand it at all. But the next day, when the election results came in, I realized it was about the loss of the female (pink) candidate. The days following the election, everywhere I went, people were stunned. I finally stopped going out to public gatherings for a while, because of the unsettledness in the community. A few nights later, I had a second dream that began much like the first, except that this time, I was looking down on the scene from on high. Then I saw an intricate and beautiful tapestry which was mesmerizing in its exquisite detail. There were patterns of *order* and patterns of *chaos* on the tapestry; the latter were at a 90° angle from the former. (Hard to explain, but that's how it was!) When I woke up, I understood that both patterns were essential to make the tapestry complete.

This dream did not conform to my idealized expectations about "how things should be" in life. Instead, it presented me with an image whose beauty defied my expectations. That's how I knew it must be real.

If faith is what we need to transcend our fears of The Devil, imagination is what we need to transcend our faith in a limited vision of what is possible. Interestingly, Key 6 is often associated with the Hebrew letter *Zain*, "sword" and Key 15 with *Ayin*, "eye." The first is about separating our ideas in a way that allows us to analyze them (into their three aspects of the Angel, the man, and the women) and the second is about *seeing through* the nature of illusion, both positive and negative.

To transcend illusion requires both courage and common sense, the same qualities that allow us to develop healthy relationships and stable communities. While we often think of family in connection with blood relatives, a family is really any closely-bonded group whose members serve as a source of loving support. In the image on Key 24, there is no grand vision of either heaven or hell. Instead, we see a couple clothed in attractive attire (better to preserve the sense of mystery that enhances mutual attraction). This is a mature relationship; the woman looks self-confident and the man seems receptive to both his wife and child. He carries a basket of food, including a fish fresh from the market.

When activity (male energy) is balanced by receptivity (female energy), the result is a zest for life (a child). The temple in the background shows us that inner balance leads to balanced relationships that in turn serve as the basis for an enlightened culture (the beautiful temple). Beyond the temple is a small path leading to the same mountain we saw in Key 6, because there is a direct relationship between inner transformation and outer culture.

Symbolically, this third octave of Six represents the state of mind achieved by those who reconcile the opposites within them. The greatest barrier to this resolution is the belief that it is an impossible task. This path tells us that nothing is impossible: anything we can dare to imagine we can become. Most of all, it tells us that this is our heritage as sovereign beings, that we have both the right and the responsibility to leave the garden of our childhood illusions.

Enneagram Sixes may initially find it daunting to contemplate the reconciliation of such polar opposites as the Angel and the Devil. But this is not only possible; it is the certain result of choosing love over fear. Sixes willing to make this choice are those capable of joining together to create harmonious families and thriving communities.

Notes

[1] Key 4 shows the mature ego, a person who has gone as far as he can using ego alone. To go further, "the King must die," as James George Frazier observes in *The Golden Bough*. Each Emperor/King symbolizes a particular season or cycle in life—a season when the sun is high and we are at the peak of our powers. But it's a season that will not last forever. This is why the King must die: both to make way for the renewal of life and to free the King from his bondage to matter.

[2] I am a Four on the enneagram. Interestingly, I once had a numinous dream where I was escorted by a phalanx of fully-armored medieval knights into the Spanish desert and left there to fend for myself. This initiated a very "dry" period in my life where I spent a lot of time alone. The experience was not always pleasant but it did provide ample opportunity for self-reflection.

[3] On the enneagram, Points 4 and 5 are separated by the "gap" at the bottom of the circle, a gap that is often likened to the Abyss, the Void, or the Nothingness. Thus, the enneagram visibly depicts the idea of that involution (Points 1–4) is followed by the move into a transitional place that is akin to death (and that is associated with a complete change of polarity, from feminine involution to masculine evolution).

[4] In Greek mythology, the Goddess Iris is the personification of the rainbow and messenger of the gods. As the sun unites Earth and heaven, Iris links the gods to humanity. She travels with the speed of wind from one end of the world to the other, and into the depths of the sea and the underworld. See https://www.princeton.edu/.../Iris_(mythology).html.

[5] There is another phase that is sometimes included in alchemical descriptions: the *peacock* or *phoenix* sub-phase of many colors that is usually seen as coming after the *nigredo*, and is associated with the iris or rainbow. It is the point where something begins to rise from the ashes—to move towards the golden crown of Wisdom at the end of the winding road that leads up a high peak in the far distance.

[6] The story goes like this: A chickpea leaps almost over the rim of the pot, where it's being boiled. "Why are you doing this to me?" The cook knocks him down with the ladle. "Don't you try to jump out. You think I'm torturing you, [but]I'm giving you flavor, so you can mix with spices and rice, and be the lovely vitality of a human being." Source: *Chickpea to Cook* by Rumi.

14:
Enneagram Paths 7-8-9

Path of Liberation – Type 7
The Chariot (7) – The Tower (16) – Merkaba (25)

THE CHARIOT (7) depicts a wonderfully bold young man who looks like he's raring to set out on an adventure. In his shiny armor and impressive crown, he looks the very image of the hero. And The Chariot is pretty impressive-looking, too: big wheels, solid body, and a starry canopy at the top. Not to mention the two amazing-looking sphinx (or is it sphinxes?) ready to do his bidding.[1] But wait. There seems to be a problem here. Although the sphinx look powerful, they aren't actually hooked up to The Chariot. And there's no reins, either. So how's the hero supposed to drive this Rube Goldberg contraption?

He does it with his *will*. For this is the Key that demonstrates the power of trained will to make things happen in the world. It's the same will that The Magician (1) exerts, only now it's been trained, polished, and prepared for real-time action in the outside world. The training is important, because without it the sphinx won't pull in the same direction (one's black and one's white, so you know they've got different priorities). So the priority at this Key is the ability to gather up one's energies in a way that allows them to go exactly where they are directed. A charioteer without self-control or a goal that inspires him can easily waste most of his time and energy on diverse activities without really getting anywhere in particular.

Sevens on the enneagram are very like the charioteer: young, excited, and raring to go. Even older Sevens seem youngish; they have a spirit of youth that Jung expressed as the archetype of the *puer*—the Eternal Youth. They see the world as their playground, and are usually avid travelers that enjoy learning about diverse cultures. Sevens especially value their freedom, the ability to be footloose and fancy-free. They are quick to adapt to changing circumstances and can usually blend into whatever environment they encounter in their travels.

Sevens have an androgynous quality that makes male Sevens seem somewhat feminine and female Sevens seem somewhat masculine. Because the charioteer is male, we see this feminine quality reflected in Key 7 in the charioteer's face & golden locks, the moons on his epaulets, and the prominent breasts on the Sphinx (all of which are related to The Moon, The Chariot's planetary ruler.)[2]

The biggest problem for Sevens is often "too much of a good thing." They are blessed with so many talents and interests that they can easily become overwhelmed by the task of trying to get them under control. So they can easily end up like the charioteer, all dressed up with nowhere to go (without a sense of inner direction). It is all too easy for them to spend a big chunk of their lives up in the air, never quite committing to anyone or anything. It can sometimes take a sudden shock to bring them down to earth.

That's where **THE TOWER (16)** comes in. At The Tower, anything too far up in the air (too far removed from real life) is sent crashing back to earth, because it has become ungrounded. This card depicts the kind of events with the power to separate the real from the unreal in our lives. Such events instantly bring us back to earth, allowing us see what really matters. The lightning bolt is shaped very much like the Lightning Flash on the Tree of Life, the sudden descent of divine energy that brings everything in life into physical manifestation. This tells us that it is not inherently destructive. It only seems destructive when it hits our most cherished illusions—the ones that really have to go.

Most of us are afraid of Tower experiences, because of their suddenness and intensity. But even negative Tower experiences are actually a gift, not a punishment, because they force us out of situations that make it hard to move forwards in life. (The fiery *yods*—flames—that rain down represent a shower of divine grace).

Sevens often attract Tower experiences because of their amazing tendency to glide through situations that would easily sink another type. Given the chance, the mentally agile Seven will think up some way to escape his problems, often using guile, cleverness, or even trickery; he is the perfect trickster hero, like the one we see in the RWS Seven of Swords. The only problem is that he is sometimes too clever for his own good. If he only wants the fun experiences of the hero's journey—rather than the hard ones that have the power to change him—then Tower experiences give him a

THE CHARIOT.

THE TOWER.

MERKABA.

challenge that even he can't escape. By stripping him of everything that he hasn't actually earned, they compel him to re-evaluate his actions.

But for the mature and focused Seven, Tower experiences can represent the "Eureka!" moment that comes to those who stubbornly refuse to give up their quest to achieve some result or solve some problem. It can also represent a spiritual breakthrough that comes quite suddenly. To David Allen Hulse, The Tower represents a kundalini awakening (in the East) or the manifestation of the secret fire of the alchemists (in the West): "It is the spiritual force that descends upon the seeker with such great force, and in the blink of an eye,…transforms the direction of life forever."[3]

A MERKABA (25) is the light body "vehicle" that allows embodied human beings to move beyond the confines of the physical vehicle to other dimensions of consciousness. "Merkaba" breaks down as "mer" (light), "ka" (spirit), "ba" (body), so it is the light body that is the natural companion of our denser physical body. It is the "wheels within wheels" of Ezekiel and the subject of the *merkaba* meditation widely taught by Drunvalo Melchizidek since the 1980s. More recently, it has been associated with the spirals of energy that we see in DNA, with the idea that human DNA is evolving so as to encompass more light, that humankind might be raised up to a higher level of awareness.

The figure of the *merkaba* can be portrayed in different ways, because it is extremely complex and can be used for many purposes. It brings into play the principles of sacred geometry, the esoteric properties of both the diatonic and chromatic scales, the Tree of Life, and the enneagram![4] For our purposes here, it suffices to say that it is a symbol of the divine vehicle that contains human consciousness in its embodied form. We encounter Key 25 at a point in our inner journey when this vehicle is changing—expanding in ways that makes two things possible: a greater expression of consciousness in the 3-D world and the ability to "travel" to other dimensions of embodied consciousness (the 4-D, 5-D, and even higher dimensions of being). The *merkaba* provides us with the light body we need to become a "tourist of the Cosmos."

But in a more everyday sense, the merkaba is anything that becomes the impetus for becoming more open to spontaneity, creativity, and fun, while at the same time enabling us to maintain a sense of inner attention and focus. It gives us the power to travel freely but requires us to use that power with grace and maturity. The purpose of The Tower is to show us what happens when we fail to maintain a balance between freedom and responsibility. The purpose of the merkaba is to show us what is possible when we can achieve that kind of balance.

Enneagram Sevens love to travel—both physically and mentally—but have a harder time finding a way to integrate their diverse ideas and experiences into a unified whole. It's as though their lives are "all plot and no theme." To find lasting fulfillment, they must discover the theme around which those experiences revolve. This is what is meant by cultivating the inner attention and bringing it into balance with our outer activities. Sevens who can do this are able to evolve from mere pleasure-seekers without an agenda into "messengers of the Gods" (innovators with the power and imagination to open other people to new dimensions of being).

Path of Ascension – Type 8

Strength (8) – The Star (17) – The Divine Monad (26)

Strength is an attribute ever popular with heroes. Both physical strength and courage (strength of heart) give them the necessary fortitude to both survive the journey and to triumph over adversity. But **STRENGTH (8)** as a Key depicts a strange image: a beatific woman clothed in white (for purity) with a figure-8 lemniscus over her head (a sign of eternity and reciprocity).[5] Bedecked in roses (devotion), she leans over a great red lion, holding its mouth with her hand (yes, it's really red, although it looks orange in most colored cards). This is the Red Lion of Desire: the part of our desire nature that is wild, free, and potentially predatory. Untamed, it can ruin our lives. Tempered by love, it can be a creative force that we use to accomplish the Great Work of transformation (the distant mountain).

This Key depicts the reciprocal relationship between love and the instincts. For not only does the woman love the lion; the lion loves her back. He looks at her with gentle eyes, obedient to her every command. The figure-8 lemniscus depicts the reciprocity of this relationship, showing both how love is the force that animates the physical body and how that embodied force (the kundalini) is raised in response to love. It also depicts the actual form of this "serpent-force" as it flows up the spine when the time is right. If the lemniscus over The Magician's head depicts "as above, so below," the lemniscus over Strength's head depicts "as below, so above" (the power of the feminine energy of subconsciousness, to raise up or "redeem" the animal instincts).

The reciprocity of this relationship calls to mind the medieval ideal of courtly love that helped elevate the culture of Europe by introducing a new code of conduct that defined the spiritual relationship between Lover and Beloved. It came out of the culture of the troubadours, who circulated among the courts of Europe singing songs of courtly love and chivalry inspired by the mystical love poetry of the Sufis. The following description offers a short but expressive description of the chivalric ideal:

> The ideal in courtly love was to embody the archetypal forces of Lover and Beloved. The Beloved was...to embody the ideal of the Divine Feminine, Sophia, Divine Wisdom. She was to be ever slightly out of reach, but within sight. Her presence was to draw the Lover with her presence, her goodness,

her feminine divinity....The Lover...was to seek his Beloved, his idealized Lady. He had to prove himself worthy of her, face great obstacles with humility and perseverance, in her name.[6]

The code of chivalry radically changed the culture of Europe by transforming an entire class of armed and dangerous men (i.e., knights) into high-minded lovers looking to win the privilege of kissing the hand of the ladies to whom they pledged their devotion. In so doing, chivalry sublimated the instincts in a way that greatly elevated the civilization of the times. It may have been the single greatest factor that set the stage for the emergence of the Renaissance a century later.

The chivalric code is an ideal that Eights on the enneagram can readily relate to. For while they are the most charismatic, powerful, and instinctually-driven type on the enneagram, they are potentially the most devoted. Like the knights of the Middle Ages, they instinctively seek an object worthy of their devotion, because they understand in their gut the reciprocal relationship between love and power: how balancing the two can manifest great changes.

Eights are known for their leadership, dominance, and sheer animal magnetism; they lead in a highly personal way, by asking no more of their followers than they are prepared to do themselves. However, because of their formidable physical stamina, they can often do much more than the average person, so they can be tough leaders to follow. They have no patience with half-hearted efforts and, once invested in a project, will do everything possible to bring it to fruition. The difficulty can be in finding something or someone in life that truly inspires them. It can't be any old thing; it has to be something worthy of their devotion. But they really need that inspiration, because without it, they find it hard to appropriately channel the life force within them. It is too powerful to suppress, and if frustrated can leak out as explosive anger and an overpowering lust (appetite) that is almost impossible to satisfy.

Both Type 8 on the enneagram and Key 8 in the tarot are specifically associated with the quality of lust. In the enneagram community, lust is often

STRENGTH.

THE STAR.

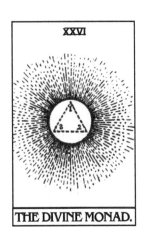

THE DIVINE MONAD.

said to be the "vice" associated with Type 8 (although Eights themselves don't necessarily see it as a vice, because it's also a powerful motivating energy). In the tarot, Aleister Crowley calls the Strength Key by the name of Lust. So it's not surprising his Thoth deck shows the woman boldly riding a lion, not just touching its mouth! (It's likely that Crowley preferred the image of "lust inflamed by passion" to the image of "lust tempered by love.") On the enneagram, Point 8 (lust) is directly linked with Point 2 (love), through the inner line that connects them. And Point 2 is said to be the "heart point" of Eight: an influence that brings out its gentler, more tender side.

If the vice for Eights is lust, the virtue is innocence: the very quality we see depicted at THE STAR (17). Love is so transformative that when it raises up the primal instincts, the results can be dramatic: a state of wonder that heals and inspires. Everything about this Key is magical: the pool, the sky, the stars, the fertile land. The woman pouring the water, the rose-covered figure at Strength, and The High Priestess are all symbols of the Goddess Isis in all of her manifestations. As The High Priestess, she is heavily veiled and hidden from sight; as Strength, she is clothed only in white (purity); as the woman in The Star, she is finally revealed in her naked and innocent glory.

Key 17 symbolically depicts the state of the individual who has found both her feminine intuition (the waters of life) and masculine inspiration (the starlit sky). This allows her to commune with her own soul (the sacred ibis) and replenish her own inner waters (by pouring water into the pool). She can also share her sense of inspiration with others (by pouring it onto the land). At this point, this is not yet a permanent state. It's a glimpse of things to come, a vision of what can happen "when you wish upon a star."

For the enneagram Eight, life can seem like an endless series of battles—power struggles to become the "top dog" in any situation. In part, this is because the Eight is a natural leader who is always ready to take charge. There is often the sense that groups without leaders need direction, and Eights are usually prepared to provide it. What they do not realize is that groups can also be participant-led, although Eights seldom wait long enough to determine whether this is in fact the situation. Thus, some of their conflicts with others come from their inability to grasp the idea that mature individuals need no leader to organize their affairs but can live by the light of their own star (according to their own intuitions). Eights often bump their heads a lot before becoming sensitized to some of the more subtle currents that play a role in life, especially in personal relationships. Often, they have been hurt when they were young and vulnerable, and as a result adopted the kind of cynical persona designed to protect their feelings. Truth be told, they are probably the most emotionally vulnerable type on the enneagram circle, although you might never know it from their action-oriented manner. The Star symbolizes the possibility that the innocence they lost early in life can be fully restored to them, so they can once again drink freely from the waters of life. For this to happen, they must willingly take down their formidable defenses, so that the walls they have erected for protection do not block the light of their own inner star. Eights who can summon up the courage to let their guard down can experience both improved relationships and a renewed sense of hope for the future.

THE DIVINE MONAD (26) represents the complete unification of the incarnated human being in all of its many aspects: the masculine self (at One), feminine self (at Two), creative self (at Three), personal self (at Four), alchemical self (at Five), balanced self (at Six), and self as light body (at Seven). There is also a pre-self at Point 0 (which represents the Fool on the cusp of becoming a self) and a post-self at Point 9 (which represents the Fool on the cusp of moving from self-hood to a state beyond the self).

Key 26 symbolizes the apex of what is possible in the evolution of a single human being: the individual with the power to fully incarnate his potential. This is the fully unified Self, such as is depicted in the archetype of the Ascended Master, a human being who exercises mastery through the power of love. This kind of mastery is the ultimate outcome of a transformational process—a process that has three aspects, as we have seen.[7]

The imagery used to symbolize The Divine Monad is designed to depict the concept of *unity in diversity*: the idea that mastery is achieved by finding a way to transform diverse activity into one unified locus of action. It comes from a 19th-century pen-and-ink drawing that shows a triangle within a circle, a triangle positioned exactly the same way that the enneagram triangle is positioned within the enneagram circle. The circle seems to be scintillating; it looks like the sun at mid-day. The numbering of the three vertices of the triangle focuses our attention on the two aspects of consciousness (masculine and feminine) that must be balanced to produce a unified psyche (the number 1 at the top). Once we have an equilateral triangle, we have by implication the circle that inscribes it.

Enneagram Eights represent both the lowest and highest potential in a human being: they have both the strongest instinctual appetites and the greatest potential to render service to all life, once those appetites been raised up and directed towards some worthwhile goal.

The path of an Eight is never easy, because it involves powerful energies that tend to push an individual to extremes. The only way to work with such power is to go beyond mere self-discipline (which will curb but never tame the beast) to discover the only force powerful enough to effect genuine transformation: the unlimited power of love. Nothing less will suffice.

But Eights who have the courage to confront the raw power of instinct and the patience to learn how to make that power his servant can realize a degree of inner development that is available to only the very few.

Type 9 – Path of Divine Possibility
The Fool (0) – The Hermit (9) – The Moon (18) – Divine Mystery (27)

This path is unique in possessing four Keys, not three. This is because it includes The Fool, which plays a unique archetypal role. **THE FOOL (0)** is the ultimate symbol of paradox in my imagined Tarot of the Enneagram. It can be either the first Key or the last Key; the "every" Key or the "no" Key; the "foolish fool" (who strives earnestly to complete the journey) or the "wise fool" (the open-to-life experiencer who has no goals). Although this Key can be described, it can never be pinned down. As a result, The Fool will always stand apart from the other 27 Keys in the major tarot. We cannot leave it out of the nine paths but cannot fully include it, either.

The discussion below describes the Fool at both the beginning and the end of the journey. But it also includes a unique image for Key 27 which highlights that aspect of The Fool that is not part of the journey but which serves as both its source and its ultimate destination (see Chapters 9 and 16 for a discussion).

As the first Key in the ordinal sequence of Keys 0–21, The Fool (0) is often said to represent a young person curious about the world, but who is also naïve and inexperienced. He's open to life but unsure of how to proceed. His colorful dress looks fun, but it's really more appropriate for a fancy dinner than a wilderness trek. But The Fool doesn't seem to care or even notice. He's not in any hurry to get anywhere, but rambles happily over the terrain, literally "smelling the roses." Of course, we as observers can't help but wonder how he can be so carefree in such dangerous terrain, especially since he's about to walk off a cliff. Even if it's just a foot high ledge, that's still enough to break a leg. If he's lucky, he'll see this as a wake-up call and begin to pay more attention to where he's going. Or maybe he'll avoid calamity altogether by paying attention to the little dog (his helpful instincts).

Key 0 offers a particularly apt representation of Type 9 on the enneagram. Young Nines tend to have exactly the same carefree, easygoing attitude about life. So they often start out by following more decisive friends with goals that Nines will happily "borrow" until they find something better. Once they get going (even on someone else's path), they tend to keep going, as long as their experiences seem agreeable. However, at some point, the Nine usually begins to realize that he really needs his own path, not another's. He finds this realization disconcerting, because it means he's going to have to start making his own decisions and taking responsibility for them. And that is often the Nine's greatest challenge, because he is happiest when just blending into his surroundings; the expression "going with the flow" must have been invented with this type in mind. Taking charge of his life will require him to step out of the flow and become his own person.

THE HERMIT (9) is the second archetype that represents Point 9 in the Arc of the Day. Here we see The Fool transformed into someone who is much more sober and inwardly attuned. Gone is the frivolous fellow clad in flamboyant attire (the youthful persona). The Hermit's outer garments are gray (showing he's more balanced); the heavy robe (his inner attention) protects his dazzling light from leaking out. He is in control of this inner light, and he can direct it into the lantern that helps fellow wanderers find their way through the wilderness of life. At this point, though, The Fool is no longer wandering. He stands perfectly still, content to serve as a beacon for the next set of lost Fools.

On the enneagram, The Hermit represents the unfolding of the mystical potential of the Nine. One of the gifts of the Nine is an innate understanding of the rhythms of the natural world. Nines almost always feel at home in nature, even in wild places far from civilization. They often find it initially hard to look within. But once they do, they find a natural oneness that appeals to their harmony-seeking nature. As Hermits, Nines discover that the world of outer experience reflects an even more interesting world within—a realization that will stay with them when they descend back into the valley of ordinary life. The ability to access their inner light will serve them well in that world. But it's going to be even more helpful during the descent into the darkness of Banzhaf's Arc of the Night.[8]

THE HERMIT.

THE MOON.

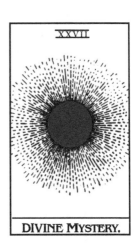

DIVINE MYSTERY.

The third Key in the journey of the Nine is **THE MOON** (18), which represents the very last stage in the Arc of the Night. As the last Key before the return of the light, The Moon naturally presents many challenges. It tests the hero's will to persevere, both mentally and physically, under extreme duress. It also tests his discernment, which he must carefully exercise if he wants to avoid getting separated from the path. Because it's a long trek back, there will be many obstacles. Some are scary, like the creepy crustacean (subconscious impulses), the wolf (the untamed will), and the ominous twin towers (mental doubt and fear). Others are more subtle, which is why they don't appear right away. These may look more alluring than frightening (like the poppy field that tempts Dorothy to leave the yellow brick road). Whatever the challenge, the hero must maintain both his focus and composure, if he wants to make it all the way home.

The need to persevere under duress tests the Nine's ability to override his "happy wanderer" tendencies. The Night journey home is arduous, and anyone either unwilling or unable to push through the pain is not going to make it to the end. And there will be pain, because any hero who arrives at this point in the journey is at the very edge of his limits. Nines find pain hard to deal with. This is not because they're wimps but because it seriously disrupts their sense of oneness with life. That's why they tend to fuzz out (let go of their inner attention): so they can go unconscious to anything that might create a sense of separation. But if they fall asleep here, their Night Journey is sure to come to an unfortunate end. A related obstacle for Nines is their natural curiosity. Normally, curiosity is fine, but not during The Night Journey! And for Nines, it can be yet another way to avoid being present in the moment. So this journey is a tailor-made test for the oh-so-distractible Nine, whose attention is by nature diffused. That quality of diffusion is great for casual strolling (the Fool) or meditation (The Hermit), but it becomes a liability at The Moon, where only the most rapt attention to one's situation will keep a hero on the path.

But Nines also have some qualities that will serve them well on the journey home. They are adaptable to changing conditions; they instinctively know how to roll with the punches and just keep going. They also know how to leave the past behind, which helps them stay focused in the moment. They are also open to advice from others (especially higher sources) and more than willing to ask for help. And their love of nature and lack of duplicity often attract help from unexpected sources, especially at the moment it's most needed.

As the last Key in the ordinal sequence of Keys 0–27, **DIVINE MYSTERY** (27) symbolizes our understanding of life at the completion of the journey (if there is such a thing as completion). It depicts the highest octave of The Fool—and thus the point of origin for not only The Fool but the entire tarot. In qabala, it is the *Ain*, which literally means "no" in Hebrew; in Sufi mysticism, *Allah* means "The Great Nothing"; in the enneagram, Key 27 symbolizes the zero point on the top of the circle. It expresses the mystery that everything in the created Cosmos (the "Cosmos of Something-ness") came from the Uncreated. It is also the First Principle that governs the existence of every human being.

We are all The Fool. We all participate in the mystery of existence but are ultimately non-existent. We are part of the One that emanates from the Nothingness. Everything about us is a paradox. We start the journey without that sense of identity which separates us from the whole; yet by realizing that identity, we return to the Whole. We return with something new, and bring this "something" to the Nothingness that is somehow enriched by it. Such a statement makes no logical sense, does it? And yet it rings true on an intuitive level. The image on Key 27 is identical to the image on Key 26, except that the three-in-one unity has become the radiant Nothingness that is the source of all things in manifestation.

It is interesting to me that there is an actual enneagram type—Type 9—that embodies the archetype of the Divine Mystery. Because if Point 0 symbolizes the Nothingness, how can it also be a temperament type? This is yet another paradox that remains unexplained.

However, Type 9 clearly exists. It serves as the root type out of which all the other eight types arise. And yet it exists in its own right (just like The Fool).Understanding this type can benefit all the other types, because it reveals something fundamental about human nature: both its ineffable origins in non-existence and its ultimate potential (to express the Divine Mystery of non-existence while actually existing in a human body).

As we have seen, it is difficult for Nines to separate from the Oneness into which we are born. But life in a body brings separation. Even if this separation is an illusion, it's a powerful illusion. And it's an illusion that exists for a purpose: so that we the chance to experience transformation. So the hero's journey is about experiencing a sense of separation from the Divine Mystery in order to return to it having experienced something new. But to experience something new, we must become individuals. That is what happens as we grow from infancy to adulthood.

However, Nines tend to resist this process, because it means becoming less identified with the Oneness. I once met a women who had saved up the funds to spend a year traveling around, looking for answers about life. She related her experience spending the winter in a remote Alaskan village where the long winters and isolation caused some of the residents to engage in incest. Most people would this find pretty shocking. But when she related her story, it was with such dispassion that I almost didn't realize what she was saying. Towards the end of the conversation, she indicated her disappointment that her trip had thus far not given her the answers she was seeking. That's when I realized she was probably a Nine: because it was so hard for her to really "take in" the experiences she was having. I also remember thinking that, no matter how long she spent traveling, she probably wasn't going to get her questions answered until she was ready to allow life to pierce the veil of her self-protective illusions.

These illusions arise from valuing peace and harmony so much that it is the only thing we see—just as the beauty of the high mountains is the only thing The Fool sees, even as he's about to step into the unknown. To actually create harmony in the world means being willing to experience its disharmony, whether we are talking about the outer environment or the world within us. To realize how disharmonious life can be is always a disconcerting experience (just ask any teen). But it need not be a shameful experience, if we see ourselves as adventurers or explorers, rather than fallen creatures in need of redemption.

Mature Nines are the ones who were brave enough to undertake the hero's journey of separation—to walk three times around the enneagram circle, finally making their way home to their point of origin. Upon their return, they find themselves able to experience the Divine Mystery in an entirely new way. Instead of unconsciously losing themselves in forgetfulness, they now remember who they are and the nature of their divine heritage. They are conscious of what they experience but do not feel the need to judge it. And they possess a sense of inner calm that harmonizes the world around them. They have become the source of the harmony they sought, rather than its perennial seeker.

The nature of this state is captured in the remarks of Chogram Trungpa Rinpoche on the last of the Zen Ox Herding pictures:

> Nirmanakaya [the absence of self-nature] is the fully awakened state of being in the world. Its action is like the moon reflecting in a hundred bowls of water. The moon has no desire to reflect, but that is its nature. This state is dealing with the earth with ultimate simplicity...[not] following the example of anyone....You destroy whatever needs to be destroyed, you subdue whatever needs to be subdued, and you care for whatever needs your care.

So ends our hero's journey through the tarot and the enneagram. See the frontispiece for a depiction of all nine paths on the enneagram. You will notice that this graphic actually shows ten paths, because there are two versions of the path for Point 0/9: one for the curious Fool who perennially seeks out new experiences and the other for The Hermit (who is in perennial meditation on the Divine Mystery).

Notes

[1] Merriam-Webster says the plural is "sphinges." No way, I'm sticking with "sphinx."

[2] This astrological assignment is from the Golden Dawn; in the Continental system described in Appendix E, Part II, The Chariot is associated with Gemini, which would focus our attention on its wandering, peripatetic character. Also, because Gemini is associated with Mercury, it emphasizes the mercurial, changing character of the charioteer.

[3] *New Dimensions of the Cube of Space: The Path of Initiation Revealed by the Tarot Upon the Qabalistic Cube* (Weiser: 2000), p. 43.

[4] According to Drunvalo's original teachings, the *merkaba* is a star tetrahedron consisting of two counter-rotating tetrahedrons, one male and one female, which all humans possess but which must be activated if these fields are to move. In a 2011 video, Drunvalo said that there is actually a third stationary tetrahedron, as well (google "Information on Ascension and the Merkaba," available on YouTube at https://www.youtube.com/watch?v=7ix149wD_IU&feature=youtu.be). Interestingly, Drunvalo's teachings equate the merkaba with the diatonic scale—which is precisely the scale that Gurdjieff mapped onto the enneagram (see p. 289 in Ouspensky's *In Search of the Miraculous*, 2001); see also Chapter 9 and Fig. E-6 in Appendix E. Drunvalo also cites Gurdjieff as speaking of a polarity switch in the middle of a scale, which would almost certainly be a reference to Gurdjieff's teachings on the enneagram as detailed by Ouspensky. Drunvalo's comments can be found on pp. 312-313 of *The Ancient Secret of the Flower of Life*, Vol. 2 (Clear Light Trust: 2000); see also my comments on the nadir of the enneagram, which is where the polarity switch occurs, in Chapter 8. My conclusion is that the two-dimensional (flat) enneagram can also be accurately represented as a three-dimensional merkaba. See Figs. E-7a and E-7b in Appendix E and the surrounding discussion for more on the merkaba and the enneagram.

[5] The following discussion of the lemniscus is worth sharing here: "Behind the woman and the lion, the analemma is drawn in the sky. Also known as the lemniscate, from the Latin Lemniscus, meaning ribbon, the analemma represents the position of the sun at noon over an entire year. Before the advent of electronic navigation, and using only a sextant and the date, mariners could calculate their latitude anywhere on earth using the information in the analemma. In the same way, if you know your inner strength, you can navigate anything that life brings you." Source: www.theschoolforwizards.co.

[6] See http://www.hopedance.org/home/awakenings/53-blogs/soul2/1809-troubadours-sufis-romantic-love-cathars-and-more.

[7] For a discussion on the threefold nature of transformational processes, see, e.g., Fig. 4-2, Table 4-1, Table 10-1, and Fig. 15-1 and the surrounding discussion. Please note that in the original version of this print, the positions of 2 and 3 are reversed; I recomposed the graphic so that it would reflect the clockwise 1-2-3 transformational progression depicted on the enneagram (just as I reversed the direction of The Fool on the front cover, so it would be moving clockwise).

[8] It is interesting that both The Fool and The Hermit stand at the very top of the world, because the Nine on the enneagram is at the very top of the world, as well—at the very top of the enneagram circle. Maybe that is why The Moon Key represents The Fool's shadow: because it takes him to the depths of the subconscious, which is the polar opposite of the superconscious peaks of Keys 0 and 9. (And what of Key 27, the black hole, which possesses neither height, depth, nor any other manifest quality?)

15:
Applications of the Model

Three things cannot be long hidden: the sun, the moon, and the truth.
– Gautama Buddha

NOW THE 27-KEY MODEL IS COMPLETE. In the last three chapters, we looked at the unique qualities of each three-octave path. In this chapter, we'll look at how this nine-path model can be used in both enneagram and tarot work. There is also a section discussing its use with a conventional 22-Key deck. But let's begin with a summary of the completed model and a description of its three Arcs.

A Three-Arc Model

Fig. 15-1 (next page) shows its three octaves—the Arc of the Day, Arc of the Night, and Arc of the Goal—on the enneagram. The images are small but large enough to reveal the overall pattern. The three enneagrams in this figure are placed on a spiral to remind us that different Arcs (octaves) are part of an endless spiral that has neither beginning nor end.

The basis for this model was discussed in Chapter 1, which introduced Hajo Banzhaf's two-Arc 22-Key tarot model consisting of the Arc of the Day and Arc of the Night, where the first Arc consists of Keys 1–9 (each representing an archetypal potential) and the second consists of Keys 10–18 (each representing an archetypal challenge). The three remaining Keys (19–21) represent the Jungian goal of reconciling the opposites to create psychic wholeness. But because there are only three cards remaining, we can only see the specific nature of the resolution phase for three of these nine paths, leaving six paths unresolved (see pp. 8–9).

Chapter 5 further explored this model, focusing on Banzhaf's depiction of the hero's journey through Keys 0–21 from a Jungian perspective. Chapter 10 discussed two existing 27-Key tarot models, Rosengarten's and Gotthold's, as well as the tarot constellations approach developed by Arrien and Greer. Chapter 11 introduced the new enneagram-based 27-Key model with six new Keys and nine three-octave paths. Chapters 12–14 provided detailed descriptions of the new Keys and paths.

What follows is a description of the model broken down by its three Arcs.

The **ARC OF THE DAY** introduces us to nine unique characters, each of which plays a different role in life. Alternatively, we can think of them as nine archetypal stages in life, since the images are arranged in an order which can

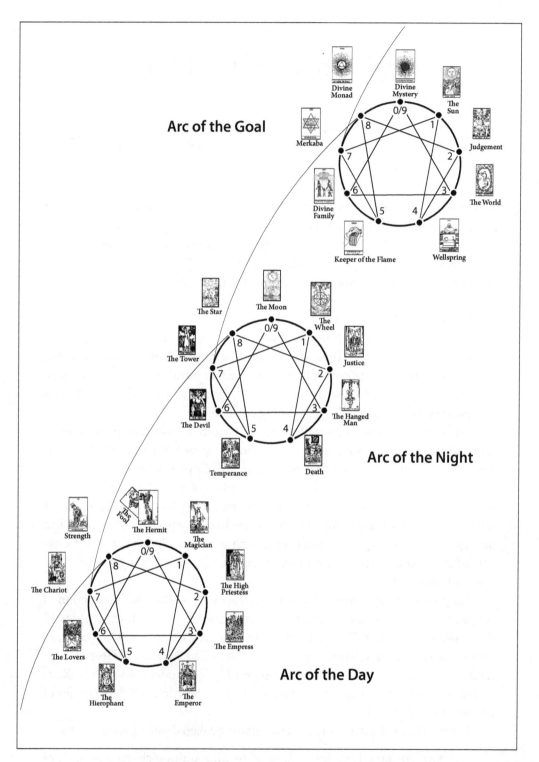

FIG. 15-1. The Three Arcs on the Enneagram.

depict the move from innocence (The Fool) to wisdom (The Hermit).* I have described them in this book as both nine temperament types and nine paths in life, both of which can be mapped onto the enneagram. In the context of the hero's journey, they represents mental ideals to which we aspire, but are not likely to fully embody, at least not when we are young. Each one offers a glimpse of what is possible, should we be willing to take on the challenges of the Arc of the Night (the shadow aspects of the psyche). This Arc also foreshadows those challenges so that we can begin to learn how to use our strengths to compensate for our weaknesses. But the first nine archetypes mainly focus on our strengths, in recognition of the fact that the first part of life is about getting inspired enough to set forth into the world, in search some new goal or dream.

The **ARC OF THE NIGHT** describes the challenges that confront us when we begin to scratch the surface of our fears and aversions. In *The Intelligent Enneagram*, A. G. E. Blake speaks of the second octave in a transformational process as the phase in which we "*have to bear the contradiction in our own work so that it can then be resolved by the third force*" (emphasis his, p. 233). Here Blake gives us a subtle clue about why the second octave can be such a challenge: because it makes us aware of the "contradiction in our own work." Jungian analyst Edward Whitmont is more direct. He observes that the shadow is that part of the personality that "has been repressed for the sake of an ego ideal. Since everything unconscious is projected, we encounter the shadow in projection—in our view of 'the other fellow.' "[1] In shadow work, the projection bounces back on the one who projects it, compelling that person to suddenly know the real truth about these projections. This is an extremely painful realization, so painful that it often has the power to turn people back early in the process. In Jung's words, "One does not become enlightened by imagining figures of light, but by making the darkness conscious. The latter procedure, however, is disagreeable and therefore not popular." (Ah, the power of understatement.) One way to carry on in the face of our discomfort is to find a goal that sufficiently inspires us to persevere despite the darkness.

The **ARC OF THE GOAL** can provide the vision that makes the difficult second octave work, if not pleasant, at least tolerable. Banzhaf notes that the final card in the major arcana "should be understood less as a final stage...and more as an image that pushes us forward" (p. 225). There are moments in life when

---

* The Lovers Key in the RWS deck doesn't look like it is depicting a character, but that's because it shows an individual from the inside-out, depicting the proper balance of the three forces within a human being: subconsciousness, consciousness, and superconsciousness. In traditional, Marseille-style decks, The Lovers depicts a single character trying to make a critical decision (either between two lovers or between Mom and his beloved). In either case, the focus is on the importance of inner balance when making outer decisions.

we genuinely need someone or something to push us forward, so that we don't beat a hasty retreat into our idealized self-images when the truth becomes too painful to bear. It's often the case that our willingness to face that truth, despite our fear, completely transforms the situation, such that our actual experience is less daunting than we anticipated. Once we face our fears even once, it becomes easier to face them in the future.

Third-octave symbolic images can inspire us to look forwards instead of backwards, just like inspirational sayings ("Courage consists of hanging on five minutes longer"). Such statements may sound corny when we're sitting in the armchair, but they have real power when we find ourselves in dire circumstances with nowhere to turn.

It's interesting that when we finally "arrive" at the third octave, it's inevitably different than we imagined. That's because there's really no way to imagine the experience of a higher octave from the vantage point of the lower. Gurdjieff tells us that someone at this point in his evolution "has the three worlds within himself"; Blake likens it to the Sufi state in which we are "in the world but not of the world" (p. 233).

One of the reasons I found it challenging to develop images for the third octave is that it takes us beyond our existing concepts of reality. The higher we go, the more subtle our experiences become (and the harder they are to convey in either words or images).

Applications of the Model in Enneagram Work

There are many ways to use the nine-path model in enneagram work. Below I describe a few of them.

The first and most obvious use for the new model is that it enables us to work with the enneagram and tarot *in tandem*. Anyone who knows both systems well will draw informally from their knowledge of them in various ways. But it's easier to work with the tarot once the seeming numerical inconsistencies between them (22 Keys vs nine types) have been resolved. A 27-Key tarot model resolves that problem.

Second, having a three-Key path for each type makes the journey more *relatable*, because it speaks to the specific concerns of different types. What matters most to Ones is simply not the same as what matters most to Fives, Nines, or Threes; they have very different priorities. Thus, just as the enneagram subtypes provide a more fine-grained description of each type, the nine paths provide a more fine-grained description of the hero's journey for each type.

Third, symbolic images makes it easier to envision and remember the characteristics associated with each type. This is especially helpful for people who do not have easy access to local enneagram teachers or workshops.

Fourth, adding visual imagery potentially opens the field to a broader cross-section of people, especially those with a humanities background: artists, designers, anthropologists, intuitives, mystics, and anyone else who is inspired by a creative, adventurous approach to inner work. It may also attract those involved in the disciplines of the Western Esoteric Tradition, such as esoteric astrology and the Hermetic qabala.

Fifth, this model provides a starting point for discussing where the enneagram might fit into the Western Esoteric Tradition.[2] The enneagram is a very new system (at least in terms of its pubic unveiling, which was just a century ago). It has yet to find its place within that Tradition, although it clearly belongs there; see the discussion in Chapter 16 and Appendix E.

Sixth and perhaps most significantly, this nine-path tarot model can help people already working with the enneagram to re-imagine the nine types as positive potentials instead of obscurations of essence (see Chapter 1). The tarot has a wonderful quality that tends to put people in a creative and playful mood. Just looking at the images in a tarot deck gets our imagination fired up, taking us out of our heads and into an open-ended, intuitive space where our biggest teacher is our own inner voice. We don't even need to know anything about the tarot images to work with them, because the inner self speaks to us in pictures. One night, my tarot teacher had two of us work with one card each for the entire evening, exploring what we saw there. I thought it would be boring. But instead, the experience was like traveling into another world; it surprised me just how much there was to discover in a single card.

I would like to think that a model like this will provide enneagrammers with a way to envision the nine types as imaginal *arche*-types on an adventure, because this lifts us up and encourages us in our inner work. What would it be like for Nines to discover how unique and special they really are? For Ones to learn about joy and self-acceptance? For Twos to know their true worth without the need for reassurance from others? For Threes to realize that it's okay to make creativity a priority? For Fours to discover the secret of authentic living? For Fives to unearth the truths that really matter? For Sixes to overcome their fear of life? For Sevens to experience true freedom? For Eights to fully embody who they are?

These are all delightful lessons to learn. Wouldn't any one of us want the opportunity to learn about joy, self-acceptance, truth, and freedom? Our work with the nine types is meant to give us exactly those kinds of experiences. But to use the opportunities we've been given, we have to be able to see the types in a whole new way. This is why I gave the paths names that focus on a key quality that each path can help us develop. The list below also includes a truth about life that each path can help us better understand.

- **Nines** on The Path of Divine Possibility – *It's possible to separate from the collective while still remaining at one with life.*

- **Ones** on The Path of Alchemy – *The purpose of incarnation is not to perfect the world but to illuminate it with our inner light.*

- **Twos** on The Path of Intuition – *The relationship we cultivate with ourselves is the fount from which all others flow.*

- **Threes** on The Path of Creativity – *The process by which things are created is what makes them worth something in the end.*

- **Fours** on The Path of Individuation – *Individualism marks the start of a journey towards individuation, which leads us home to our original self.*

- **Fives** on The Path of Wisdom – *The ultimate purpose of learning is not ultimately to acquire knowledge, but to learn how to love and honor it.*

- **Sixes** on The Path of Trust in the Goodness of Life – *Life is a blessing and trust is the quality that allows us to experience it that way.*

- **Sevens** on The Path of Liberation – *True liberation comes not from having the freedom to choose but the discernment to know what choice to make.*

- **Eights** on The Path of Ascension – *Ascension is not the ultimate goal but the state of wholeness that is a springboard for action.*

Envisioning the types as paths helps remind us that life never stands still but is always moving in some direction. This is also true of our type: it is not something static but is also moving in some direction, either towards expanded or diminished awareness—or in Joseph Campbell's words, towards *myth* or *fantasy*. But the type does not determine that direction. We do.

Applications in Tarot Work

Placing these paths and their associated images on the enneagram has somewhat different advantages for those well-versed in the traditions of the tarot. As noted above, this is in part because it attracts a different community of people—people who tend to be more artistically-oriented and less psychologically-oriented. Although people of many beliefs embrace the tarot, it seems to lack any particular religious overlay, at least as far as I can tell. Many tarotists embrace Hermetic values, which is one of the main reasons that the hero's journey is such an iconic idea in the tarot community.

But like all systems, tarot does not provide all the answers. The nine-path model is designed to make it easier for tarotists to apply the insights of the enneagram in tarot work; some of these applications are listed below.

First, the nine-path model *puts a face* on the abstract numerology of the Western Esoteric Tradition. This is because, in the enneagram, the numbers become actual people with whom we can talk. This brings them to life in an unimaginable fashion. Few if any enneagrammers have exploited this powerful feature of the system, probably because of the heavy emphasis on the types as distortions of essence. To see Types 1–9 as walking, talking exemplars of number symbolism may seem like a bit of a stretch. But that is exactly what they are. (This idea reminds me of the scene in Truffaut's film adaptation of Bradbury's *Fahrenheit 451* in which all the characters who have fled their dystopian anti-literate society become "walking books," self-identified by the book they decide to memorize for posterity.)

Second, the model gives us *a new perspective on the hero's journey*. We can imagine it as the journey of an individual whose temperament affects both the experiences he has and how he interprets them. The three-card sequences which I am calling "variants" speak to these differences in perspective (please see my comments on the characters in Tolkien's *Lord of the Rings* in Chapter 11).

Third, it extends the work done by pioneers like Angeles Arrien and Mary Greer on the *tarot constellations*. The idea of tarot constellations is of great value, but only three of the constellations have full three-octave constellations (The Fool is given a value of 22 to complete the fourth); the other five do not (see Table 10-2). This new model provides them with nine three-octave constellations. It also makes the constellations easier to imagine, so they can be applied in a more practical way.

Fourth, it allows us *to explore relationships between the nine paths*. This is because, as a geometrically-based system, the enneagram can reveal relational patterns—particularly triadic patterns—in a way that the tarot cannot. And yet, just how many tarot clients ask questions about relationships? It's probably the single most asked-about topic in a reading. More generally, the ability to handle relationship dynamics is important in any kind of inner work.

The enneagram is by far the best system I've encountered for that purpose, because it has the ability to identify subtle temperament differences that people just aren't aware of. In my two decades of enneagram work, the most oft-heard comment is "My relationships have really changed since I learned about the enneagram." Even people who have been taught the system primarily as a way to identify personality deficiencies can't help but notice its power to resolve relationship problems. It doesn't even need to be taught; anyone exposed to the system over time begins to pick up on ways to resolve ongoing conflicts or to avoid them in the first place.

The enneagram is such a powerful tool for conflict resolution because it teaches us enough about ourselves and others to develop workable strategies for getting along with people who seem completely different. This is because it doesn't just describe the differences, but teaches us *why* they exist. This helps us better see things from another person's point of view.

For example, a friend of mine who discovered the enneagram is a reserved Six who works in a highly competitive environment. He figured out that many of the people he found intimidating were Threes, a more extroverted type. Threes, of course, have their own problems. Learning the enneagram helped my friend in three ways: he better appreciated his own strengths (carefulness, attention to detail, and a good service ethic), began to notice that Threes didn't necessarily walk on water (even when they claimed to), and stopped feeling that he had to try to be like the Threes around him (because they were fundamentally different).

Another reason for improved relationships is that we learn the preferences of each type and how to accommodate them. The same friend in the story above was assigned at one point to share an office with a female co-worker that he believed was a Five. Fives like privacy, so before he moved in, he made it clear that he would respect his office mate's privacy. He also let the Five determine the layout of the office. A year later, when the two were chatting at an office party, she told him that he was the best office mate she ever had.

I had a similar experience with a One. Ones often have the endearing but annoying habit of trying to show their loving concern by criticizing those they love. My friend had this habit in spades. But since I knew he was a One, I was usually more amused than offended by his remarks. Because Ones have a connecting line to Seven (who generally have a good sense of humor), I could often lighten up the conversation with jokes or other remarks designed to express the idea that "I appreciate your help but I'm doing fine, thanks." (If that didn't work, I could always try touching lightly on one or two of *his* little problems—just enough to remind him that none of us are perfect!)

A third way that enneagram work transforms relationships is by helping people come to terms with difficult roles or relationships that can't be instantly transformed. For example, young Threes (who tend to be over-adapting) can learn how to resist family pressure to seek out high-status careers that don't meet their creative needs. Male Twos with a loving disposition can learn to feel good about their soft, "mushy" side, even when peers or parents think they should act more "manly." Parents of young Ones, who tend to behave like miniature adults from age 8 onward, can find ways to make their child feel like she is taken seriously while at the same time seeking out age-appropriate activities that help her learn how to let go and have fun.

These brief examples barely scratch the surface of the enneagram's potential to help people understand how to get along with one another. If the tarot is a Treasure House of Images, the enneagram is a Treasure House of Relationships. Accordingly, positioning the nine-path model on the enneagram circle is the first step in an exploration of the relational dynamics among both the nine paths and the 27 Keys. **Table 15-1** provides some rules of thumb for using the enneagram to explore relationships.

Table 15-1. Using the Enneagram to Explore Relationships.

Types that often get along well with one another:

▶ Adjoining types that "lean towards" one another (4w3 & 3w4, 7w8 & 8w7, etc.)

▶ Types sharing connecting points (1 and 5 both connect to 7; 2 and 5 both connect to 8; etc.)

▶ "Triangle" types (3-6-9; they tend to accommodate one another)

▶ "Hexad" types (1-2-4-5-7-8; They aren't always friends, but tend to understand one another)

▶ Types in the same "Hornevian" group (4-5-9=inward, 3-7-8=active, 1-2-6=relational)

▶ Types in the same energy center (but sometimes it can work in reverse if people get competitive)

▶ Types who use their differences to make one "whole" person (e.g., 2-5 or 8-4 pairings)

▶ SP subtypes with other SP subtypes (both tend to be matter-of-fact and practical)

Types that may have problems getting along or understanding each other:

▶ Same type with different wing preferences (1w2 & 1w9, 7w8 & 7w6, etc.)

▶ Same type with different preferred subtype arena (SP2 & SOC2, SX1 & SOC1, etc.)

▶ "Triangle" types with "hexad" types (3-6-9 types & 1-2-4-5-7-8 types)

▶ Same type with different connecting point preferences (1 > 7 vs 1 > 4, 5 > 7 vs 5 > 8, etc.)

▶ Types with very different priorities (3w2 and 4w5, counterphobic Sixes & SX Eights, etc.)

▶ SX subtypes with SX partners (Intense attraction often alternates with intense conflict)

▶ SP subtypes with SOC subtypes (SPs seek solitude while SOCs seek social interaction)

Factors that affect enneagram relationship dynamics:

▶ Social roles (Bosses with strong opinions like Eights,Ones, or Fours can direct impassive employees like Nines or Fives but not usually vice-versa)

▶ Setting (Sevens and Threes play well—but often don't work well—together)

▶ Family roles (One or Eight parents can come on too strong with sensitive types, e.g., 4-5-6)

▶ Energy intensity (Intense types can find it hard to get along with less intense types and vice-versa; but many types get along with Nines, who tend to be universally receptive, especially youthful Nines)

▶ Incompatible values (Types with really different values can have difficulties, like Fours who value personal authenticity vs Sixes who value loyalty to the group)

▶ Sociability (e.g., Sociable Twos usually want more interaction than they get from reserved Fives)

▶ Emotional balance (Balanced types get along with other balanced types)

These observations are very general and don't explain in detail the reasons for the statements made. But they do give you an idea of the kind of relational dynamics that can be explored. Helen Palmer's *The Enneagram in Love and Work* (1995) can also provide ideas for looking at type interactions; Appendix C provides specific suggestions for using the enneagram in tarot readings.

Working with 27 Keys with a 22-Key Deck

In Chapter 11, I made the point that just because we have a 27-Key model, that doesn't mean we have to have a 27-Key deck to work with the model. Most tarot readings involve looking both at images on the cards in front of us and combining what we see with symbolic associations we already have, either from our experiences in life or from working with other symbolic systems, e.g., astrology, Nordic runes, the qabala, or the I-Ching. The same approach is possible with the enneagram: once we understand the system, we can apply what we know about the nine types in our tarot work.

❖ ❖ ❖

In a conventional tarot deck, the last three Keys of the major arcana are The Sun (19), Judgement (20), and The World (21). Here, we'll be asking them to stand in for the entire Arc of the Goal. They can definitely do this, because they have both the appropriate symbology and numbers to do so.

Symbolically, all transformational processes involve three forces: an active, passive, and integrating force. And each of these cards represent one of those forces: The Sun = the active, masculine force; Judgement = the feminine, receptive force; and The World = the integration of the masculine & feminine.

Numerologically, these have the symbolic values of 1, 2, and 3. Since the new system is based on the number nine, these three cards can be patterned in several different ways: (a) as 1-2-3 (an incomplete Arc with three points); (b) as 1-2-3-1-2-3-1-2-3 (a complete Arc with nine points); and (c) as **Phases I** (1-2-3), **II** (4-5-6), and **III** (7-8-9), where each Key stands for a larger "metaphase" in a transformational process like the hero's journey (see **Fig. 15-2**).

VERSION A shows these three cards as Banzhaf depicts them: as the first three Keys of an incomplete octave. But even though the octave is incomplete, these Keys provide us with the three symbolic elements we need to create a complete octave, should we wish to. When placed on the enneagram, they depict a thesis-antithesis-synthesis pattern that invites expansion. Versions B and C depict two ways to make that expansion happen.

VERSION B shows how the pattern begun in Version A can be mapped onto the entire circle. When this is done, an interesting pattern emerges: In this pattern, the 1-4-7 triad is associated with the *initiating force* of The Sun; the 2-5-8 triad with the *preserving force* of Judgement; and the 3-6-9 triad with the

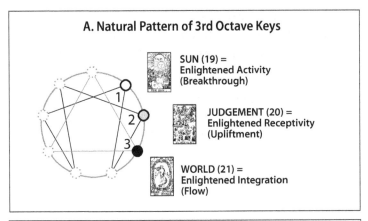

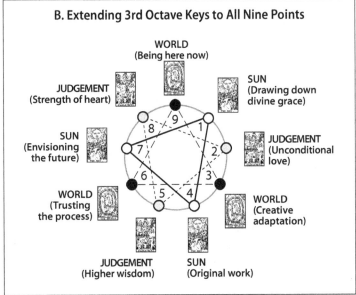

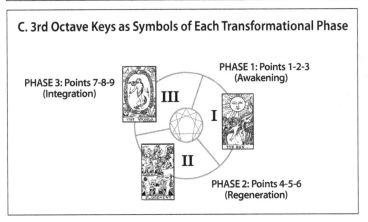

FIG. 15-2. Mapping The Sun, Judgement & The World onto the Enneagram.

adaptive force of The World. In astrology, these same relationships are described as cardinal, fixed, and mutable; in Hinduism, they are depicted by the deities Brahma (the creator), Vishnu (the preserver) and Shiva (the destroyer).

VERSION C shows the three Keys as symbols of the three major phases of transformation: Awakening (The Sun at 1-2-3), Regeneration (Judgement at 4-5-6), and Integration (The World at 7-8-9). This is akin to the three phases of the hero's journey as mapped out in Table 4-1 and Fig. D-2 in Appendix D.

When we draw any of the "third octave" Keys, we know that the focus is on some kind of resolution. But just what kind of resolution is it?

▶ With *The Sun*, it can represent a moment of breakthrough from "night" to "day" (Version A); a resolution achieved via a masculine, initiative-oriented path that involves the 1-4-7 triad (drawing down some ideal from "on high" [1], creating something original "from the deep" [4], or envisioning a futuristic result [7] = Version B); or the initial phase of resolution (where we get a vision of the big picture = Version C).

▶ With *Judgement*, it can represent being uplifted or healed through surrender to a higher force (Version A); a resolution involving the 2-5-8 triad (achieved via unconditional love [2], higher wisdom [5], or strength of heart [8] = Version B); or the second phase of resolution (where we implement our goals in a tangible fashion in the physical world = Version C).

▶ With *The World*, it can represent the ability to bring balance to everything in daily life (Version A); a resolution involving the 3-6-9 triad (achieved via creative adaptation to changing conditions [3], trusting the process to serve the world [6], or being serenely present in the "now" moment [9] = Version B); or the last phase of resolution (where we enjoy living for its own sake = Version C).

With these enneagram-informed meanings in mind, we can further pinpoint the significance of these three cards in a reading in several ways: by using our intuition, asking clients what the Key means to them, looking at their position within a spread, or drawing additional cards to obtain greater clarity. In this way, it's possible for the last three Keys in the major arcana to symbolically create an entire Arc of the Goal.

Notes

[1] *The Symbolic Quest: Basic Concepts of Analytical Psychology* (Princeton: 1969/1991), p. 160.

[2] There has been little if anything written about where the enneagram might fit into the Western Esoteric Tradition, but Chapter 16 suggests some possibilities for the future.

16:
Implications of the Model

Leave all dialectic behind and follow the path of the Powers.
– René Schwaller

THE PREVIOUS CHAPTER explored practical applications of the nine-path enneagram model. In this chapter, we'll look at how it highlights aspects of both the enneagram and tarot from an angle that reveals their power to revivify and restore the Western Esoteric Tradition. In the case of the enneagram, it is such a new system that it has not even been fully integrated into that Tradition. I hope this chapter will illustrate what the enneagram has to offer and how the enneagram and tarot together can help restore the long-fractured relationship between science and spirituality.

The Fool's Secret

And just who is the one with the most to tell us about how to reunite science with spirituality? Naturally, it's The Fool! This is a book about Fools, written by a Fool, and directed to an audience of fellow Fools who are engaged in the "excellent adventure" we call life. That's why The Fool is right there in the title and prominently displayed on the cover, stepping off his cliff into the Great Unknown. Every time he sets forth, he never knows what he will find. Of course, as the author of the book, I have seen fit to introduce him to an enneagram adventure. What neither of us know is where this adventure will take us, for that bouncing enneagram ball may be headed off yet another cliff!

I originally entitled the book *The Hero's Journey in the Enneagram & Tarot*, but the wording was awfully similar to Banzhaf's *Tarot and the Journey of the Hero*. However, one of my favorite movies is *Bill and Ted's Excellent Adventure*, which always sends me into stitches. One day, it popped into my head to call this book *The Fool's Excellent Adventure*, and I decided to go with it.

Little did I realize just how important a role The Fool would come to play—how his ability to wear so many different hats would affect my understanding of not only The Fool, but what this book is all about. But it wasn't The Fool alone; *it was The Fool on the enneagram*. Because it was when I placed The Fool on the enneagram that I began to see his special role more clearly, especially as Key 0. And that's when it began to dawn on me why it is important to make The Fool the focal point of the journey. It's because we're fast approaching a point where we need to get to know The Fool, to learn what he knows, and even to emulate him (even though he's just a fool). Because The Fool knows something we need to know: *the secret to eternal life.*

To understand what this means, we need to look at a little history. I talked in Chapter 9 about the paradoxical quality of the idea of "zero/infinity" and how it was rejected by Greco-Roman culture and subsequently by the Christian Church, whose religious doctrines dominated European culture until the scientific revolution of the 18th century Enlightenment began to undermine them. Over the next century, science began to replace religion as the new arbiter of truth. By the late 19th century, many scientists believed they had everything sewed up in a nice, neat little package.

Then came the revolution in quantum physics, which threatened to pull down the whole darned edifice by creating multiple paradoxes that no one has been able to resolve. Instead, the paradoxes keep getting worse. And their implications for our beliefs keep getting hairier. Western culture has been running from the questions that the new physics raises for a very long time. But now things have reached the point where there's no more running.

This is creating an ontological crisis in Western culture. "Ontological," by the way, is just a fancy word for "being-ness," and it's used to mean the nature of life and how it came into being. Science can refer to the Big Bang, but it cannot explain what gave rise to the Big Bang. Even the Big Bang theory has come under attack in recent years. What we thought we knew is coming increasingly into question; every new discovery seems to raise more questions than it answers.

The net effect is that, within less than three centuries, the traditional belief structures of the West—both religious and secular—have been considerably shaken up. Initially, science supplanted religion as the dominant paradigm in modern culture. But now, the very methodologies that demonstrated the limitations of Western religious doctrine are now demonstrating the limitations of scientism—the belief that science provides the only valid means of acquiring knowledge.

At this point, Western culture is fast approaching the point where there seems to be no rock left to stand on when it comes to understanding either the nature of life or the nature of human consciousness—at least from a mainstream perspective. This is because both mainstream religion and mainstream science rest upon assumptions that are simply too rigid and narrow to encompass the reality either is trying to describe. And one of the greatest false assumptions is that *religion and science are opposites, rather than complements.* Restoring Western culture will require a reconciliation of the two, as Ken Wilber pointed out in *Integral Spirituality* (2006).

My purpose here is to explore the role that the tarot and enneagram can play in restoring Western culture, especially when used in tandem and informed by Hermetic ("as above, so below") philosophy. But it's useful to start by seeing what physicists have to say about the implications of their discoveries, because this helps us see where we are right now as a culture.

The New Physics

Most physicists are not philosophers; they did not study physics in order to delve into deep philosophical questions about the nature of life or human consciousness. In fact, most assiduously avoid such topics. But in *Quantum Enigma: Physics Encounters Consciousness* (2011), physicists Bruce Rosenblum and Fred Kuttner attempt to confront the implications of the new physics for human consciousness, despite the fact that both appear to be much more comfortable with the traditional scientific method than psychology or metaphysics. Thus, it's no surprise to discover that these authors are not exactly thrilled by the "woo-woo" implications of the new discoveries in their field, especially the idea that the act of observing appears to create our physical reality:

> All of physics is based on quantum theory. It's the most battle-tested theory in all of science. And one-third of our economy involves products designed with it. However, quantum mechanics also displays an enigma. It tells us that physical reality is created by observation....The mystery presented by quantum mechanics...[is called] the "quantum measurement problem."[1]

Calling a mystery a "measurement problem" sounds like a vain attempt to make the mystery go away. It hasn't worked, but you can't blame them for trying: their entire worldview is based on the idea of mechanism (that's why they talk about "quantum mechanics," not "quantum mysteries"). Alas, quantum physics is not nearly as mechanical as Rosenblum and Kuttner would like. The problem is that it "challenges [the whole premise of] scientific realism" (p. 139) by compelling physicists to confront the idea that human consciousness has the power to change reality, whether we like it or not. And most physicists do not.

Quantum physics has inadvertently shown that observers inevitably influence the outcome of scientific experiments, which means that the two most important assumptions in the empirical method—the assumption of objectivity and independence of conditions—do not work at the quantum level. Then we have the unsettling idea of "spooky-action-at-a-distance," which implies the literal interconnectedness ("entanglement") of everything in life. (I love the way that scientists manage to take things that ought to inspire awe and mystery and use language that makes them sound like something dreadful; "entangle" is defined as "to cause to become twisted together or caught in a snarl or entwining mass.")

Mainstream physics is so averse to these ideas that there is even a whole line of experiments designed to allow physicists to "move on" so they don't have to deal with the hard question of human consciousness (see pp. 202–203). Nevertheless, these authors *do* try to tackle the question. But they do so mostly by citing the work of philosopher David Chalmers on mind/body consciousness. This doesn't help much, because philosophers have been working on the mind/body problem for centuries without success (because their speculations remain solely on the level of the mind). A more fruitful approach would have been to discuss the veritable raft of scientific studies showing empirical support for all sorts of "spooky action" involving some kind of *psi*. Anyone who looks into this area knows that this body of research exists and that many experiments have been replicated time and time again, despite the efforts of diehard skeptics to prove otherwise. Their failure to delve more deeply into this area may stem from their visceral distaste of scientists for phenomena they consider "mystical," *even when the reality of these phenomena can be empirically verified by rigorous scientific studies.*[2]

Disappointingly, the book does not really provide any answers to the questions it poses; it simply ends with the famous Shakespearean quote from *Hamlet* ("There are more things in heaven and earth, Horatio, than are dreamt of in your philosophy."). I suppose this is their way of saying, "After writing this whole book, we still have no idea what physics has to do with consciousness."

However, the authors are more forthcoming about how they feel about this lack of resolution on their website:

> The quantum weirdness is not hard to "understand"—even with zero physics background. But it's almost impossible to believe. When someone tells you something you can't believe, you might well think you don't understand. *But believing might be the real problem.* It's best to approach the subject with an open mind. That's not easy (emphasis mine).

No, it's never easy to move beyond the boundaries of what we think we know, to abandon the basic assumptions by which we live our lives. But that's the hero's journey in a nutshell. In this case, we're talking about the journey of hard-headed Western science into the Special World of Relativity and Quantum Mechanics. As with any good hero's journey, what the adventurers find in the Special World both awes and amazes them.

"I HAD NO IDEA IT WOULD LOOK LIKE **THAT**!"

But these hero physicists seem to be stuck in their amazement, unwilling or unable to accept the implications of what they see, because it threatens to turn their whole worldview upside-down (which appears to be their Ordeal). It's not just these two authors who are upset. It's the leading lights within the field. Erwin Schrödinger (of the famous cat "thought experiment") was so dismayed by the implications of his work that he admitted, "I do not like it and I am sorry I had anything to do with it." Neils Bohr said that "anyone who is not shocked by the quantum theory doesn't understand it." And an unnamed commentator in *Quantum Enigma* says that what he sees coming down the pike will leave people (that is, physicists) begging to go back to the *less* disturbing world of quantum theory. Einstein declared after one quantum physics discovery, "If it is correct, it signifies the end of science."[3]

He is right of course. The new physics *does* signify the end of science, but only science as we know it—science in the narrow, purely materialist sense. In another sense, the new physics opens science up to an entirely new way of thinking. It's the transition that's difficult, because scientists raised in the old paradigm are not looking for a new way of thinking. And a new scientific paradigm has yet to emerge.

Western Science and Eastern Religion

However, quantum physics continues to unearth evidence that has spiritual implications. As mentioned above, there's going to have to be some sort of rapprochement between science and spirituality if both arrive at similar conclusions about the nature of life. Unfortunately, the ancient wisdom traditions of the West that could have provided the ontological foundation we need to gracefully come to terms with the new physics have been repeatedly and ruthlessly stamped out, first by religious leaders (using brute force) and later by the scientific establishment (using public ridicule). It's only since the turn of the 21st century that it has become even *marginally* possible for mainstream investigators to dare to explore the relationship between science and spirituality.

In the East, there exist ancient traditions that allow science and religion to be reconciled; there exist sacred texts containing the same kind of paradoxical statements that we see in modern physics textbooks. And there exists another paradoxical idea new to the West: the idea that Being arises out of Non-being.

In Hinduism, Non-being is called the *maha pralaya*, "the [Great] Center or Zero, which is the primeval cause of the entire manifestation and to which everything will ultimately return."[4] Lao Tsu said in the *Tao Te Ching*, "All things are born of Being. Being is born of Non-being." Jalaluddin Rumi, founder of the Mevlevi Sufi order, has said, "The moon passes over the ocean of Non-being. In the desire of the One to know himself, we exist." In Buddhism, non-Being is the state of *sunyata*, "the fruit of Enlightenment."[5] "The Buddha...taught that everything we take to be solid is actually empty of any inherent nature. The apparently substantial world we perceive is in reality, without substance at all, and is akin to a dream. The full realization of this truth is the basis for enlightenment."[6]

Please note, if you will, the tone of these statements. They are graceful, poetic, and quietly inspirational. What they are *not* is fearful. The mystics of the East are not shaking in their boots over the idea of zero, infinity, the possibility of getting sucked into a black hole, or of a singularity "piercing a hole" in the fabric of the universe (all concerns expressed in either *Zero: The Biography of a Dangerous Idea* or *Quantum Enigma*). Rather, their attitude is impassively matter-of-fact—which is the kind of attitude we might expect more from scientists than mystics.

This difference in tone illustrates the huge gulf between the perspectives of East and West. The West has the jazzy technology that can produce the weird quantum effects, but not the philosophical and spiritual roots to cope with what the investigators find. As a result, the experience of discovering the truth about life is rather like opening Pandora's box. The East used a different route to discover the same truths, and they discovered them much earlier—not through scientific manipulation but through direct spiritual experience.

The mystical teachings of the East have three critical truths to share with us in the West: (a) there are two aspects of the Totality or Life: Being and Non-being; (b) Non-being gives rise to Being; and (c) Non-being is where we came from and the state to which we will ultimately return. What is more, the return is joyful; it is associated with completion, illumination, and primordial bliss.

Quantum physicists are in the process of figuring out the part about Being and Non-being; what they can't seem to grasp is the bit about illumination and bliss![7] (Modern physicists are the Messengers of the Gods, they just don't know it yet!)

Western Science and Western Esotericism

We have seen that many beliefs in Eastern religious traditions are based on direct, mystical experiences—experiences that are generally compatible with the discoveries of modern physics. This is one reason why many modern Westerners are drawn to Eastern religion: because it gives them a way to reconcile science with spirituality. But Western culture differs from Eastern culture in many ways, which is why it is unlikely that Eastern religion will ever be adopted on a large scale in the Western world. A better solution is to rediscover the lost wisdom of the West, which is just as powerful as the wisdom of the East.

One place to look is Hermetic philosophy, which provides a set of broad principles that explicate the nature of life and a vision of humankind towards which to strive. Another is sacred geometry, which delineates the hidden building blocks of creation and encompasses a number of profound Western systems, including the enneagram and qabala. A third place to look is to the tarot, which hides the wisdom of the West in archetypal images with the power to reconnect us with Cosmic Memory, both individually and collectively. These are only a few of the better-known resources that can revitalize Western culture; we can also look to indigenous shamanism, Jungian dreamwork, Celtic wisdom, and other traditions that preserve the ancient wisdom of the West.

A resource I have found particularly helpful for providing a detailed description of the nature of creation is a set of teachings dictated to Western esotericist Dion Fortune in the 1920s. Although Fortune wrote many books, she says these teachings were channeled, not her own creation. Published in 1949 as *The Cosmic Doctrine*, these teachings precisely echo the wisdom of the East when it comes to the idea that life originates in the Unmanifest (Non-being):

> The Unmanifest is pure existence. We cannot say of It that it is Not. Although it is not manifest it Is. It is the source from which all arises. It is the only "Reality." It alone is substance. It alone is stable...the Unmanifest is the Great Negation; at the same time, it is infinite potentiality which has not [yet] occurred (p. 19).

This quote is from the first page of the book. The rest of the book explains two things: (a) how the world of manifestation comes into existence (through the "unificatory principle" of Love) and (b) how the beings that come into manifestation ("Divine Sparks") can evolve from being part of the dream to being part of the reality that gives rise to the dream.

To do so requires us to learn how to love, "whether that love be intellectual sympathy on the plane of the concrete mind or physical unity on the plane of matter. Love in all of its aspects is a symbol of the Logos as One" (p. 185). To love is to open to the spirit of life and its opportunities for experience, not holding back or distancing ourselves out of fear, distaste, or a sense of superiority.

And this brings to mind The Fool and his love affair with life (**Fig. 16-1.**) He may have his head in the clouds (at least at the start) but he has not a shred of fear, distrust, or hubris. He cares not a fig for his image but listens to his inner voice and acts to satisfy his endless curiosity about life.

Recalling his "zero" position reminds us that The Fool is always an edge-walker who stands between the two worlds of the Unmanifest and the Manifest, which is a very special place

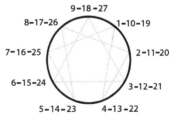

Fig. 16-1. The Fool, Happily Cliff-Diving.

in mystical lore. In Sufism, it is called "the place where the two seas meet"; it has been called the "locus of the mystical journey." This distinctive spot is a place of strange and paradoxical events, such as a cooked fish coming to life again and jumping back into the ocean—a logical impossibility, unless time can move backwards. It's also the place where we might encounter Khidr, the mysterious Green Man, who figures prominently in both Sufi and Celtic lore. In Sufism, he is the mystical teacher who instructs us through paradox and surprise, rather than according to our expectations.

There is a famous Sufi story about Khidr and Moses. Moses wants to become the student of Khidr, but Khidr warns him, "You will not be able to follow me." But Moses persists and Khidr agrees to let him try. But Khidr is a hard master to follow, because he does many things that Moses does not understand. Some of them even seem morally wrong. Each time Moses protests, Khidr patiently explains himself and Moses relents. But after the third time, Khidr reminds him of what he foretold at the beginning and sends him on his way.

In this story, Moses represents the conditioned self that is brought up in the Dream world of Being. This is where he learns the rules that govern the created world. His encounter with Khidr symbolizes the first time he becomes aware of his inner teacher, his *in-tuition*. But his conditioning makes him distrust it, and he falls back on relying upon the conventional rules he has been taught from childhood.

The story of Moses and Khidr is like the story of Sir Percival's first visit to the Grail Castle, where in a moment of clarity, he perceives the Grail Procession. But he is too inexperienced to know how to respond to the vision. Like Percival, Moses will have to have further experiences before he acquires the maturity to trust his inner voice (an attainment symbolized in the tarot as The Fool becoming The Hermit).

A Fool's Paradise

In a quantum sense, The Fool represents the "Divine Spark" as it first emerges into the Special World of Being. He may be "trailing clouds of glory," but he is also apt to trip and fall a lot, due to a complete lack of life experience! The delicate white rose that he carries attests to the purity of the world from which he comes, as does his white undergarment; his laurel wreath tells us he will win the day; and his waving feather celebrates his entrance into the dream world we call reality. His magnificent robe contains the Hebrew letter *Shin* (fire), a symbol of the eternal flame. He has no real luggage, only a very small bag that could carry practically nothing; it has on it the emblem of the eagle, the highest manifestation of Scorpio, the sign of death and rebirth.

This empty-looking bag is our clue as to The Fool's secret. It's not secret knowledge or powers that he has; it's about what he *has-not*. It's about the nothingness he carries with him wherever he goes, the spark of divine nothingness that serves to connect him to his place of origin.

The Fool is the only card in the tarot deck that symbolizes this particular quality, as shown by his special zero. That's why he is the journeyer and the joker that can become any card in any deck. It's why he always looks young and never really dies: because his life is eternal. He shows us why we do not need to fear non-existence. *Non-existence is home.*

In a tarot reading, The Fool is not considered a bad card to draw. But it often leaves us scratching our heads as to why we drew it. There are so many possible meanings attached to The Fool. To interpret the card, we can't just rely on something we memorized. We have to use our intuition.

The Fool is designed to give us a little taste of paradox, perhaps to help us get used to dealing with paradox in our own lives, just as small synchronicities allow us to see the interconnectedness of life, even when it comes to trivial events. I recently went to the store just to buy mint Tums. All I had at home were the fruity kind and I don't like them much. As I walked down the aisle, I saw a guy approaching from the other end. We were the only two people there. As I walked, scanning the shelves for Tums, I saw him scanning the shelves, too. Eventually we converged on exactly the same shelf and, finally, on the exact same spot. It turned out we had both come to the store for just one thing: a bottle of mint Tums. We had a little conversation about it, because there *were* no mint Tums and we had to settle for an inferior brand.

This encounter was not exactly a cosmic event. But it *was* unusual and oddly amusing, as are many synchronicities. Often, they don't seem very "spiritual" in the usual sense of the word. But maybe the funniness of these events might be more important than we think. We always expect spiritual stuff to be serious, even solemn. But it might be more spiritual (and loving) to learn how to laugh and have fun, even in little ways, so we can avoid getting too serious and self-important. The Fool doesn't look very self-important. In fact, he's the only character in the entire tarot who is routinely portrayed in a comedic role, often with torn pants, a harlequin outfit, or accompanied by a funny little dog, as in the RWS deck.

But let's be honest—when we draw The Fool in a reading, how many of us really want to identify with him? Not many, I'll bet. Most of us like to think we're a little more clued-in and a little less spaced-out. But are we, really? Or are we just too dense to realize the truth?

Western culture conditions us to think we're the smartest, most sophisticated, and most technologically advanced people who have ever walked the face of the earth (political correctness notwithstanding). But if humility is a virtue, how do we *really* rate on a scale of 1–10? How would we rate our ability to love, to be truly sincere, or to see ourselves in a humorous light? How many of us have

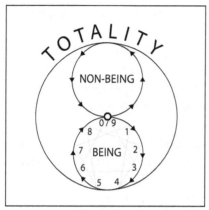

Fig. 16-2.
The Flow between Being & Non-being.

the kind of trust in life that would allow us to walk off a cliff, knowing no real harm can come of it?

To get a handle on what's really going on, a simple model may be useful; see **Fig. 16-2.** This figure depicts the equation NON-BEING + BEING = THE TOTALITY. Non-being (the top circle) and Being (the bottom enneagram circle) are in a figure-8 flow, signifying the idea that there is a continuous flow between existence and non-existence; some people call this reincarnation. When we incarnate, we begin dreaming; when we die, we come home to reality.

The two circles of Being and Non-being are connected at Point 0/9—the point "where the two seas meet." And that's why this point is associated with The Storyteller (Type 9) on the enneagram and The Fool in the tarot. Both archetypes are one and the same.

In the life cycle, Point 0/9 is where we emerge from Non-Being into Being. This is a momentous event, whether we are talking about the original emanation of Being from Non-being, the bursting forth of a universe into existence, or the birth of an individual human being. The return to Non-being is equally momentous, because it represents waking up from the dream and remembering our true identity. There is no death, no final end, to either life or to consciousness; there is just a flowing forth and receding back, according to our individual nature and the larger cycles of life (the "Cosmic Tides").[8]

This is not a complicated idea. Is it really so hard to comprehend? Eastern culture has known about it for millennia. It's we in the West who have forgotten our divine heritage, and forgotten it so completely that we have come to fear our gifts instead of developing them.

But in Jungian psychology, the more we fear something, the more we constellate it in a distorted form. We are currently constellating the technical ability to tamper with most basic elements of life, like atoms (to create bombs or missiles), genes (to create new species or clones), and silicon (to create artificially intelligent machines). We play the role of idiot savants, creating new stuff that we don't how to use. Collectively speaking, we seem to have a pretty low spiritual I.Q.

As we delve ever more deeply into the mysteries of life, what kind of understanding will inform our work? The detached mentalism of philosophy? The cruel logic of atheism? The cynical spirit of commercialism? None of these can show us the way out of fear and into the light (not even in combination with money, drugs, or zombie apocalypse flicks).

If we in the West want to get grounded in the real, we need to recover our lost wisdom teachings, to revive the Hermetic spirit that fizzled out after the Renaissance, and find a way to integrate art, science, and religion as they sought to do during that Renaissance era that many of us look back to so fondly.[9] It's time to create a second Renaissance, one that cannot be easily subverted by Church, State, or our fears of the unknown.

The nine-path model presented here is designed to offer one practical approach for rediscovering the wisdom of the West. The intent is to honor the traditions of the past while also developing innovations for the future. The tarot gives us visual images to make abstract ideas concrete; the enneagram provides nine paths of development and a matrix upon which to envision them.

> When we can dream, we can make life come true,
> When we can love, we can find our way through.
> When we can laugh, we can take back the night,
> When we can die, we can live in the light.

From the *The Cosmic Doctrine*: "Whosoever expresses Love brings Spirit, which is One, into manifestation...therefore, choose Love—and live."[10]

Notes

[1] The first part of this quote is from the authors' website (see http://quantumenigma.com/nutshell/); the second part is from their book, pp. *xi–xii*.

[2] To discover just how much empirical work has been done to verify the existence of *psi*, see, e.g., the work of respected experimental psychologist Daryl Bem (his scientific papers are available at his website, including a meta-analysis on precognition experiments); *The Biology of Belief*, by biochemist Bruce Lipton (Hay House: 2016); *Entangled Minds: Extrasensory Experiences in a Quantum Reality* (Paraview: 2006) and *Supernormal* (Deepak Chopra: 2013), both by Dean Radin, head of the Institute of Noetic Sciences. Also check out the website The Campaign for Open Science, established by Dr. Larry Dossey in 2014 to promote the fair-minded scientific assessment of consciousness.

[3] It's a bit dismaying to see such brilliant thinkers respond to the new physics with such a "tearing of hair and gnashing of teeth." Maybe these physicists would not be quite so gobsmacked if they were part of a scientific culture in which science and spirituality were not regarded as mutually exclusive. But they *are* part of that kind of culture. According to a 2009 Pew Foundation survey, 95% of Americans say they believe in some sort of higher power while only 51% of scientists say they do. The spread is even wider if we ask about a belief in God: 83% Americans vs 33% of scientists say they believe. You might think this is because scientists are naturally inclined to be less religious; and this may be true. But as someone who worked for years in that environment, I can testify that science promotes a culture of disbelief that makes it hard for anyone with a spiritual orientation to work for an extended period in a scientific environment. And there is absolutely no way to talk about religion or even spirituality at work; the topic is simply taboo.

[4] Chandra, Ram. *The Complete Works of Ram Chandra, Vol. 1* (Shri Ram Chandra Mission: 1989), p. 28.

[5] See http://buddhanet.net/cbp2_f6.htm.

[6] Aaron de Long and Kim Desrosiers; see https://westchester.shambhala.org/.

[7] That's the problem with Western science: it's superb at bloodlessly dissecting things into their bits and pieces but not so good at appreciating the beauty of the creation as a whole or the idea that it might have some kind of overarching purpose.

[8] The Cosmic Tides are one of the Cosmic forces described in *The Cosmic Doctrine*, and they have to do with the timing of Cosmic events, just like the ocean tides on earth. *The Cosmic Doctrine* includes this particularly interesting statement: "By a knowledge of these Cosmic Tides the 'illuminated' may avail himself of their forces, hence the power of a knowledge of the Numbers of the Secret Calendar" (p. 32). There is no explanation of what these Numbers are or what the Secret Calendar might reveal. But doesn't it sound intriguing?

[9] This is religion not in the narrow, doctrinal sense, but in the sense of the word *religio*, which means "sacredness, piety, holiness, conscientiousness, a sense of right, divine service."

[10] *The Cosmic Doctrine*, p. 185.

Appendixes

A – E

Appendix A:

Tarot Card Meanings

Major Arcana

I – ARC OF THE DAY

These Keys describe nine archetypes that describe themes in the hero's journey. They put a human face to concepts that might otherwise be hard to imagine.

0 **FOOL**	**An innocent journeyer sets forth into the adventure of life.** Innocence, enthusiasm, high energy, adventurous child, lack of embarrassment, adventure/travel, warning to be careful, Divine Fool, carefree way of life, wayfarer, trickster, traveler through life, wandering in the wild
1 **MAGICIAN**	**A would-be alchemist connects heaven & earth via mastery of the elements of life.** Mastery, alchemy, will, focus, the *animus*, concentration, creative power, magical/metaphysical ability, effective communication/timing, "as above, so below" perspective, alignment with Divine principles, perfectionism, precision, high standards
2 **HIGH PRIESTESS**	**Precious secrets are protected & the psyche lets flow the waters of life.** Power of the feminine, the inner voice, the *anima*, inner resources, mystery, the inner chamber of the heart, deep secrets, silent wisdom, psychic flashes, intuitive awareness, subtle nurturance, being in the flow, feminine mysteries
3 **EMPRESS**	**Nature blesses the creation and brings new life into the world.** Abundance, blessings, fertility, creativity, home life, flow, vitality, health, matriarchy, mature love, Mother Nature, cultivation of nature, creativity, outer activity
4 **EMPEROR**	**The ruler stands apart in the desert heights, sacrificing his life for the Kingdom.** Independence, individuality, intellect, will power, responsibility, standing tall, conquest, indomitable will, never backing down, dauntlessness, aloneness, the dying King, the ultimate sacrifice (of self for others)
5 **HIEROPHANT**	**The teacher dispenses wisdom in accordance with Divine Law and the needs of the student.** Wisdom, attainment, esoteric knowledge, shamanic ritual, spiritual responsibility, Higher Self, initiatic traditions, secret teachings, individual instruction, teaching through silence, "to Know, to Will, to Dare & to Keep Silent"
6 **LOVERS**	**(1) The masculine and feminine cooperate under the aegis of the Higher Self or (2) The Choice in made between sacred and profane love.** Sentimental love, inner integration, sexuality, intimate partnership, mutual trust, purity in love, faith in a higher source, resolve differences through a higher source, spiritual discernment, decisions about relationships, choosing faith over fear
7 **CHARIOT**	**Victory is achieved via focus, self-discipline, and the love of adventure.** Travel, adventure, adaptability, high spirits, enthusiasm, adventures in consciousness, travel, ability to be at home anywhere, Crossing the Great Water, moving through old limits, adaptability, creative thinking, quick action
8 **STRENGTH**	**When the heart rules the instincts, all of life rejoices.** Love mastering lust, courage of the heart, warmth & vitality, self-confidence, overcoming fear with fortitude, elevated sexuality, beauty and the beast, strength from within, kundalini rising, creative energy sublimated into masterful work
9 **HERMIT**	**Inner stillness makes us a Light in the Wilderness.** Love of solitude, inner peace, meditation, wilderness retreat, travel for growth, seclusion, way-showing to travelers, resolving unfinished business, inner realization, spiritual receptivity, enjoyment of simple pleasures & time alone

II – ARC OF THE NIGHT

These Keys represent the challenges we encounter when we seek to evolve in life. They show us what must be done, give us clues about how to do it, and reveal the unseen gifts associated with each challenge.

10 **WHEEL OF FORTUNE**	**The Wheel of Life moves, bringing fortune, opportunity, and the unexpected.** Cyclical change, destiny/fate, luck, second chances, good fortune, breakthroughs, prosperity, unexpected events, expanded vision, contending with uncertainty
11 **JUSTICE**	**The cultivation of discernment realigns our inner being.** Balance, adjustment, precision, adjudication, decisions, equality, fairness, legal matters, karma, realignment, truth, looking honestly at ourselves, spiritual calibration
12 **HANGED MAN**	**An upside-down shift brings a chance for change.** Time out, suspension, acceptance, transition, voluntary sacrifice, learning to surrender, withdrawal from old patterns, allowing, stillness, receptivity, patience, timelessness, starving old habits of the power to hold us
13 **DEATH**	**The end of a major phase brings a profound transition.** Major transition, absolute end to a situation, *nigredo* in alchemy, no going back, death of a dream or illusion, dramatic break with the past, complete surrender, transformative change, crossing the Rubicon
14 **TEMPERANCE**	**The testing & tempering of the Higher Self creates great inner strength.** Creating the alchemical container, enduring the refining fire, fine adjustments creating exquisite balance, blending of the opposites, getting tossed back & forth between extremes, being perfected by alchemical change
15 **DEVIL**	**Confronting the Dweller tests our bravery, fortitude, and sense of humor.** Facing the Dweller on the Threshold, our greatest fear, the lure of materialism, addictions, obsessions, lack of humor, enemies, self-gratification, self-delusion, trickster humor, overconfidence, hubris, learning to laugh in the face of fear
16 **TOWER**	**Sudden realization strikes down all that resists change.** Destabilizing shocks, a bolt out of the blue, massive renovation, complete restructuring, spiritual liberation, illusions blown up, Road to Damascus experience, dramatic end to oppression, intuitive flashes, sudden inspirations
17 **STAR**	**The evening star illuminates the night, bringing release and renewed hope.** Hope, relief, rescue, purification, receiving spiritual nourishment, sanctification, respite from trouble, spiritual guidance, gratitude, wonder, innocence, inner radiance, renewal, awe & mystery, inner peace, chance for complete rejuvenation
18 **MOON**	**The mysterious moon lights our way on the long journey home.** Half-illumination, night journeys, changeable conditions, uncertain conditions, moodiness, psychic impressions, dark light, subconscious images, Dark Night of the Soul, childhood fears, deep feelings & intuitions, shadow work, welling up of the subconscious, welling up of the Deep, the need for discernment

III – Arc of the Goal

These Keys represent the result of integrating the archetypes of the Day and the Night. The first three represent the paths of the Masculine (19), Feminine (20), and the Collective (21) and are seen in all 78-card decks. The remainder specify additional paths: Wellspring (22), Keeper of the Flame (23), The Divine Family (24), Merkaba (25), The Divine Monad (26), and Divine Mystery (27).

19 Sun	**The return of the light brings energy, optimism, and a sense of joy.** Return of the light, relief, release, joy, happiness, healing of the inner child, talent, celebration, self-expression, living in the light, warmth, appreciation, good health, vitality, radiance, clarification, understanding
20 Judgement	**Transcendent healing "raises us up" into the light.** Healing, resurrection, revelation, a new aeon, realization, enlightenment, transpersonal change, the ultimate re-balancing, complete acceptance and forgiveness, transcending human judgments
21 World	**We dance in the light of our inner radiance.** Joy, fulfillment, zest for life, gratitude, living in the moment, creativity, lightness of being, no sense of limits, perfect alignment, oneness with All That Is, world community, collective enlightenment and celebration
22 Wellspring	**We return to the wellspring of our being.** Individuation, Original Self, The Face Before I Was Born, Return Home, disidentification with ego, devotion/surrender to the Divine, spiritual depth, individual dominion, pristine awareness, replenishment, restoration, calmness amid the storm
23 Keeper of the Flame	**We partake of divine wisdom and share it with others.** Transcendent Wisdom, perfect understanding, knowledge infused with love, awareness beyond thought, ability to impart wisdom through one's being, Great White Brotherhood, World Teachers, preservation of esoteric wisdom, *darshan*
24 Divine Family	**Integration of our two halves brings both inner union and outer communion.** Divine Union, psychic integration, enlightened sexuality and bliss, Twin Flames, union of Soulmates, harmony in relationships brings harmonious families, communities & cultures, Christ Consciousness as established in the world
25 Merkaba	**Traveling though the dimensions, we discover the mysteries of the Cosmos.** Understanding of multidimensionality of being, ability to transcend time and space, activation and use of Light Body (*merkaba*), interdimensional travel, whole new level of discovery, innovation and synthesis
26 Divine Monad	**We fully embody our Being (the "I AM" self).** Complete alignment of vertical and horizontal potentials; mastery of mind, emotions & body; infinite power with infinite surrender; union with All That Is; enlightenment; permanent realization; the Ascension
27 Divine Mystery	**We transcend the World of Manifestation to experience the state of Non-being.** Experiencing the ineffable mystery that gives rise to All That Is, grasping the imaginal and ephemeral nature of manifestation, awareness of the relationship between Being & Non-being, experiencing the innateness of Non-being

Minor Arcana

FOUR SUITS: WANDS, CUPS, SWORDS, PENTACLES

WANDS (FIRE)	Life force, growth, energy, light, magic, intuition, charisma, attractiveness, communication, entrepreneurship, innovation, games, competition, communication, love of freedom, spiritual expression, competition, risk-taking, passion, egotism, self-centeredness, pure (impersonal) passion, lust, amorality
CUPS (WATER)	Flow, emotions, inner life, upwelling, moods, memories, spiritual nourishment, empathy, heart-to-heart communication, harmony, love, sentimentality, self-indulgence, self-pity, "giving to get"
SWORDS (AIR)	Mentality, discrimination, sharpness, force, conflict, clarity, power, beliefs, courage, self-discipline, pointedness, cruelty, mental defenses pierced, pain, delusions
PENTACLES (EARTH)	Groundedness, the concrete world, practicalities, "sensing" function, responsibilities, surface qualities, work, physical manifestation, connecting with nature, down-to-earth self, impassivity, density, insensitivity
ACES	**ROOT ENERGY, NEW OPPORTUNITIES, SINGLE FOCUS, DEPTH, ONENESS, IDENTITY, BEGINNINGS, GOALS, GIFTS**
ACE, WANDS	New energy, enthusiasm, health, high motivation, romance, quick timing
ACE, CUPS	Opportunities in Inner life, depth of feeling, luck, joy, pregnancy, silver lining, pure love, intimacy, empathy
ACE, SWORDS	Force, determination, will, mental power, principled attack, opposition and enemies, intensification, concentration, great passion, problem-solving, singular focus, seed thought, crystallization, penetrating illusions
ACE, PENTACLES	Opportunities for abundance, jobs, material or concrete help, sense of social status as self-identity
TWOS	**DUALITY, CHOICE, BALANCING THE OPPOSITES, DECISION-MAKING, INTIMACY**
TWO, WANDS	Choice of opportunities, divided lifestyle, relationship/friendship, success
TWO, CUPS	Intimate relationships, empathy in making choices, true love, cooperation, reconciliation, congenial partnerships, mutual support, emotional nurturance
TWO, SWORDS	Either/or choices, mental indecision, legal issues, negotiation (positive) or conflict (negative), boundary issues, one-to-one conflicts, taking sides, delays
TWO, PENTACLES	Need to balance competing activities or values, choosing between alternatives, juggling choices, reconciling seeming polarities by attuning to the connection between them (a figure-8 flow), communication problems, delays in manifestation
THREES	**COMMUNICATION, SYNERGY, TRIOS, MULTIPLICITY, EXPANSION, FLOW, TRIOS EMBLEMATIC OF THE QUALITY OF THE SUIT**
THREE, WANDS	Flow of communication, creative expression, widening of interests, inspired trios, expanded work opportunities, cooperative teams, visionary enterprises
THREE, CUPS	Creative energy, celebration, social pleasures, Three Graces, gracious communication, friends, social celebration (e.g., marriage), healing

THREE, SWORDS	Emotional pain, reaction to conflict, injuries to ego or emotions, third-party troublemakers, cutting to the heart of a matter, precision work, painful decisions, heartbreak, mourning, purification through suffering
THREE, PENTACLES	Applied creativity, artisan activities, translating visions into realities, abundance, careful work, community recognition, grounded manifestation
FOURS	**STABILITY, COMPLETENESS, MATERIALITY, PHYSICAL MANIFESTATION, STRUCTURE, HOME, AUTHORITY, GROUNDEDNESS, SOLIDITY, DENSITY, DOMINION**
FOUR, WANDS	Celebration, coming full circle, a moment of perfection—a bubble (the only perfect sphere in nature), home & hearth, harmony, Venus & Aries, companionship, love, marriage, independent partners who work in harmony
FOUR, CUPS	Emotional satiety with indecision, jadedness, "Is this all there is?" feeling, restlessness, dissatisfaction, need to go within, time for reflection
FOUR, SWORDS	Recovery, recuperation, withdrawal from conflict, convalescence, rest, sanctuary, healing of wounds, time-out
FOUR, PENTACLES	Material stability, conservation, caution, home life, comfort, unshakeable stability, power of the Earth, the Four Directions, reorientation to nature
FIVES	**CHANGE, INSTABILITY, NEW ORIENTATION, UNCONVENTIONALITY, ALIENATION, IN-GROUP/OUT-GROUP ISSUES, SURVIVAL ISSUES, LOSS OR DISORIENTATION**
FIVE, WANDS	New experiences, breaking away, competition, creative competition, conflict, crowds, change, novelty, contention, engagement, unusual creative impulses
FIVE, CUPS	Change in inner life, emotional sense of loss, regret, shame, sorrow, loss of status, emotional "survival" orientation, the challenge of fully integrating emotions
FIVE, SWORDS	Betrayal, disillusionment, mental conflicts or competitions, crisis of conscience, mental ruthlessness/lack of mercy, social inclusion/exclusion, learning impassivity in the face of difficulty, maintaining perspective after a loss
FIVE, PENTACLES	Job loss, financial insecurity, "out in the cold" feeling, home life disruptions, risks, money or health concerns, unconventional lifestyles, voluntary hardship, lack of popularity, learning to rise above the sense of impoverishment
SIXES	**VICTORY, ACHIEVEMENT, HARMONY, EASING OF TROUBLES, TURNING POINT, NEW DIRECTIONS, BALANCE, PEACEFUL INTERLUDE, RESTABILIZATION**
SIX, WANDS	Victory over strife, exercising leadership, harmonious work, competence, cooperation, flow, popularity, success, skill, confidence/overconfidence, good work flow
SIX, CUPS	Period of stability after instability, peaceful interlude, nostalgia, idealized past, children, gift-giving, "in-sync" relationships, recreation, childishness
SIX, SWORDS	Turning point, relief, release, travel, new directions, water journey, radical dislocation, diplomacy, conflict resolution, transitions, deliverance, travel to promote harmony, crossing over the Great Water, scientific breakthrough, temporary calm
SIX, PENTACLES	Period of peace and prosperity, giving to others, spirit of generosity, creative partnerships (2 x 3), good social life, social responsibility/community-mindedness

SEVENS	INDIVIDUALISM, DEFENDING IDEALS, LONG-TERM PLANNING, ENVISIONING, ENCOUNTERING THE UNEXPECTED, IMAGINATION, DELUSION, DREAMS
SEVEN, WANDS	Overcoming obstacles, standing firm, defending ideals, being an individual, proper positioning, success, possible delays, creative responses to opposition, defense of spiritual principles
SEVEN, CUPS	Dreams, imagination, visions, mirages, flights of fancy, fantasy, illusions, "up in the air" nature of things, too many choices, getting lost in maya, excess, too many competing attractions
SEVEN, SWORDS	Deceptive or ambiguous situations requiring discernment, sense that "things are not what they seem," possible deceit or cheating, need for indirection, subtlety or diplomacy, acts hidden from the group, covert ops, "behind the scenes" dealings, ingenuity, cleverness, sleight-of-hand, con artist tactics, sharp business practices, theft, rash acts, clever strategizing
SEVEN, PENTACLES	Challenging situations involving work, health, money; obstacles in translating dreams into reality, failure or the fear of failure, failure of potential (when possibilities fail to manifest), setbacks ("reality checks"), stagnation, reflection upon work, necessity of time for ripening, learning patience, possible need for retreat from active involvement or work, need for a mature work ethic

EIGHTS	ORDER, ORGANIZATION, HABITS (2 X 4), STRUCTURE, MOVEMENT, ALIGNMENT OF INTENTIONS AND ACTIONS, CRAFTSMANSHIP, BUILDING
EIGHT, WANDS	Energy flowing via good habit/alignment, swiftness, aligned effort, success via focus, trends, travel, everything clicks into place, coordinated efforts, productive group dynamics
EIGHT, CUPS	Emotional realignment via separation from the Collective, abandonment of unbearable habits of feeling, reconciling Truth with Feeling, time to "sing your own song", withdrawal and reflection, walking away from unproductive relationships, end of emotional stagnation (stagnant or frozen marsh) or emotional exploitation, end of unrealistic hopes or illusions, unproductive efforts, looking for meaning in life, seeking deeper relationships
EIGHT, SWORDS	Confinement, interference, frustration, oppression, being blind to solutions, feeling "stuck," other peoples' problems, sense of helplessness or hopelessness, need for inner attunement during outer confinement, learning to deal with frustration & restriction
EIGHT, PENTACLES	Cultivating good habits involving work, health, physical activity, exercising prudence, apprenticeship & mastery, acquiring skills, attention to details, satisfaction with a job well-done, job training, steady progress, awareness of the inner value of outer work, hands-on projects, willingness to let go of old habits

NINES	MULTIPLICITY (3 X 3), INTENSIFICATION, PEAK EXPERIENCES, ARRIVAL, QUINTESSENCE OF A SUIT, COMPLETION OF A PROCESS
NINE, WANDS	Knowing via actual life experience, higher level integration, mastery/balance, advocacy, strength, attainment, pinnacle of power, dynamic and coodinated creative activity, spiritual enlightenment/realization/mastery
NINE, CUPS	Blessings multiplied, mystical attractions, wish fulfillment, success, romantic fruition, imagination manifested, emotional flow, beauty & harmony, inner calm, self-satisfaction
NINE, SWORDS	Intense anxiety (anxiety multiplied), tension, harshness, burnout, complications, self-doubt, cruelty in life/self-cruelty, crucifixion by others/self-crucifixion, sacred suffering, not a time to act but to wait, opportunity to transcend suffering
NINE, PENTACLES	Improved situation in physical life, gain acquired from attunement (love, service, humility, joy); abundance multiplied, quiet enjoyment, disciplined creativity, solitude, feminine refinement & dignity, relationship with pets & nature
TENS	ESTABLISHED OUTCOME, ELABORATION, CAPSTONE, CYCLICAL PATTERNS, FINAL PRODUCT, HOW THE OLD CYCLE AFFECTS THE NEW CYCLE
TEN, WANDS	Energy imprisoned in matter, sense of burden, depression, sacrificial effort, doldrums, inability of fire to burn freely, energy yoked, the end is near, possibility of paying off a karmic debt, need to strip off extraneous obligations, oppression at the cycle's end, need to see the broader picture, need to stop fighting the physical side of life
TEN, CUPS	The Journey Home, belongingness, empowerment, emotional wholeness, harmonious participation, reunion, family harmony, marriage, fullness, need to ground emotions in a stable foundation
TEN, SWORDS	Learning through suffering, complete surrender, problems too big to handle (requiring Grace); aftermath of war, feuds, vendettas, duels, relentless patterns of abuse & persecution; outcome of "slaying" of small self (ego death, annihilation, living in the ruins of one's being); resolution of difficult or long-standing health problems; clearly indicates the end; end of suffering; new beginning
TEN, PENTACLES	Wealth established, foundation for expansion in work, the family, dynastic wealth, the entire community, enduring relationships, ongoing success, foundation established for higher work

Court Cards

PAGES	LEARNING, YOUNGER PERSON, FEMININE ACTIVITY, YOUTH, INNER CHILD, MESSENGER, ENTHUSIASM, UNASSUMING MANNER, LACK OF EMPOWERMENT, COMMUNICATION
PAGE, WANDS	Fiery, blunt, artless, auburn, impetuous, enthusiastic, hot-tempered free spirit, full of intuitional flashes and spontaneous ideas. Innovation, adventure, optimism, self-confidence, intuition, liberation, artistry, freedom from shame or artifice, abundance and joy, equality in a relationship, need to "tame the Lion" (fire energy)
PAGE, CUPS	Charming, poetic, empathic, gentle, tender, sensitive lover of life. Beginnings of a love affair, creative writing, birth of imagination on the physical plane, rapture, dreaminess, attunement to sound, prospect of great success, ability to "ground" love on the physical plane
PAGE, SWORDS	Sharp, quick, intense, and direct young thinker with a penetrating mind who may be a bit naive and quick to act. Surprising news, innovative ideas, directness, moodiness, focused, need for thoroughness and follow-through, confidence without ostentation
PAGE, PENTACLES	Practical, grounded, careful, and sensible soul who is at home in the material world and attuned to natural cycles. Balance, diligence, love of earthly delights, diligence, attentiveness, groundedness, dedication, simplicity, and lack of pretense
KNIGHTS	EMPOWERMENT, VIGOR, COMING INTO ONE'S OWN, ARRIVALS, MOVEMENT, MATURITY, GETTING INVOLVED, LOVER ENTERS YOUR LIFE
KNIGHT, WANDS	Impetuous, creative, and fiery warrior in the service of a high cause; a trickster with a sly sense of humor. Inspired creativity, dynamism, motion, mastery, creativity, expansion via trust, focused intent, concentration, effortful passion, commitment to transformation and the challenge of being able to enjoy life responsibly
KNIGHT, CUPS	Affectionate, chivalrous, and devoted lover whose sublimated feeling is profitably directed toward high-minded pursuits. Sweetness, sentimentality, evolved spirituality, sensitivity, care, home life, moving house, water travel, romantic love
KNIGHT, SWORDS	Decisive, quick-witted, quick-to-act individual who marches to the tune of his own drummer. Charging into action, active involvement, competitiveness, military action, movement, mentally-stimulating love affairs, crusader mentality, idealism
KNIGHT, PENTACLES	Steady, persistent, and mature individual with the follow-through to make things happen in the physical world; draws strength from the earth. Perseverance, practical activity, seriousness, quiet confidence, cautious but successful effort

QUEENS	QUINTESSENCE OF WOMANHOOD, FEMININE MATURITY, INTEGRATION OF INNER LIFE AND SOCIAL ROLE, NURTURING, FRUITFULNESS, MOTHER ENERGY, SUB-PERSONALITIES OF THE EMPRESS
QUEEN, WANDS	Vivacious, tempestuous, and charismatic feminine leader whose light burns brightly in creative endeavors. Boldness, dynamism, courage under fire, unconventionality, creativity, originality, inspiration, nobility, competition, passion, spontaneity, refinement, and wildness tamed through love
QUEEN, CUPS	Loving, gentle, and nurturing feminine presence who is the soul of kindness. Sentiment, sentimentality, love, sweetness, tenderness, soulfulness, devotion, depth, intuition, feminine wisdom and understanding, grace, receptivity, care, transformation through love
QUEEN, SWORDS	Sharp, independent, and shrewd feminine leader, keen on social justice and possessing diverse skills. Emotional reserve, sternness from sorrow, precise communication skills, directness, pragmaticism, proficiency in law, music, and legal matters; possible mystical inclinations
QUEEN, PENTACLES	Unassuming and patient nurturer who supports life in an everyday and practical fashion. Serenity, calmness, peacefulness, impassivity, and quiet confidence
KINGS	QUINTESSENCE OF MANHOOD, LEADERSHIP, POWER, AUTHORITY, DOMINANCE, OVERARCHING INFLUENCE, SUB-PERSONALITIES OF THE EMPEROR
KING, WANDS	Charismatic leader, explorer, entrepreneur, or promoter with the energy to actuaize his vision. Fiery, confident, warm, outgoing, commitment to spiritual growth and evolution, intense, dispassionate, abstract (pure energy, devoid of personality)
KING, CUPS	A warm, socially responsible leader who place the needs of others ahead of his own. Humanitarian, generous, emotionally genuine, open, outreaching, affectionate, loyal, caring, and possibly sentimental
KING, SWORDS	Serious and discerning leader who excels in scientific and legal thinking. Legislative, rule-oriented, principled, diplomatic, scientific, judgment-oriented, educated, knowledgeable, insightful, thoughtful, reflective, often introverted
KING, PENTACLES	Paternal, responsible and generous leader who understand the importance of creating the material infrastructure necessary to support life in the physical world. Generosity, charitable giving, financial expertise, control of material resources, material success, expression more through acts than words, diligence, hard work

Appendix B:

Discovering Your Enneagram Type

ANYONE INTERESTED IN THE ENNEAGRAM usually wants to identify their enneagram type. To many people, taking a test seems like the ideal way to gain self-insight: quick, reliable, and clear-cut. I must admit that, as a psychologist, I've always found psychological tests pretty fascinating.

But the enneagram is not a psychological instrument. It's an esoteric instrument based on the principles of sacred geometry. As a result, answering the question "What's my type?" is never as simple as just taking a test, no matter how objective it appears (and this includes tests that have been "scientifically validated"). Even if the test correctly identifies the type, that information will be useless until an individual probes deeply enough to discover what it really means.

Despite these reservations, I have developed several enneagram tests, two on the enneagram and one on the enneagram subtypes, because they provide an interactive way to explore the types. One test lists 180 statements to which the respondents can indicate their degree of agreement (0–3); an example would be "Authenticity is what I value most." This test and the subtypes test are available on my website, (www.enneagramdimensions.net). I've also developed a simpler test that is explained below.

Instructions:

On the next page are nine short paragraphs that are matched to the Answer Key on the last page. Read through the paragraphs to see which ones sound like most like you; mentally cross out the ones that definitely don't sound like you. Read through them a second time to see whether your initial impression "sticks."

a. I take a careful approach with everything I do. It's important to me to take the time to "do things right" in my work and my life. I enjoy neatness and order. Although it's hard to admit, carelessness or cutting corners—even in little ways—can really bother me. When I see other people doing it, it's hard not to say anything. I try to keep my thoughts to myself, but this can make me tense. There are times when I wish I could loosen up a little without feeling like I'm compromising my values.

b. What matters to me is authenticity and the meaning of life. I would rather have a difficult experience that helps me know myself than success without self-insight. More than other people, I feel a longing for something that is missing. At the same time, I have ways to translate my longing into some form of creative expression via the arts, writing, or just by doing everyday things in an unusual or artistic way. When I'm being creative, I feel like I'm connecting to that part of life that's missing.

c. I'm a matter-of-fact person. I enjoy the little things in life and get along well with most people, so I have a variety of friends. I do find that a regular schedule helps me stay focused and get things done. Otherwise, it's easy to get distracted and lose track of time. Then I can get behind, and it's hard to get caught up. I like to stay calm and avoid conflicts, so I try to help the people around me get along. Personal decisions can be hard for me, so getting ideas from friends can help me decide what to do.

d. What I really care about are people. I enjoy relationships so much—they make my life worthwhile. I would almost always choose to spend time with friends or family than to spend time alone. When I have a special relationship with someone, I put them first in my life. I feel most alive when serving the needs of others and I also like to connect up people that I think might enjoy one another. But I have to be careful not to "over-give," because then I feel burned out and unappreciated.

e. I'm very direct. I speak plainly: I say what I mean and mean what I say. Some people don't like that kind of directness, but that's just how I am. I'm a good friend to the people I trust—I'm always there to help them out of a jam. I look out for my people, even when it costs me. And it *does* cost me at times, because I tend to act first and ask questions later. I've got a temper that can be hard to control. But inside, I'm a marshmallow. You just have to know me well to find that out.

f. I'm exceptionally alert and observant, especially in unfamiliar or public settings. I can spot danger a mile away; I have almost a sixth sense for it. But I can also overreact at times, getting anxious, over-vigilant, or even paranoid. But a watchful disposition does have advantages. I'm a natural skeptic, so I don't get fooled easily. I'm very protective of those I care for, and I have a feisty side when it comes to sticking up for the underdog. Also, I'm extremely loyal to groups I belong to or causes I believe in.

g. Rational thinking and logic make more sense to me than emotional outbursts. When I have a problem, instead of worrying about it, I spend time thinking about it from different angles. So I often come up with an ingenious solution that no one else has thought of. I value relationships but I would usually rather show it in private than in public. I'm a shy person who needs private space and time alone to gather my thoughts. I also use that time to re-charge my batteries, because being with other people takes a lot of energy.

h. What motivates me most in life is personal achievement. I love a challenge—working hard, being the best at what I do, and getting the job done, whatever the obstacles. I'm great at multi-tasking. I can do a lot of things at the same time without losing track of my goals. But sometimes I can get so single-minded about my work that I may lose track of other things that are important, like relationships or recreation. It's possible for me to identify so completely with what I do that I'm not sure who I am apart from my work.

i. Life is such an adventure! It's filled with so many possibilities—and I want to explore as many of them as possible. I'm a high-energy optimist who likes making work into play; my biggest challenge is finding time to do all the things that attract my attention. I have lots of interests and ideas, but I tend to get involved in so many projects that I find myself juggling all the time in order to keep them all afloat. Sometimes this works and sometimes it doesn't. But I'd rather juggle than risk the prospect of getting bored.

The answer key is on the next page.

Key

a. Type 1   f. Type 6

b. Type 4   g. Type 5

c. Type 9   h. Type 3

d. Type 2   i. Type 7

e. Type 8

Next Steps

If you are a typical respondent, you were able to quickly cross off several type descriptions as possibilities but not to immediate recognize one of them as your type. Here are some suggestions for what to do next:

▶ Go back and look at the type descriptions in Chapter 7. Then check out Appendix C, which describes the types in the context of tarot readings (both for readers and clients). Appendix C also offers a "What's my type?" tarot spread.

▶ Take the longer test on my website (www.enneagramdimensions.net), if you have MS-Excel. It will generate a bar chart showing which types you rated most highly. (But don't be fooled—just because the test looks objective doesn't mean it offers the final word on your type.)

▶ Talk with someone who is experienced with the enneagram, especially if that person is trained in enneagram typing. They can ask the kind of questions that will help you better pinpoint your type.

▶ If you live in an area where there are enneagram groups, see whether they offer workshops where you can hear people of different types talk about their experiences (typing panels). The Internet search term "enneagram" with your city's name will usually reveal local groups and the activities they offer.

▶ Check out enneagram resources on the Internet; there are many sites and chat groups available. Be aware that much of this information focuses on the types as fixations. Even so, you can still learn a lot there. Celebrity typing is very popular, and while it has its limits (because these are just guesses), it can still be helpful for people trying to distinguish one type from another.

Appendix C:

Using the Enneagram
in Tarot Work

THE TAROT IS A POWERFUL TOOL for inner work. When I first used it, I knew only a little about the enneagram. When I came back to it after 15 years of enneagram study, I found my understanding of the enneagram to be extremely helpful in tarot work, especially for readings. But it was also helpful when I used tarot for other purposes, like meditation, active imagination, and dream work; it always added an extra dimension of knowledge from which to draw. In this appendix, I talk about ways I've discovered to use the enneagram in tarot work, particularly divination.

A Few Remarks about Tarot Divination

In modern pop culture, tarot is associated with fortune telling, Gypsies, and exotic-looking 19th century parlors. That's the image that shows up in fantasy comedies like *Love Potion Number 9*, where Anne Bancroft plays a hilarious fortune teller decked out in scarves, or in horror flicks like *Tarot*, where the cards in the reading (usually Death or The Devil) foreshadow the creepy events that are to come. Con artists might also be shown as fake tarot readers or psychics, trying to fleece the public with their readings. Whatever the film, movie-style tarot readings are virtually never portrayed as something in which ordinary people would take an interest.

Another place people might encounter the tarot is as a popular form of entertainment in hip restaurants or at parties (especially "girl" parties like bridal showers), where the focus is on discovering future partners or career opportunities.

But all this fun stuff involving the tarot belies its use as a tool for inner work, especially work involving divination. Divination means "to foresee, to be inspired by a god," from the Latin *divinare* and *divinus* (divine). So divination in the truest sense is about attuning to the god within us, the divine spark that holds the answer to any question we could devise. Because the deep psyche speaks most eloquently in images, the images of the tarot are especially useful for this purpose.

Tarot cards are also often used in psychic readings, where the cards serve as touchstones that help bring the energies through and ground them in the physical world. That's why they show up in movies about the paranormal. But most people who are serious about tarot are interested in the individual cards and in how they can be combined to tell a story in response to our questions about life. Using the tarot helps us learn to trust our intuition and to develop our imagination—both of which are undervalued assets in our extroverted culture.

I enjoy using tarot both as a reader and a querent. As a reader, I learn to see how the cards can tell a story and to listen carefully to the concerns of the client. As a querent, I learn how to clarify the questions I want to ask and to allow the reader to help me find answers to these questions. I do not read professionally (for money) because I don't feel it's my calling. What I enjoy most is reading cooperatively, where two tarot partners both read and are read.

One great thing about tarot is that anybody can read it, even someone who never saw a tarot deck before. This is because the images are archetypal, and our inner being knows exactly how to respond to them, even if we feel like "I don't know anything." Some of the most interesting readings I've gotten are from complete beginners.

When I read for others, I like to try to keep the reading focused as much as possible on the "now" moment. There are two reasons for this. First, it's the only moment in which we can act. Second, it reminds all present that we all create our future by our present acts. Even events that seem fateful are still affected by our actions and attitudes in the moment.

I also like to read collaboratively, i.e., *with* the person rather than *for* the person. This means asking questions, especially about how they react to a particular card. Asking the question, "What does this card mean to you?", is sure to elicit a lot of information. Even if the person says it doesn't mean much of anything, that's also information, because it may hide a strong aversion masked as indifference. People can surprise you with their responses; a friend of mine new to the tarot and going through lots of changes really liked the Tower card, having no idea that it's one that most people would prefer not to draw!

Tarot readings can range from playfully fun to incredibly serious. In the tarot group I attend, we have a once-a-year meeting where we play tarot games; these are not competitive games but playful ventures into self-exploration with the support of other players. The first time I attended, most of my fellow participants were, like myself, new to the group and the games were mainly fun and exploratory. Two years later, the people at our table were long-time participants, the discussion was self-revelatory, and the topics much more profound.

The enneagram has helped my tarot reading in at least four ways.

First, it's allowed me to more accurately identify my strengths and weaknesses as a reader. Like most Fours, I am acutely aware of somebody's emotional state, particularly when that person is in distress. (Helen Palmer once said that, if you visit a suicide hotline center, the place is filled wall to wall with Fours!) So I'm a good reader for someone in crisis who's past the point of trying to "make nice" with their situation. I'm less skillful when it comes to getting past people's psychological defenses, especially when they are trying to show me just how good they are at maintaining them!

Second, my knowledge of the enneagram has often helped me more easily grasp the querent's central issue, especially if I know or can accurately guess at their enneagram type. Assessing somebody else's type is a delicate subject which I'll talk more about below. But the fact remains that anyone who knows the enneagram often uses it to try to type other people, especially when it comes to celebrities. If it's done carefully, it can be a great aid in tarot work.

Third, it has helped me interpret what I'm being told during a reading, especially if I know or sense the type of the reader. For example, if someone is an

Eight, I'm not offended if they "take charge" and give very direct feedback; if they're a Five, I'm not surprised when they focus more on ideas than emotions; if they're a Two, I understand their emphasis on establishing rapport and their preference for exploring the emotional and intuitive aspects of the cards.

Fourth, knowing the enneagram has given me ideas for tarot spreads, a few of which I share below. There are just a few spreads because I don't want to overwhelm anyone with too much information, which is very easy to do when it comes to a complex system like the enneagram.

Reading Tarot When You Know Your Own Enneagram Type

If you are giving a reading and you know (or think you know) your type, below are some tips that may be helpful. Reading these descriptions may also help you determine your type.

▶ As a ONE with a critical eye for detail, you tend to be relatively formal and focused as a tarot reader. This can make some clients a bit uncomfortable. So you can likely benefit by using some kind of relaxation technique before the session, so that you begin in a serene and open state. Try to be supportive (rather than critical) and sufficiently non-directive that the other person will be able to tune into his or her own intuitions. This will enable clients to feel relaxed enough to openly share those impressions with you.

▶ As a TWO with a preference for emotionally connecting with people, you may be inclined to be very friendly with clients. Some people like that kind of friendliness, but not everyone. Try to go slow and watch for signs that you're getting too "chummy," especially with individuals who are reserved. Cultivating the ability to read the body language of clients will allow you to know when to speak up, when to ask questions, and when to remain silently empathetic.

▶ As a THREE with an orientation towards action, you may need to remind yourself to start by getting completely centered and inwardly still. So take the time you need to settle in, so you can be receptive to whatever is unfolding in the moment. Take the time to establish rapport. During the reading, try to focus not only on the client's practical questions, but on any unexpressed concerns, emotional shifts, or other subtle factors that are present. Let the client lead whenever possible while you support his or her explorations.

▶ As a FOUR with a preoccupation with self-expression, you may need to make a conscious shift away from your own inner preoccupations in order to be attentive to those of your client. Cultivating an open heart will make it possible to listen empathetically, which will enable you to be not only emotionally present but consciously aware of the client's needs and wishes. Try to remain attentive while at the same time diffusing your natural intensity, so that you radiate a relaxed sense of goodwill and encouragement.

▶ As a FIVE, your native shyness may be an asset when drawing out equally shy clients. But when dealing with more outgoing clients, you need to pay special attention to establishing and maintaining rapport, so your client will feel at ease. You can benefit from consciously marshaling your attention beforehand, so you can maintain a steady focus. This will allow you to exercise leadership and respond appropriately to emotional cues.

▶ **As a Six**, your natural modesty and genuine desire to serve can help you quiet the nervous energy that makes it hard to sit still and deeply listen. You can especially benefit from consciously bringing the energy of your head into your heart, so that the two are synchronized. This will allow your intuition to operate without restraint, to the benefit of both you and your clients.

▶ **As a Seven**, your love of fun and new ideas can make it something of a challenge to switch from active to receptive mode. So you can benefit from making the effort to stay quietly focused during the entire session. Clients will appreciate your upbeat attitude and positive energy, so long as you can stay grounded, patient, and attentive to the topic at hand.

▶ **As an Eight**, your natural leadership abilities give you self-confidence as a reader but may also make it a challenge to allow clients the time and space to make their own discoveries, minus your direction. The ability not only to state the truth as you see it, but to be silent and "lead from behind," gives your client the opportunity to develop insights from their own point of view and gives you the chance to notice the deeper dimensions of what is unfolding.

▶ **As a Nine**, your ability to be impassively receptive to both the client and the surrounding environment allows a space to emerge in which the truth can naturally unfold. However, you may need to cultivate the ability to be more proactive as a reader (asking questions, suggesting interpretations, and illustrating the ways the cards interact) to add some structure to the reading. This will also help you to stay on-track (not getting distracted by interesting side issues).

Reading Tarot When You Know Your Client's Enneagram Type

One of the best things about the enneagram community is its ethical stance about reading somebody's else type. Virtually no enneagram teacher I know would ever recommend telling somebody out of the blue, "I think you're Type *x*." There is also an unspoken ethical practice of using type knowledge in a constructive way (never for a manipulative or destructive purpose). That said, it is very common for enneagram-savvy people to type (or attempt to type) other people. This is not only natural, it's unavoidable.

As a cognitive psychologist, I have seen plenty of scientific evidence supporting the idea that human beings are hardwired to use whatever information they have to form hypotheses about people and their motives. We do it every day with the people we meet. So in jury cases, when the judge instructs the jury not to form any judgments before the end of the trial, he's telling them to do the impossible (one of my Ph.D. dissertation committee members did the research).

The same thing is true about "disregarding" evidence that the judge decides is inadmissable after it's already been introduced. Human beings just can't do that.

What we *can* do is to become more consciously aware of how we're doing this and the assumptions underlying our judgments—which is one reason understanding all nine types can be helpful. Another thing that helps is to adopt a scientific stance, seeing our guesses about type as hypotheses and not as facts.

My approach when typing others is not to fight my impressions, but simply to *hold them lightly*. This means keeping my assessment fluid and remaining open to new ideas. If done with care and discernment, I don't see typing others as a problem (although I usually keep my impressions to myself).

One thing that helped me develop a circumspect approach to typing was receiving training on how to interview people in a way that's designed to help them discover their type. The most important thing I got out of that course was the importance of *coming up with the right questions*—the kind that help distinguish look-alike types. But you don't need to attend a workshop to come up with useful questions. Developing good interviewing questions is a great way to teach yourself about the types.

Example: If someone says they often feel tense or worried, I start wondering if that person might be a One or a Six. Ones worry out of tension while Sixes worry out of fear. If I ask what things make them feel worried, the Ones tend to talk about their latest frustration in life, like their neighbor playing the stereo late at night. So their concern is really how to deal with their irritation, so they don't explode.

Sixes typically respond to the same question with a story about a scary thing that happened recently (or possibly, a bunch of scary things: all the latest threats from terrorism, cell phones, creepy neighbors, climate change, or climbing ladders). So in this case, the client feels out of control, not angry. But there's a caveat here: some Sixes (called counter-phobic Sixes) like to hide their fear with a lot of bluster, so they are pretty good at coming up with negative projections about other people, countries, political parties, etc. But if we really attune to the energy, not the just words, it's not that hard to tell the difference between angry frustration and anxious projection; it just takes practice.

Based on my enneagram experience, I would say that about 10–15% of the people I meet are quite challenging to type, even after years of working with them or seeing them regularly in some other context. About half of those are typable after I get to know them very well. When people are hard to type, I think it's because there's some kind of disconnect between the inner energy and the way they display it (or cover it over). Sometimes, a chance remark (often something uncharacteristic of this individual) will suddenly reveal someone's core motivation.

The reasons people are hard to type vary: sometimes they are more or less "living" at a wing point or connecting point most of the time. This was true for me in my 20s, when I acted much more like a Two (a connecting point) than a Four. Years later, when I asked myself why, I realized that I was simply not ready to take on certain type-related challenges at that point in my life.

After I found the enneagram, I was sometimes mistaken for a Five because I've got a big Five wing, which shows up especially during workshops, where I usually take copious notes and ask a lot of questions. But I'm not a Five; I simply look like one in certain contexts.

Sometimes people don't act like their real type because they are emulating someone they admire, the way that method actors try to inhabit the characters they portray. One enneagram teacher I know so admired his enneagram teacher that he thought they were the same type for five years. It took courage to tell his students he had mis-typed himself, but it's actually not uncommon. A third scenario concerns people who have a strong self-image (either in a positive or negative sense). If someone sees herself in a certain way, she may reject all evidence to the contrary—at least for awhile. Letting go of early conditioning (or our reaction to such conditioning) can take many years and be a hero's journey all by itself.

Nevertheless, most people I meet up with are not that hard to type (and do not find it that hard to type themselves). The main challenge is to get to know both yourself and the enneagram well enough to put all the pieces of the puzzle together.

Below are observations about the types as clients that may be helpful.

▶ **ONES AS CLIENTS** tend to be intense, reserved, and initially uncomfortable in a tarot reading situation, especially if they don't know the reader. They benefit from a reader who defers to their preference for a more formal and polite approach (at least initially). They seek explanations that are clear and concise, without too much ambiguity; they dislike pretense but can be painfully sensitive to personal criticism, so it's important to give feedback with care and discretion, watching carefully for strong but subtle emotional reactions. Although Ones seldom ask for emotional support, they appreciate a reader with the ability to respond calmly and without reactivity to any negative emotions that may arise. (This is true of any type but especially of Ones!)

▶ **TWOS AS CLIENTS** seek emotional rapport and are interested in those aspects of a reading that touch on relationships, feelings, and social interactions; it can at times be a challenge to maintain rapport while still retaining the professional distance that is necessary to ask fruitful questions and provide insightful feedback. Redirecting their energy into the reading (instead of developing a relationship with you, the reader) can help them understand that relationships work best when two people place their shared attention on a third activity, object, or goal (not just each other).

▶ **THREES AS CLIENTS** usually want practical, solution-oriented information given in concrete terms, so they dislike too much airy-fairy metaphysical stuff, especially if it seems irrelevant or hard to apply. However, they can sometimes become too focused on the "bottom-line," even in personal relationships, where process matters. A reader can help them focus more on process (and especially its creative potential) by inviting them to give their artistic impressions of the cards, to tell a story using them, or to explore the emotions they evoke. The idea is to help them enjoy the process of working with the cards, so they can see this kind of activity as something possessing value for its own sake rather than just as a means to an end.

► **FOURS AS CLIENTS** seek depth, meaning, and authentic engagement in a tarot reading; they really want to be seen for who they are and seldom ask about anything casually; they have excellent "bullshit detectors," so they respond best to readers who are emotionally genuine and unpretentious. At the same time, they tend to be emotionally intense and direct in a way that requires the reader to be completely grounded, in order to "hold" the space open for whatever might emerge. Four clients appreciate readers who have done their own work, are willing to allow them to go deep, and admit their limitations rather than pretending to know more than they actually do.

► **FIVES AS CLIENTS** look for mental clarity rather than emotional support, and they usually shy away from emotionally charged topics; they appreciate patience and a certain degree of reserve on the part of the reader. They will stonewall any reader who moves too far too fast into topics about which they are emotionally sensitive. So it's necessary to exercise discretion while at the same time encouraging clients to move at least a *little* bit out of their comfort zone; patient acceptance and kindness will often do wonders to draw the shy Five into a collaborative frame of mind.

► **SIXES AS CLIENTS** often have thin psychic borders, which can make them wary of tarot readings and initially skeptical. (Even if they are open to tarot readings, they might still be skeptical about *your* motives as a reader!) So they require great calmness and patience at the beginning (when they are still deciding whether or not you can be trusted to handle sensitive areas with care and respect). Underneath the skepticism is a deep curiosity about life and a powerful desire to move past their fears in order to live with greater joy, optimism, and faith.

► **SEVENS AS CLIENTS** are unusually curious about the process involved in a tarot reading and eager to explore the meanings of each card. They are usually fun to read for, because they ask lots of questions and seem impressed with your responses. But if you're not careful, their fascinated questioning can keep you discoursing on the design or history of the cards instead of honing in on the story that the cards are trying to convey to this *particular* individual. So a reader has to be careful with Sevens to maintain a steady focus on the bottom-line, patiently bringing their attention back to the messages the cards convey and how they can be concretely implemented in their daily lives. (You might notice that this is the exact opposite of the approach used for Threes, because Threes tend to focus too much on concrete results while Sevens focus too much on process and theory.)

▶ **EIGHTS AS CLIENTS** can be tough nuts to crack, because of their thick, self-protective exterior, which makes them appear intimidating or even aggressive. It helps to know that under their tough exterior lies an extremely vulnerable, childlike "inner personality" that is extraordinarily sensitive to rejection, thus necessitating the projection of the powerful "alter ego" outer self. Eights tend to test the mettle of a reader new to them by initially asking direct questions designed to determine whether the reader can (a) "meet their energy" (handle what they dish out) and (b) are worthy of their respect. Like Fours, they like direct, "no b.s." responses; unlike Fours, they seek concrete and practical solutions rather than philosophical discussions. For best results, avoid intellectual abstractions and emotionally charged topics; Eights will let you know if they are open to a deeper discussion.

▶ **NINES AS CLIENTS** tend to approach a tarot reading with openness and curiosity; they are intrigued by the actual images on the cards and the stories they have to tell. But as with Sevens, it is often easier to get Nines interested in the cards as stories than in what those cards might reveal about their *own* inner stories! Attempts to go deeper may be initially rebuffed, especially if the cards depict themes that might disturb their sense of harmonious union with the world around them. For they are the most peace-loving type, and their preference for harmony can override their desire for insight. But a reader can use their innate curiosity to help them get in touch with what the cards tell them is going on inside. It's helpful to ask the kind of questions that gently guide them to see the issues the cards reveal but encourage them to come to their own conclusions.

Enneagram Spreads

If you like to use tarot spreads for divination, here are a few ideas for using the enneagram in those spreads. I've described them from the perspective of an individual using them alone, but they can also be used in tarot readings.

SPREAD #1: Using the Law of Three to embark on your hero's journey. We've looked many times at the Law of Three, the process by which all transformation occurs. One of the simplest ways to start transforming your life—and embark on your journey—is by using the Law of Three in this simple four-card spread.

The first card, the Significator, defines some aspect of your life that is ripe for change. The other three cards reveal the process that can bring this change about: the best thing you can do (the *active principle*), the best attitude you can adopt (the *receptive principle*), and the results of combining the two (the *reconciling* principle).

Instructions: Draw four cards, face down. Turn each one up, asking the following questions:

Significator: *"What can I do right now to change my life for the better?"*

Card 1: *"What kind of action will promote a positive change ?"*

Card 2: *"What kind of attitude will support that change?"*

Card 3: *"What is the best possible outcome in this situation?"*

You may find with this spread a definite emphasis on either action or attitude, depending upon your habitual approach to life. Action-oriented types may be encouraged to become more receptive (open, attentive, and flexible) while receptive types may be encouraged to be more proactive (alert, decisive, and willing to follow through). The cards will provide hints about the easiest way to make change happen.

SUGGESTIONS:

▶ Try to adopt the mindset that big shifts begin with small changes. So don't stress yourself out by immediately globbing onto the most difficult and stubborn problem in your life!

▶ Remind yourself that *you will never be asked to do anything for which you are truly not ready.* The biggest favor you can do for yourself is remembering that life supports you in every moment and in every way possible. You are never alone and never without help.

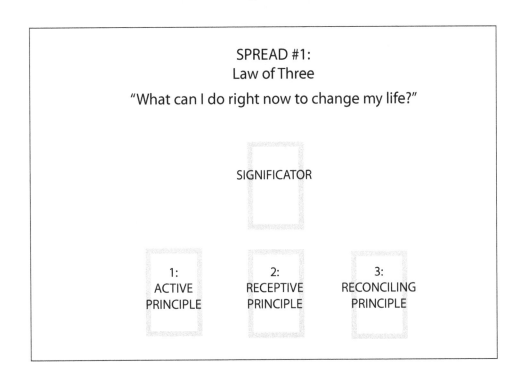

SPREAD #1:
Law of Three
"What can I do right now to change my life?"

SIGNIFICATOR

1:
ACTIVE
PRINCIPLE

2:
RECEPTIVE
PRINCIPLE

3:
RECONCILING
PRINCIPLE

SPREAD #2: Getting acquainted with your inner "cast of characters" using the enneagram. This is a more complex spread that can familiarize you with the enneagram, help you discover your enneagram type, and begin working with the tarot and enneagram together.

Instructions:

1. Arrange the first 10 Keys in the major arcana in an enneagram circle; then clear your mind of outside distractions until you are feeling calm and relaxed.

2. Start with The Fool, who symbolizes the Unknown Self. Ask him *"What can you tell me that is useful to know?"* Jot down your thoughts and impressions as you study the card, including fleeting images, music, lyrics, numbers, or voices from the past. Don't analyze too deeply at this point, just let the impressions flow.

3. Do this for Keys 1–9. When you're done, read its enneagram type description (below). *What does that add to the information you already have?*

4. *Write down a one-sentence "take home" message for each Key.* Try to stay positive and self-supporting.

5. Last step:

   ▶ **If you're trying to discover your type,** *rank the types in order of likelihood. Take the top four and ask a follow-up question (You could even try "Are you my type?" and see what clues you get.)*

   ▶ **If you're asking another question,** *jot down one small way to positively respond to each message; you could also try to come up with an overall theme for the reading (one main "take home" message).*

When I used this spread during the last week of writing this book to gain some sense of perspective, the messages collectively spoke to my weariness and encouraged me to relax, not to worry, and to look to the future.

The Perfecter (1): *A high-minded visionary who believes their actions should always embody their highest ideals.*

The Emotional Intuitive (2): *A tender-hearted, affectionate person who freely expresses their emotions and seeks to bond with others.*

The Self-tester (3): *A naturally productive person who channels their energy into creating abundance in life.*

The Deep Sea Diver (4): *An unconventional individualist who senses that something is missing in life and is always seeking to find it.*

The Puzzle-solver (5): *A mindful observer who often acts as a mentor to others.*

The Steward (6): *A service-oriented skeptic who tends to see outside authority figures as either very positive (the Angel in Key 6) or very negative (the Devil in Key 15).*

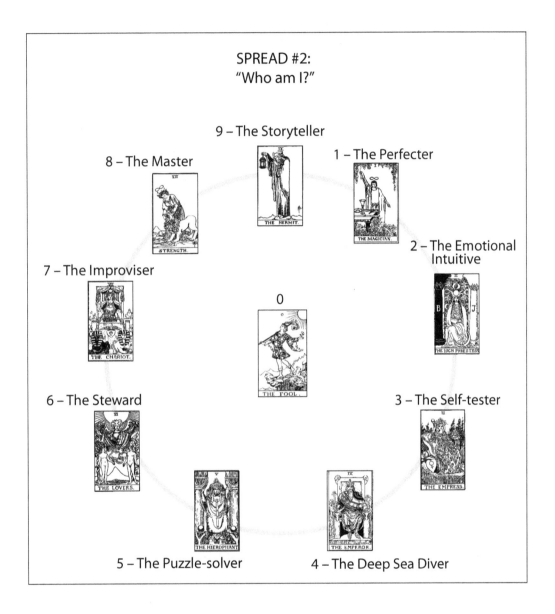

The Improviser (7): *A high-spirited optimist with a yen for travel, adventure, and all kinds of stimulating experiences.*

The Master (8): *A natural leader who can often benefit from developing greater self-discipline and a more diplomatic manner.*

The Storyteller (9): *An imaginative dreamer who loves to "go with the flow" and to blend in with the natural environment.*

SPREAD #3: **Mapping out the hero's journey on the enneagram.** This layout is similar to Spread #2, but the focus is on the nine paths introduced in Chapter 11. The card at Point 0 acts as the Significator, setting the theme for the journey. There are two ways to proceed:

OPTION A: LIFE AS A JOURNEY. The goal here is to imagine your life as a hero's journey and to explore your relationship to each stage in that journey. It's also to mentally bridge the gap between ordinary life (where it's hard to see ourselves as heroes) and the hero's journey (where anyone with enough desire can become a hero).

Instructions. Lay out the cards as shown. Turn over each card one at a time (0–9), making up a hero's story as you go, being as imaginative and free in your storytelling as possible.
What kind of a story is it? Is it the kind you would like to read? Is it anything like your life right now? If not, what is different? Can you imagine yourself as someone on a hero's journey? If not, what would need to change to make that possible? If you could imagine yourself as a hero, what kind of hero would you be?

OPTION B: QUERY ON A CURRENT PROJECT. This approach is more direct and assumes a querent who is involved in some kind of big (i.e., transformative) project: building a house, working up a major proposal, planning a wedding, writing a book, improving an important relationship, or starting a new business.

Instructions. Lay out the cards as in the diagram. Turn over each card in order (0–9). For each card, use the information below to reflect on your own hero's journey in life. Try to stay self-supportive without focusing too much on either your perceived failures or successes.

▶ The **Path of Divine Possibility** (0) *reveals our life theme (the purpose that guides our current incarnation or the creative impulse behind our current project).*

▶ The **Path of Alchemy** (1) *reveals the vision, plan, and guiding principles that allow us to transform ideas into a concrete result.*

▶ The **Path of Intuition** (2) *reveals the power of our intuition to inform our actions and inspire our creations.*

▶ The **Path of Creativity** (3) *shows us how to combine action and intuition to spark creative flow and minimize automaticity.*

▶ The **Path of Individuation** (4) *reveals how to move beyond our conditioned responses to discover our true nature.*

▶ The **Path of Wisdom** (5) *reveals what we know and how to use that knowledge wisely.*

▶ The **Path of Trust in the Goodness of Life** (6) *shows us how to let go of fear and doubt in order to rediscover what is best about life.*

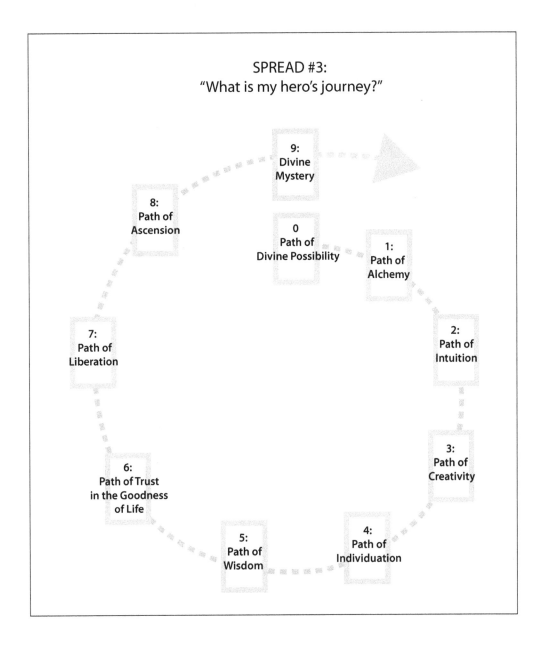

SPREAD #3:
"What is my hero's journey?"

9:
Divine
Mystery

8:
Path of
Ascension

0
Path of
Divine Possibility

1:
Path of
Alchemy

7:
Path of
Liberation

2:
Path of
Intuition

6:
Path of Trust
in the Goodness
of Life

3:
Path of
Creativity

5:
Path of
Wisdom

4:
Path of
Individuation

▶ The Path of Liberation (7) *reveals how to free ourselves from outworn beliefs or patterns in order to experience true inner freedom.*

▶ The Path of Ascension (8) *reveals how to become effective leaders who can fully actualize our potential.*

▶ Divine Mystery (9) *reveals the deeper meaning of the journey and how our experiences allow us to be more aware of the mystery behind manifestation.*

Appendix D:

The Hero's Journey
in the Minor Arcana

BECAUSE THIS IS THE FIRST BOOK linking the tarot with the enneagram, I've chosen to keep things simple by focusing mainly on correspondences between the nine enneagram points and the 22 major arcana Keys in the tarot. There are several reasons for this: the Keys represent major archetypes, they are easy to develop into a three-octave transformational model, and they can be mapped without difficulty onto enneagram Points 1–9.

But truth be told, there are useful links between the minor arcana and the enneagram, especially when we add in the qualities of their suits, which have direct correlates in the enneagram. In this appendix, we'll look at how these two distinguishing characteristics of *number* and *suit* can be used to meaningfully associate the tarot with the enneagram.[1]

We'll start by looking at how the move from Ace to 10 in the minor arcana can be viewed as a journey or progression, using the insightful model developed by Pamela Eakins as a jumping-off point.

Eakins' Approach to the Minor Arcana

Pamela Eakin's progressive approach to the minors is described in her excellent book, *The Tarot of the Spirit* (1992), which accompanies the tarot deck designed by her sister, Joyce Eakins. Unlike the "little white books" included with most decks, *Tarot of the Spirit* is anything but little. It's 448 pages of extensive commentary that relates not only to the deck, but to the deeper symbolism and patterns seen in both the major and minor arcanas.

One of the unique features in this book is Eakins' insightful discussion of the numbered minor arcana cards between Ace and 10, which she characterizes as a progression from raw energy at the Ace to the potential "arrival" at a higher level of development at the Ten.

As Chapter 5 explains, there are ten numbered cards in four minor arcana suits—Wands, Cups, Swords, and Pentacles—making 40 cards total. Each of the suits is said to express the qualities associated with one of the four elements known to the ancients: Wands = *fire*, Cups = *water*, Swords = *air*, and Pentacles = *earth*. With that information in mind, I have paraphrased Eakins' description of the progression as follows:

> At 1, something is beginning to open up; at 2, it becomes polarized; at 3, it becomes dimensional; at 4, it becomes stable; at 5, it begins to move; at 6, it restabilizes; at 7, it becomes highly complex; at 8, it grows; at 9, the suit comes into its highest point. At 10, the suit is completed, a cycle has fulfilled itself, and new ideas or elements begin to enter....At the 10 in any suit, the querist moves on to a new plane of existence (p. 7).

Next, she lists the characteristics of each stage; these are listed in **Table D-1** on the top of the next page. Finally, she depicts this information on a "linear graph of experience," which I have more or less recreated in **Fig. D-1**. She starts by

Table D-1. Pamela Eakins' Minor Arcana Progression.

1. raw energy	6. solution, exaltation, seeing
2. will, purpose, initial understanding	7. feeling, deepening, mystery
3. conception, manifestation	8. repose, consideration, retreat, ripening
4. production, mastery, clinging to achievement	9. understanding beyond words, strengthening
5. surrender, release, destruction	10. processing, moving to a new level

discussing the initial progression from numbers 1–4, noting that 4 represents an "initial peak." At 5, "problems arise," which appear to be resolved at 6. But this resolution is only temporary—as we see by the dramatic "back-to-the-drawing-board" dip at 7. At 8, a more lasting resolution begins; at 9, most of the issues are actually resolved; and at 10, there's a move to a "new level or new way of knowing" (p. 8).

She concludes that the "meaning of numbers 1 through 10 is uniform in every tarot deck," but adds that the four suits are also meaningful (p. 9). Thus ends Eakins' discussion.

When I looked at Fig. D-1, what I saw was a pattern which begins with a stable stage, followed by an unstable stage, followed by the return to stability at a higher level, which yields a three-stage process:

▶ STAGE I: Stable but modest growth: 1–4

▶ STAGE II: Destabilization phase: 5–7

▶ STAGE III: Re-stabilization phase 8–10

Juxtaposing this pattern onto the enneagram yields **Fig. D-2**, which divides the enneagram into three developmental phases. This is extremely similar to the three-stage pattern of the hero's journey pattern discussed in Chapter 4; see Fig. 4-2 and Table 4-1.

Eakin's minor arcana model begins with an easy progression from 1 to 4 followed by an area of instability between 4 and 5; then there is a sharp and difficult climb from 5 to 8 followed by a noticeably gentler up-and-down progression from 8 to 10. On the enneagram, we see the same progression from Points 1–4, the unstable crossing from 4 to 5, a similarly steep climb between Points 5–7, and a gentler progression to Points 9 and 1.[2]

The main difference is that in the hero's journey on the enneagram, the first major shift begins to happen around Point 3, when the hero makes his decision to proceed on the journey, thus setting events into motion.[3] In the minor arcana, we don't really see the effects of that fateful decision right away (although it may be foreshadowed by both the Three of Swords and the Four of Cups). In the minor arcana, both Threes and Fours are usually positive cards, because Threes

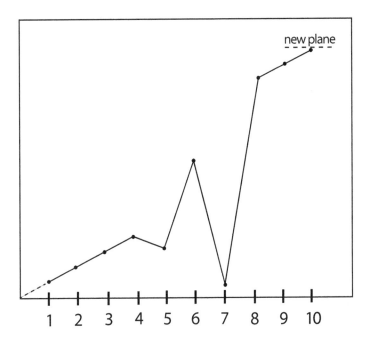

Fig. D-1. Pamela Eakins' Minor Arcana Progression.

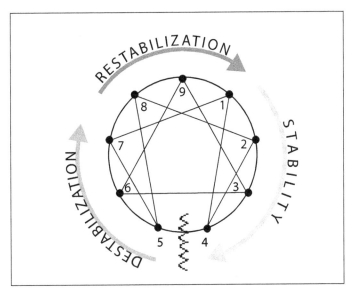

Fig. D-2. Enneagram Three-phase Progression.

Now if we look for a moment at the major arcana in the tarot, we find that these three elements of fire, air, and water are assigned in the Golden Dawn system as follows: fire to Judgement; water to The Hanged Man; and air to The Fool. According to the qabala, these three elements combine to create the fourth element of earth. So there is an exact correlation between the enneagram, tarot, and qabala in this regard (see Appendix E for more on the links between these three systems).[5]

Mapping the Minors onto the Enneagram

Because I'd already linked the three elements of fire, air, and water to the three enneagram energy centers in 2009, when I resumed my study of tarot, I immediately realized it was possible to link specific minor cards to the enneagram using a combination of numbers (1–9) and the elemental properties associated with the three energy centers (fire, air, and water). **Fig. D-3** shows how this works:

▶ Points 2, 3, and 4 can be paired with the watery Two of Cups, Three of Cups, and Four of Cups.

▶ Points 5, 6, and 7 can be paired with the airy Five of Swords, Six of Swords, and Seven of Swords.

▶ Points 8, 9, and 1 can be paired with the fiery Eight of Wands, Nine of Wands, and the Ace of Wands/10 of Wands.

The discussion below details these correspondences; it also includes a brief mention of correspondences to the Keys in the major arcana that share the same number (italicized). We begin with the Ace of Wands because it represents the beginning of a new cycle; we end with the 10 of Wands because it represents the end of one cycle and the beginning of another.

ACE of WANDS.

THE ACE OF WANDS offers us the stark image of a giant hand emerging from a cloud, uprightly grasping a fertile branch. This is a good image to symbolize the raw beginning of any new venture; it can also symbolize the arising of a great creative impulse that inspires us to translate vague dreams into concrete realities, starting with the development of our inner vision and the devising of a long-range plan. *In the major arcana, The Magician (1) depicts the masculine archetype of fiery will.*

THE TWO OF CUPS symbolizes personal love and shared affection in the ordinary (worldly) sense and thus represents our ability to learn about—and

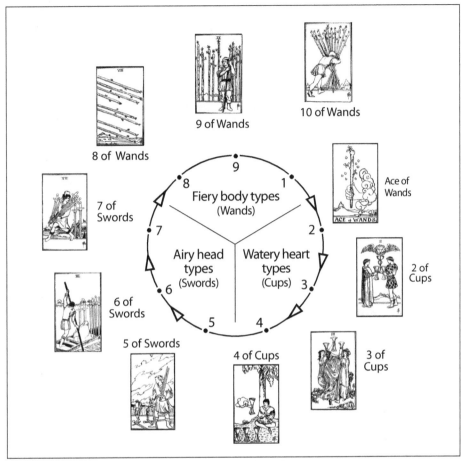

Fig. D-3. The Hero's Journey in the Minor Arcana.
*(The somewhat odd-looking card placement is intended to show
the spiral pattern beginning at the Ace and ending with the 10.)*

experience—deeply personal relationships. It focuses our attention on how the exchange of love and affection (the water in the cups) can bring about mutual healing (the caduceus). The Two of Cups thus shares an affinity with enneagram Point 2, where we learn to love and to share our love with others in close friendships and intimate relationships. *In the major arcana, High Priestess (2) represents the feminine archetype of divine remembrance and intuition.*

THE THREE OF CUPS. Here the emotional energy developed at Two becomes sublimated into creative activity, productive work, and cooperative ventures. And that is just what the image on the card depicts: congenial social interactions between like-minded celebrants. This image is entirely compatible with enneagram Point 3, where we develop the ability to cooperatively participate in interactive events while still retaining our personal goals and our identity as a separate person. The focus here is practical and success is determined

by measurable results, even in our emotional lives. *In the major arcana, The Empress (3) symbolizes the conversion of the hidden resources of The High Priestess into a tri-fold creative process that infuses life with a sense of flow.*

THE FOUR OF CUPS represents the completeness of the number four in the realm of emotion. But an overabundance of emotion can be overwhelming, which may be why the figure on the card seems ambivalent about receiving the water from the fourth cup. There may be other reasons, as well: first, the move from three to four symbolically represents the shift from *flow* to a four-square *foundation*, and emotional energy doesn't like to be static. Second, four represents the end of a cycle, which means we don't know what comes after. But a sensitive person may intuit the big shift that is coming, which is probably why this image seems disquieting. It exactly captures the energy of Point 4 on the enneagram: the place where a person confronts what is real and unreal about themselves and experiences the pain of knowing that—despite the appearance of completeness—there is still something missing from life. This image fits Point 4 so well as to be striking; the expression on the sitter's face is one that enneagram Fours know very well. *In the major arcana, The Emperor (4) also depicts a figure that looks uncomfortable: although he sits on a throne and is adorned with kingly regalia, his throne is in the middle of nowhere and he looks out-of-place in the desert landscape.*

To summarize the journey to this point: We started at the Ace of Wands (fire), with the image of a fresh and upright living branch designed to symbolize the fiery descent from spirit into matter (Point 1 on the enneagram). The next step took us into the element of water, which flows downwards from Points 2–4. The element of water (Cups) is about getting to know ourselves emotionally in a deeply personal and subjective way, and this is how we begin to develop a sense of self: by seeing ourselves as reflected in our relationships (Point 2), developing a self-image and work ethic (Point 3), and realizing the limitations of our persona, which motivates us to seek a more authentic self (Point 4). Moving ahead from this point will entail a complete shift in perspective (which means transitioning from Cups (the domain of subjective feeling) to Swords (the domain of objective thinking).

THE FIVE OF SWORDS represents a completely different world: one in which the need for mental discrimination is paramount and our personal reactions are largely irrelevant. The image on the card shows three people, each of which has developed a different strategy for dealing with this Brave New World: one becomes a predator (and smirks in the foreground), another a victim (and weeps by the water), and the third a mature adult (who has learned to walk away from such extremes). Point 5 on the enneagram is associated with mental operations and the objective mindset; it's where we learn to exercise discrimination and to become impassive rather than to take offense. *In the major arcana, The Hierophant (5) is the ultimate seeker of mental clarity and, later, the dispenser of knowledge (especially arcane or hidden wisdom).*

THE SIX OF SWORDS represents our next step into the world of mental constructs and objective knowledge. But judging by the image, venturing forth into this new world of objectivity is distressing to the more feminine and child-like aspects of the psyche (the seated figures); only the masculine part of the self feels confident in its ability to steer the boat. Air is the element associated with thought; and thought often engenders fear, especially when cut off from the energy of the heart or body. Thus, Point 6 on the enneagram is where we confront our greatest fears: like the previous point, it is the sword ("sacred word") that rends our garments (beliefs), exposing us to life as it is, not as we imagine it to be. This image depicts a moment of solace, telling us that help is always available when truly needed. But it also tells us that our difficulties are not yet resolved, for we are only 2/3 of the way through our journey, and that is always a critical point when failure is likely (that is, unless we can surrender our fears and find a way to trust the process). *In the major arcana, The Lovers (6) is associated both with the paradisiacal Garden of Eden but also with the fateful events that caused our expulsion from the Garden (so it also effectively captures the ambivalence*

of this number). The higher octave of Key 6 is The Devil (15), which again alerts us to the need for tempering trust with discernment.

THE SEVEN OF SWORDS is the last of the Swords (air elements) to be encountered; and like all of them, it is tricky and hard to read. What is the figure on the card up to? Is he stealing swords? Or just playing a practical joke of some kind? (The scene looks more festive than menacing.) Although often associated with deception or trickery, the Seven of Swords can also indicate ingenuity, practical genius, or a talent for making sudden mental leaps. The ambivalence of the image tells us that a lot depends on how we work with the mysterious energy of the number seven—which is especially hard to grasp in the realm of air! Point 7 on the enneagram is also associated with mental quickness and flashes of insight, but also restlessness, guile, and often flexible ethical standards (the archetype of the Trickster). *In the major arcana, The Chariot (7), is associated with youthful power and energy but also with opposing desires that must be reconciled if the vehicle is to actually move forward. (Although the figure in the chariot looks confident, the two funny-looking sphinx capture the "tricky-ness" and humor of striving to look more masterful than we really are!)*

POINT 8: EIGHT OF WANDS symbolizes the move from air to fire—and from mental uncertainty to decisive action. It also symbolizes the move from youth to maturity, to that phase in life when we can fully manifest who we are through our being and our actions. Thus, the Eight of Wands is associated with something coming into imminent manifestation, and this fits the energy associated with Point 8 on the enneagram to a tee. Note the precisely coordinated formation of the flying wands; this is a symbol of perfection in manifestation. This perfection is not an ideal but is embodied as a real-life skill set developed over time and expressed in actions that are achievable but difficult to attain. It is about power developed to a very high level of refinement, a level demonstrated by the great masters in every field of endeavor. *In the major arcana, Strength (8) is associated with the power of patience and devotion to transform undisciplined potential into the mastery that underlies all strength.*

THE NINE OF WANDS is associated in the RWS tarot with the ability to be grounded (unmoving) wherever one is situated, and this is certainly one of the characteristics associated with Point 9 on the enneagram. The RWS image even captures the grumpiness sometimes associated with Nines, especially those who are in the process of waking up. What this particular image does not reveal as obviously is the hidden fire at Point 9, the inner flame that burns eternally, whether visible or not (the power of the triplicity or 3 x 3). Point 9 is the place where *Being* touches *Non-being*, so it represents the ultimate resolving of the opposites. *In the major arcana, The Hermit (9) is associated with solitude and meditation—which is how the opposites get resolved: by allowing them to exist*

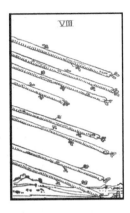  

together without reactivity until all reactivity is dissolved and we know ourselves to be a part of All-That-Is and All-That-Is-Not.

THE TEN OF WANDS is a bit like a *coda* or postscript, in that it is not actually part of the 1–9 cycle but rather the first step in a new cycle. But as a result, it reveals the outcome of the previous cycle and how it sets the stage for the next. The Ten of Wands in the RWS deck is associated with bearing an onerous burden while struggling to (finally) reach home. It has often been qabalistically interpreted as depicting the manifestation of the most ethereal energy (fire) in the densest world (Assiah or physicality), which explains the heaviness of the image: for it can be perceived as a burdensome challenge to bring the subtle energy of spiritual fire into the dense physical world. But the image also provides clues that this task needn't be quite so burdensome as it is currently depicted, if only the figure would rearrange his awkward load or look ahead to his destination, which is now in sight. It might also help to recall the initial impetus for the work—the Ace of Wands—which was to create something new (not to become over-identified with a sense of burden). This is also the lesson to be learned at the higher octave of Point 1 on the enneagram, where willpower must give way to greater flexibility. *We see the same lesson reflected in the major arcana, where the determined Magician (1) encounters The Wheel of Fortune (10), which offers him the chance to adapt to the things in life that cannot be immediately changed.*

❖ ❖ ❖

In this appendix, I've explored one way to link the enneagram with the tarot using minor arcana cards. I foresee the possibility of linking the entire minor arcana with the enneagram, but that would involve some more ambitious explorations into its symbology, especially as depicted in the RWS deck (please see Endnote D-1 or the discussion at the beginning of Chapter 5). My goal here was more modest: simply to open the door to the minors and invite readers to further explore these relationships for themselves.

Notes

[1] As alluded to in Chapter 5, in addition to the suits and numbers of the cards, the Order of the Golden Dawn uses two additional characteristics to interpret the meaning of the cards in the minor arcana: its theorized astrological associations and the qualities associated with the qabalistic sephiroth 1–10. These latter two associations are controversial, because they are not traditional to the tarot. Rather, they are based on ideas set forth by the founders of the Golden Dawn in their efforts to "marry" the tarot with the qabala. However, in this case, the marriage seems a bit forced; as Joseph Gurney has pointedly noted in "The Tarot of the Golden Dawn," (http://www.jwmt.org/v2n17/gurney.html), their method for determining astrological assignments is idiosyncratic and "does not correspond to conventional astrology." As for the idea of assigning the minor cards of each suit with values of 2–10 to the 10 sephiroth on the Tree of Life (starting with sephira 2 and ending with sephira 10), this is also potentially problematic for at least three reasons. One is that sephiroth are ineffable emanations of the Divine while the minor tarot cards are traditionally associated with the affairs of ordinary life; this means there is a *conceptual mismatch* between the two. Another problem is that the sephiroth are arranged *hierarchically*, with the higher-numbered sephiroth being *lower* on the Tree (and therefore symbolizing a denser level of existence); we may question whether this same symbolism ought to be uniformly applied to the cards of the minor tarot. Third, the GD method of assigning meaning to the major and minor cards differs sufficiently that it actually breaks the symbolic connection between majors and minors sharing the same root number (as determined by the numbers printed on each tarot card). Such propositions deserve further discussion. But until now, the Golden Dawn and its successor organizations have simply asserted the validity of their approach without providing any real arguments or evidence to support their assertions; see Part II of Appendix E for a general discussion on the Golden Dawn's approach to tarot correspondences.

[2] On the enneagram, the 1–4 progression represents the involutionary move from spirit to matter while the 5–9 progression is the evolutionary move from matter back to spirit. I have written extensively about the two aspects of transformation on the enneagram; see Chapter 7 in *Archetypes of the Enneagram* (2011) or Chapter 8 in *The Integral Enneagram* (2013).

[3] The enneagram describes three process stages. In Table 4-1, the demarcation between stages occurs at Points 3, 6, and 9; in Fig. D-2, it occurs at 4, 7, and 10. This difference illustrates the slight variations in the way that transformational processes can be conceptualized. On the enneagram, although the destabilization process begins at Point 3 with the decision to move into unknown territory, changes are not really seen at that point. It is only when we get somewhere in the vicinity of Point 4 that a real shift finally begins, as discussed in Chapter 4. It tangibly manifests on the enneagram at the nadir, between 4 and 5, when some kind of irrevocable shift occurs (a shift embodied in the minor arcana as the "dire" scenarios depicted in all the Fives, which portray the dismay we typically experience in the face of change). At Five, there commences a period during which stability alternates with instability (because of the "air" element that tends to introduce fear and doubt). It's not until Point 8 that things begin to crystallize in a way that indicates the final outcome of a transformational process.

[4] Tarot decks that use the Golden Dawn attributions associate the Fives in the minor arcana with the sephiroth Geburah, which describes the quality of severity—another reason the Fives often describe situations which appear adverse from a limited human perspective.

[5] Interestingly, the elemental correspondences I used for each enneagram energy center in *The Positive Enneagram* did not come from any enneagram teacher or published source; I deduced them from studying the properties of the energy centers. At the time, I had not studied qabala and did not know about the three mother letters and the elements they represent (fire, air, and water) or the fact that they combine to create the fourth element of earth. It just made sense to me that this is how the three enneagram centers must work.

Appendix E:

Tarot, Qabala and the Enneagram

THIS APPENDIX FOCUSES ON THE QABALA and its relationship to both the enneagram and the tarot. Although I did not originally intend to discuss the qabala in this book, the deeper I got into my research, the more I realized it was necessary.

One reason is that the tarot and the qabala have become quite intertwined in the minds of many esoterically inclined tarotists. A second is that there's a definite relationship through sacred geometry between the enneagram and qabalistic Tree of Life—which means that there is also a relationship waiting to be delineated between the tarot, the enneagram, and the Tree of Life (**Fig. E-1**). The third and most salient reason is that the most well-known approach used in the English-speaking world to link the tarot with the Tree of Life is the one devised by the original Hermetic Order of the Golden Dawn. However, this approach is not especially helpful for linking the enneagram with the tarot in the way I am proposing in this book (where Key 1 in the tarot can be meaningfully associated with Point 1 on the enneagram, Key 2 with Point 2, and so forth). Why this is true cannot be explained in a few sentences—hence, this appendix, which is divided into two sections.

Part I gives a brief introduction to the qabala and how it has been previously linked to the enneagram, first by a rabbi focusing on the Jewish qabbalah and more recently by me, using sacred geometry principles.

Part II provides a brief history of earlier efforts to link the tarot and qabala, focusing mainly on the Continental system developed by French tarotists in the early to mid-1800s and the Golden Dawn (GD) system launched in England during the last decade of the 19th century. While the GD approach has since become very popular in the English-speaking world, it associates the Keys of the major arcana with symbolic number values derived entirely from the qabala—values that systematically differ from the number values actually printed on the cards. Moreover, its core claim is that their revised system provides the (only) true set of tarot correspondences. This claim is problematic, however, in that it is substantiated by very little credible evidence, as we will see. Thus, my purpose in Part II is to explore the GD approach and how it came to be so widespread, with the aim of re-opening the discussion about the relationship between the tarot and qabala.

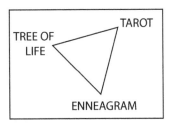

Fig. E-1.
Linking Three Systems.

Part I: The Qabala and the Enneagram

THE DISCUSSION BELOW introduces the qabala and two approaches to linking it with the enneagram.

Qabala 101

The qabala is a complex system that is often considered to be the centerpiece of the Western Esoteric Tradition. According to the modern leaders of the Golden Dawn, Chic and Sandra Cicero, it "professes to describe and categorize the universe, and encompasses knowledge of the universe's fundamental essence, composition, and evolution" (*The Golden Dawn*, p. 96). The qabala (also spelled cabala or kabbalah) can be seen from a Jewish, Christian or magico-Hermetic perspective; the "qabala" spelling usually connotes the last approach.[1]

Just as with the tarot and the enneagram, the origins of the qabala are shrouded in mystery; its deepest roots are likely older than we will ever know, because it is said to be a form of ancient wisdom passed from teacher to student, possibly for millennia. Core qabalistic teachings are described in three written sources: the *Sepher Yetzirah* or *Sefer Yetzirah* (Book of Formation), the *Bahir* (Book of Illumination), and the *Zohar* (Book of Splendor). Because the teachings in all of these books have roots in an oral tradition, it is unclear when they were actually written down for the first time, perhaps in the immediate centuries preceding or following the Common Era (birth of Christ). The ideas they express became better known after the dissemination of the *Zohar* by Rabbi Moshe de Leon in 13th century Spain.[2] Most modern writers consider the qabala to be rooted in Jewish wisdom[3] or mysticism,[4] although there are dissenters, such as Sufi author Idries Shah, who claims that it was part of older Sufi teachings that were later adopted by Jewish mystics.[5]

The source most relevant for our purposes here is the *Sepher Yetzirah (SY)*, a very short work which is widely acknowledged to be the oldest teaching. This is because the *SY* contains the specifications that are used to generate the qabalistic Tree of Life, which is used by Hermetically-oriented qabalists for inner work. The founders of the Golden Dawn were particularly intrigued by the idea that it might be of Egyptian origin—which is not outside the realm of possibility, since it is widely attributed by Hebrew sources to the patriarch Moses. And Moses was not only a Jewish patriarch but someone raised in the royal Egyptian family; he would therefore likely have had access to sources of esoteric wisdom not readily available to other Jews. Regarding the possibility that the qabala is of Egyptian origin, perhaps the attitude of Israel Regardie is the most common: although he acknowledges the key role played by Jewish mystics and the lack of authenticated evidence pointing to Egyptian roots, he says that despite everything, "the practical Theurgy [ceremonial magic] of the Egyptians harmonizes remarkably well with the philosophical theories of the qabalah" (p. 43). This comment echoes the intuitions of 18th and 19th century esotericists who believed both the tarot and the qabala to have Egyptian roots.

The same claim has been recently revived by sacred geometry teacher Drunvalo Melchizedek. Drunvalo adds another dimension to qabala discussions by focusing particularly on the sacred geometry of its primary symbol—the Tree of Life—in the context of sacred geometry and such figures as the Seed of Life, Egg of Life, Flower of Life, and Fruit of Life.[6]

By the 1800s, the qabala—especially in its Jewish and Christian forms—had been known to the public for at least 600 years. Widely esteemed by mystics and esoteric scholars alike, its Tree of Life provided a powerful symbol around which the nascent esoteric renaissance of the late 1700s began to coalesce. As Pamela Eakins puts it in *Tarot of the Spirit*, "the Tree of Life forms the ground-plan, blueprint, or master pattern of the Western Mystery Tradition" (p. 34).

Fig. E-2 shows the qabalistic Tree of Life as envisioned by Christian kabbalist Athanasius Kircher and later adopted by the Golden Dawn.[7] It depicts the ten Divine emanations (*sephiroth* in Hebrew), each of which is numbered; the numbers signify the order in which these emanations issued forth from the Unmanifest to create the world of Manifestation, a process that ultimately culminates in the creation of the entirely physical domain of Malkuth.[8] The Golden Dawn makes the claim that these 10 sephiroth can be linked to the 10 numbered cards of each minor suit in the tarot (although we will not be exploring the merits of that claim here).[9]

The sephiroth are connected by 22 lines (called *paths*), each of which is associated in the *Sepher Yetzirah* with one of the 22 letters in the Hebrew alphabet. Other path attributions have been added over the years; what appears in this particular depiction are the Hebrew letters, the transliteration and meaning of the Hebrew letters in English, and the path numbers.[10] The *Sepher Yetzirah* also speaks of astrological associations which can also be added to the paths.[11]

It's not too hard to see why this figure has been called a Tree: it is vertically-oriented with a narrow base which widens into three vertical branches called *pillars* which are designated as *active* (the right side), *receptive* (the left side), and *equilibrating* (the middle pillar). The active pillar is masculine; the passive pillar is feminine; and the equilibrating pillar is neutralizing. The Tree or its pillars appear in either literal or symbolic form in many of the Keys in the major arcana (e.g., Keys 2, 5, 6, 7, 11, 15, and 20—although in Key 20, the right/left order is reversed).

The Tree of Life is said to describe the four worlds of creation—Atziluth, Briah, Yetzirah, and Assiah—each of which also corresponds with one of the four elements of the ancient world (fire, water, air, and earth, respectively).

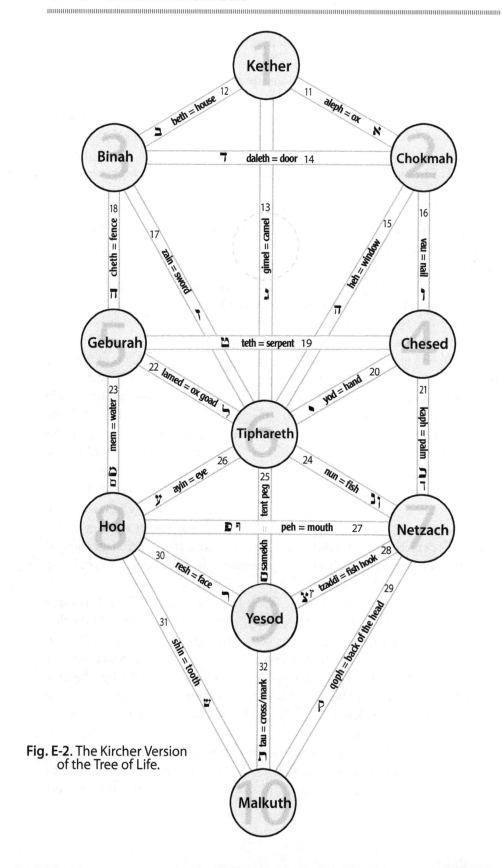

Fig. E-2. The Kircher Version of the Tree of Life.

Atziluth is the fiery spiritual world and includes the sephiroth 1, 2, 3; Briah is the watery creative world and includes the sephiroth 4, 5, 6; Yetzirah is the airy mental world and includes the sephiroth 7, 8, 9; and Assiah is the earthy material world and includes only sephira 10 (the physical world represented by Malkuth); see **Fig. E-3a.**

Fig. E-3b shows the involutionary descent of the Divine energy that created the material world we know at Malkuth. This descent is called the Path of the Lightning Flash and it's the same one we see hitting The Tower in Key 16. We who dwell in the material world find our way back to Source by ascending up the Tree through the process of *pathworking*, a technique that involves meditating deeply on the nature of each path in a way that inwardly connects the individual with that path, so that its energies can be worked with and mastered. In this way, one can gradually work from the bottom to the top of the Tree.

Another way to depict the qabala is by grouping the sephiroth within the top three worlds into three categories, represented by the Supernal, Ethical, and Astral Triangles (**Fig. E-3c**). The Supernal Triangle represents the triadic energies of the Divine, whereas the other two triangles are said to be reflections of the Divine. The Ethical Triangle represents the higher mind, feeling, and imagination, while the Astral Triangle represents the everyday personality self (its reasoning, emotions, and imaginings).

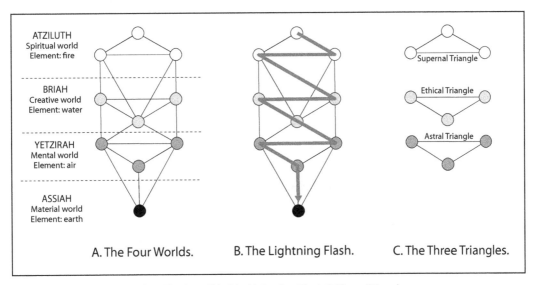

Fig. E-3. The Four Worlds, Lightning Flash & Three Triangles.

The Enneagram & the Qabala (Dualistic Perspective)

Generally speaking, there has not been a lot written about the relationship between the enneagram and qabala, probably because—esoterically speaking—the enneagram is a newbie system that only made its first public appearance (courtesy of G. I. Gurdjieff) about a century ago.[12] But to both Gurdjieff and Idries Shaw, the enneagram is only new in the sense of being newly *revealed*. (Like many esoteric systems, its roots are said to be ancient but well-hidden.)

The only historical attempt that has been made to link the enneagram with the Tree of Life comes from Rabbi Howard Addison, who published *The Enneagram and Kabbalah* in 1998. Although I was initially intrigued by the title, the book turned out to be less useful than I had imagined.

For starters, the author links the enneagram with the Hebrew kabbalah, not the Hermetic qabala. This is not surprising, since he is a rabbi. Thus, his interpretation is based on a very traditional Judeo-Christian point of view, with a strong emphasis on the Fall of humankind into a state of sin as the result of disobeying God's commands.

The author appears to see this view as universal, allowing him to state with confidence that "religions classically depict saints and sinners as having fairly specific virtues or vices" (p. 41)—a statement that lays the groundwork for discussing the virtues and vices attributed to the nine enneagram types by enneagram teachers who hold a dualistic view of human nature.[13] But what Rabbi Addison states is not true of all religions, just dualistic religions (just as the division of enneagram type characteristics into "good" and "bad" categories only makes sense from a dualistic point of view).

From Rabbi Addison's point of view, then, it makes sense to suppose that people start out in a state of original innocence but "fall" into a state of ego-personality, as the result of social conditioning and cognitive development: "Like the Adam [and Eve] tales, the narrative that underlies the Enneagram theory of personality presupposes both Original Rightness and a Fall," p. 21.

He is indeed correct in his assertion if we are talking about the theory of the personality enneagram as taught by Oscar Ichazo and subsequently inherited by later generations of enneagram teachers. But this is precisely why I do not use this model in my enneagram work.[14] It's for the same reasons that I embrace a Hermetic view of the qabala—one that focuses not on our self-limiting beliefs but on what we can become.

But even apart from these philosophical differences, there are other problems involving the way that Rabbi Addison seeks to link the nine enneagram types with the ten sephiroth, which he does by associating Type 1 with Chokmah (2), Type 2 with Binah (3), Type 3 with Chesed (4), Type 4 with Tiphareth (6), Type 5 with Geburah (5), Type 6 with Netzach (7), Type 7 with Hod (8), Type 8 with Yesod (9), and Type 9 with Malkuth (10).[15]

You might notice here that the numbers of the type and the sephiroth do not match up (except for Type 5). But of course not all correspondences are numeric, so this is not necessarily a fatal problem, although it does seem rather odd. You might also notice that he switches the order (by associating Type 4 with Tiphareth and Type 5 with Netzach). This switch in order definitely bothers me, because when it comes to both the sephiroth and the enneagram points, *order matters*. But the author offers no other justification for making this change other than the idea that Type 4 seems to match up well with "Beauty," the attribute traditionally associated with Tiphareth (6).

Another problem for me is that I did not find the comparisons made between the types and the sephiroth very compelling. When I first became aware of the Tree of Life, I also looked for parallels between the sephiroth and the nine types, but could not fit them together in a way that seemed truly "on point." For one thing, the sephiroth are described in the *Sepher Yetzirah* as cosmic emanations or dimensions, which makes them extraordinarily abstract in nature. But the enneagram points are described as personality types, which (while complex) are not abstract. If they are to be meaningfully related to the sephiroth, the parallels between the two must be carefully justified.

Another problem is that the Tree of Life is depicted as a hierarchical model of reality, which means that the sephiroth in the Supernal Triangle are considered to be purer/highest/closer to Source than those in the "lower" two triangles. This is also true of the paths: anyone who works with the qabala sees frequent references to the idea that, while the paths close to Malkuth may be important, they lack the spiritual status of those higher up the Tree. The ranking procedures in the Golden Dawn also embody this assumption: the higher up the Tree you go, the higher your grade.[16]

Thus, when we liken the enneagram points to the sephiroth, it's hard to avoid implying that those assigned to the higher sephiroth must somehow be more evolved than those assigned to the lower sephiroth—even if that is not our intention.

Given the limitations of *The Enneagram and Kabbalah*, I would not consider it a useful starting point for exploring the relationship between the enneagram and qabala, especially from a Hermetic perspective.

The Enneagram & the Qabala (Sacred Geometry Perspective)

But there is another way to link the enneagram with the qabalistic Tree of Life, one based on sacred geometry. In *The Doctrine of Transcendental Magic*, Éliphas Lévi describes the three triangles of the qabala as examples of the Law of Equilibrium, which is the same principle that Gurdjieff has called the Law of Three—a principle which has been extensively referenced throughout this book, because it is the basis for the enneagram. At the end of his description, Lévi observes that "such, according to the Kabalah, is the groundwork of all religions and all sciences—*a triple triangle and a circle* [emphasis mine]."[17]

A triple triangle and a circle? That description sounds to me a lot like the enneagram! (See Fig. E-9, at the end of this section.) Such a quote points to a probable relationship between the two systems. However, sacred geometry provides an even more direct pointer. This is the relationship we'll explore below.[18]

The first thing to observe is that, although the *Sepher Yetzirah (SY)* describes the Tree of Life, it does not describe its exact appearance, only its specifications. It's as if the teachers of the *Sepher Yetzirah* were actually looking at the Tree of Life and describing it in words. If so, this suggests that the Tree is older than the *SY.* One well-known modern teacher of sacred geometry, Drunvalo Melchizedek, says that the Tree of Life is not Hebrew in origin but is "outside of any race or religion. It's a pattern that is intimately part of nature." He goes on to observe that there are carvings of the Tree in Egyptian pillars that are about 5000 years old.[19]

While I was recently re-reading Drunvalo's two-volume book series, I realized that it revealed a way to directly link the enneagram with the Tree of Life. The paragraphs below explain how this works.

The section I was reading was about the sacred geometry of the human chakra system, starting on page 310. Drunvalo likens the eight human chakras to the Egg of Life, a figure that depicts the first eight cells of a human embryo. He shows a drawing of the Egg of Life like the one in **Fig. E-4a.**

A. Egg of Life
(3-D Seed of Life)

B. Seed of Life on
the Flower of Life

C. Tree of Life on
the Flower of Life

Fig. E-4. The Flower of Life and its Derivations.

Please notice in this figure that, geometrically speaking, the Egg of Life is identical to the Seed of Life (**Fig. E4b**); the only difference is that the Egg of Life looks 3-D while the Seed looks either 2-D or like a transparent version of the Egg. Notice also that both the Seed of Life and the Tree of Life can be placed on the Flower of Life (FOL) (**Fig. E4c**). This tells us that all these figures are closely related. Now to give you an idea of where we're going, what I propose to show is that the Egg of Life is one way of depicting the enneagram in 3-D. If so, then the enneagram and the Tree of Life are intimately related through their geometric roots in the Flower of Life.

The following discussion will explain how this works. Some parts are fairly technical; if there's anything you don't understand, just skip over it and read the bits that make sense.

Continuing with Drunvalo's discussion, after he talks about the Egg of Life, he talks about the human chakra system, which has eight main chakras. He says that if we start with the Egg of Life and carefully unfold it, we will see an upright pattern of eight circles representing the eight main chakras in the human body (**Fig. E-5**). He explains the chakras in this way:

> You have the same change-in-direction half steps between the third and fourth chakras and the seventh and eighth chakras. And there's still that special change between the fourth and fifth chakras, the heart and the sound chakras. These movements are also found in the harmonics of music (p. 311).

At this point, Drunvalo mentions the polarity change as something "that Gurdjieff talks about," noting that "it is the place where the polarity reverses, changing from female to male" (p. 312). He illustrates this idea using the musical scale (**Fig. E-6**). This figure shows the two changes of direction at the half-steps and the change of polarity between *fa* and *sol*.

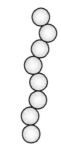

Fig. E-5.
The Eight Chakras.

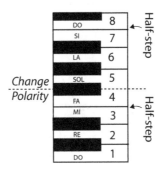

Fig. E-6.
The Diatonic Scale.

He also provides a third approach to look at the same principle: by reference to the 3-D figure of the *star tetrahedron*. The star tetrahedron is very interesting, because it is a composite figure having two complete tetrahedrons (one male and the other female), each of which has four points, which can be likened to the four notes on the scale in Fig. E-6. Thus, together they create the same eight notes that we see on the diatonic scale (**Fig. E-7a**).

Drunvalo provides a detailed breakdown of how the movement from point to point (1–8) is like moving up the scale from *do* at 1 to *do* at 8 (**Fig. E-7b**). This figure also shows the movement through the void between 4 and 5, a void represented on the enneagram as the chaotic nadir between Points 4 and 5.

When I was initially exposed to this material in Drunvalo's FOL workshops in the 1990s, this material didn't very mean much to me. But when I returned to these ideas after working with the enneagram for a long time, I suddenly saw something that amazed me. I knew that the star tetrahedron is known as the *merkaba* (chariot), which is the light body which encompasses each human being—and which acts as a vehicle for moving between different dimensions of reality. We have already talked about this in Chapter 14, in the discussion of Key 7 (The Chariot) and Key 25 (Merkaba). But what I did not know until that moment of realization is that *the merkaba is the enneagram as it was first introduced by Gurdjieff.*

There are several unmistakable clues that support this assertion.

The first is Drunvalo's casual reference to Gurdjieff on page 312. What he does not say is just how much emphasis Gurdjieff placed on the musical scale in his teachings—how it is the central metaphor used for describing the enneagram. This is why *In Search of the Miraculous* (ISM) contains extensive references to Gurdjieff's fascinating but often obscure allusions to the diatonic scale and the role of octaves in human evolution, all leading up to the unveiling of the enneagram. It is crystal clear from Gurdjieff's teachings that the enneagram and the diatonic scale are one and the same. So anything that

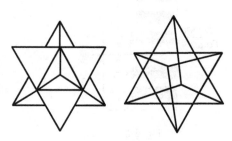

Fig. E-7a.
Front & Side View
of a Star Tetrahedron.

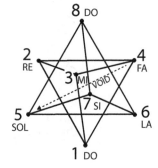

Fig. E-7b.
The Star Tetrahedron
as a Sequence.

is true of this scale will be true of the enneagram. (See the discussion in "The Turn at the Bottom of the Enneagram" in Chapter 7 and Fig. 9-1 in Chapter 9, which shows the enneagram depicted as a scale; this figure is very like Fig. 51 on p. 291 of *ISM*).

The second clue is that, according to Drunvalo, Gurdjieff describes a polarity switch from female to male in the middle of the scale—which is precisely the place where we switch from the female to male in the creation of a star tetrahedron *and* the enneagram. Although I do not recall seeing a direct reference by Gurdjieff to a polarity switch between Points 4 and 5—and believe me, I have looked—I intuitively realized long ago that such a switch must occur, and have written about it quite a bit. It is also discussed in "The Turn at the Bottom of the Enneagram," in Chapter 8, where I characterize the nadir as the place where there's a crossover from (feminine) involution to (masculine) evolution. For other discussions of the masculine and feminine halves of the enneagram, see Chapter 8 in *The Integral Enneagram*, especially Tables 8-1 and 8-2.

But the third and most definitive clue concerns the strange placement of the "shock points" on the enneagram. Gurdjieff taught that the enneagram consists of seven tones and two shock points that are associated with the semitones. In an ascending diatonic scale, these occur between *mi-fa* and *si-do*, a fact that Gurdjieff readily acknowledges. But he actually places the second shock point on the enneagram between *sol-la*, **not** *si-do*, remarking that "the apparent placing of the interval in *its wrong place* itself shows to those who are able to read the symbol what kind of 'shock' is required for the passage from 'si' to 'do'," (*ISM*, p. 291, emphasis his). (See Figs. 8-2 and 9-1 and the discussions around them for more on the shock points.)

While I cannot pretend to have solved the mystery of "what kind of shock is required," I *have* discovered that it is possible using a 3-D star tetrahedron to visually perceive the whole steps and half steps where Gurdjieff actually placed them on the enneagram (i.e., in the "wrong" place).[17] It can be done using Drunvalo's instructions on pp. 312–313, which are designed to allow someone to map the diatonic scale (and by inference, the Egg of Life and the human chakra system) onto a star tetrahedron.

The only caveat is that the star tetrahedron must be held at the correct angle (an angle that will need to change slightly after the first tetrahedron interval of *do–fa* is completed). You'll need a 3-D star tetrahedron to see how it works.

If we think in terms of 3-D reality, we know that the half-step we perceive when we follow Drunvalo's instructions is, in fact, an optical illusion. But if we think in 2-D reality (by imagining the star tetrahedron as a flat figure), then the illusion becomes real.[18]

This exercise convinced me that the enneagram is a flat version of a three-dimensional star tetrahedron, which—in its 3-D version—is the light body of a human being. When activated, it is said to serve as the vehicle that will allow humankind to experience a much expanded sense of awareness (to travel "between the worlds") while remaining in physical incarnation, a process known as Ascension. It is the existence of the Light Body at Key 25 that allows Ascension to occur at Key 26 (see Chapter 14).

This is why I said at the beginning of this section that the enneagram must be directly and intimately related to the Tree of Life: because the enneagram is the Egg of Life (and thus, also the Seed of Life). Drunvalo links the two by juxtaposing the Tree of Life on the Seed of Life (**Fig. E-8**). His comment: "See how perfectly they fit? They become like a key, one fitting directly over the other."

They do indeed fit perfectly together—demonstrating the direct relationship between the enneagram and the Tree of Life. All that remains is to work out the details of such a relationship. However, Lévi's earlier mention of three triangles and a circle (**Fig. E-9**) could easily refer not only to the three triangles within the enneagram circle, but the three triangles on the Tree of Life (Fig. E-8).

Since my primary focus is on linking the enneagram with the tarot, I will leave this subject for the time being. I invite the reader to ponder the exact nature of the correspondences between the enneagram and the Tree of Life, and what it might reveal about the relationship between the enneagram, the tarot, and the qabala.

Fig. E-8.
The Tree of Life &
Seed of Life
Juxtaposed.

Fig. E-9.
The Three
Triangles.

Part II: The Qabala and Tarot

NOW THAT WE'VE TAKEN A LOOK at the qabala and how it can be related through sacred geometry to the enneagram, let's take a look at the qabala and how it is potentially related to the tarot. Unlike the enneagram or Tree of Life, the tarot is not a geometric construct. So if it is to be related to the qabala, a different approach must be used. In Part II, we'll look at two different approaches: one advocated by French occultists and Continental deck designers and the other advocated by the Order of the Golden Dawn. We'll also look at how the two came to differ and what modern tarot authors and deck designers have to say about the best way to describe the relationship between the tarot and qabala.

Historical Roots

Ever since the Antoine Court de Gébelin first noticed the esoteric potential of the tarot in the last quarter of the 18th century, esotericists have been trying to link it with the qabala, a system of great antiquity often said to have originated with Moses. A contemporary of de Gébelin's, the Comte de Mellet, was the first to point out that, since there are 22 major Keys in the tarot and 22 connecting paths on the qabalistic Tree of Life, perhaps the two were related. He was also the first to attempt to link the major Keys of the tarot with the qabalistic paths. Later French occultists such as Etteilla, Papus, and Éliphas Lévi were also intrigued by the possibility of linking the tarot with the qabalistic Tree of Life.

However, it is Lévi (1810–1875) who is best remembered for his efforts to match up the two systems. As a charismatic magician and prolific writer, Lévi was an enormously influential individual in the world of 19th century esotericism. He was a born synthesizer who searched diligently for correspondences between the tarot, qabala, and astrology. He obviously had a deep respect for the tarot, which he reverently referred to as "that miraculous work which inspired all the sacred books of antiquity."[19]

Given Lévi's veneration of the tarot, it is not surprising that the approach he developed to link the tarot with the qabala was designed to preserve the original number symbolism of the tarot as much as possible. This was not an easy task, because like the tarot Keys, the Hebrew letters also have numeric meanings. The Hebrew letter *Aleph* is associated with the number 1, *Beth* with the number 2, *Gimel* with the number 3, and so forth. Furthermore, the numbering system is different, in that the numbers associated with the tarot Keys range from 0–21 while the numbers associated with the Hebrew alphabet range from 1–22.

Lévi took the approach of pairing *Aleph*, the first letter of the Hebrew alphabet, with Key 1 (The Magician); the second letter *Beth* with Key 2 (The High Priestess); and so forth. Linking *Aleph* to The Magician gives it a symbolic value of 1—which is identical to the traditional value associated with the card. The same is true for The High Priestess and, indeed, for all 21 Keys having positive integers as values. The only tarot Key not already assigned to a positive integer is The Fool; if the tarot is to be mapped to the qabalistic paths on the Tree, The Fool must be assigned a positive integer *because there is no zero in the Hebrew alphabet.*

This might seem like a small point, but symbolically, it is a problem, because zero is very different from all the positive integers, as discussed in Chapter 9. The zero value of The Fool in the tarot is what numerically distinguishes it from all the other Keys, conferring upon The Fool the ability to symbolize either the *allness* of life, (both manifest and unmanifest) or nothingness of life (its unmanifest state of *emptiness,* the word "zero" being derived from the Sanskrit word "sunya," meaning empty or void). However, the paths on the Tree of Life are all part of the manifest world. Once we assign The Fool a positive integer, we place it 100% into the manifest world, thus depriving it of its uniquely dual symbolism.

Lévi's solution was a compromise. He assigned The Fool to the Hebrew letter *Shin,* which comes second to last in the Hebrew alphabet and has a value of 300. Although this assignment does not preserve the symbolism of the zero, it does allow the rest of the tarot Keys to be assigned to numbers that match their face value. So in a very real sense, we could say that Key 0, The Fool, was sacrificed for the sake of the other 21 Keys.

But the fact that such a sacrifice is necessary means that the match between the 22 Keys and the 22 Hebrew letters is far from perfect. This is a critical point, because it calls into question the root assumption that qabala and tarot are parallel systems that can be perfectly reconciled. Maybe they can—but to date, no one has completely solved the pesky problem of what to do with The Fool.

Lévi's approach generates what has been called the *French, Continental* or *Marseille system of tarot correspondences.* It is distinguished by its emphasis on retaining the traditional values of the Keys (the ones printed on the cards). It remains the system most favored to this day by tarotists on the European Continent and is often associated with the older French Marseille-style decks and the tarotists who prefer them (e.g., Irene Gad in *Tarot and Individuation,* 1994; Elizabeth Haich in *Wisdom of the Tarot,* 1983; Oscar Wirth in *Tarot of the Magicians,* 1927/2012; and Papus in *Tarot of the Bohemians,* 1892). Its correspondences can also be seen in newer decks that rely on Lévi's system of correspondences (e.g., Manly P. Hall's New Art Tarot,[23] Luis Pena Longo's El Gran Tarot Esoterico, or Christine Payne-Towler's Tarot of the Holy Light).[20]

One of the weaknesses of Lévi's approach is that, like his predecessors, he does not provide any real conceptual rationale for linking the 22 Keys with the 22 qabalistic paths; he simply relies on the coincidence that both systems have 22 important elements to make his argument for him. So Lévi's exploration into the idea of linking the tarot with the qabala through their numbers falls more into the category of a tentative exploration than a definitive argument. This may be why Lévi never physically positioned the 22 major arcana Keys on the 22 paths on the Tree of Life: because he knew the problems of linking the two systems had not been fully worked out.[21]

As we shall see, the founders of the Golden Dawn (GD) devised a much more radical solution: to solve the problem by simply not considering it a problem! Instead, they assigned a value to each Key that differed from its face value and didn't bother to justify this departure from tradition. However were they able to do this? That is a question we'll explore below. But first we'll take a closer look at the differences between the traditional Continental approach and the Golden Dawn's revision.

The Golden Dawn's New Tarot Correspondences

We have already looked at the Continental approach in some depth in the previous section. But to sum up, in the Continental approach, the numbers actually printed on the tarot cards are assumed to be there for a reason. Thus, an effort is made to retain those values for all the major arcana Keys except The Fool.

If you recall the comments from tarot authors in Chapter 9, when the tarot is considered in isolation, most of these authors express the view that numbers convey symbolic information, which means that the numbers on the cards are meaningful, not arbitrary. This view is thus logically consistent with the Continental approach to tarot correspondences.

By contrast, in the Golden Dawn's system, the numeric values assigned to all 22 Keys are derived entirely from the qabala. This is because of the way in which the values are assigned: by starting with the first element in each system and assigning values in sequential order from that point onward. So the first three assignments look like this:

The Fool (0) = *Aleph* (1)

The Magician (1) = *Beth* (2)

The High Priestess (2) = *Gimel* (3)

The same pattern prevails for the other 19 Keys: each is systematically assigned to a Hebrew number-letter that is not the same as the face value of the tarot card.[22]

In addition, a defining characteristic of the Golden Dawn's approach is its claim that the proposed attributions are the "only true attributions"—despite the fact that the Golden Dawn has never presented any compelling evidence to substantiate that claim. And yet, this system of attributions has become extremely influential among modern English-speaking tarotists and qabalists for reasons we'll explore below.

But first let's take a comprehensive look at the differences between these two systems, shown in **Table E-1** on the next page. The Continental approach (the one also embraced by A. E. Waite in his design of the RWS tarot)[23] is shown in the shaded columns on the *left*; the approach promoted by the Golden Dawn is shown in the unshaded columns on the *right*. It is easy to see how the Continental approach links the tarot to the qabala in a way that preserves 21 of the 22 numeric values of the Keys while the GD approach alters them.[24]

You might expect that both these tarot attribution systems would be mentioned as possible alternatives in tarot books that also discuss the qabala. But in the great majority of books published in English, the GD system is presented as though it is the only real option available, especially in books intended for the mass market. A diligent researcher can however find at least a brief mention of the two systems in more esoteric works such as Stuart Kaplan's *The Encyclopedia of Tarot, Vol. 1* (pp. 15–16); *The Underground Stream* (1999) by Christine Payne-Towler (pp. 15–16, 118–119); *A History of the Occult Tarot* (2002) by Decker and Dummett (pp. 82–84); *A Cultural History of the Tarot* (2009) by Helen Farley (pp. 129–136); or Appendix A in Mary Greer's *Who Are You in the Tarot?* (2011). But such discussions tend to be hard to follow; often, there is just a chart showing the different attributions, but with little accompanying discussion about the circumstances that created two different systems.[25]

The result is that the majority of people who become interested in qabalistic tarot in English-speaking cultures are initially aware of only the Golden Dawn system of tarot correspondences. That was certainly true in my case. When I was new to the tarot and thirsty to gain a deeper knowledge of the system, one of the first things I did was to dutifully memorize the GD correspondences.

But every once in a while, I would encounter a book or a deck which used the Continental system (e.g., Gad's excellent *Tarot and Individuation*). I did not know what I was seeing, just that the Hebrew letter attributions were different. Therefore, I found books like these confusing. I put all the ones that didn't use the GD system on a back shelf and even considered ditching them altogether. But I decided instead to wait until I understood the reason for the difference in approach.

However, at the same time I was memorizing the GD tarot attributions, I was also beginning to notice the correspondences between the tarot Keys and enneagram types sharing the same number. To me, these correspondences were not something I read about in a book; they were based upon my direct experiences with people of all nine enneagram types and my growing understanding of the 22 tarot Keys.

What I could not have known at the time was that the GD attributions that I faithfully learned were actually at odds with the correspondences I was noticing between the enneagram and tarot, because they discounted the significance of the numbers printed on the tarot cards. I also did not yet realize that the ap-

Table E-1. Continental vs Golden Dawn Tarot Correspondences.									
Tarot Key Printed Value & Card Name	CONTINENTAL APPROACH (LÉVI,* WIRTH, PAPUS, RWS DECK) *Values printed on TAROT KEYS predominate*				GOLDEN DAWN APPROACH (Cipher MSS/Book of T) *Values of HEBREW LETTERS predominate*				
	ORDER	TAROT VALUE	HEBREW LETTER/ NUMERIC VALUE	HEBREW MEANING*	ORDER	TAROT VALUE	HEBREW LETTER/ NUMERIC VALUE	HEBREW MEANING
0 – Fool	After Key 20	none or 0	Shin (300)	Tooth	1st	none or 0	Aleph (1)	Ox
1 – Magician	1st	1	Aleph (1)	Ox	2nd	1	Beth (2)	House
2 – High Priestess	2nd	2	Beth (2)	House	3rd	2	Gimel (3)	Camel
3 – Empress	3rd	3	Gimel (3)	Camel	4th	3	Daleth (4)	Door
4 – Emperor	4th	4	Daleth (4)	Door	5th	4	He (5)	Window
5 – Hierophant	5th	5	He (5)	Window	6th	5	Vau (6)	Nail
6 – Lovers	6th	6	Vau (6)	Nail	7th	6	Zayin (7)	Sword
7 – Chariot	7th	7	Zayin (7)	Sword	8th	7	Cheth (8)	Fence
8 – Strength**	8th	8	Cheth (8)	Fence	9th	8	Teth (9)	Snake
9 – Hermit	9th	9	Teth (9)	Snake	10th	9	Yod (10)	Hand
10 – Wheel of Fortune	10th	10	Yod (10)	Hand	11th	10	Kaph (20)	Grasping hand
11 – Justice	11th	11	Kaph (20)	Grasping hand	12th	11	Lamed (30)	Ox goad
12 – Hanged Man	12th	12	Lamed (30)	Ox goad	13th	12	Mem (40)	Water
13 – Death	13th	13	Mem (40)	Water	14th	13	Nun (50)	Fish
14 – Temperance	14th	14	Nun (50)	Fish	15th	14	Samech (60)	Tool
15 – Devil	15th	15	Samech (60)	Tool	16th	15	Ayin (70)	Eye
16 – Tower	16th	16	Ayin (70)	Eye	17th	16	Peh (80)	Mouth
17 – Star	17th	17	Peh (80)	Mouth	18th	17	Tzaddi (90)	Fish hook
18 – Moon	18th	18	Tzaddi (90)	Fish hook	19th	18	Qoph (100)	Back of head
19 – Sun	19th	19	Qoph (100)	Back of head	20th	19	Resh (200)	Face
20 – Judgement	20th	20	Resh (200)	Face	21st	20	Shin (300)	Tooth
21 – Universe	21st	21	Tau (400)	Cross/mark	22nd	21	Tau (400)*	Cross/mark

* The positioning of the Fool in the penultimate position is Lévi's.

** Please note however that many Continentalists use the older approach of assigning Strength a value of 11 and Justice as value of 8; see, e.g., pp. 72–77 in Pollack's *Seventy Eight Degrees of Freedom* or pp. 9–11 in Banzhaf 's *Tarot and the Journey of the Hero* for a discussion.

proach used to assign values to tarot cards was not developed in a manner that would have earned my respect had I understood the motives or methods of its developers. The last thing I didn't yet know about was the strong but unsupported claim made by the original magicians of the Golden Dawn: that they had been gifted with the *one and only correct set of attributions* (attributions either undiscovered or unrevealed by their French predecessors such as Lévi).

To a casual user of the tarot, the existence of such claims might not matter much. But to someone who uses the tarot for qabalistic work in the Golden Dawn tradition, it might matter a lot. Case in point: a friend of mine who is well-versed in the Golden Dawn system. When I told her about this book, she wondered aloud whether it's possible to link the tarot with the enneagram using the values printed on the cards, because these are not their "real" values (i.e., the values assigned by the Golden Dawn).

Hmmm....although I was aware at that point that the GD had linked each Key with a Hebrew letter, I was less aware of the extent to which the values associated with those letters would be seen as more important than the values actually printed on the cards. So her comments initially took me aback.

At the same time, it remained my strong conviction that the numbers on the cards have great symbolic significance. It dawned upon me, however, that to the extent that modern tarot culture has been influenced by the teachings of the Golden Dawn, this "obvious" assumption may not be obvious at all. I realized I had to do the historical research necessary to understand how the numerology of the tarot as an independent system had seemingly become subsumed by the numerology of the qabala (or at least, the GD's version of the qabala).

Synchronistically, it was at just about that time that I discovered Christine Payne-Towler's *The Underground Stream: Esoteric Tarot Revealed* (2000). This is the first book I encountered that talks extensively about the Continental system, which Christine favors over the one devised by the Golden Dawn. I had the opportunity to talk with her about these ideas during and after the 2017 Northwest Tarot Symposium in Portland, Oregon. She said that, although the Golden Dawn approach is the one that everyone in English-speaking cultures knows, she prefers the Continental approach because it is more true to the historic spirit of the tarot. It was our discussions that paved the way for my discovery of other books that explore the same topic.[26]

Those same discussions made me aware of the pivotal role that prominent Golden Dawn members (notably, William Westcott, Aleister Crowley, and A. E. Waite) played in shaping the way that English-speaking esotericists in the late 19th and early 20th centuries came to view the historic works of the French school, with whom they were in direct and fierce competition. These three authors were prolific translators of esoteric Hebrew and French works, and in their translations, they often included disparaging comments about the works they were translating. One of the chief targets of those comments was the system of tarot correspondences developed by Lévi. As Payne-Towler pointedly observes, these GD authors

> are not just saying "we like our correspondences better" or that "there are other versions than Lévi's." No, they are saying that...the English fellows [of the Golden Dawn] have "the correct attributions" known only to "full initiates" like themselves.[27]

It is likely that the Golden Dawn took such an aggressive approach because as a newly minted secret society, their leaders needed members. To get them, they had to demonstrate that their group was privy to knowledge that others lacked (especially since their new tarot attributions constituted such a radical departure from those they sought to discredit). Over time, the new attributions became popularized to the extent that many modern-day English-speaking tarotists know no others.

But tarot historians are fully aware of just how radically different these new attributions were from the historical attributions, as the following comments reveal:

▶ "[The Golden Dawn] attribution...was quite new, contradicting that propounded by Éliphas Lévi and everybody else" (Ronald Decker and Michael Dummett, *A History of the Occult Tarot*, p. 82).

▶ "This [Golden Dawn] theory of tarot attributions was at odds with all kabbalistic theories of tarot that had preceded it" (Helen Farley, *A Cultural History of the Tarot*, p. 132).

▶ "[Although] the creators of the Golden Dawn tarot system were familiar with the French tradition [used by Lévi]...[they] deviated markedly from it in creating their own tarot lineage" (Mary Greer, in "Golden Dawn Correspondences for Astrology and Tarot").[28]

Greer's last line is particularly instructive, in that she speaks of the Golden Dawn as "creating their own tarot lineage." To the extent that the Golden Dawn really did create a new tarot lineage, where does that leave the "old" tarot lineage (i.e., the old numbering system and the ideas that created it)?

It appears to leave them twisting slowly in the wind. According to Christine Payne-Towler,

> the effort made by the Golden Dawn undertook to create the impression of having an authentic body of teachings and practices was so convincing and so thorough that they single-handedly managed to call into question the veracity of two previous centuries of esoteric scholarship.[29]

Given the number of books that now seem to accept the Golden Dawn's teachings as "givens," it's hard to characterize this conclusion as overstated—especially when one becomes aware of exactly how the Golden Dawn came to adopt their new set of tarot correspondences. When I delved into the origins of the Golden Dawn and their teachings, it was like chasing the White Rabbit into Wonderland: as the story unfolded, it got curiouser and curiouser.

The *Cipher Manuscripts*: The Foundation of the Golden Dawn

It all began with a mysterious series of documents known as the *Cipher Manuscripts* (*MSS*), documents that played a foundational role in the establishment of the original Hermetic Order of the Golden Dawn. Their role was so important that it led esoteric historian Darcy Kuntz to flatly state that

> the key to understanding the magical system of the Hermetic Order of the Golden Dawn is contained in the deciphering and comprehension of the Cipher Manuscript.[30]

So what exactly are the *Cipher MSS* and why are they the key to understanding the Golden Dawn?

This question is easier to ask than to answer. But it's useful to start by summarizing the story originally told about the *Cipher MSS*, in order to understanding the mythic theme that informed the original vision of the Golden Dawn:

> William Westcott, a Master Mason, told two of his fellow Masons, S. L. M. Mathers and William Robert Woodman, the story of finding a set of 60 faded, seemingly medieval folios revealing graded initiation rituals plus the "true" set of tarot correspondences between the major arcana Keys and the 22 paths of the Tree of Life. Out of these folios fell a scrap of paper containing the name and address of a German initiate ("Anna Sprengel") presumed to have contacts on the Inner Planes. She authorized the establishment of a secret society—the Order of the Golden Dawn—based on the esoteric information in the folios, which came to be called the *Cipher Manuscripts* (*Cipher MSS*).

This story proved to be sufficient to accomplish the purposes for which it was intended. Within a year, Westcott, S. L. M. Mathers and Robert Woodman established the Hermetic Order of the Golden Dawn, relying on the information in the *Cipher MSS* as the basis for its core teachings. As mentioned above, this information consisted mainly of fragments of rituals (which were elaborately fleshed out by Mathers) and the new tarot correspondences. Thus, the tarot correspondences provided the only information that was truly new and different, which is why it had to be touted as a newly unveiled secret.

But in order for would-be initiates to gain access to this hidden knowledge, they first had to take a solemn membership Oath agreeing that, should they violate this oath of secrecy, they would accept "the awful penalty of voluntarily submitting myself to a deadly and hostile current of will set in motion by the chiefs of the Order, by which I should fall slain and paralyzed without visible weapon as if blasted by the lightning flash."

This is a serious-sounding oath, so it's obvious that those who required it were serious about keeping their secrets hidden—sufficiently so to try to make potential violators believe they possessed both the power and will to inflict the supreme penalty for revealing GD secrets. At the same time, such an oath might sound darkly glamorous to some would-be members, making the teachings seem even more mysteriously attractive.

However, the teachings on the tarot correspondences were not imparted until members had reached the Practicus grade, three grades above the entry-level Neophyte grade. **Table E-2a** shows a facsimile of the encoded Folio 35 that I traced from the original; **Table E-2b** shows the English translation, with a few extraneous notes deleted. Below Table E-2b is a key to the cipher, a cipher that was well known to 19th century esotericists and could have been found by anyone in the British museum (Source: *Polygraphiae, by* Johann Trithemius, 1462–1516).

Notice that both The Fool and The Juggler (the original author's term for The Magician) were designated as "Key 1"; no reference is even made in Folio 35 to the value of zero traditionally attributed to The Fool. (My rendition is not a copying mistake; the "1" is right there in the original.) Notice also the switch between the Key numbers for Strength and Justice (where Strength becomes Key 8 and Justice becomes Key 11). This is a major change made by the Golden Dawn which first shows up publicly in the RWS deck. Although this is not our primary focus here, it's a very famous innovation that has engendered much discussion ever since. In this book, I used the RWS designation (where Strength is Key 8 and Justice is Key 11) because I am using the RWS deck. But it would not have been difficult to use the original attributions of Justice at Key 8 and Strength as Key 11 and still demonstrate a link between the enneagram and tarot because, on the enneagram, Points 2 (the cross-sum reduction of 11) and 8 are intimately related.[31]

It is important to note the context in which the tarot correspondences from Folio 35 were presented to GD members. These were not just theories (or even just ordinary teachings), but were given to members as if they were secret, sacred truths coming from an unnameable Source. Thus, it is not surprising to discover that this material plays a critical role in the Practicus initiation ceremony, where candidates are shown the GD tarot correspondences, after which the initiator intones the following:

> *Behold the true attribution of Tarot.*
> *Ponder it in thy heart.*
> *Reveal it not to the profane.*"[32]

Such a proclamation is designed to produce awe and reverence. Who would dare question the veracity of the teachings after this kind of experience?

Table E-2a. Encoded Golden Dawn Tarot Correspondences (letter order reversed).*

(cipher)	(cipher)	(cipher)	(cipher)
♀⋔⋔⏀	A	11	I
...	▽	23	XII
...	△	31	XX
...	☿	12	I
...	☽	13	II
...	♀	14	III
...	4	21	X
...	♂	27	XVI
...	☉	30	XIX
...	♄	32	XXI
...	♈	15	IV
...	♉	16	V
...	♊	17	VI
...	♋	18	VII
...	♐	19	XI
...	♍	20	IX
...	♎	22	VIII
...	♏	24	XIII
...	♐	25	XIV
...	♑	26	XV
...	♒	28	XVII
...	♓	29	XVIII

*This is my slightly simplified handwritten version of Folio 35, *Cipher MSS*.

Table E-2b. Exact Translation of Table E-2a.				
"Sunonums [Synonyms] in Tarot Divination"				
[NAME]	[SYMBOL]	[PATH]	[KEY]	[HEBREW LETTER]
Fool	△ (open)	11	I	Aleph
Hanged Man	▽	23	XII	Mem
Judgment	△	31	XX	Shin
Juggler [Magician]	☿	12	I	Beth
High Priestess	☽	13	II	Gimel
Empress	♀	14	III	Daleth
✴ ROTA Wheel	♃	21	X	Kaph
Tower Struck [by lightning]	♂	27	XVI	Peh
Sun	☉	30	XIX	Resh
Universe	♄	32	XXI	Tau
Emperor	♈	15	IV	Heh
Hierophant	♉	16	V	Vav
Lovers	♊	17	VI	Zayin
Chariot	♋	18	VII	Cheth
Strength	♌	19	XI	Teth
Hermit	♍	20	IX	Yod
Justice	♎	22	VIII	Lamed
Death	♏	24	XIII	Nun
Temperance	♐	25	XIV	Samech
Devil	♑	26	XV	Ayin
Star	♒	28	XVII	Tzaddi
Moon	♓	29	XVIII	Qoph

Cipher Key:

a ⊙	d ◌	g ⌒	k ⅋	n ⋺	q ∩	t X	y ⅄
b ⊢	e ⊃	h ⚲	L ♀	o ⋔	r ⚡	u ⚷	z ⋒
c ⊖	f ⚽	i ⊢	m e	p ∪	s X	x ⋔	

Apparently, few if any did. GD members who were fortunate enough to receive this knowledge simply accepted what they were told and memorized the correspondences.

Decker and Dummett explain the importance of these new correspondences thusly:

> When the Order of the Golden Dawn was formed, it had to have secret doctrines, gradually revealed to initiates as they advanced through the grades, that could not be found in any published books; as Aleister Crowley later sardonically remarked, it is no use swearing people to terrible oaths not to reveal what they are going to learn and then teaching them the Hebrew alphabet.[33]

The "back story" of the *Cipher MSS* was apparently compelling enough to gain the Order several hundred new GD members, among them prominent people in the arts (such as poet W. B. Yeats) and theater (such as famed actress Florence Farr). But eventually, both the Sprengel letters and *Cipher MSS* eventually became the subjects of closer scrutiny. As R. A. Gilbert observes,

> there was much...about both the letters and cipher manuscripts that was highly suspicious, and they would eventually prove to be a millstone around Westcott's neck. The cipher manuscripts, which masked a text wholly in English, were written in brown ink on sheets of old paper [to give the appearance of age]...but the presence of expressions borrowed from the *Egyptian Book of the Dead* [first published in 1842] and Tarot Trump attributions taken from Éliphas Lévi's *Dogme et Rituel de l'Haute Magie* [1954–1956] rules out any possibility that the text is earlier than 1870" (p. 42 of 250).[34]

Doubts about the letters from Sprengel came fully to light in early 1900, after S. L. M. Mathers (who was apparently known for his dramatic outbursts) wrote an agitated letter on February 16th to Florence Farr charging that Westcott "either forged or procured to be forged the professed correspondence." In that letter, he says that he had actually known about the forgery, but could not previously reveal it because of an earlier oath of secrecy made to Westcott.[35] According to Mary Greer, Farr wrote to Westcott, hoping to clear up the matter; he wrote back is that the allegations were untrue but that he could not prove it because the witnesses were deceased.[36, 37]

The controversy that swirled around these documents was not the only problem that plagued the Golden Dawn at that time—there were power struggles, personality clashes, and the awful scandal involving the Horos deception[38]—but it arguably broke the spirit that held the organization together. After a major meeting of the group in May 1903, the group "dissolved in chaos." Thus ended the original Order of the Golden Dawn.[39]

Later discussions of the Sprengel letters and *Cipher MSS* by both academic and esoteric historians confirmed the dual ideas that (a) the letters from Sprengel were almost certainly falsified and (b) it was impossible to verify the provenance of the *Cipher MSS*. For example, in Chapter 32 of his last book, *Shadows of Life and Thought* (1938), A. E. Waite discusses a variety of evidence indicating that the *Cipher MSS* was a recent creation, probably less than a decade old at the time of the founding of the Golden Dawn.

In 1972, Ellic Howe offered the first modern historical account of the Golden Dawn in his book *Magicians of the Golden Dawn*. While he compliments their ability to develop a "practical and effective system" of magical teachings, he also cites the Order as a prime example of what can happen to those who seek occult power but fall victim to both ego and the power of their creative imagination (p. *ix*). He unapologetically observes that "it was founded on a fraud" (p. *xvii*), which he proceeds to explore in detail in the first chapter of the book, "Suspect Documents," where he offers a devastatingly thorough critique of both documents, in particular, the Sprengel letters. He summarizes his finding with the statement that

> the textual evidence suggests that Westcott organized a series of faked documents in order to give the impression that the Hermetic Order of the Golden Dawn derived its authority and status from an enigmatic German source" (p. 7).

Although some authors have attempted to offer a more sympathetic view of past events (e.g., R. A. Gilbert, in *The Twilight of the Magicians*, 1983), no one since that time has been able to cite convincing evidence showing the following:

▶ that Anna Sprengel definitely existed

▶ that she was ever in correspondence with William Westcott

▶ that she had the authority to authorize the establishment of a secret society with the blessing of "inner contacts"

▶ that the *Cipher MSS* existed prior to 1856

▶ that the tarot correspondences in the *Cipher MSS* were devised by someone who knew them to be the "true attribution" of the tarot

By the time that Darcy Kuntz published *The Complete Golden Dawn Cipher Manuscripts* (1996), he didn't even bother trying to make the case that the *Cipher MSS* might be real; he instead focused on trying to determine who might have written them (since most people who have looked into the matter don't think it was one of the founders of the Golden Dawn). In his article "Provenance Unknown," Kuntz says he believes it was written by esoteric scholar Kenneth Mackenzie, an associate of Westcott's who was well-versed in esoteric knowledge. Mackenzie had died several years previously, but his wife still had his papers. She was an early member of the Golden Dawn, but never advanced past the first grade of initiation. Kuntz believes that she was admitted to the Golden

Dawn at its inception in order that she should take the Membership Oath, thus guaranteeing her silence.

The only source that staunchly defends the provenance of the *Cipher MSS* is the reconstituted Order of the Golden Dawn (revived by Chic and Sandra Cicero in the 1970s). Its website makes the claim that it was obtained from the widow of a Masonic scholar who was given them by a certain Count Apponyi "together with Hermetic and Rosicrucian lineages, with which to found the Hermetic Order of the Golden Dawn."[40] However, the writer offers no evidence to substantiate that claim, the implication being that this remains "behind the veil" information that must remain concealed. But even the Golden Dawn website acknowledges that the account of the Sprengel letters given by William Westcott is false; the falsehood is deplored but not accepted as sufficient evidence for rejecting the validity of the teachings as given in the *Cipher MSS*.[41]

The Golden Dawn from the 19th Century to the Present

It's easy to criticize those who joined the Golden Dawn for their naïveté, given these recent revelations. But the Golden Dawn was the right organization at the right time, a time when people were searching for answers and optimistic about finding them. The Occult Revival that blossomed in the mid-1800s inspired people to explore exotic ideas and activities that had previously been off-limits—mesmerism, spiritualism, magic, communalism, theosophy, psychic phenomena, and the brand new discipline of psychoanalysis. In England, new organizations sprang up to bring like-minded people together with an interest in the world of the unseen: spiritualist churches began to appear in the 1850s; the Theosophical Society was founded in 1875; and the Society for Psychical Research was founded in 1882.

So the launching of the Golden Dawn in 1888 came at an opportune moment in history. The GD offered a philosophical alternative (Hermeticism) to traditional religious doctrine; intriguing ceremonies and practices that promised transformational change (the graded initiations, tarot teachings, and magical techniques); and enough mystery to spark the imagination of potential members (the *Cipher Manuscripts*, Anna Sprengel, guidance from wise but unseen "inner contacts" from whom they could purportedly receive esoteric wisdom).

As Helen Farley observes in *A Cultural History of the Tarot* (2009),

> the Order was the crowning glory of the occult revival, synthesizing into a coherent whole a vast body of disparate material including Egyptian mythology, kabbalah, tarot, Enochian magic, alchemy, Rosicrucianism and astrology....People from all walks of life were attracted to the promise of power and knowledge (p. 129).

As a mysterious document with what seemed to be Rosicrucian provenance, the *Cipher MSS* would have provided the membership of the GD with the justification necessary to embrace an exciting new system of correspondences, despite its counterintuitive tarot assignments. Ironically, the very fact that the numerological assignments seemed counterintuitive may have been seen as a sign that they must have great esoteric significance!

But despite its auspicious start, the original Golden Dawn disbanded 15 years after its inception. However, its rituals and tarot correspondences did not die away, but lived on in the splinter groups associated with individuals who were part of the original Order: S. L. M. Mathers' *Alpha et Omega*, Robert Felkin's *Stella Matutina*, Aleister Crowley's *Ordo Templi Orientis*, Dion Fortune's *Fraternity of the Inner Light*, and Paul Foster Case's *B.O.T.A.* (Builders of the Adytum).

Many of the esoteric groups originally inspired by the Golden Dawn and their offshoots were active in the first half of the 20th century, certainly through the 1920s and into the 1930s. But the worldwide Depression of the Thirties, WWII, and its Cold War aftermath seems to have diminished public interest in *esoterica* of all kinds. It is not until the countercultural generation came of age in the 1960s that interest in occult topics began to take off again, initiating an Age of Aquarius-style revival that created a new and growing fascination with hidden knowledge, magic, and the tarot.[42]

During the 1970s and 80s, the RWS deck became so popular that it spawned a host of imitators; its popularity also did much to publicize the original Order of the Golden Dawn, since both its designer A. E. Waite and artist Pamela Colman Smith were members; the same can be said of Aleister Crowley's deck, which finally became available to the public in 1969. Books about both decks proliferated, along with books on magic, especially those by Israel Regardie, Aleister Crowley, and Dion Fortune. The establishment in 1978 of a new Hermetic Order of the Golden Dawn, Inc. by Chic and Sandra Cicero no doubt boosted interest in the GD system, which became the most popular system for "magical advancement" in the world.

It might be argued that the popularity enjoyed by the GD approach is due to its natural superiority as a system. Modern tarotists who know about the bogus *Cipher MSS* may continue to embrace its correspondences even so, because they find practical value in them. I understand where they are coming from, because I've also found value in them. But I see a big difference between finding value in an approach vs bestowing upon it hegemonic status based on claims that fall apart under close scrutiny.

Consider the possibility that any system of correspondences has the potential to serve as a useful tool for qabalistic work, especially for pathworking. This is because the images of the tarot offer such a powerful memory aid for envisioning each path. I realize that such an assertion flies in the face of the idea that esoteric work involves precise calculations, knowledge, etc., such that one must possess exactly the right images for each path.

But that is a very masculine way of thinking! Masculine disciplines are inevitably based upon the assumption that discovering truth means finding the one and only correct way of apprehending it. However, genuine truth is often much more slippery than we would like to think; it may depend upon universal truths but it also relies upon situational variables that can only be accessed through intuition. In feminine approaches to inner work, claims made for specific teachings and techniques often matter less than one's awareness of what is unfolding in the moment. From that point of view, truth is always changing, because what is true in one moment is not true in the next. All the tools we use and the way we use them is in a state of flux.

As Rachel Pollack observes in *The Forest of Souls* (2005), "the occult tradition tends to see the Tarot as a *scientific* instrument," i.e., as having a fixed meaning that must be properly decoded [especially if we are to consider the deck "esoteric"—SR]. She likens this to viewing the tarot the way we would view classical music, with its many formalities and rules for composition. But she says that we could also think of the tarot as folk music, which has much more flexibility built into it (pp. 38–39). (I used to sing in Eastern European a cappella groups, where there is so much flexibility built in that some of the songs did not even have time signatures.)

Gareth Knight introduces a similar idea when he observes that "by its very nature, [the tarot and its]…pictorial symbols can be interpreted in the light of various contexts."[43] In other words, *the tarot is such a rich treasury of symbolic wisdom that its images will tend to advance our understanding, whatever set of attributions is employed.*

However, the fact remains that the tarot attributions set forth in the *Cipher MSS* are the ones that are now the best-known. And at least in English-speaking countries, they are also the ones against which all other proposed systems are now measured. Case in point: A story told by William Gray in the postscript at the end his book, *Growing the Tree Within*. In a nutshell, this book was initially rejected for publication because it advocates a set of tarot correspondences that departs from that used in the Golden Dawn system. But to understand why this matters, it's useful to understand who Gray was in British tarot culture and to hear what he has to say about the reasons cited for the rejection of his book.

William Gray (1913–1992) was a well-respected occultist who wrote over 30 books on esoteric topics, especially the qabala. So when he originally wrote the book in question—during the 1970s (when it was called *The Talking Tree*)—he was already a very well-known and respected writer in occult circles.

In the postscript at the end of this book, he discusses the implications of the rejection letter he received from a publisher who turned down the book for publication simply because his tarot attributions were not "traditional" (i.e., not the Golden Dawn attributions). After receiving this letter, Gray became incensed by the idea that the Golden Dawn attributions should be accorded the kind of status we would associate with the wisdom of the ancients. Thus, in his postscript, he notes that

> queries have often been raised concerning why this [new]…system of Path-working should differ in any way from what is sometimes styled the "Traditional" [Golden Dawn] method, because of increasing familiarity with its last century lay-out. The implications seem to be that an immutable and infallible set of Path attributions have already been officially fixed by some unquestionable authority, and any deviancy from that decree smacks of heresy, blasphemy, and other unmentionable occult aberrations (p. 429).

He goes on to directly quote the rejection letter from the publisher, who observes that

> you have changed the traditional [Golden Dawn] Hebrew letter attributions, and altered the way in which the Tarot trumps are allotted…[which would make this book] meaningless to a lot of readers. *I am sure your way is probably correct,* but because it is not the traditional one, I fear we would find it very difficult to publish" (emphasis his, p. 429).

Here the publisher is admitting that Gray's attributions are probably better than the Golden Dawn's! But he indicates that, nevertheless, his company is afraid to take a chance on them, because the GD correspondences are so much more well-known.

Gray does not accept this argument, noting that

> the reputed "Traditional" [Golden Dawn] connections between the Tree and the Tarot…[depend upon] the Trump numberings *being forced into unreasonable relationships with Path positions determined by Hebrew numerology* (p. 433, emphasis mine).

Here Gray explicitly rejects the GD correspondences as "unreasonable," using essentially the same argument I am employing in this appendix. He then expresses his strong disagreement with the thesis that the Golden Dawn's version of the Tree is "traditional" in the sense of being so venerated and ancient that we dare not tamper with it. He ends by observing that

> tradition should be a *living spirit*…[leading people] from past learning to future illumination (p. 433).

The implication here is that if tradition is truly a living spirit, it should serve as a springboard for evolving ideas rather than a gate that bars the way to thoughtful innovation.

From my standpoint, it's not only that the GD system is just a century old (and therefore not old enough to qualify as a "tradition"); it's that the GD system does not qualify as a tradition in any real sense of the word. A tradition is a set of practices that evolves organically in a family, community, or culture over a long period of time. Real traditions are based upon practical wisdom acquired by many generations. That is why traditions are venerated: because their value has been repeatedly validated by many different people in varying circumstances.

The system of tarot correspondences adopted by the GD is in no way a tradition of that sort. It is most probably the work of a single human being whose identity we don't know and likely never will. It was aggrandized as "received wisdom" from the inner planes by at least one individual (Westcott) who knowingly deceived members of the Golden Dawn not only by declaring the system to be of divine origin, but to be the one and only correct teaching on the topic. Then he and other GD leaders imparted these teachings to rank and file members in a manner designed to ensure that they would never be questioned. As a result, by the time that it was possible to openly question the provenance of the GD system of correspondences, it had become too well-established to question!

So rather than calling it a tradition, I would call it one potential framework for inner work, a framework that deserves to be openly discussed, not enshrined. To open such a discussion, it's useful to start by surveying what well-known tarotists have already said about the possible link between the tarot and qabala in the post-Original Golden Dawn era. That's what we'll look at next.

Tarot and Qabala: A View from the Field

It is interesting to see that even after the Golden Dawn system became well-known, it was not adopted by everyone. Opinions among tarotists still vary when it comes to the question of how to relate the tarot and qabala (or even whether there exists a relationship at all).

When I went searching for direct quotes, I found that tarot authors generally fell into one of two groups. In the first are people who view the tarot and qabala as intrinsically related and possibly different aspects of a single underlying system. In the second are people who see the two as independent entities and tend to favor keeping them separate, although some (though not all of them) favor exploring potential parallels between them.

Let's start by looking at the comments of those who see the tarot and qabala as *very closely related*:[44]

► Dion Fortune describes the qabala, tarot, and astrology as so intimately inter-twined that they are actually "three aspects of one and the same system."[45]

► Paul Foster Case, closely following the Golden Dawn, says "every major trump corresponds to one of the twenty-two letters of the Hebrew alphabet," and uses exactly the same correspondences as the GD as well as the same approach to assigning them to paths on the Tree, additionally commenting that the astro-logical attributions in the *Sepher Yetzirah* were blinds [unlike the ones used in the Golden Dawn teachings].[46]

► Chic and Sandra Cicero, the heads of the modern Hermetic Order of the Golden Dawn, tell us that "the two systems of the Qabalah and tarot are so strikingly similar that they easily complement and describe each other, mak-ing a perfect and coherent system for psychic/spiritual growth."[47]

► Isabel Radow Kliegman says that "the Kabbalistic Tree of life provides the archetypes by which the Tarot can be understood."[48]

► Pamela Eakins states that "the tarot is Qabalistic in orientation."[49]

► Amber Jayanti sees the tarot as "rooted in the teachings of the ancient mystery school tradition known as the Qabalah."[50]

► Aleister Crowley makes the claim that "the Tarot...was designed as a practical instrument for Qabalistic calculations and for divination. In it is little place for abstract ideas."[51]

As we can see by Crowley's remarks, those who adopt this view often see the qabala as the more foundational system. To the extent this is true, this would place the tarot in a supportive rather than collaborative relationship with the qabala.

But not everyone agrees either that (a) the tarot and qabala share common roots or (b) the qabala is the more foundational system. It was interesting to discover that many tarotists view the tarot and qabala as entirely separate sys-tems which can perhaps—but not necessarily—be used collaboratively.

For example, *Alejandro Jodorowsky* says that "[the twenty-two Major Ar-cana have encouraged a concordance with the Hebrew alphabet...[but] in the final analysis, these comparisons are useful only if they are temporary."[52] This comment seems to reflect the view that we should exercise caution when mak-ing analogies involving essentially independent systems, analogies that may be useful for gaining momentary insights but less useful if we take them to mean that two separate systems should be made into a single combined system.

Esoteric scholar *Manly P. Hall* takes a similarly cautious attitude regarding the relationship between the tarot and qabala, noting that most writers on the tarot…have proceeded upon the hypothesis that the 22 major trumps represent the letters of the Hebrew alphabet….Assuming the Qabbalah to hold the solution to the Tarot riddle, seekers have often ignored other possible lines of research.[53]

By the time Hall penned this statement in the mid-1920s, the GD attributions had become standard in various offshoots of the Golden Dawn. *Yolanda Robinson*, author of a modern interpretation of Hall's 1920's tarot deck, the New Art Tarot, notes that

> the Rosicrucian movement gave birth to different and sometimes conflicting approaches to the use of Tarot with Qabalah and the Tree of Life. Even more challenging are the contradictory connections to alchemy and magic. The assignment to Hebrew letters to the twenty-two Majors, for example, became a controversial issue that is still debated today. Manly P. Hall was never convinced that a solid esoteric connection between letter and card had been fully established or revealed. [54]

Although Irene Gad says that "we have reason to speculate that the Tree of Life is the frame of reference needed to complete the impressive graphic symbolism of the major arcana" in her introduction,[55] her exploration of the relationship between the qabala and tarot is subtle and searching. Many of her comments are more speculative than definitive, and she includes ideas from many sources in her thoughtful commentary throughout the book (see especially pp. *xxviii–xxxvi*). Because she feels strongly that a relationship between the tarot and qabala must exist, I originally put her in the first category but later moved her to the second, because she clearly sees the qabala and tarot as separate systems (for example, insisting that we must "trust the images [of the tarot] themselves," p. *xxxvi*), rather than deriving their meaning from the qabala. She is a good example of a careful scholar who is conservative in her claims.

Authors *Cynthia Giles* and *Robert Wang* both take the position that the tarot and qabala are clearly separate systems, but that their very separateness illustrates how the same truth manifests in different forms. Giles observes that "there is no evidence at all to suggest that the qabalah and the Tarot were ever linked in any intentional or dependent way" but then goes on to say that "the similarities between the two systems are important not because they indicate a common source, but because they reveal certain basic esoteric concepts embodied in both."[56] Wang says that although the tarot and qabala are two separate systems, they "are mutually explanatory. And, actually, the likelihood that the two systems developed independently gives far greater authority to the ideas of both because it points toward their mutual roots in universal Truth."[57]

On her website Tarot Heritage, tarotist *Sherryl E. Smith* flatly states that "associating tarot with Cabala, the grail legend, alchemy, or other divination systems is an artificial overlay," not an inherent feature of the tarot.[58]

C. C. Zain, founder of The Church of Light in 1932, cites Lévi as saying that the qabala is a sealed book to anyone unfamiliar with the tarot, going on to add that "not only is this true, but the tarot, as here presented, will be found a key to unlock all other sacred books as well."[59] Thus, Zain sees a relationship between the tarot and qabala, but—like Irene Gad—tends to interpret the Hebrew letters through the prism of the tarot, not the other way around. Also, like Gad, he uses Continental attributions and does not position the tarot Keys on the Tree of Life.

Additionally, there are two authors who take a very strong stand against linking the tarot with the qabala, although their reasoning is very different.

The first is Jewish scholar *Gershom Scholem* (1897–1982), who was a well-known and bitter opponent of the whole approach employed in Hermetic qabala; he says it creates "considerable confusion," and refers to the "alleged kabbalistic origin of the Tarot-cards" as a total invention of 19th century figures such as Lévi, Papus, and Crowley.[60] He obviously regards the Hermetic qabala as a bastardization of the Hebrew Kabbalah, so it's not surprising that he is not interested in tarot correspondences.

The second is tarot historian *Robert Place*, who expresses strong reservations about linking the tarot with the qabala for entirely different reasons. As a champion of the tarot, he is concerned about the potentially negative effects of assigning Hebrew letters to the tarot:

> If the Tarot keys are the Hebrew letters then meditation on them will move one up the Tree of Life and toward the mystic experience. However, *the images and symbols suggested by the [Hebrew] letters are not the images on the cards and the correlations do not naturally flow together...*[so] as ingenious as Lévi is, he seduces us away from a true understanding of the icons in the tarot. It never occurs to him to ask what these images represented in Renaissance art. He assumes they are secret messages from the ancient Kabalists (emphasis mine).[61]

Here Place is pointing out that focusing most of our attention on how the tarot images relate to the Hebrew letters means *not focusing our attention on the actual images on the cards*. Therefore, he regards the entire project of attempting to link tarot with qabala as ill-advised. Although he admits that "many people derive benefit from using this system, it moves one away from understanding the actual historic Tarot and unlocking its wisdom," because the "memorized meanings" become more important than the pictures.[62] Later, he reiterates the idea that the tarot is emphatically its own system, a system based on Neoplatonic ideas. To understand the symbols of the tarot, he says, one must look not to the tradition of the qabala, but to the mystic vision of Plato.[63]

Place's arguments constitute a plea for seeing the tarot as something unique and precious in its own right, not as a hidden aspect of the qabala. His comments intrigue me for three reasons. The first is that they call to mind the enneagrammatic idea that there are multiple points of view from which to see any one thing, points of view that embody fundamental differences, despite superficial similarities.[64] The second is that they remind us that the tarot is traditionally interpreted from a Platonic/Hermetic point of view, which is quite different than the dualistic Judeo-Christian "Fall of Man" myth that informs both religions.[65] The third is that they point out how linking the tarot too closely to any other system can direct our attention away from interacting with the actual images on the cards.

I understand where Place is coming from. I also value the tarot as tarot, regardless of what it might tell us about other systems. Thus, I would proceed very carefully when exploring potential links between the tarot and qabala.

❖ ❖ ❖

I started this appendix by saying that there seems to be a relationship between the enneagram and qabala and between the enneagram and tarot, which means there is also a relationship between the tarot and qabala. But the precise nature of that relationship remains a mystery at this point.

The fact is that we have one system with a 0–21 numbering scheme and another with a 1–22 numbering scheme. I'm not at all convinced that it's possible to set aside this difference and still retain the essence of either system. The "pesky problem of The Fool" may be what saves us in the end: because it's the Fool who reminds us that when we're putting together a jigsaw puzzle, if even one piece doesn't quite fit, we haven't solved the puzzle.

In my view, the Golden Dawn tarot correspondences represent an attempt to "whistle past the graveyard"—to ignore the pieces in their approach that don't quite fit. While this system may serve admirably for some purposes, it's not perfect. And it's certainly not a system that deserves to be considered a standard by which all others are judged. To say that it represents one way of working is not problematic. But to say that it offers the best or only approach goes too far.

Notes

[1] Much of the material in this section is drawn from Robert Wang's excellent work, *The Qabalistic Tarot* (Marcus Aurelius: 1984/2004). Anyone interested in a more in-depth discussion will find it there.

[2] As John Michael Greer notes on p. 10 of his book *Paths of Wisdom* (Weiser: 1984), the qabala means "oral tradition" and that "it's notoriously hard to pin down an oral tradition by way of written sources!"

[3] Dion Fortune, *The Mystical Qabalah* (Weiser: 1984), p. 1.

[4] Robert Place, *The Tarot: History, Symbolism, and Divination* (Tarcher: 2005), p. 58; Ronald Decker, *The Esoteric Tarot* (Quest: 2013), p. 19; John Michael Greer, *Paths of Wisdom* (Weiser: 1984), p. 10.

[5] *The Sufis*, locations 5690–5716 of 6810, Kindle edition (or p. 385 in the Anchor Books 1971 version). Shah's arguments are interesting, because he supports them with references to the *Jewish Encyclopedia*.

[6] *The Ancient Secret of the Flower of Life* (Light Technology Publishing: 1998), Vol. 1, pp. 40-41, 97-98; Vol. II, p. 414.

[7] It is not clear why the founders of the Golden Dawn adopted the Kircher model of the Tree of Life, which is based on the Christian view of human beings as fallen beings in need of redemption (as opposed to the Hermetic view of humans as potential heroes embarking on the adventure of life; see Chapter 3 for a discussion). It is probably because Athanasius Kircher (1602–1680) was a well-known Egyptologist during the late Renaissance. But he was also a Jesuit, and would naturally have had to at least nominally embrace Christian teachings, including the doctrine of The Fall. I am not sure whether there was an "unfallen" version of the Tree available at that point; such a version of the Tree was developed by Rabbi Elijah ben Shlomo Zalman (1720–1797), also known as Vilna Gaon or "the GRA," but he was not born until 40 years after Kircher's death. See Rawn Clark's introduction to his video "An Examination of the GRA Tree of Life," at http://www.abardoncompanion.de/Gra/index.html; see Chapter 5 in Picknett and Prince's *The Forbidden Universe* (Skyhorse: 2011) for a short biography of Athanasius Kircher; see the final note in this appendix for a discussion of non-duality and Hermeticism.

[8] The sephiroth have also been linked by the Golden Dawn to the four court cards—Kings to Chokmah, Queens to Binah, Princes to Tiphareth, and Princesses to Malkuth—although this linking is not based on symbolic numerology, since the court cards don't have numbers.

[9] How the Golden Dawn links the minor arcana to the 10 sephiroth on the Tree of Life is problematic in my view, because it so suborns the meaning of numbered minors to the sephiroth to which they are assigned—a situation that Yolanda Robinson refers to when discussing how the minors "appear to work in a rigid format according to the specific Cabalistic structures [to which they have been assigned]," p. *xxi*, *The Revised New Art Tarot* (Circe's Whisper: 2015, black and white ed.). See also the discussion at the start of Chapter 5.

[10] There are said to be 32 paths on the qabala. The ten sephiroth are considered Paths 1–10; the 22 links between the sephiroth are considered Paths 11–32.

[11] Although the *Sepher Yetzirah* describes the general specifications for the Tree of Life regarding both the assignment of astrological symbols (signs and houses) and the 22 Hebrew letters, it does not specify the exact form of the Tree—its precise appearance or which paths go with which symbols. As a result, the "right" way to depict the Tree or to assign the symbols/letters to the paths is an endless source of speculation among qabalistic scholars.

[12] See Chapters 1 and 8 for a discussion of Gurdjieff's introduction of the enneagram; see Chapter 9 for a discussion of Gurdjieff's ideas on symbolic numerology.

[13] See Chapter 1 for a discussion of the dualistic approach to enneagram work.

[14] See my first published article on the enneagram, "Let's Depathologize the Enneagram," available on my website (http://www.enneagramdimensions.net/articles/lets_depathologize_the_enneagram.pdf).

[15] It should be noted that Rabbi Addison discusses the sephiroth using traditional Jewish names, such that Chesed is referred to as Gedulah, Geburah as Din, and Malkuth as Shekinah.

[16] I am not at all sure that the sense of hierarchy often attributed to the Tree of Life is necessarily implied by the teachings in the *Sepher Yetzirah*, which have also been used to generate the 3-D Cube of Space; see, e.g., the discussion in David Allen Hulse's *New Dimensions for the Cube of Space: The Path of Initiation Revealed by the Tarot upon the Qabalistic Cube* (Weiser: 2000).

[17] This "wrong" placement of the shock points on the enneagram is briefly alluded to in the Chapter 8 endnotes and concerns the fact that, in an ascending scale, the second half-step occurs between *si* and *do*, as shown in Fig. E-6. But on the enneagram, it is actually positioned between Points 5 and 6 (between *so* and *la*) as shown in Fig. 9-1. This placement has puzzled many people over the years, including me. But when we follow Drunvalo's instructions, we can visually perceive the half-step as occurring in the interval between *so* and *la*. It may be an optical illusion, but it clearly shows the half-steps exactly at the where Gurdjieff placed them on the enneagram.

[18] Anyone who has never heard of this placement problem may be completely lost at this point, as I was when I first encountered these ideas. Although this concept sounds obscure, it is part of the esoteric teachings on the enneagram. If you are interested in seeing what Gurdjieff has to say, check out the discussion on pp. 290–292 of *In Search of the Miraculous*.

[19] *Doctrine of Transcendental Magic*, A. E. Waite, trans. (Redway: 1896), p. 196.

[20] The Continental approach is not one approach, but a school of approaches that vary slightly (mostly in terms of where they position The Fool in the deck) but that share in common the practice of seeking to preserve the traditional numerological values of the tarot.

[21] In *A Cultural History of the Tarot* (Tauris: 2009), Helen Farley attests that "Éliphas Lévi was the first to specifically associate the tarot trumps with the letters of the Hebrew alphabet, the Golden Dawn was the first to align correspondences between the pathways of the Tree of Life and the trumps" (p. 132).

[22] Please note that because of the way the Hebrew alphabet assigns letter values, after the number nine, the values change, such that the value of Key 10 would be 10, Key 11 would be 20, Key 12 would be 30, etc., as Table E-1 shows.

[23] To understand why I placed the RWS tarot deck in the "Continental" column of Table E-1, please see Waite's discussion on pp. 70–71 of his *The Pictorial Guide to the Tarot* in the 1997 U. S. Games edition or pp. 34–35 in the 2005 Dover edition.

[24] To see how the Continental approach preserves the values of the traditional tarot, it is necessary to use cross-sum addition to convert the values of the Hebrew letters that are higher than nine to single-digit numbers.

[25] Christine Payne-Towler's discussion on tarot attributions is more extensive than may be evident from this citation, but occurs in the context of a complex discussion of the historic roots of the esoteric tarot and thus requires an esoterically informed reader. Greer's discussion is easier to follow in some ways, but is more or less buried in an appendix on a related but different topic (the "8-11 Controversy"), and would thus be found by very few readers. I only stumbled upon it because I was looking for information on this controversy and was surprised to find a table very like Table E-1 in that appendix. The discussion there, however, strongly favors the GD set of tarot correspondences, which is characterized as "brilliant" (p. 259); the reordering of Strength and Justice is presented as a "rectification of a teaching that had lost its balance" (p. 260). However, Greer *does* note more neutrally at the end of the appendix that "variations in tarot order reflect variations in world view," and specifically mentions the conflicting visions

of the French vs English magical Orders. (p. 262). What is missing , however, is the idea that the pre-Golden Dawn tarot correspondences used by Lévi and other French (and European) esoteric writers are still very much in use in non-English-speaking cultures; see Payne-Towler's discussion in "The Spanish School," in *The Underground Stream* and in "The Continental Tarots, Part 3," at http://noreah.typepad.com/tarot_arkletters/2006/11/continental_3.html.

[26] Interestingly, Christine Payne-Towler is the first person who ever talked to me about the tarot. This was over 40 years ago, when I lived in the little town of Cheshire near Eugene, Oregon, and she lived in Deadwood, along the same highway but further into the mountains. We were introduced by a mutual acquaintance, and she offered to give me a tarot reading. I enjoyed the reading but didn't get interested in tarot study at that time. Christine and I lost touch when I moved to Portland several years later, but reconnected at precisely the point when I was struggling to understand the tangled history of the tarot and the efforts made by different parties to explore its relationship with the qabala.

[27] *The Underground Stream* (Noreah: 1999), p. 134; see the entire chapter, "The English School" (pp. 132–135) for a full account of how key members of the Golden Dawn used their collective editorial voices as translators to influence their readers to favor the Golden Dawn's interpretation of the tarot over that of European esotericists.

[28] Source: https://marygreer.wordpress.com/2008/02/01/21/.

[29] *The Underground Stream* (Noreah: 1999), pp. 133–134.

[30] "Introduction," *The Golden Dawn Sourcebook* (Holmes: 1996), p. 21.

[31] On the enneagram, Points 2 and 8 are joined by a connecting line, reflecting their close relationship. If I had associated Justice with the number Eight (and Eights on the enneagram), this would point to an aspect of Eight that relates to its role as Leader and Judge, for although Enneagram Eights have an innate understanding of fairness, it is the connecting line to Point 2 that enables them to temper justice with mercy. Conversely, if I had associated Strength with the higher octave of Point 2 (derived from the cross-sum of 11), this would point to the need for High Priestess Twos to develop the ability to control and channel their wayward emotions in a way that consolidates their energies and empowers their actions. Bottom line: either approach works, but each stresses different aspects of the numbers 2 and 8. For more on the 8/11 controversy, see also Note 25 (above), Note 7 in Chapter 5, and Notes 24 and 25 in Chapter 9.

[32] For an exact copy of the original Folio 35 as it was discovered (or created), see p. 122 in Darcy Kuntz' *The Complete Golden Dawn Cipher Manuscripts* (Holmes: 1996).

[33] *A History of Occult Tarot: 1870–1970* (Duckworth: 2002), p. 82.

[34] *Revelations of the Golden Dawn* (Foulsham: 1997), the Scrbd EPUB version. It is unclear whether the pagination used is the same as in the original, but this quote is taken from the chapter entitled "Order Out of Chaos: the Birth of the Golden Dawn."

[35] Why S. L. M. Mathers felt it was acceptable to break his solemn oath to William Westcott (an oath not to reveal the Anna Sprengel deception) in 1900—but not earlier—is not revealed; nor are Mathers' original motives for taking an oath to keep silent about documents that he knew to be forgeries. The obvious answer, however, is that Mathers took the oath for the same reasons that Westcott arranged for the forgeries: to enhance the credibility of a then-fledgling Order of the Golden Dawn.

[36] *Women of the Golden Dawn* (Park Street Press: 1995), pp. 237–239.

[37] For the complete text of Mathers' letter to Florence Farr, see Darcy Kuntz' *The Golden Dawn Sourcebook* (Holmes: 1995), pp. 72–75, or Mary Greer's *Women of the Golden Dawn* (Dark Street Press: 1995), pp. 237–238.

[38] See R. A Gilbert's *The Golden Dawn: Twilight of the Magicians* (Aquarian Press: 1983) for both an account of the Horos affair and an exceptionally readable history of the Golden Dawn.

[39] Ibid, p. 41–45.

[40] Here is the statement in full from the Golden Dawn website (http://www.golden-dawn. org/truth_ciph1.html): "It is clear that the true lineage of the Hermetic Order of the Golden Dawn derives from the Continental European order of Adepts represented by Count Apponyi, who initiated Kenneth Mackenzie and are the true source of origin of the Hermetic Order of the Golden Dawn." It is interesting that the claim is made for a Continental lineage when the set of tarot correspondences given in the *Cipher MSS* is so different from other Continental sources; see Christine Payne-Towler's discussion of the Continental schools in her book, *The Underground Stream* (Noreah: 1999), beginning on p. 110.

[41] An account of the response by the current Golden Dawn to the *Cipher MSS* controversy can be found at http://www.golden-dawn.com/eu/displaycontent.aspx?pageid=283-cipher-manuscript-mystery.

[42] Chapter 1 of Lee Irwin's *Gnostic Tarot* (Weiser: 1998) contains a condensed but detailed history of the esoteric tarot, especially after 1960; alternatively, you can consult Rachel Pollack's *The Forest of Souls: A Walk Through the Tarot* (Llewellyn: 2005) for more lyrical treatment of changes in the way tarot began to be viewed during this same period (see especially Chapter 3).

[43] *A Practical Guide to Qabalistic Symbolism, Vol. II: On the Paths and the Tarot* (Weiser: 1965/2001), p. 222.

[44] I apologize in advance to anyone whom I have placed in one group who would prefer to be in the other; it is always difficult to get to the core of someone's ideas, and I am far from a perfect analyst. My purpose is not to pigeonhole people but to discuss how people have weighed in on the question, "What is the relationship between the tarot and qabala?"

[45] *The Mystical Qabala* (Weiser: 1935/1977), p. 73.

[46] *The Tarot* (Builders of the Adytum: 1940/1990), pp. 17–19. Paul Foster Case claims to have independently intuited these tarot attributions. However—much as I respect Dr. Case and his B.O.T.A. organization—this seems unlikely to me. The attributions were published anonymously in an obscure form in Aleister Crowley's book 777 in 1909 and more explicitly in the Sept. 1912 edition of Crowley's periodical, *The Equinox* (although Case incorrectly attributes it to the March edition of the *Occult Review*, which contains only a short poem by Crowley). I doubt very much whether Case would have wanted to admit that he found the attributions in *The Equinox*, because as he plainly says, Crowley broke his GD oaths when he published these correspondences. This would be an act that Case would not have wanted to endorse, in that his own organization B.O.T.A. also has oaths of secrecy.

[47] *The Essential Golden Dawn* (Llewellyn: 2014), p. 196.

[48] This information comes from an online article, "Tarot and the Tree of Life," originally printed in the July-August 2008 of *Quest*, a publication of the Theosophical Society; it is now available at https://www.theosophical.org/publications/42-publications/quest-magazine/1358-tarot-and-the-tree-of-life.

[49] *The Tarot of the Spirit* (U. S. Games: 1992), p. 4.

[50] *Living the Tarot* (Wordsworth: 2000), p. 15.

[51] *The Book of Thoth*, Chapter 3, "The Tarot and the Universe," subsection "The Tarot and the Tree of Life," available online at https://www.bibliotecapleyades.net/crowley/libro_thoth02. htm; see also p. 34 in the print version (Weiser: 1944/1995). This may be a good place to mention another comment by Crowley on tarot correspondences, from his book *777*, written in 1909: "Another class of number is of immense importance. It is the series usually expressed in Roman numbers which is printed on the Tarot Trumps. Here … the number is … one less than that of the letters of the [Hebrew] alphabet, when they are numbered according to their natural order from 1 to 22. These numbers are very nearly of the same order of idea as those of the numerical value of the letters; but they represent rather the *active magical energy of the number* than its essential being" (p. 131/149, emphasis mine; available at https://archive.org/ details/Liber777Revised). Crowley's comment is interesting, but my first response was "Say more." But there is no more; all we have is this one comment. While it's encouraging to see that Crowley considers the numbers printed on the cards to be "of immense importance," and he tells us they represent "the active magical energy of the number," he does not tell us enough to understanding his meaning.

[52] *The Way of the Tarot: The Spiritual Teacher in the Cards* (Destiny: 2004), p. 55.

[53] *The Secret Teachings of All Ages* (Philosophical Research Society: 1977), p. *cxxix*.

[54] *The Revised New Art Tarot*, black and white edition (Circe's Whisper: 2015), p. *xxi*.

[55] *Tarot and Individuation* (Nicholas-Hayes: 1994), p. *xxix*.

[56] *The Tarot: History, Mystery, and Lore* (Paragon: 1992), p. 32. Author Cynthia Giles also adds this charmingly tarot-centric comment: "Once one begins to pick up the threads that run between the Kabbalah and the Tarot, it's possible to follow these threads in many different directions—to alchemy, to astrology, to Native American religion. The Greek mystery religions, Hawaiian Kahuna magic, Chinese Taoism, Tibetan Buddhism—all of these systems of thought (and many more) have elements in common with those of the tarot."

[57] *The Qabalistic Tarot* (Marcus Aurelius: 1978/2004), p. 1.

[58] Source: https://tarot-heritage.com/history-4/.

[59] *The Sacred Tarot* (Church of Light: 1994/2004), p. 27.

[60] *Kabbalah* (Keter: 1974), p. 203.

[61] *The Tarot: History, Symbolism, and Divination* (Tarcher: 2005), p. 72.

[62] Ibid, p. 73.

[63] Ibid, p. 99.

[64] The idea that seeming similarities may not be more than skin-deep is important to consider when comparing any two things. In the enneagram, many types look superficially similar, but they are only similar within a certain context. See Chapters 6 for a discussion of look-alikes and Chapter 7 for examples.

[65] Regarding non-dualism and the qabalistic tarot: It is possible to work with the tarot

from many points of view, but the imagery lends itself to a Platonic/Hermetic ("as above, so below") view of life and, indeed, is the philosophy that traditionally informs tarot work. Looking for books or articles which have actually discussed Hermeticism as non-dualistic proved to be a challenge; however, I did find a short piece, "Giordano Bruno's Science of Nonduality, "by Keith Turausky, at http://scienceandnonduality.blogspot.com/2009/09/giordano-brunos-science-of-nonduality.html, which affirms that idea (in case we weren't sure) that Hermeticism is a thoroughly non-dualistic philosophy.

However, Hermeticism as we know it today was revived during the Renaissance at a time in which Christianity was still powerful enough to execute with impunity its foremost proponent, Giordano Bruno. Most Hermeticists at the time (both before and after Bruno) tried very hard to make Hermeticism "blend in" as much as possible with Catholicism; the same is true of the Christian kabbalah and its depiction of the Tree of Life. But what this means is that, here we are 400-500 years later, still dealing with a Judeo-Christian legacy going back on the Christian side to the doctrines adopted by the Council of Nicaea and on the Jewish side to the teachings associated with the Old Testament—teachings that are clearly dualistic. My question is this: Now that the Inquisition has lost its power to terrorize people into renouncing the truth, isn't it time to think about what it would be like to look at both tarot and qabala from an entirely non-dualistic perspective? (Please see the end of Chapter 9 and all of Chapter 16 for a discussion that points in that direction.)

References

All references are for books and articles published in hard-copy form, as Kindle/online publications, or as titled Internet articles with cited authors. For untitled information from Internet websites, check the chapter endnotes.

Addison, Howard. *The Enneagram and Kabbalah* (Jewish Lights: 1998).

Almaas, A. H. *Facets of Unity: The Enneagram of Holy Ideas* (Diamond Books: 1998).

Arrien, Angeles. *The Tarot Handbook: Practical Applications of Ancient Visual Symbols* (Tarcher: 1987/1997).

Auger, Emily. *Tarot and Other Meditation Decks: History, Theory, Aesthetics, Typology* (McFarland: 2004).

Bamford, Christopher. *Homage to Pythagoras: Rediscovering Sacred Science* (Lindisfarne: 1980).

Banzhaf, Hajo. *Tarot and the Journey of the Hero* (Weiser: 2000).

Bem, D. J., & P. Tressoldi, T. Rabeyron, & M. Duggan. "Feeling the Future: A Meta-analysis of 90 Experiments on the Anomalous Anticipation of Random Future Events" (2014); available at http://dbem.ws/.

Bennett, J. G. *Enneagram Studies* (Weiser: 1983).

Bernier, Nathan. *The Enneagram: Symbol of All and Everything* (Gilgamesh: 2003).

Blake, A. G. E. Preface to *Enneagram Studies*; J. G. Bennett, author (Weiser: 1983).

Blake, A. G. E. *The Intelligent Enneagram* (Shambhala: 1996).

Boulting, William. *Giordano Bruno: His Life, Thought, and Martyrdom* (Hardpress: 2012).

"Breaking the Tyranny of the Ego," an interview with Oscar Ichazo by Sam Keen, in *Interviews with Oscar Ichazo* (Arica: 1982).

Briggs, Isabel Myers. *Gifts Differing* (Consulting Psychologists' Press: 1980).

Campbell, Joseph. *The Hero with a Thousand Faces* (Princeton: 1940/2000).

Campbell, Joseph. *The Power of Myth* (Anchor: 1991).

Case, Paul Foster. *The Tarot: A Key to the Wisdom of the Ages* (Builders of the Adytum: 1940/1990).

Chandra, Ram. *The Complete Works of Ram Chandra*, Vol. I (Shri Ram Chandra Mission: 1989).

Cicero, Chic and Sandra Cicero. *The Essential Golden Dawn* (Llewellyn: 2014).

Clark, Rawn. "An Examination of the GRA Tree of Life," [YouTube video], available at http://www.abardoncompanion.de/Gra/index.html.

Crowley, Aleister. *777 Revised* (1909); available at https://archive.org/details/Liber777Revised.

Crowley, Aleister. "The Tarot and the Universe," in *The Book of Thoth* (1944); available at www.bibliotecapleyades.net/crowley/libro_thoth02.

Csikszentmihalyi, Mihalyi. *Flow: The Psychology of Optimal Experience* (HarperCollins: 1983).

De Becker, Gavin. *The Gift of Fear* (Dell: 1999).

Decker, Ronald, & Michael Dummett. *A History of the Occult Tarot, 1870–1970* (Gerald Duckworth: 2008).

Decker, Ronald. *The Esoteric Tarot* (Quest: 2013).

Dubs, Joe. "Nine, the Ultimate Mystery," available at http://joedubs.com/nine-the-ultimate-mystery/.

DuQuette, Lon Milo. *The Chicken Qabalah of Rabbi Lamed Ben Clifford: Dilettante's Guide to What You Do and Do Not Need to Know to Become a Qabalist* (Weiser: 2010).

Eakins, Pamela. *Tarot of the Spirit* (U. S. Games: 1992).

Evola, Julius. *The Hermetic Tradition: Symbols and Teachings of the Royal Art* (Inner Traditions: 1931/1971).

Farley, Helen. *A Cultural History of Tarot: Entertainment to Esotericism* (I. B. Tauris: 2009).

Fortune, Dion. *The Cosmic Doctrine* (Society for the Inner Light: 1949/1995).

Fortune, Dion. *The Mystical Qabalah* (Weiser: 2000).

Frazer, James George. *The Golden Bough: A Study of Magic and Religion* (Oxford: 2009).

Gad, Irene. *Tarot and Individuation: A Jungian Study of Correspondences with Cabala, Alchemy, and the Chakras* (Nicholas-Hayes: 1994).

Gilbert, R. A. *Revelations of the Golden Dawn* (Foulsham: 1997).

Gilbert, R. A. *The Golden Dawn: Twilight of the Magicians* (Aquarian Press: 1983).

Giles, Cynthia. *The Tarot: History, Mystery, and Lore* (Paragon: 1992).

Goodrick-Clarke, Nicholas. *The Western Esoteric Traditions* (Oxford: 2008).

Gotthold, Shirley. *The Transformational Tarot* (Foolscape: 1995).

Gray, Eden. *A Complete Guide to the Tarot* (Bantam: 1970).

Greer, John M. *Paths of Wisdom: Cabala in the Golden Dawn Tradition* (Weiser: 1984).

Greer, Mary. *Tarot Constellations* (Newcastle: 1987).

Greer, Mary. *Who Are You in the Tarot?* [an update of *Tarot Constellations*] (Weiser: 2011).

Greer, Mary. *Women of the Golden Dawn* (Dark Street Press: 1995).

Gurney, Joseph. "The Tarot of the Golden Dawn," available at www.scribd.com/document/52261506/The-Tarot-of-the-Golden-Dawn-Joseph-Gurney.

Haich, Elizabeth. *Wisdom of the Tarot* (Aurora Press: 1983).

Hall, Manly P. *The Secret Teachings of All Ages* (Philosophical Research Society: 1977).

Hamaker-Zondag, Karen. *Tarot as a Way of Life* (Red Wheel: 1997).

Howe, Ellic. The *Magicians of the Golden Dawn* (McNaughton and Gunn, 1972/1984).

Hulse, David Allen. *New Dimensions of the Cube of Space: The Path of Initiation Revealed by the Tarot upon the Qabalistic Cube* (Weiser: 2000).

Initiates, Three. *The Kybalion* (Yogi Publication Soc.: 1908).

"Inside the Savant Mind: Tips for Thinking from an Extraordinary Thinker," Interview with Daniel Tammett by Jonah Lehrer, *Scientific American*; available at https://www.scientificamerican.com/article/savants-cognition-thinking/.

Irwin, Lee. *The Gnostic Tarot: Mandalas for Spiritual Transformation* (Weiser: 1998).

Javane, Faith, & Dusty Bunker. *Numerology and the Divine Triangle* (U. S. Games: 1971/1980).

Jayanti, Amber. *Living the Tarot* (Wordsworth: 2000).

Jodorowsky, Alejandro. *The Way of the Tarot: The Spiritual Teacher in the Cards* (Destiny: 2004).

Jung, Carl. *Memories, Dreams, and Reflections;* Aniela Jaffe, ed. (Vintage: 1989).

Jung, Carl. "The Development of Personality," in *The Development of Personality: Papers on Child Psychology, Education, and Related Subjects.* R. F. C. Hull, trans. (Princeton Univ. Press: 1954/1981).

Kaplan, Stuart R. *The Encyclopedia of Tarot, Vol. 1.* (U. S. Games: 1978).

Keirsey, David, & Marilyn Bates. *Please Understand Me* (Promethius-Nemesis: 1978/1984).

Keirsey, David, & Marilyn Bates. *Please Understand Me II* (Promethius-Nemesis: 1998).

Kingsley, Peter. "Knowing beyond Knowing," *Parabola*: Spring 1997, pp. 21–25; available at https://goldensufi.org/a_pk_knowing.html.

Knight, Gareth. *A Practical Guide to Qabalistic Symbolism, Vol. II: On the Paths and the Tarot* (Weiser: 1978/2001).

Konraad, Sandor. *Numerology: Key to the Tarot* (Para Research: 1983).

Kripal, Jeffrey. *Esalen: America and the Religion of No Religion* (Univ. of Chicago: 2008).

Kuntz, Darcy. *The Complete Golden Dawn Cipher Manuscripts* (Holmes: 1990).

Kuntz, Darcy. *The Golden Dawn Sourcebook* (Holmes: 1996).

Lane, Belden. "The Power of Myth: Lessons from Joseph Campbell," (*The Christian Century*: July 5–12, 1989, pp. 652–654); available at http://www.religion-online.org/article/the-power-of-myth-lessons-from-joseph-campbell/.

Lawlor, Robert. "Pythagorean Number as Form, Color, and Light," in *Homage to Pythagoras*; Christopher Bamford, ed. (Lindisfarne: 1980).

Lerner, Isha & Mark. *Inner Child Cards* (Bear: 2002).

Lévi, Éliphas. *The Doctrine of Transcendental Magic*, A. E. Waite, trans. (Weiser: 1968).

Lipton, Bruce. *The Biology of Belief* (Hay House: 2016).

Mehrtens, Sue. "Jung on Numbers," available at http://jungiancenter.org/jung-on-numbers/.

Mehrtens, Sue. "Jung's Hero: The New Form of Heroism," available at http://jungiancenter.org/jungs-hero-the-new-form-of-heroism/.

Melchizidek, Drunvalo. *The Ancient Secret of the Flower of Life*, Vols. I & II (Clear Light Trust: 1998).

Murdock, Maureen. *The Heroine's Journey: Woman's Quest for Wholeness* (Shambhala: 1990).

Naranjo, Claudio. *Character and Neurosis: An Integrative View* (Gateway: 1994).

Naranjo, Claudio. *Ennea-type Structures* (Gateway: 1994).

Nicoll, Maurice. *Psychological Commentaries on the Teaching of Gurdjieff and Ouspensky*, Vol. 2 (Weiser: 1996).

Opsopaus, John. *The Pythagorean Tarot* (Llewellyn: 2001).

Ouspensky, P. D. *In Search of the Miraculous: The Teachings of G. I. Gurdjieff* (Harvest: 1949/2001).

Palmer, Helen. *The Enneagram in Love and Work* (Harper: 1995).

Papus. *Tarot of the Bohemians* (Wilshire: 1927/1978).

Payne-Towler, Christine. *Tarot of the Holy Light: A Continental Esoteric Tarot* (Noreah: 2015).

Payne-Towler, Christine. *The Underground Stream: Esoteric Tarot Revealed* (Noreah: 1999).

Picknett, Lynn, & Clive Prince. *The Forbidden Universe: the Occult Origins of Science and the Search for the Mind of God* (Skyhorse: 2011).

Place, Robert. *The Tarot: History, Symbolism and Divination* (Tarcher: 2005).

Pollack, Rachel. *Seventy-Eight Degrees of Wisdom: a Book of Tarot* (Red Wheel: 1980/2007).

Pollack, Rachel. *Tarot Wisdom: Spiritual Teachings and Deeper Meanings* (Llewellyn: 2015).

Pollack, Rachel. *The Kabbalah Tree: A Journey of Balance and Growth* (Llewellyn: 2004).

Porter, Tracy. *The Tarot Companion: An Essential Reference Guide* (Llewellyn: 2000).

Radin, Dean. *Entangled Minds: Extrasensory Experiences in a Quantum Reality* (Paraview: 2006).

Radin, Dean. *Supernormal: Science, Yoga, and the Evidence for Extraordinary Psychic Abilities* (Deepak Chopra: 2013).

Regardie, Israel. *The Golden Dawn: The Original Account of the Teachings, Rites and Ceremonies of the Hermetic Order* (Llewellyn: 2016).

Renée, Janina. "Other Uses for Meditation," available at https://www.llewellyn.com/journal/article/1678.

Rhodes, Susan. *Archetypes of the Enneagram: Exploring the Life Themes of the 27 Subtypes* (Geranium Press: 2010).

Rhodes, Susan. "Let's Depathologize the Enneagram," in the *Enneagram Monthly*; Jack Labanauskas, ed. (Oct. 2006); available at http://www.enneagramdimensions.net/articles/lets_depathologize_the_enneagram.pdf.

Rhodes, Susan. "The Circle, Triangle, and the Hexad" (2007); available at http://www.enneagramdimensions.new/articles%circle_triangle_hexad_pt1.pdf.

Rhodes, Susan. "The Enneagram of Individuality," in the *Enneagram Monthly*; Jack Labanauskas, ed. (Sept. 2008); available at http://www.enneagramdimensions.net/articles%5Cenneagram_of_individuality.pdf.

Rhodes, Susan. *The Integral Enneagram: a Dharma-based Approach for Linking the Nine Personality Types, Nine Stages of Transformation & Ken Wilber's Integral Operating System* (Geranium Press: 2013).

Rhodes, Susan. *The Positive Enneagram: A New Approach to the Nine Personality Types* (Geranium Press: 2009).

Roberts, Richard. *Tarot Revelations* (Vernal Equinox: 1982).

Robinson, Yolanda. *The Revised New Art Tarot: Mysticism and Qabalah in the Knapp-Hall Tarot* (Kindle edition: 2015).

Robinson, Yolanda. *The Revised New Art Tarot: Mysticism and Qabalah in the Knapp-Hall Tarot* (paperback edition, Circe's Whisper: 2015).

Rosenblum, Bruce, and Fred Kuttner. *Quantum Enigma: Physics Encounters Consciousness* (Oxford: 2011).

Rosengarten, Art. *Tarot and Psychology: Spectrums of Possibility* (Paragon House: 2000).

Rosengarten, Art. *Tarot of the Future: Raising Spiritual Consciousness* (Paragon House: 2018).

Sadhu, Mouni. *The Tarot: A Contemporary Course of the Quintessence of Hermetic Occultism* (Hermetica: 2007).

Schneider, Michael. *A Beginner's Guide to Constructing the Universe: The Mathematical Archetypes of Nature, Art, and Science* (HarperPerennial: 1995).

Scholem, Gershom. *Kabbalah* (Keter: 1974).

Searle, Judith. "The Gap at the Bottom of the Enneagram" (1997); available at http://personalitycafe.com/enneagram-personality-theory-forum/180553-gap-bottom-enneagram.html.

Seife, Charles. *Zero: The Biography of a Dangerous Idea* (Penguin: 2000).

Shah, Idries. *The Commanding Self* (Octagon: 1994).

Shah, Idries. *The Sufis.* (Anchor: 1971).

Smoley, Richard, and Jay Kinney. *Hidden Wisdom: A Guide to the Western Inner Traditions* (Quest: 2006).

Smoley, Richard. "Hermes and Alchemy: the Winged God and the Golden Word," in *The Inner West: A Guide to Western Inner Traditions*; Jay Smoley, ed. (Tarcher: 2004).

Tweedie, Irina. *Daughter of Fire: A Diary of a Spiritual Training with a Sufi Master* (Golden Sufi Center: 1995).

Urbanski, Julie, and Matt Urbanski. *A Long Way From Nowhere: A Couple's Journey on the Continental Divide Trail* (CreateSpace: 2014).

Vogler, Christopher. *The Writer's Journey: Mythic Structure for Writers* (Michael Wiese: 2007).

Waite, A. E. *Shadows of Life and Thought* (Kessinger: 1938/1992).

Waite, A. E. *The Pictorial Key to the Tarot* (Dover: 2005).

Waite, A. E. *The Pictorial Key to the Tarot* (U. S. Games: 1909/1997).

Wang, Robert. *The Qabalistic Tarot: A Handbook of Mystical Philosophy* (Marcus Aurelius: 1978/2004).

Whitmont, Edward. *The Symbolic Quest: Basic Concepts of Analytic Psychology* (Princeton: 1979).

Wilber, Ken. *Integral Spirituality* (Shambhala: 2006).

Wilber, Ken. *The Eye of Spirit*, 3rd ed. (Shambhala: 2001).

Wirth, Oswald. *Tarot of the Magicians* (Red Wheel: 1927/2012).

Worrel, Thomas. D. "The Quest of the Magus: A Summary of the Western Magical Tradition," in *The Inner West: An Introduction to the Inner Wisdom*; Jay Kinney, ed. (Tarcher: 2004).

Yates, Frances. *Giordano Bruno and the Hermetic Tradition* (Univ. of Chicago: 1964/1979).

Yates, Frances. "The Hermetic Tradition in Renaissance Science," in *Renaissance Magic, Witchcraft, Magic and Demonology,* Vol. II; Brian P. Levack, ed. (Univ. of Chicago: 1992).

Zain, C. C. *The Sacred Tarot* (CofL Press: 2005).

Index

CPSIA information can be obtained
at www.ICGtesting.com
Printed in the USA
BVHW091916260620
582145BV00003B/121

9 780982 479254